The Shaming of Sexual Offenders
Risk, Retribution and Reintegration

Anne-Marie McAlinden

·H A R T·
PUBLISHING

OXFORD – PORTLAND OREGON
2007

Published in North America (US and Canada) by
Hart Publishing
c/o International Specialized Book Services
920 NE 58th Avenue, Suite 300
Portland, OR 97213-3786
USA
Tel: +1 503 287 3093 or toll-free: (1) 800 944 6190
Fax: +1 503 280 8832
E-mail: orders@isbs.com
Website: www.isbs.com

© Anne-Marie McAlinden 2007

Hart Publishing, 16C Worcester Place, OX1 2JW
Telephone: +44 (0)1865 517530 Fax: +44 (0)1865 510710
E-mail: mail@hartpub.co.uk
Website: http://www.hartpub.co.uk

British Library Cataloguing in Publication Data
Data Available

ISBN-13: 978-1-84113-592-2 (paperback)
ISBN-10: 1-84113-592-5 (paperback)

Typeset by Hope Services, Abingdon
Printed and bound in Great Britain by
MPG Biddles Ltd, King's Lynn, Norfolk

THE SHAMING OF SEXUAL OFFENDERS

Sex offenders, particularly those who offend against children, feature prominently in contemporary law and order debates. Child sexual abuse is a small component of the broader category of 'gendered and sexualised violence' which causes significant trauma for victims yet continues to evade conventional approaches to justice. This is evidenced not only by the low number of prosecutions, due mostly to low levels of reporting and evidential difficulties at trial, but by the failure of the justice system to prevent re-offending, largely due to the limited availability and effectiveness of prison treatment programmes.

Following Braithwaite's dichotomy of 'reintegrative' and 'disintegrative' shaming, this book argues that contemporary popular and state-led responses to the risk posed by sex offenders are largely disintegrative in nature. At best, the offender may be labelled, stigmatised and ostracised from the community, while at worst, he may be subjected to violence and vigilante action and ultimately return to offending behaviour. The failure of these retributive responses means there is considerable scope for exploring alternative forms of justice and their potential for improving the outcome for victims, offenders and communities affected by sexual offences.

This book examines the controversy of whether restorative justice can be applied to child sexual abuse as one of the most intractable of contemporary societal problems, and if so, what special considerations might apply. Although restorative schemes with sex offenders are in short supply, a few initiatives have developed in Canada and parts of the United States which have effected significant benefits in 'reintegrative shaming.' The book examines whether such ad hoc schemes may be of general application with child sexual abuse and whether they may be implemented on a more holistic basis.

For Stephen, Maria and Pat

Acknowledgements

I owe a huge debt of gratitude to the family, friends and colleagues who have provided support and encouragement throughout the completion of this book. To Professors Sean Doran and Kieran McEvoy who supervised the original PhD thesis, on which it is partly based. I am extremely grateful for their patience and guidance. Kieran McEvoy, in particular, has been a constant source of support and friendship and an important influence on my thinking.

Particular thanks are due to Professor Keith Soothill (also the thesis external examiner), Dr Nathan Harris, Dr Shadd Maruna and Professor Kieran McEvoy for reading draft chapters of the book and providing thoughtful and insightful comments and helpful suggestions for improvement. Any errors, of course, remain my own.

To my family and friends, Pat, Maria, Patrina, Stephen F, Katie, Kathleen and Ita, and others, your love and support have helped me persevere. Finally, and above all, sincere thanks to my husband and best friend, Stephen, who put up with me working late nights and weekends, and who has always been there for me.

Some passages have been extracted from the publications below. I thank the editors or publishers for permission to use the following works: (1999) 'Sex Offender Registration: Some Observations on "Megan's Law" and the Sex Offenders Act 1997' 1 *Crime Prevention and Community Safety: An International Journal* 41; (2001) 'Indeterminate Sentences for the Severely Personality Disordered' *Criminal Law Review* 108; (2005) 'The Use of Shame with Sexual Offenders' 45 *British Journal of Criminology* 373; (2006a) 'Are There Limits to Restorative Justice? The Case of Child Sexual Abuse' in D Sullivan and L Tifft (eds) *Handbook on Restorative Justice: A Global Perspective* (New York, Routledge); (2006b) 'Managing Risk: From Regulation to the Reintegration of Sexual Offenders' 6 *Criminology & Criminal Justice* 197; (2006c) ' "Setting 'Em Up": Personal, Social and Institutional Grooming in the Sexual Abuse of Children' 15 *Social & Legal Studies* 339.

Anne-Marie McAlinden
July 2006.

Contents

Acknowledgements   vii

PART I: THE THEORETICAL CONTEXT

1 Introduction   3

The Failure of Formal Criminal Justice   4
Managing Risk: The Case for Restorative Justice   7
Sexual Offending: Definitional Matters   10
Recurrent Themes   12
Structure of the Book   13

2 Retribution: The Political and Policy-making Context   15

The Historical Perspective   16
The Contemporary Perspective   18
The Media, 'Moral Panic' and 'Populist Punitiveness'   18
  'The New Penology': Public Protection, Risk and Preventive
    Governance   23
  The Legislative Framework   25
  Multi-Agency Work on the Assessment and Management of Risk   29
  The Problematic Nature of Multi-agency Relations   32
Conclusion   34

3 Restorative and Reintegrative Theory   37

Restorative Justice   37
  What is Restorative Justice?   37
  International Restorative Practices   39
Shaming   42
  Reintegrative Shaming   42
  Conceptualisations of Shame and Shaming   45
  Shaming as a Psychological Process   46
Resettlement   47
The Relationship with Formal Criminal Justice   51
Conclusion   57

PART II: THE REINTEGRATION OF SEXUAL OFFENDERS
IN THE COMMUNITY

4 Managing Sexual Offenders in the Community: Current Problems   61

The Criminal Justice System   61

The Decline of the 'Rehabilitative Ideal'	62
Release on Licence	70
Vetting Procedures: Preventing the Unsuitable from Working with Children	75
The Offender	78
Sex Offender Recidivism	78
The Problems with 'Tracking' Sex Offenders	81
'Grooming Behaviour'	84
The Community	90
Conclusion	95

5 Sex Offender Registration and Community Notification — 97

The History of Registration and Community Notification	98
The Main Provisions	101
'Megan's Law'	101
The Sexual Offences Act 2003, Part 2	102
ViSOR	104
Public Disclosure of Information	105
The Rationale of Registration and Notification: Deterrence and Protection	107
The Competing Perspectives of the Victim and the Offender	108
The Victim	108
The Offender	110
From Rhetoric to Reality	116
Notification in Action: Public Shaming of the Offender	117
Practical Limitations	119
Conclusion	124

6 Control in the Community — 127

Shame Penalties	127
Signs and Apologies as Public Exposure	128
The Disintegrative Effects of 'Naming' and 'Shaming'	130
The Sexual Offences Act 2003: New Preventive Orders	131
Sexual Offences Prevention Orders	131
Risk of Sexual Harm Orders	135
Electronic Tagging	137
Tagging Programmes	137
The Use of Tagging with Sex Offenders	139
What Happens When Control in the Community Fails?	144
Chemical Castration	145
Secure Accommodation	151
Indeterminate Detention	154
Conclusion	160

PART III: TOWARDS A RESTORATIVE OR
REINTEGRATIVE APPROACH

7 **Reintegrative Shaming Practices**   165

'Stop It Now!'   165
Circles of Support and Accountability   168
  Are Circles Truly Restorative?   169
  Reintegrative Shaming   171
  Resettlement   173
  Extending the Use of Circles   174
The Effectiveness of Reintegrative Justice   177
  Victim-Offender Mediation and Family Group Conferencing   177
  Circles of Support   180
From Theory to Practice: Implementing Reintegrative Shaming Practices   184
  An Additional or Alternative Form of Justice?   184
  Public Education and Awareness   188
  A 'Partnership' Approach to Justice   191
Conclusion   194

8 **Reintegrative Justice: Addressing the Critics**   197

Contextualising the Debates   197
Restorative Justice and Child Sexual Offences   200
  Minimisation of Serious Criminal Offences   201
  Failure to Promote Offender Accountability   202
  Reinforcement of the Power Imbalance in Abusive Relationships   203
  Precipitation of Repeat Victimisation   204
  Encouragement of Vigilantism   205
Shaming   206
  Lack of Empirical Research   207
  Lack of Social and Norm Cohesion   208
  Difficulties in Promoting Social Inclusion   209
  The Problematic Nature of 'Community' and 'Partnership'   210
Conclusion   213

9 **Managing Risk: From Retribution to Reintegration**   215

Retributive Justice: The Failure to Manage Risk   215
Retribution and Restoration: Bridging the Gap   218
Restorative Justice: The Effective Management of Risk   220

Bibliography   225
Index   269

PART I:
THE THEORETICAL CONTEXT

1

Introduction

During a week of disturbances on the Paulsgrove Estate, residents demonstrated outside the homes of suspected paedophiles, issued threats and destroyed local property. Children even joined in with banners such as 'Don't House Them Hang Them.' As a result of these protests, a few families fled, one convicted paedophile went underground and two suspected paedophiles committed suicide.[1]

IN RECENT YEARS, there has been acute popular and official concern with managing those perceived to be a danger to society. Paedophiles in particular have captured the public imagination and have become in a sense the new 'moral panic' (Cohen, 1972/ 1980). The media have tapped into this public anxiety and fear with the adoption of 'name and shame' campaigns. As a result, the management of risk posed by sexual offenders, particularly those who offend against children, has become an issue which features prominently in the 'law and order' debate.

A plethora of legislation to both control and manage the dangerous has been enacted within a relatively short space of time, most notably, sex offender registration and community notification. As Rose (2000) argues, however, there is considerable divergence and seeming contradiction in contemporary strategies for crime control (Garland, 1996, 2001; O'Malley, 1999, 2002; Pratt, 2000). These range from punitive demands for preventive detention of dangerous individuals to the development of multi-agency work on the assessment and management of risk and the use of rehabilitative alternatives via community programmes and reintegrative shaming (Rose, 2000: 321). The current focus of criminal justice policy therefore is seemingly on a 'what works' approach (McGuire, 1995) which may help to explain the wide variation of measures used. That is, emphasis is placed on evidence-based policy and practice where the formulation and implementation of crime prevention measures is primarily empirically rather than theoretically driven. When it comes to sexual offences, however, particularly those against children, the traditional retributive form of state justice does not seem to be working (McAlinden, 2006a).

---

[1] For a detailed account see Ashenden (2002) and Williams and Thompson (2004).

THE FAILURE OF FORMAL CRIMINAL JUSTICE

Child sexual abuse is a small component of the broader category of 'gendered and sexualised violence' (Hudson, 2002), including domestic violence and rape, which causes significant trauma for victims (Herman, 1997) yet continues to evade conventional approaches to justice. One of the underlying facets of child sexual abuse is its hidden nature and the fact that it is often allowed to remain a secret. Contrary to popular belief, a high proportion of child victims, figures suggest between 80 (Grubin, 1998: 15) and 98 per cent (Leggett, 2000: 7), are abused by someone known to them rather than predatory strangers. Children or their carers often feel a sense of shame or embarrassment in coming forward to report the abuse let alone confront their abuser. This problem is even more manifest when the abuser is a trusted intimate of the child or their family. Sex offenders themselves are often devious and manipulative in nature and are able to make pervasive use of 'grooming' techniques to gain the trust of the child or their carers to both facilitate abuse and prevent its discovery (Salter, 1995, 2003; McAlinden, 2006c).

These difficulties are compounded by the fact that the traditional justice system is often limited in its response to these types of offences (McAlinden, 2006a). In tandem with significant increases in levels of recorded sexual offending, there is a parallel disillusionment with the ability of the criminal justice system to curb it.[2] This is evidenced not only by the low number of prosecutions, due mostly to low levels of reporting (Grubin, 1998; Myhill and Allen, 2002) and recording of sexual offences, and evidential difficulties and victim anxieties about the consequences of prosecution (Hudson, 2002),[3] but by the failure of the justice system to prevent reoffending, largely due to the limited availability and effectiveness of prison treatment programmes (Furby et al, 1989; Beech et al, 1998).

Research shows that while overall levels of sexual victimisation are increasing,[4] reconviction rates for sexual offenders have declined (Friendship and Thornton, 2001). More recent research shows that fewer than 5 per cent of sex offenders are ever apprehended (Salter, 2003). Moreover, evidence from self-report studies also suggests that those convicted of sexual offences often reveal the commission of many more offences than are reported to authorities by their victims (Groth et al,

---

[2] Recorded crime statistics show that the total number of recorded sexual offences has increased by 9.6% in the period 1999–2000 to 2001–02 and by 94.4% in the last 25 years ('Recorded Crime Statistics: 1898–2001–02', <http://www.homeoffice.gov.uk/rds/pdfs/100years.xls>).

[3] A recent study of attrition in rape cases found an all-time low conviction rate of just 5.6% in 2002. Around one-quarter of reported cases were 'no crimed.' Evidential issues and victim withdrawal each accounted for over one-third of cases lost. Only 14% of cases reached the trial stage, with a further proportion of these not eventually proceeding due to withdrawal or discontinuance at court (Kelly et al, 2005).

[4] The British Crime Survey, for example, estimates a high prevalence of sexual victimisation. According to the 2001 self-completion survey, 24% of women and 5% of men had been subject to some form of sexual victimisation at least once in their lifetime. Among women, 7% had also suffered a serious sexual assault at least once in their lifetime (including rape) since the age of 16 (Walby and Allen, 2004).

1982; Abel et al, 1987). In this respect, Home Office research estimates that actual recidivism rates for sexual offenders are 5.3 times the official reconviction rate (Falshaw et al, 2003).[5] The very nature of the system means that, at best, it can only ever hope to deal effectively with those offenders who have already come to the attention of law enforcement authorities. In practice, this actually covers very few offenders, since as was argued above the majority of abuse remains hidden and undisclosed.

At a more basic level, cases continuously appear in the media of children abused or murdered by habitual sex offenders. Some of the most high profile cases in recent years such as those of Sarah Payne, and Holly Wells and Jessica Chapman, known euphemistically as the 'Soham murders,' demonstrate the failure of the authorities to protect children from even known sex offenders. As Cowan et al argue: 'the sovereign act of punishment is itself regarded as an incomplete method of rehabilitation because these people are regarded as too risky and untrustworthy' (2001: 451). The sum of these difficulties means that there is a need to re-examine and perhaps redefine the current regulatory framework in respect of these offences.

The overall purpose of this book is to analyse critically the current retributive response to the management of the risk posed by released sex offenders, particularly those who offend against children, and the problems presented by their reintegration into the community. More specifically, the book will examine the state's response to sex offending via a retributive legislative framework, the highly emotive popular response by the media and the public, which can also be framed in punitive terms, and ultimately what alternative responses there might be to manage the risk presented by sex offenders in the community and reintegrate them more effectively. All of these issues are explored on a comparative basis in the primary contexts of the United States and the United Kingdom, although other jurisdictions such as the Republic of Ireland, Canada, Australia and New Zealand are referred to for the purposes of comparison and illustration.

The central argument is therefore, that since the traditional retributive framework has failed in these respects, there is considerable scope for exploring the use of other forms of justice in tackling the sex offender problem. These approaches may provide a viable means of dealing with the offender's needs in terms of risk management and successful reintegration, but also of addressing the concerns of victims and communities in terms of effective public protection. As such, a primary focus is the application of restorative justice to child sexual abuse as a serious and persistent form of offending and the potential contribution of the community in particular to the reintegration of the offender. Key initial elements to implementing such a 'partnership' approach to justice between state agencies and the community are the theory and practice of reintegrative or 'restorative

---

[5] Reconviction rates for sex offenders based on government crime statistics are generally low. Estimates range from 3–9% over a 2–6 year follow-up period (Falshaw et al, 2003); 10% after 6 years (Hood et al, 2002) and 20% over 20 years (Grubin, 1998).

community justice' (Bazemore and Schiff, 1996) and public education and awareness campaigns.

The issue of the application of restorative justice to the area of sexual offences is, to say the least, a highly contentious one. Restorative justice, however, is envisaged throughout as both a pragmatic response to the failings of retributive justice and as a way of extending the theoretical thinking on the use of restorative justice in 'hard cases.' Retributive justice has failed to hold offenders accountable and secure their rehabilitation. Similarly, the popular response to the presence of sex offenders in the community has also prevented the reintegration of offenders. Total impunity for these offenders is not an option. The failings of current approaches therefore create a moral, social, political and practical imperative to be creative, to test received wisdoms, and to draw, as appropriate, from the theoretical, policy and practical experiences of other jurisdictions, in order to devise a more effective response to these types of offences.

This book explores, in particular, the use of shaming mechanisms with sex offenders, particularly those who offend against children. Shaming, a central concept in the broader theory of restorative justice, may be of two varieties. Following Braithwaite's (1989) dichotomy of 'reintegrative' and 'disintegrative' shaming, this book will argue that within the traditional retributive framework of justice, contemporary popular and state-led responses to the risk posed by released sex offenders in the community are largely disintegrative or stigmatising in nature. These include legislative and judicial measures to control sex offenders in the community on release from custody, such as sex offender registration and community notification and novel probation conditions imposed in the United States. The media have followed suit with the adoption of 'name and shame' campaigns, which encourage public outcry and often vigilante justice. Far from securing the offender's rehabilitation or reintegration into society and the prevention of future offending, the net result is often the opposite. At best, offenders may be negatively labelled and stigmatised, serving to heighten their isolation and ostracise them from the rest of the community. At worst, they may be subjected to violence and vigilante action and may ultimately return to offending behaviour (Maxwell and Morris, 1999; Edwards and Hensley, 2001b; McAlinden, 2005).

In effect, contrary to the major arguments put forward by the critics, it is contended, albeit controversially, that some sex offenders against children may actually be suitable for a restorative approach in carefully managed contexts. In the main, it will be argued that unlike traditional retributive measures which make up the current criminal justice response to sexual offences, the theory and practice of restorative justice may offer a more meaningful, progressive and ultimately more effective response to the problem. These potential benefits include improving the safety of victims, providing relief for communities, rehabilitating and reintegrating offenders and ultimately offering a realistic prospect of breaking cycles of abuse.

MANAGING RISK: THE CASE FOR RESTORATIVE JUSTICE

In brief, as noted above, the case for restorative justice as applied to sexual offending, for its advocates, commonly rests on the perceived failings of the current regulatory framework and the greater potential of restorative justice for providing satisfactory outcomes for victims, offenders and communities affected by sexual offences in more cases (Finstad, 1990; Braithwaite and Daly, 1994; Hudson, 2002: 621). Restorative approaches in various jurisdictions may differ but are often based on the following common aims: engaging with offenders to help them appreciate the consequences of their actions and the impact they have had on their victims; encouraging appropriate forms of reparation by offenders towards their victims, if they agree, or the wider community; seeking reconciliation between the victim and offender where possible; and the reintegration of the offender within the community. It is these broad aims which are evidenced in 'reintegrative shaming' (Braithwaite, 1989) efforts with sex offenders.

Although restorative schemes with sex offenders are in short supply, a few piecemeal initiatives have developed in several jurisdictions such as Canada and parts of the United States which are based on reintegrative or restorative principles. There are considerable variations in approach, but at a broad level these programmes involve the development of restorative support and treatment networks for sex offenders where the community works in partnership with the offender and state and voluntary agencies. These schemes have been effective in managing the risk posed by sex offenders on a number of levels: in reducing reoffending (Wilson et al, 2002) and promoting 'reintegrative shaming' (Braithwaite, 1989), and in engaging communities to play a constructive, supportive and positive role in this process (Quaker Peace and Social Witness, 2005: 5). The book examines whether such ad hoc schemes may be of general application with child sexual abuse and how they may be implemented on a more widespread and holistic basis.

In the United Kingdom, the Government has embraced the restorative justice paradigm, albeit on a piecemeal basis, and consequently changed the emphasis of criminal justice in key areas such as youth justice.[6] Elsewhere, there is a growing recognition that restorative justice, which is routinely confined to low-level forms of offending in this jurisdiction, can be used for the most serious social problems. For example, it has been used in the Truth and Reconciliation Commissions of South Africa (Villa Vincenzo, 1999; Christodoulidis, 2000; Skelton and Frank, 2001) and Rwanda (Drumbl, 2000) with respect to genocide, mass torture and rape. Within this context, this book will explore whether restorative or reintegrative justice can actually be applied to child sexual abuse as one of the most

---

[6] By virtue of a range of provisions under the Crime and Disorder Act 1998, the Youth and Criminal Evidence Act 1999 and further legislation, an array of restorative options are initially explored with first time young offenders, with the formal criminal justice system as the backdrop which can be used as a last resort with more persistent offenders (Crawford and Newburn, 2003).

abhorrent yet ubiquitous of contemporary social problems, and if so, what special considerations might apply.

Some may feel that child sexual abuse is inappropriate, unsuitable or too delicate an area within which to use a restorative response and may criticise this book's arguments as either naive or somewhat Utopian. Advocates, in this respect, have addressed some of the traditional critiques concerning restorative justice as applied to 'hard' cases and how they can be overcome (Hudson, 1998, 2002; Daly, 2002a, 2006; Morris and Gelsthorpe, 2000a; Morris, 2002a; McAlinden, 2005). There is a danger of oversimplifying the principal arguments here, but in the main advocates have focused on a range of claims including that restorative justice trivialises what are very serious criminal offences, particularly where children and the vulnerable are concerned; it fails to promote offender accountability and allows the offender to reject responsibility for the offence; it reproduces and reinforces the imbalance of power entrenched in abusive relationships and leads to possible re-victimisation; and it encourages vigilantism.

Such claims have been countered theoretically (Hudson, 1998, 2002; Morris 'and Gelsthorpe, 2000a; Daly, 2002a) and empirically (Morris, 2002a; Daly, 2006) by arguing conversely that even though the criminal law remains as a symbolic signifier and denouncer, in fact restorative processes which involve the abuser's family and the wider community can meet the affective or expressive need for censure in sexual offences cases; that while the criminal justice system does little to hold offenders accountable and address ingrained patterns of offending behaviour, restorative justice seeks genuine engagement with offenders to help them acknowledge the harm done and appreciate the consequences of their actions; it focuses on the empowerment of victims in a supportive, fair and uncoerced environment in which the victim can make clear to the offender the effects of the abuse on them; that by offering constructive rather than penal solutions, it may be opted for at an earlier stage in the victim's experience of abuse; and finally, that distortions of power, including community control, are addressed when programmes adhere closely to restorative values and principles.

In addition, critics of shaming theory, in particular, also argue that a number of interrelated difficulties such as the lack of empirical research, the lack of social and norm cohesion in contemporary society, the difficulties in promoting social inclusion, and the problematic nature of the terms 'community' and 'partnership', mean that such schemes will not easily be implemented in mainstream Western society. Conversely, however, advocates contend that restorative justice schemes have outcome measures that are broader than a consideration of reoffending rates (Christie, 1977; Maxwell and Morris, 1999, 2002; Bazemore and Griffiths, 2003); popular responses to sex offending demonstrate that there is striking consensus concerning the wrongness of sexual relationships between adults and children (Hacking, 1999); the provision of accurate information about the nature of sex offending against children and approaches to it, would hopefully dispel the commonly held misconceptions, shift cultural attitudes and help to promote social inclusion (Grubin, 1998; Leggett, 2000); and finally, that the involvement of statutory and voluntary agencies in community-based schemes will help to keep the local community in check while at the same time ensuring state and organisational accountability (Crawford, 1999). This book seeks to underline these supporting arguments and comprehensively address the key concerns put forward by critics of restorative justice as applied to sexual offences.

The central importance of risk to social and political theory generally (Beck, 1992; Ericson and Haggerty, 1997) is a well-rehearsed theme in mainstream criminal justice debates (Feeley and Simon, 1992, 1994; Braithwaite, 2000; Shearing, 2000) and has been particularly evident in relation to concerns over the risk posed by released sex offenders living in the community (Kemshall and Maguire, 2003; Matravers, 2003). Given the failure of traditional risk-based approaches to sex offender management it is contended that criminal justice policy and practice need to recognise the opportunities offered by restorative justice in order to better manage risk and protect the public more effectively.

In this respect, the book will ultimately argue that moving from a purely retributive response to sex offending, to one where retribution and restoration are integrated, will facilitate the management of both known and unknown risks posed by sex offenders against children. In conjuction with the formal criminal justice system, restorative justice is itself presented as a regulatory approach to the management of risk and future danger posed by sex offenders. As will be disucssed in some detail in the final chapter, research by Soothill and colleagues (Soothill 2005, Soothill et al 2005a, 2005b) has identified three main typologies of offender: 'known and high-risk'; 'known, but low-risk'; and 'unknown risk.' Restorative justice is presented as a practical means of managing the risk posed by each of these categories of offender. It will be argued, for example, that 'known and high-risk' offenders could continue to be prosecuted in the normal way and then reintegrated into the community via circles of support on release. For 'known and low or low-middle risk' offenders, circles could be used as an effective alternative to the formal state sanctioning process. Much in the same way as happens in the youth justice system in England and Wales, the legal framework and more punitive sanctions, however, can be retained as a backdrop or as an option of last resort with more persistent offenders (Crawford and Newburn, 2003). This approach is similar, in some respects, to Braithwaite's 'enforcement pyramid' where restorative justice is regarded as part of a regulatory framework that includes deterrence and incapacitation, but pointedly not retribution (Braithwaite, 1999, 2002b; Braithwaite and Braithwaite, 2001). Moreover, it will also be argued that by encouraging more perpetrators and victims to voluntarily come forward, mainly by reducing the public villification of offenders and the threat of punitive state sanctions, it may also offer an important way of probing and managing the 'unknown risk,' where offenders may be strongly suspected of sexual offences by the authorities but have not actually been prosecuted.

SEXUAL OFFENDING: DEFINITIONAL MATTERS

Sex offenders are not a homogeneous group. Sexual offences encompass a wide range of offences, which include male and female, child and adult, victim and offender. Indeed, sexual offences range from those at the less serious end of the spectrum, such as indecent exposure, to the more serious offences which include child sexual abuse, rape and sexual murder (Fisher and Beech, 2004). In recent times, in the United Kingdom in particular, new categories of offence have emerged such as 'stalking',[7] 'trafficking',[8] and 'abuse of trust' offences,[9] and those which may involve use of the internet such as 'child pornography'[10] and 'grooming.'[11]

Indeed, following a review of the law on sexual offences (Home Office, 2000), the Sexual Offences Act 2003 has widened the definition of sexual crime.[12] Increasing emphasis, however, has also been placed on the protection of children. These new and emerging forms of deviant sexual behaviour towards children include the exploitation of children using prostitution and pornography; offences which do not involve physical contact yet which still cause the child psychological harm such as 'grooming', as discussed above, and indecent exposure, voyeurism, and sexual behaviour in a public place. As will be argued in chapter 2, however, while child physical abuse has been recognised as a specific issue of concern for many years in the United Kingdom and elsewhere, child sexual abuse and the management of offenders against children in the community have only been conceptualised as distinct social problems within the last two decades.

Despite the diversity of offences which can be classified as 'sexual' in nature, there is a recognised danger of equating sex offending against children with sex offending in general. Contemporary popular and political discourses, in this respect, have increasingly conflated the two categories and have highlighted in particular the threat posed by 'stranger danger'—male adult predatory 'paedophiles'[13] who offend against either male or female child victims who were previously unknown to them—as being symptomatic of the wider evils of sex offending in general. The focus of this book is also primarily on the management of sex offenders in the community who pose a danger to children.

---

[7] Protection from Harassment Act 1997.

[8] Sexual Offences Act 2003, ss 57–60.

[9] Introduced in the Sexual Offences (Amendment) Act 2000 and re-enacted by the Sexual Offences Act 2003, ss 16–24.

[10] Protection of Children Act 1978 (as amended by the Criminal Justice and Public Order Act 1994, ss 84–87).

[11] Sexual Offences Act 2003, s 15.

[12] This has included, for example, extending the definition of rape to include oral penetration so that it applies to both male and female victims.

[13] The term 'paedophile' comes from the Greek language and literally means 'love of children.' In a strict sense, the term is a medical one which is generally taken to mean a diagnosable psychiatric syndrome characterised by sexual attraction to pre-pubescent children or gratification from sexual intimacy with them (Berlin and Meinecke, 1981; Finkelhor and Araji, 1986; Stelzer, 1997: 1677–78).

As will also be discussed throughout the book, however, these popular and official concerns are misplaced on at least two important levels. First, the media have contributed to the creation of a myth, which has been readily absorbed by the public, that society is full of sexual predators known to the authorities who are ready to prey on the vulnerable, in particular women and young children who were previously unknown to them (Sampson, 1994; Greer, 2003). In reality, the majority of child sexual abuse is in fact intra-familial in nature. That is to say, most children who are sexually abused are offended against by family members, or at the very least, someone well known to them. As noted at the outset of this chapter, Home Office research indicates that the majority of perpetrators, approximately 80 per cent, sexually assault children known to them, with these offences taking place in the home of either the offender or the victim (Grubin, 1998: 15). Moreover, research also suggests that fewer than 5 per cent of sex offenders are ever apprehended (Salter, 2003).

Secondly, while the majority of known sex offenders are men, sexual offences against children are also committed by women and, in a growing number of cases, young people and children (Grubin, 1998).[14] A third of all reported cases are committed by those under eighteen (Richardson et al, 1997; Grubin, 1998; Masson, 2004). Although female sex offenders account for approximately only 0.5 per cent of sex offenders in prison,[15] and less than 5 per cent of sex offences as a whole (Grubin, 1998),[16] the actual number is thought to be considerably higher (Fergusson and Mullen, 1999).[17]

Both of these common misconceptions nonetheless have also become embedded in much of the legislation, from the late 1990s onwards, to control sex offenders in the community. Many of the recent political and legislative innovations, such as sex offender registration and sexual offences prevention orders, have fed into this fallacy by concentrating on a few known offenders and, as such, can never hope to protect children adequately. In fact, this misplaced focus on perceived sites of danger may serve to detract attention and resources from the real dangers and problems.

As noted above, this book by the adoption of a more holistic approach is able to include within its remit not just 'known' offenders who have been cautioned or

---

[14] Throughout this book, the author has most often used 'their' when referring to the offender. Where this has not been possible, the use of the masculine pronoun is also deemed to include the feminine.

[15] As of November 2003, there were 28 females as opposed to 5550 male sex offenders in prisons in England and Wales. See monthly prison population brief, England and Wales, <http://www.hmprisonservice.gov.uk>.

[16] More recent American research has placed this figure as low as 1–2% (Vandiver and Walker, 2002).

[17] Although little empirical research regarding female sex offenders exists, there are a number of possible reasons for this (Hudson, 2005: 2). The actual extent of female sex offending may be difficult to determine in Western societies where women are 'permitted greater freedom than men in their physical interactions with children' (Grubin, 1998: 23). Moreover, it may also be disconcerting to think that either women or children, those traditionally thought to be vulnerable to abuse, are capable of committing such acts (Hetherton, 1999; Kemshall, 2004).

convicted of sexual offences, but also a consideration of the management of those offenders who pose a danger to children but may never have been apprehended. Perpetrators who offend against someone well known to them, and who may not yet have come to the attention of the authorities account for the majority of abuse (Grubin, 1998). This issue of how also to respond to the 'unknown risk,' which is absent from existing approaches, is a crucial issue which must be addressed if the problem of child sexual abuse, in particular its hidden nature, is to be dealt with in a meaningful and effective way.

RECURRENT THEMES

The book will consider some of the principal themes and debates concerning popular and state-led responses to the reintegration of sex offenders in the community, particularly those who offend against children. A predominant theme is the relationship between retributive and restorative justice (von Hirsch et al, 2002). In this vein, some criminologists continue to emphasise the difference of the restorative justice vision as a paradigm shift in criminal law (Zehr, 1990, 1995; Bazemore, 1996; Barnett, 2003; Walgrave, 2003). Others, however, call for recognition of alternative forms of justice and highlight the compatibility of restoration and retribution. These two concepts may in fact be integrated as part of the same system of justice where they would complement and work in tandem with each other rather than operate as opposing or alternative systems (Zedner, 1994; Levrant et al, 1999; Daly, 2000; Duff, 2002, Hudson, 2002).[18] The tension between these paradigms has yet to be fully resolved but is one which must be addressed if restorative justice is to be extended in particular to serious forms of offending.

Unlike much of the existing research, which concentrates on the criminal justice response, this book also looks at the pivotal role of 'the community' in the successful reintegration of offenders (Meienholder, 1977, Sampson and Laub, 1993; Laub et al, 1998; Farrall, 2002; Farrall and Sparks, 2006). The community, as a key player in the process of assessment and management of the risk posed by sex offenders in the community, must also be part of any future solutions. Indeed, one of the central issues in this book is whether the community may be helped to play a more constructive role than at present in managing sex offenders in the community (Crawford, 1999). Pivotal to this discussion is, inter alia, the complexity of the notion of community itself, as discussed in chapter 7.

A further theme is the need to appropriately balance the rights of victims and offenders, which underlies much of contemporary criminal justice policy and debate (O'Malley, 1996: 25–31; Cox, 1997). This points to the need to protect vulnerable members of society on the one hand and the need to safeguard the rights of offenders on the other who in many cases will have served their prison sentence.

---

[18] Some restorative justice commentators, however, have argued that in fact restorative justice systems are corroded by their partnership with a retributive framework. (See eg: Boyes-Watson, 1999).

Such concerns are particularly potent in light of the 'Halliday report' (Home Office, 2001a) and its proposed emphasis on record-enhanced sentencing.

Finally, there are the competing notions of treatment and punishment of offenders (Geiran, 1996a). These have been played out not only at policy level in the formulation of successive legislative measures, but in society's responses to the problem of sexual offending. These responses have been framed in terms of an increasingly punitive response on the one hand, and a view of sex offenders as somehow ill and requiring treatment on the other.

STRUCTURE OF THE BOOK

The book is divided into three main parts, the first of which provides the theoretical context. Chapter 2 elaborates more fully on some of the themes raised in this introductory chapter. It initially attempts to locate contemporary punitive approaches to the reintegration of sex offenders within the context of the historical background to child abuse. The chapter primarily examines the socio-political context of the current retributive framework for managing the risk posed by sex offenders. This includes the range of political and ideological pressures that shape the international debate on crime and justice. Finally, the chapter provides a brief critical overview of the multi-agency approach to the reintegration of released sex offenders, which seeks to reconcile some of these competing pressures. Chapter 3 outlines the central theoretical components of the restorative or reintegrative paradigm—restorative justice, 'shaming' in particular, and the related resettlement literature—as a necessary backdrop to a fuller discussion of practices and critiques in later chapters. The chapter further considers the theoretical and policy debates on the relationship between restorative and retributive justice.

Part II seeks to examine the range of specific issues raised by the state's response to the reintegration of sex offenders in the community. This includes a critical analysis of the problems involved in managing sex offenders in the community as well as a detailed examination of current measures to control sex offenders within the traditional retributive framework including, most notably, sex offender registration. Indeed, these initiatives were conceptualised largely as a result of the perceived management problems with sex offenders on release from custody. Chapter 4 examines the specific management and reintegration problems which relate to sexual offending. These are grouped into those which relate to the criminal justice system, the offender and the wider community.

Chapter 5 looks specifically at sex offender registration and community notification as a prime example of disintegrative shaming with sex offenders. Such schemes will be analysed primarily in the context of 'Megan's Law' in the United States and Part 2 of the Sexual Offences Act 2003 in the United Kingdom. It examines the history and rationale behind the measures and the debate over the opposing rights of victims and offenders which surfaced at the time the legislation was being implemented. The chapter also considers early indications about what the actual practical impact of such legislation might be in terms of the effective management of risk and the reintegration of sex offenders.

Chapter 6 examines other mechanisms within the formal criminal justice framework which have been formulated to manage sex offenders in the community more effectively yet which are also largely disintegrative in nature. It initially considers novel probation conditions imposed on sex offenders in the United States in the form of 'public exposure' or 'sign' penalties. It also critically assesses in practical, ethical and legal terms recent innovations in the United Kingdom including the range of new preventive measures enacted under the Sexual Offences Act 2003 as well as the more generic measure of electronic tagging. Chemical castration, secure accommodation and indeterminate detention are examined as options of last resort with more persistent offenders.

The final part of the book outlines alternative responses to managing the risk posed by sex offenders in the community and ultimately attempts to advance the case for the application of restorative justice to child sexual abuse within a reintegrative framework. Chapter 7 outlines examples of reintegrative shaming practices with sex offenders in Canada and parts of the United States such as circles of support and accountability and the 'Stop It Now!' programme. It then explores how such schemes could be further extended in practice in other jurisdictions, including the United Kingdom.

Chapter 8 addresses the principal concerns put forward by critics of restorative justice as applied to sexual offences. Many writers accept that restorative justice may have a role to play in dealing with low-level crime, yet continue to highlight the particular unsuitability of restorative justice programmes in the domain of sexual or domestic violence (Johnstone, 2003). This chapter argues, within this context, that some victims, offenders, families and communities affected by child sexual abuse could gain significant benefits from the fuller adoption of such an approach.

Finally, chapter 9 will seek to pull together some of the major themes discussed in previous chapters and their implications for public policy and practice concerning the efficient management of the risk posed by sex offenders in the community. It will outline in particular how we can move from retributive, punitive responses to sex offenders towards the reintegration, support and treatment of offenders in order to ultimately manage the risk they present in the community more effectively.

It is a reality that, at some point, most sex offenders will be released from prison having served their sentences and will be retuning to live in the local community. By ignoring the potential of the restorative paradigm in responding to sexual offences, we risk an escalation of the current problems, which are embedded in a punitive response, as outlined at the outset of this chapter. The practical issue of community reintegration, which is vital to offender resettlement (Sampson and Laub, 1993; Maruna, 2001; Petersilia, 2003) and desistance from crime (Farrall and Bowling, 1999; Farrall, 2002; Maruna and Farrall, 2004; Maguire and Raynor, 2006; McNeill, 2006), via restorative measures, can therefore no longer be sidestepped but must be meaningfully addressed.

2

Retribution:
The Political and Policy-making Context

T HE MANAGEMENT OF child sex offenders in the community has had a
short history. This can, for the most part, be attributed to the fact that child
sexual abuse has only been publicly recognised as a specific social problem
in the United Kingdom, and elsewhere, in recent times. In effect, we have moved
from a situation where child abuse was institutionalised, or at the least, tolerated
in many societies for hundreds of years (Radbill, 1968; Eisenberg, 1981; Corby,
1987: 1) to one where concern about sexual offending, especially that against children, has become panic (Cohen, 1972/1980; Sampson, 1994: x). During this time,
the management of sex offenders has been transformed into a major societal issue
as a result of a combination of several factors. Domestic proposals to establish
regulatory schemes to manage sex offenders in the community have not emerged
in a vacuum, but can be seen as part of a general trend of following initiatives
derived from the United States.[1]

Recent years have seen the politicisation of child sexual offenders as political
parties vie for ever more punitive sanctions. The general failure of rehabilitative
approaches and extensive media coverage of particular cases of child sexual abuse
or murder of children by released sex offenders has sparked public concern and led
to popular campaigns for the authorities to reveal the identity of convicted sex
offenders living in the community. Faced with these problems, governments are
abandoning rehabilitative strategies in favour of more retributive approaches to
give the public the impression that something is being done to protect them from
dangerous, violent and sexual offenders in the community and to manage the risk
they are seen as presenting. Paedophiles, in particular, have been the focus of
the criminal justice policy of recent successive governments, based largely on a
punitive crime control 'law and order' ideology of risk penality and incapacitation.

---

[1] A related topic in this context, which has increasingly captured the attention of criminologists, is
that of the globalisation of crime control initiatives and the transfer of criminal justice and penal policy between the United States and the United Kingdom (Christie, 2000; Garland, 2001; Newburn,
2002). Such developments have included, for example, innovations in 'zero tolerance' policing and the
increased use of incarceration (Jones and Newburn, 2002, 2006).

THE HISTORICAL PERSPECTIVE

It is only in the last two decades that there has been a dramatic increase in public attention and professional activity with regard to child sexual abuse (MacIntyre and Carr, 2000: vii). As La Fontaine has said:

> Sexual abuse was not even mentioned in the Department of Health circulars until 1980 ... It is only comparatively recently that the general public in Britain has begun to realise that, far from being an extremely rare phenomenon, the sexual abuse of children is much more widespread (1990: 38–39).

As will be outlined below, there is a longer history of concern, however, about cruelty to children and physical injury inflicted by parents, particularly in the United States (Radbill, 1968; Parke and Collmer, 1975; Kalisch, 1978).

In most pre-industrial Western societies fathers had absolute power over their children. Increasing industrialisation, however, brought about a change in family relationships (Corby, 1987: 1). Donzelot (1979), drawing on French social history sources, describes the process by which paternal power has gradually been eroded over the last two centuries and replaced by a focus on the role of the mother. This, he argues, has been achieved, inter alia, by means of the influence of philanthropic societies and the medical profession. Behlmer's (1982) historical analysis of child abuse between 1870 and 1910 gives a similarly detailed account of the early stages of this process in Great Britain.

In relation to child sexual abuse, social change in this area has been slow and it was not until the twentieth century that child abuse and the rights of children came to public notice (Bagley and King, 1990), and even then only intermittently (La Fontaine, 1990: 39–40). This reconceptualisation of childhood was initiated by the formation of the humane movement and the development of the juvenile court system (Olafson et al, 1993). As Kennedy et al (1990) note, for centuries the Common Law only recognised three serious breaches of sexual morality: rape, sodomy and bestiality (1990: 3). In the United Kingdom, legislation relating to other types of sexual offence, including those involving children, was only added during the Victorian age in the latter part of the nineteenth and early twentieth centuries.

The National Society for the Prevention of Cruelty to Children (NSPCC), which was founded in 1884, highlighted public awareness of the maltreatment of children at that time. During this period, for example, the age of consent for girls was raised from 12 to 16 years because of mounting concern about child prostitution (Howard League for Penal Reform, 1995). Severe prohibitions against incest are now almost universal but prior to the Punishment of Incest Act 1908 such cases were dealt with by the ecclesiastical courts, as offences against morals and religion (Turner, 1952; Wolfram, 1983). Between 1910 and the late 1960s, the issue of child sexual abuse as a major societal problem virtually disappeared in Great Britain (Corby, 1987: 2). Indeed, it was not until the enactment of the Children and Young Persons Act 1968 that the issue again came to the fore. In fact, this remained the primary legislation for regulating child sexual abuse and the appropriate punishment for child sex offenders in the United Kingdom until the passing of an abundance of legislation in the early 1990s.

In the United States, in the early 1960s, Henry Kempe and his colleagues publicised the physical abuse of children in the paper 'The Battered Child Syndrome' (Kempe et al, 1962). This was later extended to include neglect, non-organic failure to thrive[2] and emotional abuse (Garbarino and Gilliam, 1980). However, it was not until the late 1970s in the United States that awareness of the possible extent of the problem of child sexual abuse heightened among professionals and indeed the public (Kempe, 1978; Finkelhor, 1979). Finkelhor suggests that this recognition came about as a result of the growth of two popular movements—feminism, and campaigns for the protection of children which particularly highlighted children's vulnerability in the private sphere. Indeed, this perspective was also given impetus by the development of the wider concept of family violence and several subcategories of this more general rubric, such as domestic violence (Straus, 1974; Pfohl, 1977).

Although these concerns surrounding child physical abuse predate the most recent recognition of child sexual abuse, the issues being discussed then closely resemble those being debated with respect to child sexual abuse some 40 years later. There was a similar reluctance on the part of the public to accept that parents could be responsible for injury to their children, and a parallel debate over children's rights and the freedom of parents and carers to raise their children with minimal state interference or supervision (La Fontaine, 1990: 40).

Although reports on cases of incest and child sexual abuse date back to before the advent of the twentieth century,[3] in Europe, in general, an awareness of child sexual abuse did not come about until some years later (Jones et al, 1987: 42–50; Bagley and King, 1990: 25–37). Catholic cultures such as France and southern Germany were slow to recognise sexual abuse as a moral, legal and social problem, compared with Protestant or secularised cultures such as the United States, England, Canada, Sweden, Norway, the Netherlands and northern Germany (Chesnais, 1981). Even these countries failed to record occurrences of the sexual abuse of children with other criminal statistics until the late 1970s (Chesnais, 1981).[4]

Indeed, it was only in the early 1970s and late 1980s in England and Wales that child sexual abuse was 're-discovered' (Murphy, 1995: 9–16). A number of public inquiries following the deaths of children who had been subjected to child physical and sexual abuse, such as those of Maria Colwell (DHSS, 1974) and Jasmine Beckford (Brent Borough Council, 1985), placed child abuse firmly back

---

[2] This is defined as decelerated or arrested physical growth associated with poor developmental and emotional functioning. It occurs usually where a child is under 2 years and has no known medical condition that causes poor growth. Psychological, social or economic problems in the family almost always play a role in the case of NOFTT (Skuse, 1985).

[3] In France, for example, Tardieu (1878) describes post-mortem findings of sexual abuse.

[4] The first survey on the incidence of child sexual abuse was carried out in Britain between 1977 and 1978 (Mrazek et al, 1981). The rest of Western Europe lagged someway behind, although an earlier German study of incest offenders implied that many of the victims had been children (Maisch, 1973).

on the policy-making agenda. The Colwell case in particular 'proved crucial in establishing the issue as a major social problem and introducing fundamental changes in policy and practice' (Parton, 1985: 12).

However, where Great Britain is concerned, 'the problem of the sexual abuse of children exploded into the public domain through the events at Cleveland in 1987' (La Fontaine, 1990: 42). The Butler-Sloss Report of the Cleveland inquiry, into the work of some paediatricians who had diagnosed sexual abuse and of the social services who took the children into care (DHSS, 1988), was the first major official report to deal specifically with the issue of child sexual abuse. The report made a number of recommendations in relation to child protection. It emphasised, in particular, the prevailing need to develop inter-agency co-operation in terms of multi-agency disclosure, effective communication between organisations, clearly defined areas of responsibility and overall co-ordination of efforts in child protection (DHSS, 1988: 245–54). Since the late 1980s, the issue of sexual offending against children has moved from the closet of dark hidden secrets to become a full-blown 'moral panic' (Cohen, 1972/1980).

THE CONTEMPORARY PERSPECTIVE

A number of interrelated factors have contributed to the social and political conceptualisation of managing sex offenders in the community as a serious social problem. These themes combine to form a climate in which stricter controls on sex offenders have become increasingly prominent. These include media reporting of sexual crime which may promote a moral panic about the danger posed by released sex offenders and encourage punitive public attitudes; and the emergence of a 'new penology' based on public protection, risk and preventive governance which in turn has been reflected in the legislative and multi-agency framework for managing sex offenders in the community (McAlinden, 2006b).

The Media, 'Moral Panic'[5] and 'Populist Punitiveness'[6]

The increased public prominence of sexual offending must first be seen in the broader context of media construction and representation of sexual offences

---

[5] Cohen (1972/1980) coined the phrase 'moral panic' wherein he argued that the very actions of the media together with magistrates and the police designed to eradicate the delinquent activities of 'mods' and 'rockers', were in reality counterproductive in that they ultimately created and sustained a much larger 'problem.' Similarly, Hall et al's (1978) analysis documents the development of a 'moral panic' about a supposed new type of robbery, 'mugging'. This is the self-fulfilling spiral of 'deviancy amplification' as part of labelling theory where the social reaction on the part of control agents, which is aimed at stamping out or controlling deviance, in fact leads to an increase in amounts and frequency (Young, 1971, 1974). Since these pioneering works many other studies have documented the deviance construction and amplifying activities of the media in the area of sexual offences (Nava, 1988; Barak, 1994; Lees, 1995; Skidmore, 1995).

[6] This phrase was first used by Bottoms (1995) to describe the enactment of retributive criminal justice policy based on a populist view of crime and justice.

(Thomas, 2000: 15–24; Silverman and Wilson, 2002; Greer, 2003). Sexual crime increasingly dominates the headlines (Caputi, 1987; Soothill and Walby, 1991; Benedict, 1992; Soothill and Grover, 1995). The word 'paedophile', in particular it seems, has become synonymous with sexual offending against children. Journalists, who readily manipulate the label in their reporting of cases of sexual crime involving children, have seized on the term. A computer search by Soothill and colleagues (1998) revealed that over the first four months of 1998 there were 712 articles including the words 'paedophilia' or 'paedophiles' in six leading British newspapers. As will be outlined below, moreover, there is also a marked international dimension to this phenomenon.

In the last two decades a number of tragic cases have attracted widespread publicity, provoked public outcry and provided the impetus for legislative and organisational change. An examination of some of the most high profile of these cases suggests a number of common themes. First, there were revelations about paedophile rings[7] and the vulnerability of children in environments traditionally considered secure such as churches, homes, clubs and schools.[8] Indeed, this issue of 'professional perpetrators' (Sullivan and Beech, 2002)—sex offenders who use their employment as a cover to target and sexually abuse children with whom they work—is highly prevalent in a number of jurisdictions including Canada (Law Commission of Canada, 2000) and Australia (Jokovich, 2003). In England and Wales, in particular, as will be discussed in chapter 4, there have been many high profile cases of the disclosure of institutional physical and sexual abuse in care homes which have captured the media's attention[9] and resulted in a number of public inquiries (Williams and McCreadie, 1992; Kirkwood, 1993; Waterhouse, 2000) and official reviews (Warner, 1992; Utting, 1998; Nolan, 2001). In Northern Ireland, the Kincora scandal (DHSS (Northern Ireland), 1982; HMSO, 1985; Moore, 1996)[10] and the case of care worker Martin Huston (DHSS (Northern Ireland), 1993)[11] resulted in a series of enquiries, reports and guidelines which underlined the importance of developing effective procedures to prevent unsuitable individuals from working with children.[12] In the Republic of Ireland,

---

[7] 'Police Investigate Public School Paedophile Ring' *The Times*, 25 August 1996; 'Paedophiles Jailed For Porn Ring' *BBC News Online* <http://news.bbc.co.uk/1/hi/uk/1168112.stm> (13 February 2001).

[8] 'Scout Master Jailed For Reign Of Child Abuse' *The Guardian*, 24 February 1998; 'Nun Found Guilty Of Raping Girl, 10, In Her Care' *The Times*, 12 June 1999; 'Teacher Is Jailed For Sex Abuse' *The Irish Times*, 31 March 2000; '109 Years In Prison For Swim Pervert' *The Mirror*, 27 May 2000.

[9] 'Sex Abuse Claim At Boys' Homes' *The Guardian*, 20 January 1998; 'Final Deadline For Abuse Cases' *BBC News Online* http://news.bbc.co.uk/1/hi/special_report/395540.stm (16 July 1999).

[10] The Kincora case involved the systematic abuse of boys through vice rings and prostitution in Kincora hostel in East Belfast which finally came to light in the early 1980s but which could be traced back at least two decades.

[11] Huston was convicted in 1992 on 25 counts of sexual offences against children. He had been on probation for 2 years between 1987 and 1989 for committing sexual offences, yet was able to find employment with a voluntary agency involving work with children.

[12] One of the most recent cases in Northern Ireland was the Barnardo's case in 2004 where two individuals were later acquitted on appeal of a total of 70 sexual offences against 8 children which took place at a Barnardo's home between 1977 and 1981. See: 'Pair Jailed For Child Sex Crimes' *BBC News Online* http://news.bbc.co.uk/1/hi/northern_ireland/3676714.stm (21 September 2004).

'paedophile priests,' in particular, have been the objects of media concern.[13] In the mid-1990s, the highly publicised 'Fr. Brendan Smyth affair' attracted widespread attention (Ferguson, 1995; Moore, 1995).[14] This was followed more recently by the Ferns Inquiry, which identified more than one hundred allegations of child sexual abuse, made over a 30-year period, against 21 priests (Murphy et al, 2005).[15] This phenomenon of clerical abuse, however, is a worldwide one, resulting in a considerable number of claims against the Roman Catholic Church, particularly in the United States (Berry, 1992; Plante, 1999; Nolan, 2001).[16] Accusations, moreover, have also been made against a number of other religious denominations.[17] As will be discussed further in chapter 4, the organisational culture of such institutions may be conducive to abuse of power and erosion of the primary functions of care and protection, and has consequently contributed to the covering up of allegations of abuse before subsequent public revelations.

A second broad theme is the prevalence of 'stranger danger' cases which have highlighted the dangers posed by convicted or suspected sex offenders living in the community. In England and Wales, the abduction and murder of Sophie Hook by suspected paedophile Howard Hughes,[18] and the murders in Soham of Holly Wells and Jessica Chapman by Ian Huntley, another known sex offender (Bichard, 2004),[19] drew attention to the need to manage sexual offenders in the community more effectively.[20] Similarly, the release in previous years of convicted child sex offenders Robert Oliver and Sydney Cooke provoked hysteria over the whereabouts of their release and highlighted the inadequacies of current arrangements for managing sex offenders in the community.[21] In Belgium, Marc Dutroux, a repeat sex offender who was released from prison in 1992 on the condition that he would enter therapy, abducted as many as 15 young girls before raping and torturing them and then starving them to death in a dungeon.[22] The preponderance

[13] 'Priest Abuses 10 Children' *The Irish News*, 14 December 1996; 'Sins Of the Father' *The Sunday Times*, 27 July 1999; 'Priest Given 12 Years For Sex Assaults' *The Irish Times*, 7 April 2000; '100 Dublin Priests Accused Of Abuse Since 1940' *The Guardian*, 9 March 2006.

[14] Smyth was sentenced to 12 years in prison after pleading guilty to the sexual abuse of 20 young people over a period of 36 years. He previously served 4 years in a Northern Ireland prison for similar offences. His case achieved notoriety not only for his actions, but because the then Taoiseach, Albert Reynolds, was forced to resign after revelations that his Attorney General delayed processing requests for Smyth's extradition.

[15] 'Ferns Report Will Stress Need To Strengthen Child Protection' *The Irish Times*, 22 October 2005; 'Inquiry On Abuse May Become A National Audit' *The Irish Times*, 26 October 2005; 'Church Set For More Abuse Shame' *Irish Independent*, 9 November 2005.

[16] 'Patterns Of Abuse Found Nationwide' *The Boston Globe*, 14 December 2002; 'Around The World, Clerical Sex Abuse Takes A Toll' *The Boston Globe*, 14 December 2002.

[17] See: 'Danger Of Trusting The Clergy' <http://www.reformation.com/CSA/wolfe1.htm>.

[18] 'The Devil You Know Still Abuses Children' *The Sunday Times*, 6 October 1997.

[19] 'How Huntley Slipped Through the Net' *BBC News Online* < http://news.bbc.co.uk/1/hi/uk/3313303.stm > (17 December 2003).

[20] The report of the Bichard Inquiry (2004: para 8) arising from the 'Soham murders' highlighted 'systemic and corporate failures' in the way in which the police managed their intelligence systems.

[21] 'For Our Children's Sake, Keep These Men In Prison' *The Daily Mail*, 13 March 1998; 'Six Evil Predators Bound For Freedom' *The Daily Mail*, 13 March 1998.

[22] 'The Making Of A Monster' *The Sunday Times*, 25 August 1996.

of these types of cases in the print media also means that an automatic link between the sexual assault of a child and their murder is firmly cemented in public consciousness.

Thirdly, one of the most prominent themes of media coverage of sexual offences has been the media led cry for a more punitive criminal justice response. In Scotland, for example, the Dunblane shootings of 16 primary school children by a suspected paedophile, Thomas Hamilton,[23] and the reoffending of released sex offenders, John Cronin and Gavin McGuire, sparked a *Daily Record* campaign entitled 'Charter for Our Children' (25–29 January 1997). Organisers, in particular, called for the authorities to reveal the identity of convicted sex offenders living in the community. Perhaps the most well known case in this respect is the kidnapping, molestation and murder of 8-year old Sarah Payne by Roy Whiting. In tandem with the *News of the World*'s 'Name and Shame' campaign, which will be discussed further below, the case led to calls for a new 'Sarah's Law,' prompted by the media and supported by Sarah's parents, to be the equivalent of 'Megan's Law' in the United States.[24] As will be discussed in more detail in chapter 5, the public demand for a much greater degree of community notification of the identity and whereabouts of known registered sex offenders as happens in the United States, has so far been rejected by the UK Gvernment (Rutherford, 2000; Thomas, 2001).

A popular image of the sex offender is therefore created, based on the notion of a mobile yet anonymous offender, which implies a homogenous category of perpetrator. In a form of 'criminal apartheid' (Soothill et al, 1998), the sex offender is demonised as a monster or fiend and is singled out above other dangerous offenders in society (Soothill and Walby, 1991: 146; Sampson, 1994: 43–44; Thomas, 2000: 15–24). Media coverage of sexual crimes also helps to create the impression that sexual crime is a narrow band of activity committed by a narrow band of offenders who have been convicted in the past for sexual offences and would be a danger in the future if released from prison too soon (Hebenton and Thomas, 1996a: 101; 1996b: 429). The underlying theme of newspaper stories about keeping track of convicted sex offenders is that if only adequate records could be maintained then women and children could be protected (Soothill and Walby (1991: 95–96).[25]

Media coverage of sexual offences has also had a number of undesirable effects on the popular imagination. As Greer (2003) has argued, media representations of sex crime give the public important cues about how they should perceive the nature and extent of sex crime, how they should think and feel about it, how they should respond to it and the measures that might be taken to reduce risk.

[23] Focus Special: 'Why?' *The Sunday Times*, 17 March 1996.

[24] See: <http://www.forsarah.com/html/welcome.html>; 'Parent Power' *News of the World*, 30 July 2000; 'Argument Rages Over "Sarah's Law"' *The Guardian*, 13 December 2001; 'Do We Need A "Sarah's Law"?' *BBC News Online* < http://news.bbc.co.uk/1/hi/uk/1708212.stm> (13 December 2001).

[25] 'Sex Attacker Struck While On Parole' *The Times*, 23 August 1994; 'Freed Paedophile Still A Threat To Children' *The Times*, 3 December 1994; 'Murderer Was "High Risk" Offender' *BBC News Online* < http://news.bbc.co.uk/1/hi/northern_ireland /4905370.stm> (13 April 2006).

Newspaper reporting of sexual offences, in this respect, has given the impression that there has been an unprecedented explosion in sexual crime and that women and children are increasingly at risk of attack by sexual monsters (Sampson, 1994: 42).[26]

This current popular focus on the dangers posed by child sexual offenders in the community, however, is significantly misplaced. As discussed at the outset of this book, the underlying reality is that the majority of child sexual offences happen within a domestic context where the offender is either related or known to the victim. Contrary to media portrayal and popular belief, children are far more at risk from parents and relatives and family friends than from strangers (Grubin, 1998). As Jackson and Scott (1999: 92–93) point out, media coverage of the risks posed by adults to children actually 'reverse[s] the order of danger' in that so-called 'stranger danger' is given more media coverage than cases of assault on children by intimates.

Moreover, the media are also influential in prompting or sustaining vengeful public attitudes in relation to sex offenders. In this respect, the press and public campaigns for the 'naming and shaming' of paedophiles provide a microcosm for the analysis of popular responses to the perceived threat posed by sex offenders in the community. As noted above, in response to the abduction and murder of 8-year old Sarah Payne in Sussex in July 2000, the *News of the World* developed its 'Name and Shame' campaign.[27] This campaign centred on the 'outing' of suspected and known paedophiles by printing their photographs, names and addresses, along with brief details of their offending history (Silverman and Wilson, 2002: 146–66). The newspaper promised to continue publishing such details until they had 'named and shamed' all the child sex offenders in Britain.

This media crusade provoked widespread hysteria and vigilante activity in Portsmouth where a number of residents protested nightly at the presence of paedophiles in their community and the failure of the authorities to notify them of their identities and whereabouts (Williams and Thompson, 2004). Angry protesters demonstrated outside the homes of suspected paedophiles, smeared slogans on their walls, issued threats and overturned and burned cars. As a result of this activity, several families fled, one convicted paedophile disappeared and two alleged paedophiles committed suicide (Ashenden, 2002: 208).[28] One woman's house was attacked merely because she had the same surname as a known sexual offender.

The aftermath of the 'Name and Shame' campaign underlines the potential for disintegrative shaming which may lead to harassment or even physical attack by vengeful members of the community on suspected paedophiles. As will be discussed further in chapters 5 and 6, disintegrative shaming practices are also

[26] History is littered with examples of periods when the public is obsessed by the notion that they or their children are at risk of sexual assault. For a comprehensive account of those since the Second World War (see especially: Soothill, 1993).

[27] See eg: some of the range of headlines which appeared in the *News of the World*, 23 July 2000: 'Named and Shamed'; 'If You Are A Parent Read This'; 'Does A Monster Live Near You?'

[28] 'Paedophile Kills Himself After Mob Attacks His Home' *The Mirror*, 9 August 2000.

evidenced in official discourses about sex offending in the legislative and judicial response to sexual offending.

Perceived risks about sexual offending, generated by the media, may also cause the public to view as inadequate the punishment of persistent and dangerous sex offenders and to support harsher treatment of them (Walker and Marsh, 1984; Hough et al, 1988; Sampson, 1994: 45–48; Soothill and Grover, 1995; Hough, 1996). A move from elitist to more populist penal policy-making, where governments consult the views of ordinary people prior to formulating and implementing crime policies, has ultimately resulted in harsher, less tolerant policies (Johnstone, 2000).[29] Indeed, punitive public attitudes towards sex offenders have also been reflected in recent criminal justice policy, which focuses predominantly on the need to control and manage risk and protect the public from dangerous, violent and sexual offenders in the community.

'The New Penology': Public Protection, Risk and Preventive Governance

Sex offending has also become more prominent in criminal justice agendas as a result of the centrality of the sentencing philosophy of incapacitation and the related emergence of the concept of 'risk' within social and political discourses. The concept of 'risk' has also been reflected in contemporary criminal justice debates generally, and in particular in the resulting legislative and policy framework on regulating the behaviour of sex offenders on release from custody (Hebenton and Thomas, 1996b; Kemshall and Maguire, 2003; Matravers, 2003).

In debates about social ordering, the concept of risk has increasingly furnished a discursive framework within which 'responses-to-problems' are being considered (Giddens, 1990). In post-modern society, attempts at offender-based risk-reduction strategies and the persistence of panoptic[30] principles have been prominent themes in the study of social control (Cohen, 1985; Lyon, 1994). Social order is increasingly thought of as something which cannot merely be protected and maintained but which must be actively constructed and managed. Theorists highlight what they see as the late twentieth century shift towards crime control and management of risk in the community that includes rather than excludes the offender (Brown, 1996; Hebenton and Thomas, 1996b). The 'institutionalisation of risk' in modern society is evidenced by the centrality of accurate risk prediction

---

[29] Penal populism, it seems, is not confined to the UK but has had considerable growth and influence on recent criminal justice policy in other countries such as New Zealand (Pratt and Clark, 2005). The authors argue that this phenomenon can be attributed to four factors: disenchantment with the democratic process; the dynamics of crime and insecurity in a period of considerable social change; the growth and influence of 'victimization groups'; and the emergence of a new kind of penal expertise.

[30] The concept of 'panoptican', which Foucault (1977) borrowed from Bentham, focuses on surveillance as a form of social control. The term derives from the Greek word 'pan', meaning 'all', and 'opticon' which represents the visual. Foucault views the movement towards the panoptical form as a characteristic feature of the modern prison which was typically organised around a central court yard so that a few could supervise or survey a large number (Mathieson, 1997).

and management to almost all complex organisations, including those of probation (Robinson, 2002; Hudson, 2001), social services (Kemshall et al, 1997) and
the police (Ericson, 1994; Johnston, 2000).

Indeed, the contemporary politics of crime control also place a strong emphasis on public protection, risk management and preventive governance as part of
the 'new penology' (Feeley and Simon, 1992), 'risk society' (Beck, 1992; Ericson
and Haggerty, 1997) or 'the new regulatory state' (Braithwaite, 2000; Shearing,
2000). Risk assessment and management and its association with what Feeley and
Simon call 'actuarial justice' (1994) form the basis of preventive strategies like
selective incapacitation, risk of custody scales, preventative intervention with 'at
risk' groups and community-based initiatives (Crawford, 1999: 86).

This risk penality has been particularly evident in relation to concerns over the
risk posed by released sex offenders living in the community where assessing,
managing and reducing those risks has become a central concern (Simon, 1998;
Kemshall and Maguire, 2003; Matravers, 2003). Indeed, it has been argued that the
concepts of risk management (Parton et al, 1997: 232–40; Robinson, 2002;
Hudson, 2001) and more recently, governance (Ashenden, 2002, 2004; Wargent,
2002) have become the key signifiers for the regulation of child (sexual) abuse and
managing sex offenders in the community generally, both in terms of policy development and practical decision-making.

As will be argued further below, however, while the governance or control of the
dangerous and those who pose a risk to society, particularly sex offenders, has been
a mainstay of criminal justice debates in recent years, there is conflict and wide
variation in the methods of social control deployed (Garland, 1996, 2001;
O'Malley, 1999, 2002; Pratt, 2000). As Rose argues, these range from punitive
demands for execution or preventive detention of dangerous or 'risky' individuals
such as paedophiles and persistent violent offenders to the development of multi-
agency work on the assessment and management of risk and the use of therapeutic and rehabilitative alternatives via community disposals and reintegrative
shaming (2000: 321).

The 'tracking' or management of sexual offenders in the community can also be
seen in a narrower context which emphasises both the proactive 'management' of
knowledge about offenders and the production of compensatory measures against
risk (Hebenton and Thomas, 1996a; 1996b: 430–32, 439–40). 'Knowing' offenders' activities and their whereabouts allows for both preventative action and for
risk assessment where offenders are made objects of knowledge in order to classify
them into appropriate risk categories (Hebenton and Thomas, 1996a: 108, 1996b:
440). In the context of the police (Ericson, 1994; Johnston, 2000), previously dominant values such as prosecution give way to having access to and recording knowledge about suspects or offenders in the community.

The post-prison release arrangements for managing sexual offenders in the
community can also be usefully considered in terms of the two inter-related concepts of 'risk' and 'security' (Hebenton and Thomas, 1996b: 430–32, 435).
Following Ericson and Haggerty's (1997) model of 'knowledge-risk-security,' the

primary purpose of measures such as sex offender registration is to increase public safety and security through managing the risk posed by persons convicted or cautioned of sexual offences by having knowledge of their whereabouts. The conditions attached to registration for the offender and the degree of notification permitted to the community, for example, vary depending on the assessed level of risk. The logic of this risk assessment is that it targets those offenders who pose the greatest risk to the public. As will be outlined further below, formal risk assessment is routinely undertaken by inter-agency panels comprising members of the police, social services and probation, and additonally, voluntary sector agencies involved in the provision of accommodation and training and employment initiatives.

As will be argued in chapter 5 in relation to the practical problems of registration, 'risk management' in this context is in itself paradoxical in that the process is rooted in and itself constitutes 'insecurity' (Ewald, 1986; Hebenton and Thomas, 1996b: 440). Indeed, consistent with Ericson and Haggerty's (1997) model, sex offender registration appeared to be produced, in part, from an assumption that simply having knowledge about an offender's whereabouts would make the community safe. Yet, the legislation failed, in particular, to develop a clear concept of how this knowledge could actually be used, beyond the transcarceration of the offender through registration, to reduce the risk of future offending and to protect the community. Failure to address a number of key practical issues during the formulation of the legislation has meant that the expansion and heightening of the intention of control of sex offenders, through registration and community notification, effectively ends up producing the opposite (Hebenton and Thomas, 1996b: 441).

This focus on risk, dangerousness and public protection within criminal justice agendas generally has manifested itself strongly in the law, policy and practice surrounding the management of sex offenders in the community. Successive governments, mindful of the need to deliver 'populist punitiveness'[31] (Bottoms, 1995) and to counter mounting public hysteria, have developed an increasingly punitive legislative framework which lays emphasis on the effective management of the dangerous.

The Legislative Framework

The United States, in particular, has a history of increasingly punitive legislation. The most recent and significant of these measures, known as the 'three strikes and you're out' law, was passed in 1994, first in Washington and California and then

---

[31] Criminologists have highlighted the widening gap between criminology and criminal policy (Garland and Sparks, 2000: 192). As Radzinowicz put it: 'The stark fact stands out that, in the field of criminal justice, in spite of the output of criminological knowledge, a populist political approach holds sway' (1999: 469). It has also been argued, however, that there has been a one-sided, exaggerated focus on punitiveness in recent times, since the deployment of punitive sanctions has historically been an endemic feature of the criminal justice system (Matthews, 2005).

in the majority of states (Shichor and Sechrest, 1996). Indeed, many American states have adopted legislation in response to the problems of the management of repeat sex offenders in the community. Several different laws have been enacted to deal specifically with violent sexual crime. This has included the civil commitment of dangerous sex offenders (Alexander, 1995; Lieb et al, 1998), chemical castration, and sex offender registration and community notification, eventually embodied in what has become known as 'Megan's Law' (Bedarf, 1995; Kimball, 1996).

These developments have been broadly reflected in the criminal and civil law arrangements put in place in the United Kingdom where the recent emphasis has also been on identifying individuals who are likely to commit serious harm in the future. By the end of the 1990s, a range of measures providing for extended sentences and increased monitoring and surveillance of sex offenders in the community had been enacted to protect the public, and children in particular, from the risks posed by this category of offender (Hudson, 2005: 13). In this respect, the regulatory framework for managing sex offenders can be further sub-divided into penal and mental health provision and measures on release from custody.

Penal Provision

In the United Kingdom, as the 1990s unfolded, the retributive notions of the late 1980s and early 1990s (Home Office, 1988, 1990; Woolf, 1991), were gradually eroded in favour of custody and incapacitation. The assertion by Michael Howard, the former Conservative Home Secretary, that 'prison works' showed that prison and punishment were firmly back in favour for the 1990s. The Criminal Justice Act 1991, as part of its bifurcated (Bottoms, 1987) or 'twin-track' (Cavadino and Dignan, 1992) policy, authorised 'public protection' sentences for violent and sexual offenders. Less serious offenders were to be dealt with by 'community penalties' while violent and sexual offenders could be given custodial sentences longer than their 'just deserts' in order to protect the public from serious harm.

When the Labour Government came to power in 1997, it appeared keen initially to discard some of the more punitive aspects of the criminal justice policy introduced by the previous Conservative Government and carve out 'a third way' (Hoyle and Young, 2002: 533). The White Paper *No More Excuses* (Home Office, 1997a) proposed the introduction of the principles and practices of restorative justice into the youth justice system of England and Wales. As will be discussed at the end of the next chapter, these changes were subsequently introduced through a range of legislative measures (Fionda, 1999). However, violent and sexual offenders were to remain the focus of specific targeted punitive sentencing interventions. The Crime (Sentences) Act 1997, for instance, introduced a mandatory life sentence on a second conviction for a serious sexual or violent offence. This was subsequently re-enacted in the Powers of Criminal Courts (Sentencing) Act 2000.

The current sentencing framework is also based on 'selective incapacitation' (Dingwall, 1998). The broad sentencing premise is that of 'just deserts' or proportionality, with sex offenders being singled out for special consideration (Clarkson,

1997). This has been reflected in two main ways: in the nature and length of the sentence imposed, and the compulsory period of supervision in the community as part of the extended sentence (Cobley, 2003: 52–60). In this vein, following a review of sentencing structures in the Halliday report (Home Office, 2001a; Wasik, 2004), Part 12 of the Criminal Justice Act 2003 sets out a new sentencing framework (Ashworth and Player, 2005) which introduces in particular a scheme of 'custody plus' to take account of recent and relevant previous convictions (Roberts, 2002, 2003; von Hirsch, 2002; Thomas, 2004). Under the extended sentence the offender is given an appropriate custodial term followed by a further period for which he is subject to licence. In addition, and perhaps more controversially, Part 12 of the Act also introduces an indeterminate preventative sentence for violent or sexual offenders for public protection purposes (Henham, 2003; Padfield, 2003). Offenders would remain in custody under this protective sentence until it is considered that the risk they presented has sufficiently diminished. These and other initatives will be discussed in turn throughout the book.

New Labour's tough stance on 'law and order' has ensured the continuation of a populist punitive approach as part of a viscious policy cycle. Punitive political rhetoric fuels public fear which consequently produces a greater demand for more action and a more punitive society (McCold, 1996). This has in turn, however, ultimately sustained a broader problem in terms of a 'punishment deficit' (Brownlee, 1998: 313). The public's expectations that crime can be effectively controlled by a policy of deterrence through retributive punishment are unrealistically raised. The reality is, however, that contemporary retributive mechanisms which have been put in place to manage known sex offenders will do little to protect children from abuse in the home, where they may be most at risk from hidden dangers.

Mental Health Provision

In a similar vein, the current review of the mental health legislation, contained in the Mental Health Bill 2004, proposes the introduction of an indeterminate sentence for the severely personality disordered. Traditionally, dangerous people have been dealt with by one of two routes. Those who have committed an offence have been dealt with by the criminal justice system, while individuals who are mentally ill and in need of treatment have been processed through the mental health system. In recent times, however, a new category has emerged, that of the dangerous person with a severe personality disorder who is untreatable, yet who may have committed no offence. This new measure is aimed at filling the specific gap in the law which exists in relation to untreatable severely personality disordered individuals which may also include sex offenders. As will be discussed further in chapter 6, these proposed measures have been criticised as a form of preventive detention and, as such, have been strongly opposed on both practical and civil liberty grounds (McAlinden, 2001).

Post-Release Control

This toughening in penal policy towards sex offenders, however, was most clearly reflected in proposals to control sex offenders in the community more effectively. A 1996 government white paper (Home Office, 1996a: para 8.2.) advocated strengthening the arrangements for supervising convicted sex offenders following their release from custody, with the general aim of *Protecting the Public.* These recommendations led to a consultation document on the sentencing and supervision of sex offenders (Home Office, 1996b; Cobley, 1997a). Its five main proposals have now been embodied in a range of legislation.[32]

As will be discussed in detail in chapter 5, sex offender registration—the well publicised initiative requiring sex offenders to register their name and address with the local police—has been one of the most high profile of the recent measures in the government's response to concern over sex offenders and which, perhaps as a result, has attracted considerable criticism and debate (Marshall, 1997; Soothill et al, 1997; Soothill and Francis, 1998; Cobley, 2003). These and other measures are founded on the basic premise that the best way to protect the community and potential victims is through increased restriction, surveillance and monitoring of sex offenders (Kemshall, 2001). Indeed, the other recent developments in the law, policy and practice, on the management of sex offenders in the community can also be framed within an overall retributive regulatory framework.[33]

Most of this legislation pertaining to the sentencing and supervision of sex offenders in the United Kingdom, as previously outlined, has now been strengthened or re-enacted under the Sexual Offences Act 2003. Following a twin review of the law on sexual offences generally (Home Office, 2000) and the Sex Offenders Act 1997 specifically (Home Office, 2001b), a further White Paper set out to address the issues raised by these reviews with the same broad aim of protecting

---

[32] These were as follows: Extended supervision of sex offenders on release from custody (Crime (Sentences) Act 1997 and Crime and Disorder Act 1998); DNA testing on blood samples taken from convicted sex offenders in prison (Criminal Evidence (Amendment) Act 1997); Supervised access by defendants to victim statements and photographs (Sexual Offences (Protected Material) Act 1997); Measures to prevent sex offenders from seeking employment involving access to children (Criminal Justice and Court Services Act 2000); and a system of registration (Sex Offenders Act 1997)

[33] The Sexual Offences (Conspiracy and Incitement) Act 1996—enabled Britons to be tried in the United Kingdom for sexual offences committed abroad; the Protection from Harassment Act 1997—widened the definition of sexual crimes to include stalking; the Police Act 1997—established the Criminal Records Bureau to provide a more effective means of carrying out criminal record checks; the Crime and Disorder Act 1998—introduced a civil sex offender order to restrict the behaviour of sex offenders in the community; the Protection of Children Act 1999—combined the Department of Health Pre-Employment Consultancy Service Index (PECS) and the Department of Education and Employment 'List 99' to make it easier for employers to check whether those who wish to work with children are known or suspected abusers; the Sexual Offences (Amendment) Act 2000—made it an offence for an adult to engage in any sexual activity with a child if they are in a position of trust; and the Criminal Justice and Courts Services Act 2000—strengthened the registration requirements; introduced restraining and disqualification orders to restrict the offender's movement and disqualify certain offenders from working with children respectively, and placed greater emphasis on inter-agency partnerships for managing sex offenders in the community in the form of MAPPPs (Multi-Agency Public Protection Panels).

the public (Home Office, 2002). This ultimately resulted in the drafting and enactment of the Sexual Offences Act 2003. As mentioned in chapter 1, the Act redefined and widened the scope of sexual offences in general. It also amended the registration or notification provisions in Part I of the Sex Offenders Act 1997 as well as introducing several new mechanisms to control the activities of sex offenders in the community. These developments will also be discussed as they occur throughout the book. The proliferation of legislative measures, in the United Kingdom in particular, is indicative of the high level of political attention afforded in recent years to managing the risk posed by sex offenders in the community, and dangerous people more generally, within an an overall retributive framework.[34] The key organisations in the criminal justice field that work to manage the risk posed by these offenders and to protect the public have therefore been given greater regulatory powers to carry out their work.

Multi-Agency Work on the Assessment and Management of Risk

The assessment and management of the risk posed by released sex offenders in the community is the pivotal focus of inter-agency policy and practice (Cobley, 2003). In the United Kingdom, all work in relation to the management of sexual offenders in the community takes place on a multi-agency basis and is routinely co-ordinated by the statutory, voluntary and community sectors (Kemshall and Maguire, 2001; Maguire et al, 2001). In addition to the plethora of legislation on sexual offences, there is a complex bulk of guidelines for those agencies that deal with sex offenders.

A number of recent developments in the governmental approach to crime control have contributed to the policing of sex offenders (Cowan et al, 2001) within an overall regulatory framework. Emphasis has been placed in particular on related concepts such as 'active citizenship,' 'partnership', and 'multi-agency working' (Cowan, 1997; Crawford, 1999). Within state agencies themselves, institutional change has also been introduced to promote these aims through, for example, joint decision-making between previously separate departments (Garland, 1996: 453). Previously informal initiatives by various agencies (Sampson et al, 1988) have been reinforced by the adoption of 'joined up' working (Cowan et al, 2001: 439) and 'the end to end management of the offender.'[35] This has been particularly evident in relation to sex offenders through the introduction of multi-agency panels for the assessment and management of risk (Kemshall et al, 1997). The upshot of recent

---

[34] In the Republic of Ireland, over the past 15 years there has also been increased legislative focus on the management of sex offenders. A Department of Justice discussion paper on the 'Law on Sexual Offences' (Department of Justice, 1998) also advocated strengthening the arrangements for supervising released sex offenders in the community along similar lines to the UK. Its main proposals, including post-release supervision and a registration system for all convicted sex offenders, are now embodied in the Sex Offenders Act 2001.

[35] See National Offender Management Service (NOMS) website, < http://www.noms.homeoffice.gov.uk>.

developments in the area of risk 'has been the evolution of an organisational paradigm of "protection of the public" which crosses institutional boundaries' (Cowan et al, 2001: 440).

As Crawford argues: 'In many senses inter-agency partnerships are really merely the extension of the concept of "community" to organisations' (1999: 55). In the past decade these organisational communities have become an important part of British criminal justice policy. Academics and those in government circles have endorsed the need for greater multi-agency co-operation as the most effective means of policy formulation and service delivery (Crawford, 1999: 56).[36] This is also linked to a more jaded view of the capacity of the state to 'deliver' in a host of arenas including justice. The essential argument for a multi-agency approach lies in what Young has called 'the realities of crime and social control' (1992: 45). Social control in modern society is, by its very nature, multi-agency. Different criminal justice agencies have a different 'purchase on a given crime problem' due to their particular expertise (Young, 1991).

The central role in the inter-agency approach is played by the statutory agencies of the police and probation services. Important contributions are also made by other bodies such as the Prison Service, social services, local housing authorities, mental health providers and the department of education. In addition, the notion of 'partnership' has been extended on an 'informal' basis to voluntary agencies involved in the provision of services in the community (Crawford, 1999: 58). The voluntary sector, in the United Kingdom, in this respect, includes those agencies which work towards the resettlement of sex offenders in the community after their release from prison through the provision of training and employment initiatives, such as the National Association for the Care and Resettlement of Offenders (NIACRO) and those who deal with sex offenders generally through the provision of accommodation.

These large voluntary organisations may play the role of liaison between statutory agencies and the community on the issue of the management of sex offenders in the community. The voluntary sector in Northern Ireland, for example, has provided a professional, pragmatic and considered approach to questions relating to sex offenders in the community that has prevented Northern Ireland from adopting some of the more extreme measures of the United States and other jurisdictions. The Northern Ireland Voluntary Sector Sex Offender Working Group was established in 1994 in the aftermath of the *Abuse of Trust* report (DHSS (Northern Ireland), 1993), as a consortium of voluntary sector organisations, in order to exchange information, policy and practice in this area of work. It

---

[36] The terms 'partnership', 'multi-agency' and 'inter-agency' are used interchangeably here as they are in the literature (Liddle and Gelsthorpe, 1994). Crawford and Jones, however, draw attention to the differences between conceptions of 'partnership' work. Like the distinction between 'multi-disciplinary' and 'inter-disciplinary' studies, they make the distinction between 'multi-agency' relations, which merely involve the coming together of a variety of agencies in relation to a given problem, and 'inter-agency' relations which entail some degree of fusion of relations between agencies (1996: 30–31).

produced the key inter-agency report *Sex Offenders in the Community* (Voluntary Sector Sex Offender Working Group, 1997a, b), widely recognised as an influential guide to policy on sex offenders.

In place of a model of professional 'expertise' therefore is one that emphasises shared information and the importance of diverse knowledgeable agencies and a knowledgeable public (Crawford, 1999: 59). The overall purpose of such arrangements is to facilitate the exchange of information between agencies and the formulation of risk management plans in respect of individual offenders (Maguire et al, 2001). In this respect, multi-agency arrangements in relation to the effective management and treatment of sex offenders were in part formalised as a result of Part I of The Sex Offenders Act 1997, which came into force on 1 September 1997. These provisions have since been re-enacted by the Sexual Offences Act 2003. As mentioned above in relation to the legislative framework, the 1997 Act stipulated that certain categories of sex offenders must register their name and address with the police. In accordance with the guidelines issued under the Act, agencies were now required to co-operate more closely to identify, assess, monitor and manage the risk presented by registered sex offenders in the interests of public protection and a better exchange of information (Home Office, 1997b).

Inter-agency procedures have been further formalised by sections 67–68 of the Criminal Justice and Courts Services Act 2000 (Maguire and Kemshall, 2004). These provisions place a duty on the police and probation services as 'the responsible authority' to establish arrangements for assessing and managing the risks posed by sex offenders and other potentially dangerous offenders in the community. These arrangements were enhanced by the Criminal Justice Act 2003 which extended the responsible authority to include the Prison Service.[37] The Act also established a reciprocal 'duty to co-operate' between the responsible authority and a number of other agencies such as local education, housing and health and social services authorities.[38]

Under the current arrangements, the relevant agencies meet, share information and formulate co-ordinated risk management plans relating to those individuals who pose a serious risk to public safety. This rigorous risk assessment and management procedure usually consists of specialists grading sexual offenders as low, medium or high risk based on their likelihood of re-offending. The logic of this risk assessment is that it targets those offenders who pose the greatest risk to the public. In England and Wales there are now Multi-Agency Public Protection Panels (MAPPPs) to carry out his task (Kemshall and Maguire, 2001, 2002; Maguire et al, 2001; Bryan and Doyle, 2003; Lieb, 2003).[39] These panels have the

---

[37] s 325(1).

[38] s 325(6).

[39] Current inter-agency risk assessment protocols for sex offenders are based on two basic approaches (Kemshall, 2001). One is the clinical method which is essentially a diagnostic assessment derived in part from the medical and mental health fields. The other is the actuarial method which uses statistical techniques to predict the risk of reoffending. There are weaknesses in both approaches so that their combined use is currently advocated as a more accurate, holistic approach to risk assessment. There are a number of tools for predicting sex offence recidivism which are used conjunctively: the

power to disclose information about offenders to schools, voluntary agencies and other groups in the community. More recently, members of the public are also being recruited to contribute to the strategic risk management of the MAPPP arrangements (Home Office, 2002: 15).

Indeed, one of the most difficult issues for those organisations involved in the inter-agency approach who work towards the management of sex offenders in the community is that of disclosure or the sharing of information about sex offenders with the community (Kemshall and Maguire, 2003). As will be discussed in chapter 5 in relation to sex offender registration and community notification, the question of when the community should be notified about the presence of sex offenders living in their area in the United Kingdom is certainly nowhere near as widespread as in the United States.

The difficulties related to community reaction to the resettlement of the sex offenders in the local community, as will be highlighted in chapter 4, make it clear that this is a volatile issue. In general, inter-agency procedures provide that information is released strictly on a 'need to know' basis and that only in exceptional circumstances should specific information, such as name and address, be made available to the community. Disclosure may be made where there is a specific threat of serious harm to an individual child or group of children (Power, 2003). In other words, the level of information passed to the community must always reflect the level of assessed risk.[40]

The Problematic Nature of Multi-agency Relations

Effective work with sex offenders necessitates an effective partnership approach. The success of the MAPPP arrangements have been reflected in the annual area reports first published in 2002.[41] These confirm that the new arrangements have led to more effective inter-agency working and have built on existing good practice (Home Office, 2001c: 14).[42] Co-ordination is clearly the touchstone of inter-agency processes which are based around a federation rather than a unifica-

Rapid Risk Assessment for Sex Offence Recidivism (RRASOR), widely used in Canada and the United States in post sentence detention procedures (Hanson, 1997), and the Structured Anchored Clinical Judgement (SACJ), which is used by the Prison Service and the police in England and Wales (Grubin, 1998), have now been combined into STATIC 99 which has increased predictive accuracy (Hanson and Thornton, 1999). More recently, MATRIX 2000 has refined and updated the SACJ.

[40]   In *R v Chief Constable of North Wales Police, ex parte Thorpe* [1999] QB 396 (CA), it was held that the police were only entitled to notify the community about convicted sex offenders living in their area when they reasonably conclude that this is what is required in order to protect the public. This case also echoes the dichotomy between protecting the rights of victims and offenders.

[41]   These are available online, <http://www.probation.homeoffice.gov.uk/output/Page30.asp.>

[42]   A recent review of the equivalent approach in Northern Ireland—Multi-agency Procedures for the Assessment and Management of Sex Offenders (MASRAM) also commented positively on the process. It was said to have 'undoubtedly tightened the assessment and management arrangements' that apply to sex offenders while at the same time moving 'well beyond concentrating on the "critical few" offenders who pose an imminent risk of serious harm' (Criminal Justice Inspection Northern Ireland, 2005: 5).

tion of agencies with the same core goal of public protection (Kemshall and Maguire, 2001; Parton et al, 1997). However, differences in approach to the problem of offender management may result in fragmented working practices and in a breakdown of effective communication of information about offenders. Indeed, a growing body of literature exists on the problematic nature of the inter-agency response in terms of the competing contributions, priorities and aims of the organisations involved, where a number of broad critiques emerge:

First, in practice, structural, cultural, conceptual and definitional tensions exist between different criminal justice agencies which constitute 'sites' of ideological and organisational conflict around which inter-agency relations are structured (Crawford, 1999: 94–147). The police and probation services, for example, are marked by very different training, occupational socialisation, philosophies and working practices (Crawford: 1999: 97). The notions of expertise, task specialisation and different organisational functions produce a complex web of inter-agency conflicts as well as alliances. These may be manifested in the form of mutual suspicion and distrust and differential power relations between personnel from differing organisations.

Secondly, the partnership approach appears to call into question the processes of professionalisation and the established division of criminal justice labour. The paradoxical nature of inter-agency work is that it simultaneously requires organisations to co-operate to share information across organisational boundaries but at the same time recognises the need for individual organisational autonomy with clearly defined responsibilities. The result is that 'we are left with a complex interplay between the logics of new discourses and the practices of old institutions' (Crawford, 1999: 61). The blurring of organisational boundaries may cause concern among professionals that they may lose their own distinct organisational autonomy and identity (Crawford, 1999: 113–16) and can give rise to conflicts between 'project loyalties' and 'organisational loyalties' (Crawford, 1999: 122).

Thirdly, power relations, which exist at a 'deep structural level,' are the central aspects in the study of inter-organisational networks (Blagg et al, 1988; Sampson et al, 1988, 1991; Pearson et al, 1992; Crawford and Jones, 1995). Institutional and structural power differences exist between agencies and are incorporated into multi-agency work. Human and material resources, access to information, and competing claims to specialist knowledge all affect the capacity of agencies to achieve desired outcomes (Crawford, 1999: 127). For example, specialisation in crime prevention, together with the wealth of statistical information on crimes have allowed the police to become 'experts' and 'new security professionals' in the field of crime prevention and control (Reiner, 1991; Crawford, 1999: 131). In the face of this expertise, other partners in inter-agency work are often left muted (Crawford, 1999: 131).[43] Moreover, it has also been argued that power differentials

---

[43] Others, however, argue that there has been an overemphasis on the conflicting and constraining nature of power relations and that this underestimates the creative and productive nature of action within structural constraints (Crawford, 1999: 132–33) where 'power is the means of getting things done' (Giddens, 1984: 283).

influence other symptomatic forms of inter-agency conflict, such as struggles over confidentiality and privileged access to information (Sampson et al, 1991: 132).

Fourthly, there may be difficulties in making inter-agency policies formulated at managerial and policy level actually work at the operational level where the nuances and dynamics of personal relationships on the ground may frustrate inter-agency processes. For example, claims to confidentiality in information exchange also give rise to inter-agency conflicts as individuals pursue their own agendas and are unwilling to release information (Crawford, 1999: 109–10, 112). While the partnership approach may be embraced by those at policy or manager-ial level, agreements struck there can be difficult to implement at the front-line level of service delivery where junior officers are required to re-establish and renegotiate relations. This may mean that 'partnerships' located high in the rank structure in over-formalised settings are all too often remote from the day-to-day work of officers (Hope and Murphy, 1983; Crawford, 1999: 107–8). Crawford suc-cinctly summarises all these problems which taken together indicate that the very essence of inter-agency working may undermine the effective risk assessment and management of sex offenders:

> The ethos and practice of 'partnerships' embody deep structural antagonisms and unresolved tensions. Partnerships, in all their guises place a high premium upon con-sensus, communication, mutuality, and the sharing of knowledge. And yet, the reality of competition, conflict, and organisational autonomy remain essential characteristics of criminal justice (1999: 60).

CONCLUSION

This chapter has outlined the political and policy-making context of the current regulatory framework for managing the risk posed by sex offenders in the com-munity. This framework has developed within a broadly retributive context where punitive public attitudes have in turn been reflected in official responses to sex offending via the development of a crime control 'law and order' ideology. More specifically, the current retributive paradigm has been predominantly based on concerns about the need to manage risk and protect the public from dangerous, violent and sexual offenders in the community. As a result, recent criminal justice policy and penal practice have singled sex offenders out for special attention and a large body of legislation to manage and control these individuals has been enacted within a relatively short space of time. As Cowan et al have argued, however:

> [T]his punitive stance, which essentially involves the state asserting control, directly con-tradicts the assertion that the state has failed to control crime (2001: 441).

The middle part of the book will examine the state's response to controlling the risk presented by sex offenders in the community and argue that it may in fact have succeeded in achieving the opposite. If substantial weaknesses in the present regulatory response to managing sex offenders in the community can be clearly identified, and more effective mechanisms can be formulated to enhance partnerships between statutory, voluntary and community sectors, then perhaps there is greater potential for achieving real and effective child protection strategies.

In this respect, the book will ultimately explore whether more cohesive partnerships between these various constituencies may offer a more progressive, and ultimately more effective means of protecting the public than previous legislative efforts, such as the provisions of Part I of the Sex Offenders Act 1997 and other situational attempts to manage sex offenders in the community (Wortley and Smallbone, 2006) through, for example, electronic tagging and restrictions on the movement of sex offenders in public areas via sex offender orders. The theoretical backdrop to such an approach, as will be discussed in the next chapter, is the restorative or reintegrative theory or justice.

3

Restorative and Reintegrative Theory

A DETAILED TREATMENT OF the theory of restorative justice, or related practices, is beyond the scope of this book. The central concern here is rather to examine whether it may be applied to sexual offences as a serious form of offending. As such, what follows in this chapter is a brief outline of the essential components of restorative and reintegrative theory, and the related notion of 'shaming' in particular, as a contrast to the retributive framework set out in the previous chapter. A fuller discussion of practices and critiques of these justice paradigms as they apply to sexual offences will be undertaken in the last part of the book.

Central questions for the present discussion, and one of the themes which recurs throughout this book, are the relationship between restorative or reintegrative theory and the formal criminal law and ultimately how the two forms of justice might be reconciled. Indeed, it could reasonably be asserted that the latter issues—should restorative justice be applied to serious forms of offending, and if so, how can this be reconciled in practice with formal legal structures?—are perhaps the most contentious ones within contemporary restorative justice debates.

RESTORATIVE JUSTICE

What is Restorative Justice?

In modern thinking about restorative justice, such approaches routinely comprise the three central actors of the victim, the offender and the community (Zehr, 1990; Braithwaite, 1999). As a concept, however, it is not easy to define. Daly (2002b) has noted that there is an extraordinarily wide range of understandings of the term 'restorative justice.' As will be discussed further below, some emphasise core values and key principles, some focus on aims and outcomes, while others still use the term to refer to specific programmes or substantive practices (Hoyle and Young, 2002: 527). One much used definition was proffered by Marshall as:

[A] process whereby all the parties with a stake in a particular offence come together to resolve collectively how to deal with the aftermath of the offence and its implications for the future' (1999: 5).[1]

Essentially, it focuses on 'changing the normative orientation of law from retribution to restoration' (Hudson, 1998: 238). It views crime not as a violation of a general legal category which merits punishment, but as harm to individual people and relationships and, as the term suggests, seeks to redress or restore that harm (Consedine, 1995; Van Ness and Strong, 1997/2002). The difference between state justice and restorative justice is not so much in the remedies proposed, but in the processes of decision-making. Restorative justice goes further than state justice in including a determination of 'what happened' in its process of deliberation, as well as deciding the appropriate remedy (Hudson, 1998: 251). It should be noted, however, that the restorative process generally presupposes that the offender has acknowledged responsibility for an offence. Restorative justice therefore is not a fact-finding process focused on the determination of guilt, but is concerned rather with devising an appropriate response to admitted behaviour. In other words, its realm is that of sentencing, and not that of adjudication as in the criminal trial (Hoyle and Young, 2002: 525).

The terms 'restorative justice' (Zehr, 1990, 1995) and 'community justice' (Barajas, 1995; Griffiths and Hamilton, 1996; Karp and Clear, 2002) are often used interchangeably (Clear, 2006). Indeed, a third alternative in this context is the hybrid-term, 'restorative community justice' (Bazemore and Schiff, 1996). However, although the usage of these two concepts has become blurred, there are important nuanced and conceptual distinctions between them (Crawford and Clear, 2003). In the main it has been argued that restorative justice is 'case based' whereas community justice is 'community based'—the former 'works' when key participants end up feeling restored, while the latter 'works' when the quality of life in a given place is improved (Crawford and Clear, 2003).[2]

Despite these subtle differences, there are nonetheless a number of common themes in these paradigms. These include changing the focus of justice intervention from retribution to reparation; altering the justice process to bring informal justice processes closer to local communities and increase citizen involvement in the process of restoration (and reintegration); considering the impact on victims and significant others, and empowering victims and offenders (Zehr, 1990, 1995;

---

[1] Braithwaite (1999: 5–6), however, recognises the limitations of this definition in terms of a failure to specify who or what is restored and to define the core values of restorative justice. Others have also criticised it as being too restrictive. (See, eg: Bazemore and Walgrave, 1999; McCold, 2000; Walgrave, 2000). As Zehr and Mika note, as restorative programmes become more widespread, the number of definitions has increased significantly (1998: 47). The latter provide a fundamental definition based on a 'values approach' which is comprised of three major themes: (1) crime as a violation of persons, interpersonal relationships and community that (2) create harms, obligation and liabilities and (3) justice processes that address needs and seek to heal and right wrongs. These components are also endorsed as the core principles of restorative justice practice in the context of paramilitary punishment violence in Northern Ireland (Mika and McEvoy, 2001).

[2] Alternative labels include 'relational justice,' 'positive justice' and 'reintegrative justice.'

Van Ness, 1993; Bazemore and Umbreit, 1995). These common elements are the subject of this analysis which will focus on the benefits of 'community' or 'reintegrative' justice as a whole in managing the risk posed by sex offenders in the community.

As mentioned above, there is much scholarly debate as to whether restorative justice is properly to be understood as a set of principles rather than a particular practice, with no clear answers being provided either way. In any case, there are a number of key values which are said to underpin restorative approaches which are as follows (Dignan and Lowey, 1999; Crawford and Goodey, 2000): First, the principle of 'inclusivity'—restorative approaches take account of the interests of victims in particular, in addition to those of offenders and often the wider community, in deciding how best to deal with an offence. They extend the range of those entitled to participate in the process of dealing with the offence and bring the victim and the offender more fully into the process. They also extend the range of potential outcomes of the process to include restoration for the victim and reintegration of the offender back into the community. Secondly, the balance of interests—restorative approaches recognise the need to strike an appropriate balance between the various interests at stake with mutual respect for and empowerment of all parties involved in the process. Thirdly, consensual non-coercive participation and decision-making—a key requirement is voluntary participation. Neither the victim nor the offender should be forced to participate in a restorative justice process or the outcome.[3] Fourthly, problem-solving orientation—the approach is forward looking and aims to prevent future offending which goes beyond dealing with the aftermath of the particular crime to reintegrating offenders back into the community.

International Restorative Practices

The umbrella terms of 'community' or 'restorative' justice have generally been associated with a myriad of programmes and practices that seek to respond to crime in what is seen to be a more constructive way than through the use of conventional criminal justice approaches (Galaway and Hudson, 1996). In practice, informal systems of restorative justice can take several forms. These include reparation (Cox, 1999; Wasik, 1999); restitution (Barnett, 1977; Galaway and Hudson, 1990; Karp, 1996); victim compensation (Miers, 1991) and mediation (Marshall, 1991; Wright, 1996; Davis, 1992). Restitution programmes and ideas of reparative justice are a relatively new criminal justice development, being popular in the general domain of juvenile justice (Morris et al, 1993), and are a practical means of

---

[3] There is, however, some disagreement over the element of non-coercive practice. In the case of offenders, many will have little choice but to participate in a restorative process since the alternative may often be a harsher process or sentence. In the case of victims, some may participate out of a sense of public duty to the offender or the state. Therefore, the victim's participation, while not obviously coerced, may not be truly voluntary (Hoyle and Young, 2002: 527).

increasing the victim's right to participate in the contemporary criminal justice process.

Programmes range from the broader community-based initiatives such as community policing and neighbourhood revitalisation to those more specifically associated with restorative justice (Bazemore and Schiff, 1996; Bazemore and Griffiths, 2003). For example, restorative justice has been used in a range of regulatory and social settings to deal with civil matters or a range of harmful behaviours which are not strictly criminal (Braithwaite, 1999: 9–15). These include use within schools to deal with bullying (Ahmed, 2001; Ahmed and Braithwaite, 2004), truancy, minor forms of offending and conflict between teachers and pupils (Daly, 2001); within prisons to deal with conflicts between inmates and between inmates and staff (Hoyle, 2001); and within the workplace; or within communities to deal with disputes between neighbours or between residents and the authorities (Van Ness et al, 2001). Restorative processes in this respect have been proposed (McLaughlin and Johansen, 2002) and then recently adopted as a method of informal resolution of citizen complaints against the police, where they have achieved moderately better results than conventional processes (Young et al, 2005).

The main variants, however, are mediation, conferencing, and circles (McCold, 2001). Victim-offender mediation has been used in the United States and the United Kingdom since the 1980s, and more recently in Germany and Austria (Marshall, 1991; Davis, 1992; Umbreit, 1994).[4] As the name suggests, these schemes, which can take place instead of or before or after formal processes, allow victims and offenders to meet in the presence of a trained mediator. They aim to give the victim an opportunity to tell the offender about the effects of the offence on them, to hear the offender's explanation and secure some form of reparation, which may be in the form of an apology.

Family group conferencing was first developed in New Zealand in the late 1980s and then later in Australia[5] and England for use with young offenders, where the emphasis is on individual offenders repairing social harm (McElrea, 1994; Retzinger and Scheff, 1996; Morris and Maxwell, 2000; Dignan and Marsh, 2003; Umbreit and Zehr, 2003). These schemes add further perspectives to the basic mediation model in the form of those of the families of the victim and the offender

---

[4] There are those who do not regard victim-offender mediation programmes as examples of restorative justice. (See generally: Morris and Gelsthorpe, 2000a: 419, 424, n 17). Dignan and Cavadino (1996) distinguish restorative conferencing (an example, in their terms, of a communitarian model of justice) from mediation (an example, in their terms, of a reparation model of justice) on the basis of four characteristics: the delegation of powers from the state to members of the community; the convening of a meeting to which supporters of the victim and offender are invited as a mechanism for arriving at a negotiated community response; the empowerment of the offender and his family through formulating a plan which is acceptable to the other participants; and monitoring of those plans.

[5] FGC was adopted in Australia in a variety of forms but the model most often promoted elsewhere was developed in the Wagga Wagga police department (Moore et al, 1995). Although similar in many respects, it differs principally from the New Zealand model (Maxwell and Morris, 1993) in that it uses police officers and school personnel to set up and facilitate meetings (Umbreit and Zehr, 2003). The model was refined by McDonald et al (1995) to incorporate learning from reintegrative shaming theory resulting in a definite emphasis on changing offender behaviour.

and the collective involvement of the wider community. In most of these schemes the outcome of the conference is at least subject to approval by the court, with Australia also opting for police-led conferences. Restorative conferencing in England, and in Canberra, Australia, was developed in the late 1990s as a further model under the restorative justice umbrella (Moore et al, 1995; Young and Goold, 1999; Young, 2001). This model also aims to facilitate a process of dialogue between the victim and the offender about the offence, and to elicit an apology and perhaps an offer of reparation on the part of the offender.[6]

Circles of support and accountability have been used in Canada for the last ten years to deal with the reintegration of high-risk sex offenders at the end of their custodial sentence (Kirkegaard and Northey, 2000; Cesaroni, 2001; Petrunik, 2002; Silverman and Wilson, 2002: 67–84; Wilson et al, 2002).[7] More recently, pilot schemes have been developed in England and Wales. As will be discussed in detail in chapter 7, community involvement in these schemes is considerably greater than in the previous two models. These circles, using local community resources, aim to allay the fears of the local community, and at the same time reduce the likelihood of further offending by holding the offender accountable to their commitment not to reoffend.

With few exceptions, restorative justice initiatives have generally been concentrated on lower-level forms of offending. New Zealand applies restorative practices at a nearly universal level to adult offenders who have committed relatively serious offences (Morris and Maxwell, 2003) and to all juvenile crimes except murder and manslaughter (Morris and Maxwell, 2000). The restorative conferencing programmes in England and Australia, on the other hand, deal only with adult and juvenile offenders charged with moderately serious crimes. Elsewhere, however, there are a number of other schemes which routinely use restorative interventions for adult offenders and for very serious forms of offending (Hoyle and Young, 2002: 535). In South Australia, for example, young people charged with sexual offences, who admit their behaviour, are diverted from court processes and instead participate in a family conference (Daly, 2002a; 2006). Recently, the 'family decision-making model' in Australia and North Carolina has also used a conference-style process with children and families affected by child sexual abuse and domestic violence, although usually the perpetrator is excluded from this process (Cashmore and Paxman, 1999; Pennell and Burford, 2001; Meyer, 2005; Pennell, 2006).

Indeed, in the United States, developments have gone further still with victim-offender mediation being used in cases of homicide and sexual assault and even

---

[6] A further variant on this model is one which has been termed 'restorative social justice' (White, 2003). This builds on the basic conferencing model by attempting to integrate concerns about social justice and community building within juvenile justice practices.

[7] Within the Canadian justice system, there are both 'sentencing circles' (SC) and 'circles of support and accountability' (COSA). These terms are often used interchangeably but are in fact two separate entities. SC is part of and replaces sentencing in the criminal justice system (Lilles, 2001; Roberts and Roach, 2003). COSA, on the other hand, focus in particular on the reintegration of high-risk sex offenders.

between a killer on 'death row' and the family of his victim (Umbreit et al, 1999; Kay, 2006). Although it has been argued, in my view rightly, that to describe a process involving state killing as restorative or reintegrative is 'grotesque' and 'a contradiction in terms' (Hoyle and Young, 2002: 536).[8] The RESTORE programme is using restorative justice to address date and acquaintance rape by first time adult offenders and those charged with misdemeanour sexual offences in a collaborative programme between Pima County Attorney's Office, the Southern Arizona Center Against Sexual Assault, and the College of Public Health, University of Arizona (Koss et al, 2003).[9] Similarly, intimate abuse circles have also been proposed, albeit with some controversy, and subsequently considered by American judges, as a restorative response to domestic violence (Mills, 2003).

Restorative principles have also been used to tackle historic human rights abuses and in the resolution of broader political conflicts. For example, they have been used in the Truth and Reconciliation Commissions of South Africa (Villa Vincenzo, 1999; Christodoulidis, 2000; Skelton and Frank, 2001) and Rwanda (Drumbl, 2000) in relation to genocide, mass torture and rape and with respect to paramilitary violence in Northern Ireland (McEvoy and Mika, 2001, 2002; Mika and McEvoy, 2001). These examples demonstrate that in some jurisdictions at least, restorative justice is being used to push the boundaries of what is normally considered appropriate terrain for alternative forms of justice by being applied to some of the most serious social problems.

As will be discussed in chapter 7, restorative justice schemes may operate either within or outside the traditional criminal justice system (Zehr, 1990). An example of the latter is the use of community restorative justice schemes with paramilitary groups in Northern Ireland which operate outside the formal criminal justice system (Auld et al, 1997; Conway, 1997; Winston, 1997; Dignan and Lowey, 1999; McEvoy and Mika, 2001, 2002; Mika and McEvoy, 2001). For our purposes, however, the focus is on the former only, since the type of future response to managing sex offenders in the community envisaged here, is one where community involvement in sex offender issues is integrated into and accredited by the formal criminal justice system in conjunction with the work of statutory and voluntary agencies.

<hr />

SHAMING

Reintegrative Shaming

The concept of restorative justice owes much to Braithwaite's notion of 'reintegrative shaming' (Braithwaite, 1989; Ahmed et al, 2001).[10] The key variable,

---

[8] See also: Acker (2006).

[9] See: <http://restoreprogram.publichealth.arizona.edu/concept/default.htm>.

[10] There is also a debate surrounding the exact parameters of the relationship between reintegrative shaming and restorative justice—in particular whether the terms 'reintegration' and 'restoration' are reconcilable (Matthews, 2006), interchangeable or at least complementary (Walgrave and Aersten,

'shaming', holds that the offender should acknowledge not just his own responsibility for the act, but should also appreciate the victim's perspective. The offender should acknowledge that he performed the act, that it was wrong and harmful, and should be ashamed and determined to avoid repetition of the behaviour (Hudson, 1998: 249). Braithwaite defines shaming as:

> [A]ll social processes of expressing disapproval which have the intention or effect of invoking remorse in the person being shamed and/ or condemnation by others who become aware of the shaming' (1989: 100).

Thus, the essence of the theory is that the ways in which not only the state, but society, the community and the family sanction deviance affect the extent to which their members engage in predatory criminal behaviour. According to Braithwaite, however, the shame which matters most is not 'the shame of the remote judge or police officer but the shame of the people they most care about' (1993: 37). 'Shaming' is more important to crime control than punishment (Braithwaite and Daly, 1994: 192). Punishment ought not to be the primary focus in cases which call for a broader remit; looking at the history and looking ahead to the future for the victim's safety and changing the behaviour of abusers.

Shaming therefore is not a uniform sanction, but can be done in a variety of ways and contexts (Hay, 2001: 133–35). Braithwaite makes the distinction between two types of society and two types of shaming practice. He argues that communitarian societies (that is, those with a high degree of interdependence and strong cultural commitments to group loyalties) are better able than others (where there is a lower level of interdependence and greater concern for the expression of individualism) to informally sanction deviance and reintegrate lawbreakers by shaming the offence, rather than permanently stigmatising the offender through harsh formal penal codes (Braithwaite, 1989: 84–85).[11]

In this vein, he contrasts the reintegrative shaming of the good parent, who makes clear their disapproval of bad behaviour without rejecting the child, with the stigmatising shame of modern criminal justice. Braithwaite explains how shaming contrasts with a more classical view of sanctioning:

> Shaming, unlike purely deterrent punishment, sets out to moralise with the offender to communicate reasons for the evil of her actions (1989: 100).

Shame, therefore, has negative consequences for offenders and victims unless it is joined with a ritual termination of shame in the form of reintegration ceremonies (Garfinkel, 1956; Braithwaite, 1989; Braithwaite and Mugford, 1994; Makkai and Braithwaite, 1994; Ahmed, 2001; Harris, 2001).

1996). There are those who do not see shaming as an essential part of restorative justice and suggest that emotions such as empathy and remorse may be more crucial in affecting a reparative response. (See, eg: Maxwell and Morris, 2002, 2004; Van Stokkom, 2002).

[11] More recent research in the context of juvenile justice has also confirmed that the extent of community cohesion and societal resources at neighbourhood level has a major bearing on the propensity of young people to engage in criminal and antisocial behaviour (White, 2003).

There are two facets to reintegrative shaming: (1) the overt disapproval of the delinquent act (shaming) by socially significant members; and (2) the ongoing inclusion of the offender within an interdependent relationship (reintegration) (Zhang, 1995: 251). Thus, shaming is reintegrative when it reinforces an offender's membership in civil society. This prevents the shamed individual from adopting a 'deviant master status' (Becker, 1963, 1974) and is accomplished when shaming (1) maintains bonds of love or respect between the person being shamed and the person doing the shaming; (2) is directed at the evil of the act rather than the evil of the person; (3) is delivered in a context of general social approval; and (4) is terminated with gestures or ceremonies of acceptance and forgiveness (Braithwaite, 1989: 100–1). Strategies which embody these principles are family group conferencing, discussed above, and circles of support, which will be outlined in more detail in the last part of the book.

Reintegrative shaming can be contrasted with stigmatisation which is disintegrative in nature. Little or no effort is made to forgive offenders or affirm the basic goodness of their character and thus reinforce their membership in the community of law-abiding citizens. Stigmatisation is essentially shaming in the absence of a reintegrative element and is the converse of each of the four elements mentioned above (Garfinkel, 1956). The primary relevance of stigmatisation is that it shuns offenders and treats them as outcasts and may provoke a rebellious and criminal reaction from them if, as a result of the stigma and the symbolic or literal exile from the community, offenders form oppositional subcultures that reject normative standards (Karp, 1998: 283; Maxwell and Morris, 1999). As Vagg (1998: 254) has argued, labelling therefore is the key element that separates reintegrative from disintegrative shaming.

In conjunction with Braithwaite's thesis, it is argued that shaming should be of the reintegrative variety, rather than the vengeance that is seen in some community 'naming and shaming' responses to managing sex offenders in the community (Hudson, 1998: 255). As the next part of the book will demonstrate, the theory of disintegrative shaming has, for the most part, informed contemporary state-led and popular responses to the risk posed by released sex offenders in the community within an overall retributive regulatory framework (McAlinden, 2005). This has been reflected in post-release control measures such as sex offender registration and other control in the community mechanisms enacted most recently in the United Kingdom under the Sexual Offences Act 2003.

The stigmatising process of retributive justice labels the offender rather than the offence and the offender is given more incentives to contest the label than to repent the behaviour (Becker, 1963). As the last part of the book will demonstrate, with restorative or reintegrative justice, however, the community is involved in expressing disapproval, but also in providing and guaranteeing protection and redress for victims, and in supporting perpetrators in their efforts to change and secure their reintegration into the community.

Conceptualisations of Shame and Shaming

The word 'shame' comes from old Germanic roots meaning to clothe or cover or hide oneself. Shame therefore refers to the experience of exposure (Gilligan, 1996: 64–71). Understanding and perceptions of shame have appeared across a wide range of disciplines including psychology (Tomkins, 1987; Nathanson, 1992), anthropology (Mead, 1937; Benedict, 1946), moral philosophy (Taylor, 1985; Williams, 1993), sociology (Goffman, 1959; Scheff and Retzinger, 1991), law (Kahan, 1996) and criminology (Grasmick and Bursik, 1990). The fact that theorists are 'divided by common language' (Harris and Maruna, 2006: 457), however, means that there is a distinct lack of coherence in theoretical and research typologies.

Indeed, despite the centrality of 'shaming' to Braithwaite's (1989) theory, he provided little in-depth analysis as to what the concept actually is and how it may work, beyond the primary distinction between the two types of shaming. More recently, however, theorists have attempted to refine the theory by devising conceptions of shame (Harris and Maruna, 2006) and explanations of how shame and the shaming process might operate (Ahmed et al, 2001; Harris, 2001, 2003a). Harris and Maruna (2006), for example, have espoused a framework for understanding shame and shaming which is based on three organising principles[12]: shame as social threat of rejection; shame as personal failure or worthlessness; and shame as ethical threat to the loss of self-respect and transgression of moral and social norms. The last of these incorporates elements of the previous two by combining the notion of wrongdoing that is recognised by the individual as well as society (Harris and Maruna, 2006: 455). As such, these principles are collectively based on the notion that shame or the fear of shame operates as a powerful motivation for individuals to both manage and work on relationships at the micro-level or interpersonal level, and comply with social conventions at the broader, macro-level. In effect, as will be discussed further in the next section, the interplay between individual and social variables is important for effective offender reintegration or resettlement.

These nuances and differences in how shaming is interpreted and understood are not simply conceptual, however, but of material significance in terms of how the theory of reintegrative shaming may be put into practice (Maxwell and Morris, 2002). Restorative practices that seek to apply reintegrative shaming need to be sensitive to cultural and social contexts to ensure that disapproval can be demonstrated without being stigmatising (Braithwaite and Braithwaite, 2001; Harris and Maruna, 2006: 457). As will be discussed in the last part of the book, such concerns are of particular relevance in relation to the reintegration of sex offenders.

---

[12] See also: Harris (2001).

Shaming as a Psychological Process

The role of emotion in crime and justice has been increasingly recognised in contemporary theoretical debates (Scheff and Retzinger, 1991; de Haan and Loader, 2002; Karstedt, 2002; Sherman, 2003). Scholars contend that a major benefit of restorative justice in comparison with conventional criminal justice is that it addresses the emotional dimension of crime and its aftermath (Strang, 2001; Sherman, 2003). A related body of work, in this respect, has emerged which has focused, in particular, on the functions of shame and shaming as a complex and dynamic psychological process (Tomkins, 1987; Walgrave and Aersten, 1996; Maxwell and Morris, 1999; Olthof, 2000; Harris, 2001, 2003a). This work has highlighted the importance of understanding the effects of social disapproval and the critical role that emotions such as shame and guilt play in the reintegrative shaming process (Braithwaite and Braithwaite, 2001; Harris, 2001; Harris et al, 2004).[13] Several scholars have identified shame as 'the master emotion' (Retzinger and Scheff, 1996) or 'the core emotional sequence' in family group conferencing (Moore, 1993; Harris et al, 2004). Although there is some variation between programmes, conferences usually begin with an acknowledgement of responsibility by the offender, followed by the victim's account of how they and others were affected. The victim's feelings of anger, indignation and resentment are reduced by the offender's acceptance of responsibility and acknowledgement of the harms suffered. At the same time, the victim's story leads to empathy and remorse in the offender (Harris, 2003b: 127–28). In the emotional and relational dynamics of restorative conferencing, in particular, emotions like empathy, remorse and guilt will become merged with feelings of shame, and it is ultimately the management and resolution of these moral emotions that is critical for successful restorative interventions (Ahmed et al, 2001; Harris et al, 2004).

In the recent revision of reintegrative shaming theory, Braithwaite and Braithwaite (2001) have also argued that the focus should shift from 'shaming' to 'shame management.' In effect, shaming may be important to reducing offending behaviour not because it shames offenders per se, but because it provides a means of assisting offenders to manage their feelings of shame in more constructive ways (Ahmed et al, 2001; Harris and Maruna, 2006: 459–60). Ahmed's (2001) work on school bullying, for example, suggests that the acknowledgment of shame is a good means of discharging it and that this process is associated with reduced risks of being both a bully and a victim of bullying. In the restorative process, allowing participants to tell their story (Zehr, 1990) and the ritual of apology and forgiveness, offer a means of managing the emotions of shame for both the victim and the offender and in assisting in their psychological recovery (Moore, 1993). Victim

---

[13] Others have argued, however, that given the restorative goal of repairing harm, a focus on the role of disapproval and the emotion of shame in justice processes is potentially misplaced. For these writers, empathy and remorse are much more constructive elements in achieving restorative outcomes. See especially: Karstedt, 2002; Maxwell and Morris, 2002, 2004; Morris, 2002b; Taylor, 2002; van Stokkom, 2002; Sherman, 2003. See also n 10 above.

vindication, whereby victims tell their story and communicate the harm they have suffered to the offender, is the path to displacing victim shame (Zehr, 2002). Similarly, encouraging offenders to take responsibility for their actions and to express genuine empathy and remorse and an apology to their victims (Tavuchis, 1991; Bottoms, 2003) in a supportive setting (Harris, 2001), also helps offenders to resolve their shame (Strang, 2002; Zehr, 2002) and come to enact a positive law-abiding sense of self (Leibrich, 1996; Maruna, 2001).

The revision of Braithwaite's (1989) original theory, however, does not change its central contention that shaming of the reintegrative variety reduces reoffending, whereas stigmatising or disintegrative shaming is more likely to increase it. The refinement of the theory, in fact, serves to further clarify this central proposition by underlining that the reason behind this is that individuals are more likely to manage shame constructively if they are reintegrated into society rather than being stigmatised and ostracised (Harris and Maruna, 2006: 460). This book, however, is written from a broader level of analysis than a psychological one. For the purposes of this discussion, the focus throughout is on shaming as a wider social process. Central to this discussion is an analysis in particular of how the dynamics of circles of support place considerable emphasis on forms of social disapproval that are reintegrative and restorative rather than stigmatising (Braithwaite, 1989; Braithwaite and Mugford, 1994).

RESETTLEMENT

It is useful to conclude this broad outline of the key elements of restorative and reintegrative theory by providing an overview of some of the main themes from the literature on ex-offender 'resettlement' or community 're-entry'[14] (Sampson and Laub, 1993; Maruna, 2001; Petersilia, 2003) and the related literature on 'what works' in achieving desistance from crime (Farrall and Bowling, 1999; Farrall, 2002; Maruna and Farrall, 2004; Maguire and Raynor, 2006; McNeill, 2006). It will be argued that, in many respects, this literature neatly accords with one of the central themes of this book, namely the contribution of the community to offender rehabilitation, and in particular, Braithwaite's (1989) thesis of 'reintegrative shaming.'

As outlined in the previous chapter, there have been a number of recent trends in the area of crime control, such as the rise in rates of imprisonment, particularly in the United States, and extended supervision and restrictions placed on certain categories of dangerous offender after a period of custodial detention. These developments have largely been focused on a 'risk-based' model of offender

---

[14] There have also been related recent attempts to theorise what precisely is meant by 'resettlement' (Maguire and Raynor, 2006; McNeill, 2006) and indeed, it has also been contested whether this is in fact possible, particularly where an elderly inmate population is concerned (Crawley and Sparks, 2006).

resettlement (Maruna and LeBel, 2002).[15] The upshot is, as Farrall and Sparks argue, that:

> [T]he social consequences of a criminal conviction have become not just more prevalent but also weightier and 'stickier' than in previous decades (2006: 7).

These and other policy-making developments inevitably raise questions about the social and personal consequences of conviction and have prompted a resurgence of academic interest in life after crime and punishment (Maruna, 2001; Travis and Petersilia, 2001; Farrall, 2002, 2003; Maruna and Immarigeon, 2004).

In this respect, a number of important themes emerge within academic criminology which relate to both the structural and individual obstacles to successful reintegration. The latter have been framed largely in terms of risk factors and serious social and economic disadvantages and include a history of abusive and criminal behaviour with physical or emotional abuse, persistent offending and the associated stigma, and long-term addictions; and an impoverished background resulting from lack of employment opportunities, poor education and housing provision and economic instability. The social context has had an adverse effect not only on the offender, but on the local community, thereby undermining effective informal social controls and promoting deviance (Rutter and Giller, 1983; Sampson and Laub, 1994; Hagan, 1997; Hope, 2001; Farrall, 2002: 145–92).[16] The key structural correlate perhaps which may both help and hinder effective offender management and reintegration is that of 'the community' to which almost all offenders are inevitably returned at the expiration of their sentences. As Farrall and Sparks argue in the general context but which, as this book will hope to demonstrate, has particular resonance with sex offenders:

> [A]t some level a 'reconnection with' the community is an important step in the process by which they put their 'pasts behind them' (2006: 8).

Very few scholars have, however, directly addressed the axis between crime, persistent offending and the local community setting. One early notable exception is Mays (1952) in the UK context who noted that few young offenders in his study were likely to become habitual offenders due principally to their awareness that an involvement in crime may have negative consequences, not just for themselves, but other people.[17] For some time afterwards, however, criminal career research

[15] The other type of 'deficit' model is 'needs-based' strategies which focus on helping ex-offenders to overcome addictions or learn basic skills which will usually reduce the risk of reoffending (Maruna and LeBel, 2002).

[16] This thesis is also akin to that of strain theory which attempts to explain crime as a process whereby those with limited social and individual resources are more likely to resort to illegal or deviant activities because of the tension between material goals and social advantages (Merton, 1993).

[17] Other classic studies which have addressed the interplay between long-term individual criminal offending and the local social fabric are Hobbs' study of entrepreneurs in the East End of London (1988). He found that local support for the criminal activities of offenders elevated their status in the community. Similarly, MacLeod's 8-year follow-up study of two delinquent gangs in the US (1995) suggested that an individual's aspirations for a better life are reduced in tandem with the reduction in social opportunities and as a result, social and criminal behaviours are altered.

on both sides of the Atlantic retained a considerable offender-based focus and rather neglected the social dimension (West, 1969, 1973; Osborn, 1980).

Indeed, apart from these few isolated studies which have examined the inter-relationship between the community forum and the criminal careers of local individuals, academic interest in this specific area has only been sparked comparatively recently. A body of work by Sampson and Laub (Sampson and Laub, 1993, 1994; Laub et al, 1998; Laub and Sampson, 2003), in this respect, shifted the parameters of thinking about persistent offending by refocusing attention away from individual factors towards the social processes and relationships that underlie 'trajectories of change' (Laub et al, 1998). As will be discussed in chapter 7, circles of support and accountability, by focusing on establishing reintegrative social processes, have helped to shape the offender's relationships with the local community and provided an effective forum in which the interchange between local community structures and the offender's rehabilitation has been successfully played out.

A further related aspect of these discourses on 'community', which also has a bearing on the transition from criminal behaviour, is the importance of place (Farrall and Sparks, 2006: 11). Criminological scholars, in this respect, have underlined the significance of specific social spaces in the onset of criminal offending (or reoffending) (Giddens, 1984; Hagan, 1997; Bottoms and Wiles, 2002; Farrall, 2002, 2003; Farrall and Maltby, 2003) and specifically the influence which they have on individual motivation or ability to reoffend or desist (Meisenhelder, 1977). According to this view, some places such as bars or gambling establishments have a negative effect in confirming the individual's status as an ex-offender by suggesting that they remain firmly linked to undesirable or illegal activities which were associated with their old ways (Farrall and Sparks, 2006: 11). Other respectable social spaces, however, such as churches, a stable home life, reputable employment or civic forums, may strongly suggest that the offender has suitably made the break with crime and is a reformed individual by engaging in constructive activities (Farrall and Sparks, 2006: 12–13). As will also be discussed in chapter 7, circles of support provide the offender with many of these 'benevolent' (Farrall and Sparks, 2006: 12) factors and a suitable social space in which offenders can publicly affirm to themselves and others their commitment to a future non-offending identity.

At the same time, however, individual or offender-centred factors also have a bearing on the extent to which offenders can 'make good' (Maruna, 2001). These relate chiefly to the offender's subjective thought processes and degree of self-motivation (Zamble and Quinsey, 1997; Farrall and Bowling, 1999; Farrall, 2002; Giordano et al, 2002; Farrall and Calverley, 2005: ch 8) and ultimately the construction of offending 'narratives' (Maruna, 2001: ch 2) or 'redemption scripts' (Maruna, 2001: ch 5) whereby ex-offenders attempt to 'account for and understand their criminal past' (Maruna, 2001: 7). This leading work by Maruna (2001) demonstrates that even the most persistent offenders can manage to become non-offenders and useful members of the community by making sense of their lives. Some of the most recent work on the process of desistance, however, has focused on the role of hope in the reintegration of offenders (Burnett and

Maruna, 2004; Farrall and Calverley, 2005). These studies, while different in their methodological approaches, both contend that 'hope' for the future seems to play a significant role in predicting reintegrative and rehabilitative success. It provides ex-offenders 'with the vision that an alternative "normal" life is both desirable and, ultimately . . . possible' (Farrall and Calverley, 2005: 192–93). This 'hope' can be found in a range of social situations, from successful employment or returning to the emotional support of a relationship with a partner, to continued involvement in rehabilitation or support programmes (Farrall and Sparks, 2006: 13). For these writers, hope is undermined by retributive custodial experiences (Burnett and Maruna, 2004) but restored and sustained by aspects of local community life (Farrall and Calverley, 2005).

As will also be discussed in chapter 7, community forums like circles may be able to provide these crucial ingredients of emotional support, help with practical aspects of reintegration such as accommodation and employment, and psychological or cognitive support in terms of effective treatment or rehabilitative programmes. In short, they may provide both a symbolic and actual means of hope of offender desistance and reintegration by supporting the ex-perpetrator in his efforts to change. Indeed, the general research literature on offender resettlement demonstrates that reintegrative approaches which combine cognitive-motivational programmes with practical services have produced encouraging early results (Maguire and Raynor, 2006: 19).

A final theme to emerge from the resettlement and desistance literature which has a direct bearing on the reintegration of individual sex offenders is that of 'shaming' itself (Leibrich, 1996). This in a sense takes the discussion full circle to where it began at the outset of this chapter. Some scholars have specifically applied Braithwaite's (1989) dichotomy beyond the macro-level of social processes and its impact on overall societal crime rates to its impact at the micro-level on individual reoffending or desistance (Maruna, 2001: ch 7). The reality is, however, that reintegrative shaming processes combine elements of both the structural and the individual in creating vivid 'connections between action and local context' (Farrall and Sparks, 2006: 14). That is whether the public shaming of the offender becomes reintegrative or disintegrative ultimately depends on the reaction of the local community and the social infrastructure put in place and the offender's interaction with and response to these. What Maruna calls 'The Rituals of Redemption' (2001: ch 8) demonstrates the importance of the 'social and interactional processes of empowerment and reintegration' (2001: 13). Desisting offenders themselves also testify to their exoneration and 'certification' of their rehabilitation by a number of authorities such as judges, family members and significant others (Maruna, 2001: 13). I concur with Maruna who ultimately argues that:

> [S]uch rituals, if they were to be institutionalized as part of reintegration practice, might improve efforts to reintegrate ex-offenders into society (2001: 13).

As will be discussed further in chapter 7 in relation to reintegrative shaming practices, the dynamics of initiatives such as circles of support fully address these central facets of reintegrative shaming processes, chiefly by empowering sex offenders to take responsibility for what they have done in a context of positive reinforcement.

In sum then, what restorative or reintegrative approaches bring to the resettle-ment discourse is the possibility of what Maruna and Lebel (2002) have called a 'strengths-based' approach[18] which is characterised by the themes of repair, rec-onciliation and community partnership (Farrant and Levenson, 2002; Burnett and Maruna, 2006: 84). The central idea behind this model is that it should involve 'earned redemption' (Bazemore, 1999) in the sense that genuine offender reinte-gration involves 'more than physical re-entry into the community' (Burnett and Maruna, 2006: 84). It should also involve '"earning" one's place back in the moral community' (Burnett and Maruna, 2006: 84). Opportunities are provided, in par-ticular, for offenders to develop pro-social concepts of self and their identity, usu-ally in the form of socially useful activities, such as rewarding work (Simon, 1993; Burnett and Maruna, 2006: 84). By shaming the offender rather than the offence (Braithwaite and Mugford, 1994) and by helping the offender find his place again in civil society, measures such as circles of support encapsulate the strengths-based philosophy. As Burnett and Maruna put it, they recognise that:

> [I]ndividuals emerging from a shameful past need high levels of support in nurturing their pro-social inclinations, to restore their sense of belonging, mastery, independence (2006: 101).

These approaches are fundamentally different from retributive coercive risk-based agendas by focusing instead on developing intrinsic motivations for per-sonal change. Such a model or process may ultimately offer a means of moving away from current risk-management discourses which may lead to public disclo-sure of offender status with all its attendant negative consequences towards the real and effective reintegration of sex offenders in the absence of prejudice and stigma (Goffman, 1963). A difficulty, however, as even proponents recognise, is that the current popular and political concern with public protection and risk management which lies at the heart of managerialist retributive approaches has the potential to undermine strengths-based restorative policies (Burnett and Maruna, 2006: 102). Indeed, a final polemic in the theoretical debates concerns the relationship between restorative or reintegrative justice and the formal criminal law.

THE RELATIONSHIP WITH FORMAL CRIMINAL JUSTICE

The relationship between restorative justice and formal criminal law is a con-tentious one that has yet to be satisfactorily resolved. As mentioned at the outset

---

[18] Others, however, alternatively use the label 'restorative re-entry' in this context (Tucker and Cadora, 2003; Anderson and Karp, 2004).

of this chapter, one of the greatest tensions in contemporary restorative justice discourses is the question of whether restorative justice should be integrated into mainstream retributive criminal justice, and if so, to what extent (Hoyle and Young, 2002: 540). In this respect, there are potential conflicts and debates about what is appropriate territory for restorative justice on a number of interrelated levels—in the general academic restorative justice debates; in criminal justice policy-making; in discussions on the theoretical aims of 'justice' or 'punishment'; in the use which has thus far been made of restorative justice within the traditional system of state justice; and in debates about the legitimate role of the state in restorative processes.

First, a key issue for the academic restorative justice community, as von Hirsch et al (2002) put it, is whether restorative justice and criminal justice are 'Competing or Reconcilable Paradigms'? In this respect, some writers argue that restorative justice should be kept separate because their priorities and practices are too different, while others argue that restoration should be an essential part of criminal justice and could even help to transform it. As acknowledged in chapter 1, some theorists continue to emphasise the difference of the restorative justice vision as a fundamental paradigmatic change in criminal law (Zehr, 1990, 1995; Bazemore, 1996; Barnett, 2003; Walgrave, 2003). Zehr, for example, summarises the response of the retributive framework to crime as follows:

> Crime is a violation of the state, defined by lawbreaking and guilt. Justice determines blame and administers pain in a contest between the offender and the state directed by systematic rule (1990: 181).

By way of contrast, the restorative justice model is described as viewing crime through a different 'lens' and as approaching the problem in a fundamentally different way:

> Crime is a violation of people and relationships. It creates obligations to make things right. Justice involves the victim, the offender and the community in a search for solutions which promote repair, reconciliation, and reassurance (1990: 181).

Zehr, like other advocates of restorative justice views the criminal justice system in extremely negative terms and argues for a shift in policy towards restorative thinking which is seen as a solution to many of the ills of the traditional system.[19]

Others, however, have argued that the supposed conflict between retributive and restorative justice has been overstated (Daly and Immarigeon, 1998; Daly, 2000, 2002b; Duff, 2002). They call for recognition of alternative forms of justice and highlight the compatibility of restoration and retribution, which both have positive features to offer. Marshall, for example, argues that restorative justice 'is complementary to criminal justice, not antithetical to it' (1997: 9) and that Zehr's dichotomy does an injustice to both. According to this view, restorative and

[19] Within this broad stream of thought, there are those who go further and argue that restorative justice systems are in fact corroded by their partnership with a retributive framework. (See, eg: Boyes-Watson, 1999).

retributive justice may in fact be integrated as part of the same system of justice where they would complement and work in tandem with each other, rather than operate as opposing or alternative systems (Zedner, 1994; Levrant et al, 1999; Barton, 2000; Miller and Blackler, 2000; Hudson, 2002). This is a fundamental issue which will be returned to below and later in chapter 7 of this book in relation to the discussion of how we may move from theory to practice in implementing restorative justice for sexual offences.

A second level of potential conflict between these two paradigms is evident in criminal justice policy-making. In the main, there are tensions between new Labour's retributive and socially exclusionary criminal justice policies and those policies which are restorative and socially inclusive (Brownlee, 1998). As discussed in the previous chapter, when new Labour came to power in 1997 they demonstrated a willingness to move away from the punitive, exclusionary policies of the previous Conservative Government towards more inclusive, integrative and restorative measures (Hoyle and Rose, 2001). This transition, however, has not been easy and remains incomplete (Hoyle and Young, 2002: 535).

This tension between the two types of criminal justice policy is readily highlighted in the statutory reforms that have introduced restorative justice practices into the contemporary youth justice system of England and Wales (Hoyle and Young, 2002: 533–34). By virtue of a range of provisions under the Crime and Disorder Act 1998, and the Youth Justice and Criminal Evidence Act 1999, as well as subsequent legislation, an array of restorative options are initially explored with first time young offenders, with the formal criminal justice system as the backdrop which can be used as a last resort with more persistent offenders (Dignan, 1999; Crawford and Newburn, 2003).[20]

The messages contained within the Crime and Disorder Act 1998 are particularly contradictory (Hoyle and Young, 2002: 534). While there are clear restorative elements within the legislative framework, there are also many punitive measures such as antisocial behaviour orders, curfew orders, referral orders, reprimands and warnings and the use of imprisonment for persistent young offenders. The measures as a whole embody the values of crime control and punishment rather than those of restorative justice and social inclusion (Evans and Puech, 2001). Indeed, for some commentators, the restorative aspects of the Act do not go far enough (Ball, 1999; Fionda, 1999). Attempts to introduce elements of restorative justice into the mainstream youth justice system have highlighted a fundamental tension between the representative and participatory nature of restorative justice and the more managerialist character of the contemporary youth system in England and Wales (Crawford and Newburn, 2002). Recent empirical research on young

---

[20] Eg: the 1998 Act replaced police cautions for young offenders with 'reprimands' and 'warnings' (ss 65–66); it introduced reparation orders as a non-custodial order for young offenders (ss 67–68); and action plan orders as another form of restorative intervention (ss 69–70) (Dignan, 1999). Part I of the Youth Justice and Criminal Evidence Act 1999 introduced referrals to young offender panels. Part IV of the Powers of Criminal Courts (Sentencing) Act 2000 made further provision with respect to such orders.

offenders' experiences of social exclusion and restorative justice in the South West of England demonstrates that restorative justice has become harnessed to the interests of reinforcing 'moral discipline' rather than engaging with 'social justice' (Gray, 2005). It has been said in particular that the coercive nature of the various orders available detracts from the 'balanced approach' which is at the heart of restorative justice and which mandates that equal attention should be afforded to victims and offenders, as well as the wider community (Hoyle and Young, 2002: 534). As Morris and Gelsthorpe note 'restorative justice [is] just one theme in a broadly punitive and controlling piece of legislation' (2000b: 18). Such specific criticisms, it seems, could equally be applied to the broader tensions between restorative justice and the criminal justice system as a whole.

The relationship between restorative justice and the existing criminal justice system therefore is an awkward one, as the former seeks both to fit into a larger criminal justice portfolio, in which many of the policies are still very strongly influenced by more traditional and retributive ideals (Dignan 1999; Crawford, 2006). In the current political climate, there is constant pressure for the main political parties to appear 'tough on crime' and avoid being seen as advocating a 'soft' option (Hoyle and Young, 2002: 534). This has been outlined clearly in the last chapter in relation to the punitive regulatory policies enacted to control sex offenders via both sentencing disposals and control in the community initiatives. Similarly, policies on antisocial behaviour generally, and drugs, also make clear the Government's 'zero tolerance approach.' Arguably the evolution of restorative justice, in the United Kingdom and abroad, remains in its infancy both in terms of implementation and in understanding its effects (Crawford and Newburn 2003). Overall, however, the direction of the Government's criminal justice strategy is not entirely clear as current restorative practices are occurring within a 'no excuses' political climate, which seems to go against the grain of restorative principles (Hoyle and Rose, 2001).

A related difficulty is how to reconcile the theoretical values and aims of restorative justice with those of formal criminal law. Indeed, as Hoyle and Young argue there are 'undeniably tensions created by attempts to graft restorative justice on to established systems of criminal justice' (2002: 546) As outlined above in relation to the tensions surrounding the youth justice system in England and Wales, when restorative justice is fitted into the general rubric of the criminal law, it has to be delivered in line with the general goals of the traditional system. There are also disagreements as to the exact parameters of the two paradigms and the extent to which they are theoretically reconcilable. It is hoped, however, that the outline of restorative and retributive justice, provided in this and the previous chapter respectively, has at least demonstrated that they are rather too different entities to be simply mapped on to one other. The key then is to determine how, in practical terms, the two systems may fit together.

Some scholars have also argued that not only does restorative or reintegrative justice meet the traditional ends of punishment, but that it could carry out the main functions of criminal justice—retribution, rehabilitation/ reintegration, individual and public protection—and achieve a better balance between these aims than formal criminal justice does (Daly, 2000; Hudson, 2002: 626). Hudson (1998), in this respect, has argued that restorative and retributive aims need to be integrated so that there can be a fuller recognition of the concerns of due process and proportionality but also of discursiveness, reintegration and empowerment. Indeed, it will be argued in the third part of the book that restorative approaches to justice in the form of 'reintegrative shaming' share many of the aims of the traditional regulatory framework, most notably community protection and offender rehabilitation. Measures such as circles of support and accountability combine elements of meaningful censure of deviant behaviour and protection of the victim against further abuse, alongside measures to reduce the likelihood of reoffending and reintegrate the offender into society (Hudson, 2002: 626).

Criminal justice and restorative justice may have common aims, but they are intrinsically different, however, in terms of how they seek to achieve those aims (Walgrave, 2003; Harris et al, 2004: n 5). Retribution or punishment does appear to be integral to formal criminal justice (Willemsens, 2003), as contended in the previous chapter in relation to the current legislative framework. The retributive path consists of the infliction of humiliation and suffering on the offender, whereas the restorative path points to the reduction or compensation of suffering caused by the offence (Harris et al, 2004: 200).[21] It is the idea, therefore, that criminal justice should involve retribution that seems to make it incompatible with restorative justice. In this respect, perhaps the most compelling approach regarding the possibility of combining restorative justice with the traditional regulatory framework is Braithwaite's (2002b) idea of responsive regulation. In brief, restorative justice may be part of a regulatory framework that includes deterrence and incapacitation, but not retribution. By adopting a more holistic and all-encompassing approach to sexual offences, restorative justice also potentially offers the possibility of moving beyond traditional oppositional criminal justice and penological dualisms such as retribution/ restoration; rehabilitation/ public protection and even the rights between victims and offenders (Zimring, 2001; Daly, 2002b: 72; Hudson, 2002: 626). In essence, whatever the tensions between the different perspectives, it becomes difficult in practice to clearly separate justice developments for victims from those affecting offenders, communities and the state (Goodey, 2000).

A further area of contention is the use which has been made to date of restorative justice in responding to particular types of offending. As mentioned above, although there are some isolated examples of restorative justice being applied to serious offences, it has been largely confined to so-called 'low-level crime' that

---

[21] The place of punishment in a justice system based on restorative justice has been the subject of much debate among restorative justice proponents. There are those who believe that punishment is an integral part of restorative justice. (See, eg: Barton, 2000; Daly, 2000; Duff, 2002), and those who argue that punishment has no place at all in such a system. (See, eg: Wright, 1996; Walgrave, 2001). In an attempt to reconcile these differences, it has also been argued that these discourses seem 'almost to be a bickering about words' (Willemsens, 2003: 24) in that what some term 'punishment', others term 'restorative sanctions'.

commonly concerns local communities. However, as will also be discussed in detail in chapter 8, even those proponents who are willing to accept these uses are usually less willing to extend this paradigm to more serious and persistent forms of offending (Johnstone, 2003). In many jurisdictions, not least the United Kingdom, restorative justice has operated, as Garland argues, 'on the margins of criminal justice, offsetting the central tendencies without much changing the overall balance of the system' (2001: 104). 'The result is that mainstream criminal justice has tended to minimize or try to ignore it' (Shapland et al, 2002: 10). The difficulty is that if restorative justice is not to be stuck at the margins but instead move into mainstream criminal justice, it will have to transcend the confines of minor offences and first time and young offenders (Braithwaite, 1999; Morris and Maxwell, 2001), which is common in some jurisdictions. Current orthodoxies, therefore, about what is and is not suitable for restorative justice and how it should look in practice need to be challenged. Ultimately it will have to be accepted as being suitable to be applied across a range of offences, including those at the most serious end of the spectrum like sexual offences, and in particular those against children. As Walgrave has suggested:

> To actualise its potential fully, a maximalist version of restorative justice must be developed, with the aim of providing restorative outcomes to a maximum number of crimes in a maximum number of situations and contexts, including those where voluntary agreements are not possible and coercion is needed (2001: 34).

Finally, if restorative justice is to realise its full potential and be incorporated as a legitimate response to sexual offending behaviour along with the formal administration of justice, there are also a number of difficult practical issues that will have to be addressed. As will be discussed in chapter 8 in relation to the critique of reintegrative justice, removing the state completely from the process introduces concerns about due process and adequate procedural safeguards, and in particular how to ensure accountability and the legitimacy of the process (Van Ness, 1998; Braithwaite, 1999). However, at the same time, if the state is to be involved, which is what is envisaged in this book, there are also legitimate concerns about the extent and nature of its role (Hoyle and Young, 2002: 540–17). As Hoyle and Young have argued:

> An institutionalised response to criminal offences, in particular to the more serious offences, ultimately requires input from one or other of the criminal justice agencies— even if only for societal recognition of the legitimacy of the process (2002: 546).

These concerns include (1) who should facilitate the programmes—possibilities include the police, social workers or other state or voluntary agencies or neutral facilitators in the form of an entirely independent agency (Sandor, 1994; White, 1994; Cunneen, 1997; Ashworth, 2001; Maxwell and Morris, 2001; Young, 2001); (2) whether legal advice or representation should be made available—this is in recognition of the fact that the offender may effectively confess to the commission of an offence (Meier, 1998; Lord Chancellor's Department, 2001: para 68; Young,

2001) and is regarded as perhaps the most important due process check on the process and outcomes (Warner, 1994; Shapland, 2001). There are others, however, who question the necessity or appropriateness of involving lawyers in the restorative process, pointing chiefly to the need to safeguard against partisan, advisory and representative roles which may monopolise the process and reduce the offender's involvement and the opportunity to confront his offending and take responsibility for his actions (Ball, 1999; Wright, 1999; Crawford, 2002); (3) how to ensure proportionality—there should not be a disproportionate burden placed on the offender, and equally the victim or the wider community should not be allowed to unduly influence the process which could lead to inconsistency and injustice (Zedner, 1994; Cavadino and Dignan, 1998; Wasik, 1999; Ashworth, 2000). Others suggest that the concept of proportionality is incompatible with restorative justice (Braithwaite and Petit, 1990) and that the fairness of outcomes must reflect other core values of restorative justice such as mutual respect or empowerment (Hoyle and Young, 2002: 545); (4) what if the influence of the state controls the agenda and consequently limits community involvement?—a legitimate and accountable process would properly protect the rights of all participants. This is part of the state's agenda. At the same time, care needs to be taken to avoid vengeful or disruptive communities from taking over the process.

These and other concerns will be addressed in chapter 7 in relation to implementing restorative or reintegrative practices. It will be argued that many of these concerns are removed or at least alleviated if the restorative process does not take place as an alternative fact-finding process, but rather as a reintegrative treatment and support programme in conjunction with the formal criminal justice system. In addition, the implementation of a measure such as circles of support and accountability, which allows for a measure of community involvement, would strengthen the decision-making process of the state in relation to resettlement of the offender and also help to improve the accountability of both sectors.

CONCLUSION

It has been argued that restorative justice has different aims, values and priorities from those of traditional retributive justice. Moreover, there are a number of difficulties at both the theoretical and practical level in reconciling these paradigms. It is argued, however, that their inherent differences and potential difficulties do not preclude them from being reconciled. To paraphrase the title rubric of von Hirsch et al's (2002) book, referred to above, it is contended that, in short, restorative justice and criminal justice may be competing paradigms, but they are not totally irreconcilable.

Given the level of potential conflict and debate, it is acknowledged that further integration of these forms of justice is far from being unproblematic and will not be accomplished without some difficulty. In addition, as will be discussed in chapter 8, there are also a number of key critiques which are routinely put forward when restorative justice is applied to serious forms of offending, in particular sexual offences, which must be satisfactorily addressed. If restorative or reintegrative justice is to be meaningfully and effectively applied to sexual offences, there are a number of tensions that will have to be resolved. As Hudson has argued:

> The key to reconciling the problems and possibilities of restorative justice lie in creative consideration of its relationship to formal criminal law. Problems of how to deal with recalcitrant offenders; how to ensure that restorative procedures are not seen as second-class justice; how to balance expressive and instrumental functions of justice; and above all, how to ensure that the voice of any party does not become submerged in an emergent unitary consensus all turn on the relationship between the discursive processes of restorative approaches and the role of the formal law in modern societies in relation to defining relationships and allocating rights (1998: 255–56).

These tensions illustrate the fact that it is impossible to understand both the possibilities and limitations of justice responses to sexual offences, without simultaneously engaging in political, philosophical, and indeed practical debates about both the meaning of justice in relation to sexual offences, and the role of the state, victims, communities and offenders in the process (Brownlie, 2003).

PART II:
THE REINTEGRATION OF SEXUAL OFFENDERS IN THE COMMUNITY

4

Managing Sexual Offenders in the Community: Current Problems

THIS CHAPTER EXPLORES the current problems involved in managing the risk posed by sex offenders in the community. The range of legislative measures that exist to control sex offenders in the community has been broadly outlined in chapter 2. In addition to the problems inherent in much of this legislation, which will be dealt with in subsequent chapters, there is a range of difficulties involved in successfully rehabilitating sex offenders and reintegrating them into the community. These factors have, in turn, been used to justify singling sex offenders out as different from other dangerous offenders.

It will be argued that a dynamic tripartite relationship pertaining to the criminal justice system, offenders themselves and the communities in which they are placed, combine to make problematic the release of convicted sex offenders and to ensure that many continue to pose a high-risk to society. It is this problematic nature of efficient risk assessment and management of sex offenders that has led, in part, to the legislative enactment of a number of retributive measures to control their whereabouts, such as sex offender registration.

The sum of these problems, however, indicates that the current state-led and popular retributive responses to managing the risk posed by sex offenders in the community do not appear to be working and that the traditional justice system is ill-designed to secure the rehabilitation and reintegration of sex offenders. The initial focus will be on the myriad of problems posed by the criminal justice system, before turning to examine the role played by offenders themselves and finally the wider community.

THE CRIMINAL JUSTICE SYSTEM

There are a number of problems posed by the contemporary retributive justice system which have negative consequences for the management of sex offenders in the community on release from custody. These relate to the decline of rehabilitation and treatment in prisons, increased resort to early release procedures, the inherent weaknesses of supervision and the difficulties of preventing unsuitable individuals from working with children.

The Decline of the 'Rehabilitative Ideal'[1]

The construction of sexual offending as a specific social problem, as discussed in chapter 2, appears to have fuelled society's demands for a 'pound of flesh' in dealing with sex offenders (Geiran, 1996a: 142). However, side by side with this primitive retributive response in the need to exact vengeance, there is also evidence in conceptualisations influencing the policy process of a view of sex offenders as somehow ill and requiring treatment (Berliner, 1996: 295; Geiran, 1996b).

The complexity of choice between treatment and punishment often lies in the wide divergence of views of sexually deviant behaviour (Melella et al, 1989: 224). The legal system views sexual deviation as a violation of the criminal law resulting in appropriate punishment through incapacitation, retribution, deterrence, rehabilitation or a combination of these. In contrast, sexual deviation is also viewed by some as a medical problem for which punishment is neither morally appropriate nor effective in accomplishing a continuing deterrent or rehabilitative effect. In any event, it is generally agreed that both society and the offender would receive a greater benefit if the offender were rehabilitated or 'cured' and able to desist.

Allen (1981) traces the roots of 'the rehabilitative ideal' to the Old Testament and argues that it can only be properly understood in the context of the particular social and political culture of the period. Indeed, sentencing aimed at reformation of the offender's character can be traced back to the early days of probation and borstal institutions (Garland, 1985). This 'treatment model' reached its zenith in the United States in the 1960s. Sentences were no longer to be short and of a fixed term, but of indeterminate length so that the offender could only be released when, in the opinion of the experts, a cure had been affected (Blumstein et al, 1983). The early 1970s saw the decline of rehabilitation as a basis of penal policy (Bottoms and Preston, 1981) due to the changing socio-political atmosphere (Allen, 1981; Shichor, 1992) though it is still a leading rationale in many European countries today.

One of the principal arguments expounded in favour of managing sex offenders in the community, however, is the fact that rehabilitation is not routinely imposed as part of a prison sentence (Sampson, 1994; 100–4; Parliament of the Commonwealth of Australia, 1995; para 4.23; Applegate et al, 1997). In prisons today, it appears that there is a broad commitment to the rehabilitation and treatment of the offender, but that this has not been realised in practice. In the current crime control 'law and order' ideology, there is apparently more concern with removing the offender from society to protect the public than with reforming him, since people have largely lost faith in the idea of the reformation of the offender (Simon, 1998). Indeed, as Henham argues, 'the treatment needs of sentenced sex offenders have been subsumed to the wider goals of system objectives and political agendas' (1998: 70). The latter seems to represent the contemporary view of rehabilitation at least in so far as imprisonment is concerned (O'Malley 1996: 292).

---

[1] See: Allen (1981).

Therapeutic Treatment for Sex Offenders

Conceptualisations of sexual offending as an illness, requiring psychological treatment for pathological offenders within a punitive framework, have a lengthy history (Howitt, 1996: 189–228; Geiran, 1996a: 137–39). The assessment and treatment of sex offenders by medical, mental health and social service professionals dates back to the last century (Geiran, 1996a: 138). Initially, based largely on medical and psychiatric approaches, significant developments and growth in sex offender treatment began, especially in the United States, in the 1960s and 1970s, following innovations in behaviourally-based treatment for a range of psychological and behavioural problems. These movements resulted in an increasing focus on deviant sexual arousal as a treatment target in work with sex offenders. Another significant influence on sex offender treatment in the 1970s and 1980s was the feminist movement. This resulted in treatment programmes increasingly addressing issues such as power, control, sex-role-stereotyping and attitudes to women and children.

Therapeutic treatment of sex offenders is now generally taken to include a range of interventions with individual offenders that are intended, either as a primary or secondary goal, to help them modify their behaviour in order to avoid or reduce reoffending (Howard League for Penal Reform, 1995: 87). Intervention methods may involve 'talk therapies' (individual or group psychotherapy) or 'bioimpedance measures' (including surgical operations and 'chemical castration') (Geiran, 1996a: 139). Surgical methods are now rarely if ever used, while 'chemical castration' (pharmacological treatments to suppress sexual activity), as will be discussed in chapter 6, remains popular in some jurisdictions today.

Treatment of sex offenders in the last decade, however, mainly comprises individual and group psychotherapy, with an increasing emphasis on the structured group work approach (Knopp, 1984; Laws, 1989; Marshall et al, 1990; Strain and Sheath, 1993; Sampson, 1994: 18–22). In fact, group therapy may be a key factor in the treatment and rehabilitation of sex offenders. Some sexual deviants are diagnosed with 'sociopathic' personalities, and are therefore unresponsive to psychotherapy because they do not respond to therapists on an individual level. Furthermore, it has been suggested that many offenders are suspicious of their therapists and perceive them as adversaries because they suspect that they are connected with the state (Carpenter, 1998: 454–55). The small-group approach, therefore, often works best because peers with similar problems can confront and challenge each other, thereby making unresponsive individuals more likely to participate in the programme. In addition, small group therapy helps sex offenders through their initial denial phase because many of their peers have already acknowledged their own criminality (Carpenter, 1998: 455). Consequently, the group therapy approach alleviates the offender's social isolation and may enable therapists to get to the root of the offender's problem more quickly.

In many cases, such influences may stem from sexual abuse when the offender was young (Horowitz, 1996: 94). As such, any effective treatment programme must examine an offender's psychological motivations head on. Most pro-grammes, in this respect, describe themselves as operating within a 'cognitive-behavioural' therapeutic framework (Sampson, 1994: 19–20; Geiran, 1996a: 139; 1996b). They typically include interventions to address denial and minimisation and distorted thinking errors, to increase awareness and empathy for victims, to control deviant sexual arousal, and incorporate behavioural schedules designed to identify high-risk situations for offenders and help them prevent reoffending (O'Malley, 1996: 402–5; Department of Justice, 1998: 88; Brown, 2005: ch 6). However, programme content may vary depending on characteristics of partici-pants, type of offending, needs and problem areas, as well as other factors such as agency context, professionals' training and therapeutic orientation (Cotter et al, 1991). Essentially, there are two basic provisions for treatment of the adult sex offender. One is treatment in prison (Hollin and Howells, 1991; Perkins, 1991), the other, treatment in the community. Respect for individual rights entails that participation in treatment programmes be voluntary and that their duration be within the remits set by proportionality, a key concept for retributive theory (von Hirsch, 1994).

Treatment in Prison

Several prisons specialise in dealing with sex offenders and offer a comprehensive treatment and therapy programme. In many Anglo-American and Common Law jurisdictions, however, problems of under-funding and staffing mean that only a very small minority of imprisoned sex offenders are actually in a treatment pro-gramme designed specifically for these types of offenders. These facts would also appear to suggest that the traditional justice system is, in reality, more concerned with the current trend in penal policy of removing offenders from society than with reforming them.[2]

Over the years many American states have adopted a diverse range of treatment programmes in response to the problems posed by repeat sex offenders (Brown, 2005: ch 3). In 1994, there were 20 prison-based treatment programmes for ado-lescent and adult sex offenders and 710 in total throughout the US (Freeman-Longo et al, 1995). Washington State maintains one of the largest prison-based treatment programmes in the United States, with places for 200,000 offenders (Department of Corrections, 1997). Comprehensive programmes are also offered in Avenol prison in California. In California, however, as in many other states, therapy is not generally available in prisons simply because there are too many inmates (Carpenter, 1998: 448). In 1998, in addition to the 6000 sex offenders on parole in California, its prisons housed about 16,000 sex offenders, but only offered one treatment programme to 46 rapists and child molesters (Fromson,

---

[2] For a detailed overview of the current use of cognitive-behavioural sex offender treatment pro-grammes in Canada, Australia, New Zealand, Europe and the rest of the world, see eg: Brown (2005: ch 3).

1994: 317). Similarly, in Texas, only about 200 of the more than 25,000 imprisoned sex offenders are in a sex offender treatment programme (Russell, 1997: 431). Indeed, as will also be discussed in chapter 6, to compensate for the distinct lack of rehabilitative programmes in prisons, California's chemical castration law advocates propose medical remedies to deter offenders from committing further offences when their period of incarceration has expired. Restricting programmes in this way, however, to a narrow band of offenders may limit their overall effectiveness in reducing sex offender recidivism and the incidence of sexual offending.

In England and Wales specialist treatment programmes for sex offenders are offered at Grendon Underwood prison (Taylor, 2000; Wilson and McCabe, 2002). In 1991, the Home Office set up a national Sex Offender Treatment Programme (SOTP) at prisons throughout the country (Grubin and Thornton, 1994; Mann and Thornton, 1998; Brown, 2005: 56–68). The programme allows for systematic treatment of a large number of sex offenders using a cognitive-behavioural model of treatment. The five accredited components of the SOTP are comprised of a Core Programme (which normally takes one year to complete), the Extended Programme (which is usually for high-risk offenders who have completed the Core Programme but still have significant problems to address), the Adapted Core Programme (for low-IQ offenders), the Booster Programme (which is a pre-release course) and the Rolling Programme (for lower-risk offenders) (Beech and Fisher, 2004; Hudson, 2005: 39–41). There is also a Denier's Programme for those offenders who do not acknowledge that they have a problem, but where sexual offences form part of their offending history. Offenders undergo a series of psychometric tests, in addition to structured risk and needs assessments, to ensure that they are matched to the appropriate programme (Hanson and Thornton, 2000; Thornton, 2002; Grubin, 2004). Participation in the programme is voluntary.

However, the SOTP programme has not been without its critics, particularly in that lack of resources has resulted in treatment only being offered to all sex offenders serving longer sentences, usually of seven years or more (Cobley, 1997a: 99). As mentioned above, sentencers operate within the philosophical and practical constraints of the current retributivist system to which the specific treatment needs of individual sex offenders are often subordinated (Henham, 1998: 77–78).[3] This limitation on programme availability may be justified on the grounds that the most serious offenders, and consequently perhaps the ones most in need of therapeutic intervention, are likely to receive treatment. Nonetheless, this failing is significant given that for some repeat sex offenders, sexual abuse and violence has been their way of life for many years, and it will take time for them to change their attitudes and learn to control their deviant sexual behaviour.[4]

[3] It has also been suggested, in this respect, that sentencing jurisprudence and practice need to be rethought and restructured to take account of current developments within the theory and research on sex offender treatment in order to achieve continuity between policy and practice and ultimately a more holistic approach to the sentencing and treatment of sex offenders. (See eg: Henham, 1998; Edwards and Hensley, 2001a).

[4] The Northern Ireland Prison Service has adopted this national model and currently provides treatment programmes for sex offenders at Maghaberry and Magilligan prisons. In the Republic of

Indeed, there has been a preponderance of research aimed at establishing or refuting the rehabilitative effect of various forms of treatment. Research by Martinson et al (1974) demonstrating that 'nothing works,' suggested that different types of treatment made no difference to reconviction rates. This, however, was followed by a subsequent retraction towards the position that everything works in certain circumstances (Martinson, 1979).[5] As will be discussed further below, the most recent studies demonstrate that treatment can produce small but significant reductions in levels of reoffending for some sex offenders. This shift in emphasis to 'what works' (McGuire, 1995) has led to a renewed treatment ethos in offender rehabilitation beyond mere containment, and has further formed the basis of contemporary evidenced-based policy and practice (Friendship et al, 2001; Home Office, 2001c).

As will be discussed further below, however, the prospects of empirically supporting a utilitarian justification for the imprisonment of sex offenders, based on their individual rehabilitation, seem remote (Lacey, 1988: 30–31). As Lacey has also argued in a general context, it is not clear whether the absence of strong corroborative data is due to the intractable nature of sex offending or to the fact that rehabilitation in a prison setting is likely to be unsuccessful with these types of offenders (1988: 30–31). Criminology, in this respect, provides many arguments regarding the difficulty of combining treatment and punishment (Finstad, 1990: 176; Sampson, 1994: 108–12; O'Malley, 1996: 406). Indeed, it cannot be assumed that just because an offender goes to prison he will emerge reformed (Finstad, 1990; Ditchfield and Marshall, 1991). Instead, as outlined above, reformation of the sex offender is usually dependent on specialist treatment facilities. Prison is an institutional setting and difficulties may arise in attempting to transfer what has been learned there into a real situation on the outside (Sampson, 1994: 117–18). The success of therapy also depends largely on the accurate targeting of high-risk offenders, treatment and therapist characteristics, group cohesion, and each patient's individual circumstances and their motivation to change (Brown, 2005: ch 9).[6] Indeed, it is generally accepted that coercive treatment programmes do not work and that the effectiveness of therapeutic interventions is improved when offenders become involved voluntarily (McIvor, 1992; McLaren, 1992; McGuire, 1995).

Ireland, there are approximately 300 sex offenders in Irish prisons at any one time. Ten of these at a time participate in an intensive offence-focused group work treatment programme at Arbour Hill prison in Dublin (Geiran, 1996a; Murphy, 1998). Approximately 15–20% of sex offenders in Irish prisons are sufficiently motivated to apply for a place on a treatment programme, 42% of whom have been convicted of offences against children (Department of Justice 1998: 81).

[5] The Brody Report (1975) also gave a qualified judgment. It found that rehabilitative programmes sometimes did work by having a discernible effect on reconviction rates but often only for highly selected 'good risk' offenders who may well not have reoffended anyway, in rather specialised situations, and over rather short follow-up periods.

[6] In this respect, one of the most recent developments in the 'what works' literature has focused on the perspectives of sex offenders themselves on their treatment and management. (See eg: Wilson and McCabe, 2002; Hudson, 2005). The use of this 'voice' provides the literature with not only a deeper understanding of how the therapeutic process operates, but raises issues which have not previously been described in the prison literature or within the 'what works' debate (Wilson and McCabe, 2002).

While early studies of the effectiveness of sex offender treatment programmes in reducing offending behaviour were pessimistic, the most recent evaluations have been more positive (Kemshall, 2001). These overwhelmingly suggest that cognitive-behavioural approaches are the most effective (Marshall and Barbaree, 1988; Marques et al, 1994; Vennard et al, 1997). This treatment model, which has been described as the 'cornerstone of the "what works" enterprise in the United Kingdom' (Vanstone, 2000: 171) has reduced reconviction rates by between 10 per cent (McGuire, 2000) and 14 per cent (Friendship, Blud et al, 2002).[7]

In the United Kingdom, studies of traditional treatments reveal a moderate success rate. An early evaluation of the prison-based SOTP demonstrated a significant treatment effect (Thornton and Hogue, 1993). A more detailed study by the Sex Offender Treatment Evaluation Project (STEP) Group (Beech et al, 1998) of SOTP examined the extent to which treated child abusers showed statistically significant changes in their levels of denial, pro-offending attitudes, and acceptance of accountability. Both shorter treatment (80 hours) and longer treatment (160 hours) produced statistically significant reductions in these areas. Two-thirds of men were successfully treated with regard to reduction in pro-offending attitudes with one-third of men showing an overall treatment effect, which was sufficient to make them largely indistinguishable from the profile of a non-sexual offender. Treatment was particularly effective with low deviancy men who were relatively open about their offending: 84 per cent showed significant reductions in pro-offending attitudes and 59 per cent showed an overall treatment effect, compared with 43 per cent and 14 per cent respectively of the high deviancy men.

One of the most recent studies on the treatment impact of the SOTP compared two-year reconviction rates for a group of male adult sex offenders serving four years or more who had voluntarily participated in the programme, and those for a group with similar characteristics who had not participated in the SOTP (Friendship et al, 2003). While the treatment group had lower reconviction rates than the comparison group for a further sexual offence, and also for any offence type, these differences were not statistically significant. The study concluded that although the Core Programme appears to have a significant impact on sexual and violent reconviction for low-risk and medium-risk offenders, the areas targeted by the programme do not seem sufficient for reducing reconviction in high-risk sex offenders, who should be provided with additional treatment.

Studies of programmes in the United States and Canada, particularly in the 1990s, have found lower recidivism rates for those who received treatment and have demonstrated that treatment is up to 40–50 per cent effective (Freeman-Longo and Knopp, 1992; Brown, 2005: 192–202). In Kentucky, for example, the recidivism rate for treated sex offenders was three times lower than the control group (3.4 per cent compared with 8.7 per cent) (Barnes and Peterson, 1997).

---

[7] Note, however, that it has also been contended that this approach is not universally applicable with all groups of offenders outside the adult mainstream such as females, adolescents and indigenous offenders (Cameron and Telfer, 2004). This could be a significant failing since, as noted in ch 1, the sex offending population increasingly includes both women and young offenders (Grubin, 1998).

Similarly, in Canada, treated offenders had a recidivism rate of 14.2 per cent compared with a figure of 33.9 per cent for the untreated group (Nicholaichuk and Gordon, 1996). One study of an outpatient programme in the US state of Vermont concluded that treatment does in fact work to some degree. Although treatment did not work equally with all offenders, treatment was found to be helpful under the right conditions (McGrath, 1995: 26; McGrath et al, 1998). The most recent published American research on recidivism indicates lower sexual offence rearrest rates for treated offenders over five-year (Marques et al, 2000) and six-year (McGrath et al, 2003) follow-up periods.

Some argue that no one is sure how well various types of sex offender treatments work, even though they are fairly well established. Indeed, there are a number of recognised difficulties in evaluating treatment programmes including, for example, those which relate to the use of a particular research design and outcome measures (Brown, 2005: ch 7). One argument is that many of the suggested treatments for sex offenders are not proven methods (Kaihla, 1995: 57) as they have not all been validated externally. In addition, as will be discussed further below, it has also been shown that actual recidivism rates for sex offenders are 5.3 times the official reconviction rate (Falshaw et al, 2003). As such, broader and more sensitive outcome measures should be more fully incorporated into the future evaluation of treatment programmes for sex offenders (Marshall and Barbaree, 1988; Marques et al, 1994; Friendship et al, 2001, 2003; Friendship, Beech et al, 2001; Friendship and Thornton, 2001; Francis et al, 2002). Moreover, there are also dangers in using recidivism data, which can be an imprecise and uncertain concept, as a measure of successful intervention (Matthews and Pitts, 2000). Indeed, as the final part of this book will argue, the effect of programmes on overall levels of engagement—on an offender's acknowledgement of their deviant behaviour and on levels of victim empathy and awareness—are equally important outcome measures.

On the whole, therefore, sex offender treatment in its various forms has so far been shown to be only marginally effective with some groups as opposed to others (Marshall et al, 1991; Marshall, 1993; Quinsey et al, 1993; Beckett et al, 1994; Sampson, 1994: 121–24; Finn, 1995; Nagayama Hall, 1995). As Furby et al have concluded 'There is as yet no evidence that clinical treatment reduces rates of sex offences in general' (1989: 27). These weaknesses in the provision of sex offender treatment may mean that high-risk sex offenders are often released without the benefit of an effective programme. This failing also underlines the importance of effective multi-agency work which enables rehabilitative and reintegrative work with sex offenders to continue on release.

There is a clear need to extend the use of therapeutic programmes with sex offenders both within prison and the community. The problem with gathering further support for therapy, however, is that no statistical evidence exists to corroborate the beneficial long-term results. As will be discussed below in relation to the offender, the various recidivism rates that have been touted have led the public to believe that sex offenders are untreatable or unchangeable (Simon, 1998). Furthermore, many people in society do not like to 'give' free therapy to sex offenders, because they want to punish them for what they have done and give them something more punitive so that they will pay for their crimes (Carpenter, 1998: 453). Some form of psychiatric help, however, may be the only way to protect society from habitual offenders. Some treatment professionals favour a middle ground that combines traditional rehabilitative therapy which deals with an offender's psychological motivations with chemical injections which suppress the sexual drive. Indeed, as will be outlined in chapter 6, statistics demonstrate that recidivism rates do decrease when sex offenders are treated in this way.

Treatment in the Community

In cases where a custodial sentence is not imposed, the court has the power to attach conditions to a probation order which may include a requirement that the offender undergoes a treatment programme (Cobley, 1997a: 99–100). In the United States, sex offenders, especially those who have offended against children, may receive a suspended sentence which is usually accompanied by the condition that the offender takes part in treatment under court supervision (Berliner, 1998: 1212). One such scheme is the Special Sex Offender Sentencing Alternative (SSOSA) in Washington which provides a community-based treatment alternative for those who have not been convicted of rape, have no prior convictions, and whose sentence does not exceed a certain length (Berliner, 1998: 1212).

Recidivism rates for both SSOSA and non-SSOSA offenders showed a low and comparable rate of recidivism of 5 per cent (Berliner, 1998: 1212–13). However, despite the evidence that the community is not at greater risk, these schemes have been undermined in recent years in response to public outcry about perceived leniency in the 'treatment' of sex offenders. As a result, some states have been forced to impose mandatory minimum sentences that negate such community-based programmes (Berliner, 1998: 1212).

In recent years, probation services in the United Kingdom have also taken up the challenge and initiated various community-based treatment programmes.[8] There are currently a number of programmes within the Probation Service, though these are generally run in a community as opposed to residential setting (Brown, 2005: 58–59, 62–68; Hudson, 2005: 41–43).[9] Barker and Morgan (1993)

---

[8] In Northern Ireland, the principal scheme is The Alderwood Centre, a day centre funded by probation, which provides individual and group programmes for sex offenders. Internal evaluations, which are not publicly available, have revealed positive outcomes with some offenders, though this was over a relatively short follow-up period. In the Republic of Ireland, a number of programmes are provided at St Conal's Psychiatric Hospital, Letterkenny, an outpatient programme for adult males, most of whom had abused children, the Northside Inter-agency Project in Dublin (McGrath, 1992), a community-based programme catering for male juvenile or adolescent offenders (Geiran, 1996a: 139) and the programme, primarily for intra-familial offenders, run by the National Forensic Psychiatric Service at the Central Mental Hospital in Dundrum in Dublin (O'Connor et al, 1994).

[9] There are also three independently accredited programmes for sex offenders run by the Probation Service: the Thames Valley Programme, the Northumbrian Groupwork Programme, and the West Midlands Community Sex Offender Groupwork Programme (Brown, 2005: 65–68; Hudson, 2005: 41–43).

reviewed the literature on the provision, nature, evaluation and efficacy of community-based sex offender treatment programmes in England and Wales. They found that all but 13 of the probation services were running some form of sex offender treatment programme. However, of the 63 probation-led pro- grammes in existence, only three had been running for more than five years. There appeared to be three main models of treatment: full-time attendance for one or two weeks, two hours weekly for eight weeks to six months, or two hours weekly for a year to indefinitely. The main treatment approach being used was 'cognitive-behavioural' therapy and such programmes were primarily under- taken in groups. Just over half the sample appeared to have benefited from treat- ment (Beech et al, 1993).

The second phase of evaluation found that probation-run programmes had some success with low-deviancy offenders but had little impact with the more deviant ones. Overall these programmes enabled offenders to understand their offending behaviour but had little success in helping them develop strategies to minimise or even acknowledge future risk (Beckett et al, 1994). The third phase of evaluation produced more positive results. The majority of the 133 offenders referred for treatment had not been reconvicted of a further offence within two years. Only six (5 per cent) had been reconvicted of a further sexual offence within this period, compared with 9 per cent who did not receive treatment, and a further five were reconvicted for a non-sexual offence (Hedderman and Sugg, 1996). A follow-up study found that only 10 per cent of those classed as 'benefiting' from treatment were reconvicted after six years, compared with 23 per cent who were classed as 'not having received treatment' (Beech et al, 2001).

These studies of non-custodial treatment programmes admittedly demonstrate slightly more success with reforming offenders than their custodial counterparts. However, unlike other community-based reintegrative treatment and support programmes like circles of support, which will be discussed in chapter 7, they appear to be failing overall to promote significant levels of offender engagement with the rehabilitative and reintegrative process and to successfully identify and manage risky behaviour. Indeed, recidivism is most likely to be prevented when interventions attempt to address the lifelong potential for reoffending and do not expect sex offenders to be permanently 'cured' following a single course of treat- ment (Hanson et al, 1993).

Release on Licence

As outlined in chapter 2 in relation to the current retributive framework, the crim- inal justice systems in the United States and the United Kingdom have, for some time, been centrally concerned with public protection and the incapacitation of sex offenders. However, almost all sex offenders are inevitably returned to society at some point. Indeed, the length of time an offender serves in custody is only partly determined by a prison sentence. A large proportion of it is determined by the operation of the parole and life sentence procedures (Sampson, 1994: 61–63; Hebenton and Thomas, 1996a: 99; Cobley, 1997a: 99).

In general, parole or release on licence is an administrative procedure whereby a review board permits an offender who has already begun part of a prison term to serve the remaining part of the sentence in the community, usually under supervision.[10] The offender, however, is required to abide by a set of release conditions that if breached may result in his return to prison for the remainder of the original sentence. In the context of the United States, the recognised goals of parole are said to be rehabilitation and public safety,[11] although deterrence and condign punishment are also acceptable ends.[12] Other permissible goals include incapacitation, retribution, favourable impact on prison management, equalisation of sentencing, and 'fine tuning' of sentences (Stelzer, 1997: 1692), although these goals have generally gone without mention by the courts.

In the United States, in particular, it seems that there has been a substantial increase in the number of sex offenders released from custody (Hebenton, 1997: 7). In many states, although a judge may give the maximum prison term for an offence, most convicted child sex offenders are being released after only half their sentence is served due to prison overcrowding and a lack of funding, and the fact that the correctional system tends to allow good behaviour to count towards early release (Carpenter, 1998: 449). One of the most comprehensive overviews of statistical information on sex offenders in the United States was undertaken by the Bureau of Justice in 1997 (Greenfeld, 1997). This found that on a given day in 1994 there were approximately 234,000 offenders convicted of a sexual offence under the care, custody or control of corrections agencies. Nearly 60 per cent of these were under conditional supervision in the community, on parole or probation.[13] Other figures suggest that of the 16,000 convicted sex offenders currently housed in California's prisons, 2000 of these individuals are released from custody each week whose supervisory periods may extend over several years (Stadler, 1997: 1297). As will be outlined in chapter 6, in response to the problem of early release and the lack of rehabilitative measures, chemical castration has been implemented or proposed in many US states to catch a few sex offenders before they are released and to monitor those who are on parole (Carpenter, 1998: 449). Moreover, in some states for those convicted of child molestation, a split sentence of lifetime supervision with electronic monitoring, following a minimum 25-year prison term, has recently been introduced as an alternative to life in prison.[14]

In the United Kingdom, Part II of the Criminal Justice Act 1991 provided for general changes to the early release procedures and post-custodial supervision

[10] The term 'parole' comes from the French, *parole d'honneur*, meaning 'word of honour,' which would appear to reflect something of the procedure itself.

[11] *United States v Consuelo-Gonzalez*, 521 F.2d 259, at 265 (9th Cir. 1975).

[12] *United States v Tonry*, 605 F.2d 144, at 148 (5th Cir. 1979).

[13] See full report, < http://www.ojp.usdoj.gov/bjs/pub/pdf/soo.pdf>.

[14] See The Jessica Lunsford Act of 2005 (Chapter 2005–28; House Bill No 1877), as enacted originally in Florida, and then Louisiana and Arizona, and in similar form in a number of other states (Arkansas, Oregon, Virginia and Washington).

(Davies 1997; Maguire and Raynor, 1997). The effect of these changes has been an increase in the number of sex offenders released from custody into the community (Home Office, 1991; Hebenton and Thomas, 1996a: 107, 1996b: 433–34).[15] Prior to the 1991 Act, 190 persons convicted of sex offences started probation orders and 150 community service orders, with about 400 sex offenders on parole licence (Home Office, 1991: 31). One estimate suggested that changes resulting from the 1991 Act would more than quadruple the number of sex offenders on licence in the community (Sampson, 1994: 66).[16] Increasing the number of sex offenders at large in the community, however, is regarded by many as problematic. The spectre of the mobile sex offender, as discussed in chapter 2, holds a special place both in official discourses and in the demonology of the popular imagination (Hebenton and Thomas, 1996a: 101, 107; 1996b: 429).[17]

Under a series of legislative amendments judges in England and Wales in particular have increased powers to direct that sex offenders be supervised until the end of their full sentence (Kemshall, 2001).[18] Early indications, however, were that this element of continued supervision only occurred in approximately 10 per cent of cases (Hebenton and Thomas, 1996a: 100; 1996b: 433). The Powers of Criminal Courts (Sentencing) Act 2000, as a piece of consolidating legislation, had a limited life of only three years, with the passing of the Criminal Justice Act 2003. The 2003 Act, which applies for the most part to England and Wales only, reformulates much of the sentencing framework which was created in 1991 and consolidated in 2000.

Part 12, chapter 6 of the Act repeals the early release provisions contained in the 1991 Act for offenders sentenced under the new regime.[19] However, the release of prisoners sentenced prior to the 2003 Act will continue to be governed by the 1991 Act which will ensure that it remains a relevant piece of legislation for some time to come. On release, fixed-term offenders in general are now subject to a period of licence which will extend throughout the term of the whole sentence and not, as previously, terminating at the two-thirds point.[20] Under chapter 5 of Part 12 of the Act, offenders who have committed 'non-serious' violent or sexual offences, that is where the maximum tariff is less than ten years' imprisonment, may also be sub-

---

[15] 'More Than 100,000 Paedophiles At Large Says Home Office' *The Times*, 20 February 1997

[16] Similarly, in the Republic of Ireland many prisoners are released before three-quarters of their sentence has expired (O'Malley, 1996: 270). The pressure on prison accommodation since the early 1980s has had to be countered by extensive resort to early releases, most of which did not meet the traditional criteria and were not accompanied by traditional supervision arrangements (O'Malley 1996: 272; Department of Justice, 1997: 109–10). In addition, up to 60 sexual offenders are released every year on completion of their sentences most of whom would not have availed of the group treatment programme at Arbour Hill prison (Department of Justice, 1998: 81).

[17] 'Change in Law Came Too Late To Prevent Release' *The Times*, 23 August 1997.

[18] ss 58–60 of the Crime and Disorder Act 1998, eg, amended the 1991 Act by extending the licence period following a custodial sentence in the case of sexual offences for a total aggregate of up to 10 years where the court considers that this is required to prevent further offences or secure the offender's rehabilitation on release.

[19] For a comprehensive account of the law, policy and practice in this area, see Cobley 2000/2005: ch 6).

[20] s 249.

ject to a new form of extended sentence, which is similar in many respects to the previous law.[21] Where the court considers that there is a significant risk of serious harm to members of the public, it may impose a sentence comprising a custodial term plus a further period of licence ('the extension period') for not longer than eight years.[22] In addition, as will be discussed further in chapter 6, serious sex offenders may also be subject to a life sentence or term of imprisonment for public protection purposes.[23] An offender sentenced under this provision will remain on licence for at least ten years after which he may apply to the parole board for his licence to be terminated.[24]

As Thomas (2004) notes, the current situation in relation to licence provisions in the United Kingdom, therefore, is one of considerable confusion. It seems that the Act is being brought into force in the usual piecemeal manner, and it has consequently been argued that there will be critical problems of transitional provisions, in particular those relating to dangerous offenders (Thomas, 2004). In the main, given that sexual offences may not come to notice until years after their commission, and that the old law, as noted above, is likely to remain in operation alongside the new, there will be obvious problems when an offender is convicted of a series of offences, which have been committed both before and after the commencement of the Act (Thomas, 2004).

In the United Kingdom, arrangements have long been in place to allow local authorities to have notice of the discharge from prison of a person convicted of offences against children (Home Office, 1964: paras 6–7; Sampson, 1994: 64–82; Home Office et al, 1995). The recent National Offender Management Service (NOMS) in England and Wales brings together the work of the main correctional agencies of the prison and probation services. The basic focus of the NOMS is on the 'end to end management' of offenders which should presumably facilitate a greater degree of co-operation between the elements of release from custody and control in the community (Hough et al, 2006).[25] However, as will be discussed further below, there are concerns even with such enhanced arrangements, in terms of both effective inter-agency co-operation and consequent offender management.

The primary official objective of supervision is seen as the protection of the public (Hebenton and Thomas, 1996a: 105). Secondary purposes are the prevention of reoffending, successful reintegration of the prisoner into the community (HMPS, 1994: para 8.13), and to enable the assessment of the risk of any danger to the public (Home Office et al, 1995: paras 7.3–7.5). Even after the 'community'

---

[21] ss 227–28, s 247.

[22] In the Republic of Ireland, until relatively recently sex offenders could not be mandatorily supervised after release from prison unless the original sentence was one of life imprisonment. The Sex Offenders Act 2001, however, made provision, inter alia, for a system of post-release supervision so that courts, at the time of conviction, will be able to sentence a sex offender to a determinate sentence comprising a term of imprisonment and a period of post-release supervision in the community.

[23] ss 225–26.

[24] Sch 18.

[25] See: <http://www.noms.homeoffice.gov.uk/>.

part of the sentence has been undertaken and probation officers have ended their involvement, surveillance may still be undertaken by social services staff.

The supervision of sex offenders in the community after their release from prison has, in fact, two principal aims (Department of Justice, 2000). The first is to help offenders maintain internal self-control over their offending behaviour, and the second is to provide external monitoring of their post-release behaviour. The supervision will be tailored on a case-by-case basis according to the individual offender's needs. All offenders may also be subject to extra negative or positive licence conditions being imposed as part of the supervision arrangements. In appropriate cases, offenders could be prevented from engaging in any work or organised activity involving children or from living in the same household as a child. They could also be obliged to live in a 'halfway house' for a period after their release or to enter psychological counselling or other treatment programmes as part of the supervision regime (Home Office et al, 1995: s 7, Annex A; Thomas, 2000/2005: 106). This latter aspect could be particularly important in supporting and observing those sex offenders who did not receive treatment in prison (Department of Justice, 1998: 87–89). Equally, a major benefit of post-release supervision will also arise in those cases where the sex offender has actually participated in a programme while in prison, as licence conditions may include a requirement that offenders subject themselves to further treatment on release (Department of Justice, 2000).

While police and probation supervision have continued over the years in various forms, for example the role of the juvenile liaison officers in the 1950s (Oliver, 1978: 36–37), it is the establishment and growth of the criminal record system in England and Wales which has provided a key 'supervisory point' (Hebenton and Thomas, 1993). As will be discussed further below, the aims of legislative measures enacted on criminal records, such as the Police Act 1997 and the Protection of Children Act 1999, are to allow improved arrangements for communication within the criminal justice system, and a more rational and comprehensive procedure for checking the criminal background of ex-offenders wishing to work with vulnerable members of society, especially children. Such a supervisory role for the criminal record also has parallels in the United States (Gordon, 1990).

However, the adequacy of the current arrangements in England and Wales for managing sex offenders in the community on release from custody has been increasingly questioned both by the professionals and a concerned public (Hughes and Parker, 1994; Hebenton and Thomas, 1996a: 107–8; Cobley, 1997a: 101). This is especially the case in the policing of child sexual abuse where police, practitioners and some academics share a number of interrelated concerns (Hallett and Birchall, 1992; Hughes et al, 1996). First, that the practice of disclosing to other agencies appropriate information about offenders, especially by the probation services, varies considerably. Secondly, there is a perception that personal data protection provisions limit what information can be collected and shared on known and suspected offenders (Hughes et al, 1996: 31). Finally, that the current local arrangements cannot deal with suspects or the known behavioural strategy or modus operandi of many sex offenders. These offenders are extremely mobile, often searching out families and likely targets in different police jurisdictions (Hebenton and Thomas, 1996a: 107–8; Hughes et al, 1996: 34). It is the limitations of the current arrangements for monitoring sex offenders in the community that led, in part, to the emergence of the sex offenders' register.

Indeed, as will be discussed in the next chapter, the registration and notification procedures, currently contained in 'Megan's Law' in the United States and Part 2 of the Sexual Offences Act 2003 in the United Kingdom, go some way towards addressing these particular concerns (Bedarf, 1995: 909). They provide for a uniform, though albeit limited, disclosure of information about sex offenders and their whereabouts to appropriate agencies and attempt to provide for a more up to date and comprehensive computer database on sex offenders. The recent advent of the national database of violent and sex offenders (ViSOR) in the UK, in this respect, should facilitate a single centralised record of addresses which enables information to be shared by a large number of police forces. However, as will be discussed further below in relation to 'tracking' problems pertaining to offenders, it is the third concern about the mobile sex offender which continues to provide the most problems.

Vetting Procedures: Preventing the Unsuitable from Working with Children

A further difficulty which relates to the management of sex offenders in the community, and which pertains to the criminal justice system, is the difficulty of preventing unsuitable individuals from working with children. In England and Wales in particular, as noted in chapter 2, a number of public inquiry reports or official reviews, have resulted from the disclosure of institutional physical and sexual abuse in care homes (See Corby et al, 2001; Birch and Taylor, 2003).[26] These confirm that the abuse normally took place over a number of years and its extent went unrecognised for some time; usually more than one victim was involved, and often more than one offender (Finkelhor et al, 1988; White and Hart, 1995; Gallagher, 1998, 1999; Waterhouse, 2000); the victims were afraid to disclose the abuse; or when they did no action was taken, either because there was a conspiracy to keep allegations quiet or a ready acceptance of the denial by the alleged perpetrator (Sullivan and Beech, 2002: 161).[27]

[26] The inquiries have included the Ty Mawr Inquiry following allegations of misconduct in Gwent children's homes (Williams and McCreadie, 1992); the Leicestershire Inquiry into allegations of sexual abuse by management and staff in children's homes (Kirkwood, 1993); and the Waterhouse Report (2000) of the tribunal of inquiry into the abuse of children in care homes in North Wales. The reviews have included the Warner Report (1992) on the selection, development and management of staff in children's homes; the Utting Report (1998) on the safeguards for children living away from home; and the Nolan Committee Report (2001) on child protection policies in the Roman Catholic Church in England and Wales.
[27] These factors are also confirmed by the literature on the prevalence of abuse within childcare institutions which suggests that, predominantly, the complaints appear to be of a sexual nature, involving both boys and girls, and that the majority have not been reported (Barter, 1999; Gallagher, 1998).

A familiar response when organisational failures are identified is that things have been rectified and that there is no longer any cause for concern (Soothill et al, 2005b: 38). As is typical of all child abuse inquiries, however, many of these appear to have made similar recommendations to protect children in the future, which have not always been acted on (Parton, 2004). For example, several inquiries have questioned the accuracy of vetting procedures and the consistency with which various agencies use the system. The Warner Inquiry (1992) found that 10 per cent of the heads of homes and a third of care workers were able to take up their posts before any references were received. The Utting Report (1998), some six years later, also expressed serious concerns about the manner in which police checks were handled and highlighted that insufficient consideration was given to references. The Waterhouse Report (2000) also listed a catalogue of inadequate procedures and breaches of policy, from recruiting staff informally without obtaining references, to failure to check foster families or employees before they commence work. Indeed, the report of the Bichard Inquiry, arising from the 'Soham murders' also highlighted 'systemic and corporate failures' in the way in which the police managed their intelligence systems (2004: para 8). As Sullivan and Beech (2002) argue, this raises questions not only about the speed and process of organisational change, but more worryingly, whether any lessons have actually been learned.

Other recommendations have resulted in a plethora of legislative developments within a few short years, which have attempted to improve childcare practice and prevent offenders from making contact with children through organisations. These have included the Sexual Offences (Amendment) Act 2000 which made it an offence for an adult to engage in any sexual activity with a child if they are in a position of trust.[28] The Criminal Justice and Court Service Act 2000 made it a criminal offence for convicted abusers to seek employment with children or for employers to knowingly appoint such people. The majority of these measures, however, are based around pre-employment vetting. For example, Part V of the Police Act 1997 established the Criminal Records Bureau to provide a more effective means of carrying out criminal record checks. In addition, the Protection of Children Act 1999 combined the Department of Health Pre-employment Consultancy Service Index (PECS) and the Department of Education and Employment 'List 99' to make it easier for employers to check whether those who wish to work with children are known or suspected abusers.

More recently, the furore surrounding the sex offenders in schools row and the decision of Ruth Kelly, then Secretary of State for Education, to approve a number of known sex offenders for work within schools have reopened this debate.[29] These cases have prompted a further review of current systems for the vetting of

---

[28] This offence has now been extended considerably by the Sexual Offences Act 2003, ss 16–24.
[29] 'Sex Offender Offered Teaching Job' BBC News Online <http://news.bbc.co.uk/1/hi/england/norfolk/4591850.stm> (8 January 2006); 'This Child Sex Offender Was Given Teaching Jobs In Three Schools' *Daily Mail* (London), 14 January 2006; '7 Perv Teachers . . . 1 Dunce Minister' *The Sun*, 16 January 2006.

teachers and other individuals who work with children (Scorer, 2006), including the sex offenders register and 'List 99', as a follow-up to the recommendations of the Bichard Inquiry (Bichard, 2004). The Bichard Report recommended, in particular, the introduction of a national registration system for those deemed suitable to work with children, as opposed to having a number of lists compiled according to different criteria, and improved information sharing between agencies. Although many of Bichard's recommendations have yet to be implemented,[30] reform of police intelligence and inter-agency procedures and further legislation to prevent unsuitable individuals from working with children now seem likely.

As will be discussed further below in relation to 'grooming behaviour' and problems which relate to the offender, the danger is that these legislative and policy developments have largely been reactive responses to the problem. Moreover, they have also been focused on developing external controls to prevent known sex offenders from making contact with children. What is needed, however, is greater understanding of the internal process of how sex offenders actually operate in order to develop proactive responses to problems before they occur (McAlinden, 2006c).

The Utting Inquiry (1998), for instance, as one of the major reports in the last few years proposed a 'protective strategy' comprised of four main elements: (1) a threshold of entry to paid and voluntary work with children which is high enough to deter committed abusers; (2) management which pursues overall excellence and is vigilant in protecting children and exposing abuse; (3) disciplinary and criminal procedures which deal effectively with offenders; and (4) an approved system of communicating information about known abusers between agencies with a need to know. However, this strategy does not fully acknowledge the characteristics of the offender and the nature of their behaviour within institutions on a number of levels. The focus on an entry threshold misses the point that sex offenders will use grooming techniques in order to cross any threshold in their quest to access children. Moreover, the emphasis on a vigilant management and swift disciplinary measures does not take account of the fact that sex offenders may actually constitute the management in an institution. This may allow them to make use of existing environments of pervasive secrecy (Sullivan and Beech, 2002) and the subsequent onset of abuse to go undetected or unpunished. Finally, the value placed on information sharing is based on the known, identifiable and preventable risk and not the unknown, hidden and therefore the most dangerous one (McAlinden, 2006c).

---

[30] 'Changes After Soham "Fall Short"' BBC News Online <http://news.bbc.co.uk/1/hi/uk/4349135.stm> (15 March 2006); 'Review Of Sex Offenders In School' BBC News Online <http://news.bbc.co.uk/1/hi/education/4602060.stm> (11 January 2006); 'Kelly To Tighten Sex Offender Law' BBC News Online <http://news.bbc.co.uk/1/hi/uk_politics/4604490.stm> (12 January 2006).

THE OFFENDER

Offenders themselves also present related problems for statutory and voluntary agencies which work towards their resettlement and reintegration. In the main, difficulties arise in relation to sex offender recidivism, the resulting need to 'track' the offender in the community and, more recently, the prevalence of 'grooming' behaviour.

Sex Offender Recidivism

The supposedly high rates of reoffending among sex offenders once they are released from custody also makes problematic the effective management of risk. Indeed, it would appear that both popular and official discourses have focused on sex offender recidivism in order to justify a punitive retributive response to controlling sex offenders in the community.

In the United States, legislatures, courts and advocates all agree that current legislation mandating sex offender registration and notification in particular are intended to address the high recidivism rate of sex offenders (Bedarf, 1995: 885, 893; Pallone, 2003; Sample and Bray, 2003). During the formulation of the legislation at both state and federal level, the focus was on former child sex offenders due to their perceived risk of recidivism (Hebenton and Thomas, 1996b: 437–38; Hebenton, 1997: 7). Analysis of the Congressional Record makes it clear that legislators in Congress were influenced by two studies submitted.[31] One found that 74 per cent of imprisoned child sex offenders had a previous conviction for a similar offence and that they were the most difficult class of offenders to rehabilitate. The second study claimed that the average child sex offender molests 117 children during his lifetime. In California, the appeal court in the 1985 case of *People v Tate*[32] held that that state's registration requirement is based on the assumption that sex offenders are more likely than other criminals to repeat their crimes. Similarly, in Arizona in 1992, the court in *State v Noble*[33] cited research studies on sex offender recidivism to support the assertion that registration statutes serve the important goal of aiding law enforcement in apprehending recidivists.

In a similar vein, the public also continues to perceive that the threat from sex offenders is greater than it actually is (New Jersey Commission on the Habitual Sex Offender, 1950: 13–14; Roberts and White, 1986).[34] Advocates of the various pieces of legislation which provide for the control of sex offenders in the community, such as registration, notification and tagging, continue to fuel this public

---

[31] 139 *Cong. Rec.*, H10, 320 Nov. 20 1993.
[32] 210 Cal. Rptr. 117, 119.
[33] 829 P.2d 1217, 1224.
[34] 'Crime and Embellishment' *LA Times Magazine*, 10 April 1994.

misperception by touting high recidivism rates as the reason why such laws are necessary (Bedarf, 1995: 897–98). These statistics simultaneously increase the public fear of sex offenders and provide a rationale for statutes meant to allay these fears (Bedarf, 1995: 898). Purportedly high recidivism rates are thus crucial to the existence and popularity of these laws (Hebenton and Thomas, 1996a: 102; Hebenton, 1997: 5). That not only the public but more crucially the official perception of sex offender recidivism rates may be false or misleading, however, is reason to question the validity of this body of legislation (Bedarf, 1995: 893).

Indeed, despite this shared perception that recidivism is a more serious problem among sex offenders generally than other criminals, recidivism research over the last few decades has produced mixed results (Furby et al, 1989; Nagayama Hall, 1995). This research has concentrated intermittently on both sex offences in general and offending specifically against children. Prior to the 1970s, the majority of studies concluded that sex offenders had a lower recidivism rate than the average criminal. In 1950, the New Jersey Commission on the Habitual Sex Offender reported that based on subsequent arrests for sexual offences, sex offenders had a recidivism rate of only 7 per cent. This rate was lower than all other serious offences except murder (New Jersey Commission on the Habitual Sex Offender, 1950: 14). Various researchers in subsequent years agreed with this conclusion, finding that serious sex offenders, such as rapists and child molesters, were not serious recidivists (Radzinowicz, 1957; Groth et al, 1982; Grunfeld and Noreik, 1986). One of the most comprehensive studies concluded that only 10 per cent of sex offenders were convicted for another sexual crime within 12–24 years (Christiansen et al, 1965: 43). In a similar vein, a more recent United States Department of Justice report found that only 7.7 per cent of convicted rapists were rearrested for rape within three years of their release from custody (Beck and Shipley, 1989).

In the late 1970s, criminologists reassessed their conclusions about sex offender recidivism (Soothill et al, 1976; Burgoyne, 1979). Soothill and Gibbens (1978) in a 20-year follow-up study of 86 rape offenders found that 24 (23 per cent) were reconvicted for further sexual or other crimes of violence. Indeed, Groth et al (1982: 456–57) asserted that sex offenders commit an alarming number of sexual offences for which they are never arrested or convicted. A 1985 study of the correlation between recidivism and the type of sexual crime found that over half the sample were rearrested within the 10-year period for some offence (Romero and Williams, 1985). The average rate of rearrest was 11.3 per cent, although this rate varied significantly with the type of offender; paedophiles at 6.2 per cent, sexual assaulters at 10.4 per cent, and exhibitionists at 20.5 per cent. In 1988, the California Department of Justice, as part of an assessment of the effectiveness of the California sex offender registration statute, found that 19.7 per cent of the subjects were rearrested for a registrable offence within fifteen years (Lewis, 1988). Similarly, Van der Werff (1989) in a general study of the 6-year reconviction rate of a sample of Dutch offenders prosecuted in 1977 found that of 119 rape offenders, 66 per cent were reconvicted for any offence and 17 per cent were reconvicted for a subsequent sexual offence.

Furthermore, evidence from self-report studies also suggests that those convicted of sexual offences often reveal the commission of many more offences than are reported to the authorities by their victims (Groth et al, 1982; Abel et al, 1987). Whereas these experts agree that the recidivism rate for untreated child sexual offenders is high, there is disagreement as to the precise figure. Some studies indicate that paedophiles most prone to recidivism, non-incestuous paedophiles, targeting boys, may have an average of approximately 280 victims in their lifetime (Abel et al, 1987: 15–16). Other studies have found a differing number of victims per sex offender (Riesenberg, 1987: 900; Stadler, 1997: 1288, n 15). A study of sex offender drug treatment for example (Kravitz et al 1995) found that, among 22 child molesters in the study, the median number of victims admitted by the men was 13. The number of actual victims ranged from 1–200. Moreover, there is also a positive correlation between the number of sexual crimes committed and the likelihood of future reoffending (Ortmann, 1980: 443–44).

Notwithstanding these two broad spectrums of opinion, Furby et al (1989) in a comprehensive and detailed review of 42 studies of sex offender recidivism, found that the wide variations in method, samples and categories of sexual offences studied, meant that few studies could be compared and little was known (Barker and Morgan, 1993; Nagayama Hall, 1995). They noted that longer follow-up increased the number of men found to reoffend and that recidivism rates may differ for different types of offenders, with the data showing that factors such as age, criminal history (Rice et al, 1991; Barker and Morgan, 1993; Marshall, 1994) and offence type are important. Due to the 'vast' under-reporting of sexual offences and the resulting fact that known sex offenders are a highly select population (Barker and Morgan, 1993), they concluded that many studies lacked sufficient follow-up and recommended a minimum period of ten years (Soothill and Gibbens, 1978).[35]

The most recent research on sex offender recidivism has taken a more nuanced approach. This shows, for example, that while overall levels of sexual offending are increasing, reconviction rates for sex offenders have declined (Friendship and Thornton, 2001) and are relatively low in comparison with other types of offender. A Home Office study which surveyed a range of studies found that about 20 per cent of those who are convicted of sexual offences against children, and 25 per cent overall, are reconvicted for similar offences over a 20-year period (Grubin, 1998: 32–40). This is much lower than recidivism rates for offenders generally which run at about 50 per cent over two years and 60 per cent over four. Indeed, the rate of reconviction for sexual offences remains fairly constant: as little as 10 per cent even

---

[35] All these studies refer to the recidivism of offenders released from incarceration or conventional criminal justice programmes. For the sake of completeness, it is proposed to make some mention of psychiatric treatment evaluation studies. Furby et al's (1989) review of studies suggests that the results are not as consistent as studies of offenders released from custody. A 4-year follow-up study of 54 Canadian rapists released after treatment from Penetanguishene, a maximum security psychiatric hospital, reveals that 28% had been convicted of a further sexual offence and 43% for a sexual or violent offence (Rice et al, 1989).

after a 6-year follow-up period (Hood et al, 2002).[36] These findings, however, are subject to the caveats outlined above in relation to the effectiveness of treatment programmes that actual recidivism levels may be 5.3 times greater than the official reconviction rates (Falshaw et al, 2003) and that fewer than 5 per cent of sex offenders are ever apprehended (Salter, 2003).

In addition, as noted above, there are also sub-groups of offenders for whom reoffending rates are substantially higher, including those with previous convictions for sexual offences and violence. Indeed, research has also shown that sex offenders of different types exhibit different reoffending behaviour. While Broadhurst and Maller (1992) in their study of Australian offenders found little support for the notion of sexual offenders as 'specialists', they found relatively high proportions of those who eventually repeat offences which are sexual or violent in nature. Similarly, it has also been argued that sex offenders can be both 'generalists' and 'specialists'—they may range widely across a spectrum of offences but still specialise within sexual offending (Soothill et al, 2000; Hood et al, 2002). Whatever sets of figures are cited, it would appear that certain classes of sex offender, particularly paedophiles, are at a significant risk of reoffending, in the absence of appropriate mechanisms for treatment and support which fully address the causes and consequences of their offending behaviour. As Murray argues: 'regardless of the estimate used, recidivism rates of child molesters are a serious concern' (1998: 734).

It has also been argued that if actual recidivism rates motivated registration legislation and other such control in the community mechanisms, then surely drug dealers or robbers should be the prime targets rather than sex offenders (Bedarf, 1995: 898). One response to this criticism may be that sexual offences cause so much harm to the community that punitive control in the community measures are justified regardless of recidivism rates. Such an argument, however, does not consider that legislatures have failed to impose registration requirements, for example, on other violent offenders, such as robbers or assaulters, who arguably also inflict serious harm on the community. Indeed, the statistical prominence of repeat sexual offences alone may not necessarily account for a policy response. On the contrary, several other factors pertaining to the offender may also help to explain how the management of sex offenders in the community has been conceptualised, both within popular and official discourses, as a problem or issue requiring specific action.

The Problems with 'Tracking' Sex Offenders

Public and official perceptions about high levels of sex offender recidivism generates a further justification for legislation governing sex offenders in the community.

---

[36] There were discernible differences, however, between intra-familial offenders, where none were reconvicted in the 6-year follow-up period and extra-familial offenders, where nearly a quarter were reconvicted of a child sexual offence (Hood et al, 2002).

If sex offenders are perceived to be high-risk recidivists then there is a subsequent need to regulate their behaviour in the community on release from custody (Martin and Sherman, 1986; Hebenton and Thomas, 1996a, 1996b; Cobley 1997b; Cox, 1997). The policy and practice of past and present tracking arrangements in the form of early release procedures and supervision provisions have been outlined above, as has the wider concept of 'managing risk in the community.' It is not proposed to repeat those arguments here in any detail.

However, it was noted that in the United States, in particular, there has been a substantial increase in the number of sex offenders released from custody due to prison overcrowding and a lack of funding. In the United Kingdom, some of the provisions of the Criminal Justice Act 1991 provided for changes to the early release procedures which also resulted in an increase of the number of sex offenders released from custody into the community (Home Office, 1991; Hebenton and Thomas, 1996a).[37]

In response to these problems, as will be discussed in the next two chapters, a number of control in the community mechanisms designed to manage sex offenders and the risk they are seen to present more effectively, have been formulated in recent years. In particular, the requirement that a released sex offender should register his name and address and any subsequent changes with the police was intended to be useful in 'keeping track' of his whereabouts (Bedarf, 1995; Cobley 1997b).[38] Moreover, registration schemes involve a reconceptualisation of and a far greater proactive approach to tracking (Parliament of the Commonwealth of Australia, 1995: paras 4.15–18; Hughes et al, 1996: vii; Hebenton and Thomas, 1996a: 108). The assumption underlying this mode of thinking is that if offenders remain largely unchecked in the community, free to access victims, then people are not protected and crime is neither reduced nor prevented.[39] Offender detection therefore is at the centre of this approach (Hebenton and Thomas 1996a: 108).

In the past, sex offenders were being released from prison and could essentially disappear with statutory authorities having no idea of their whereabouts, unless they had contact with probation by virtue of a probation order. Until relatively recently, there was a distinct gap in the legislative provision for sex offender registration which, as will be discussed in the next chapter, initially only required the specified categories of offender to register their details with the police every 14 days. This created consequent problems for the police in keeping track of released sex offenders who could technically shift addresses within this period. Under Part 2 of the Sexual Offences Act 2003, which strengthens and replaces the provisions of Part I of the Sex Offenders Act 1997, sex offenders currently have to register their details with the police within three days of their release from custody. This at least gives the police the ability to assess the area they are residing in and evaluate what risks they may present to the local community.

---

[37] 'More Than 100,000 Paedophiles At Large Says Home Office' *The Times*, 20 February 1997.
[38] See also: John Hutton, *Hansard* HC Deb, vol 289, col 64 (27 January 1997).
[39] *id.*

A related problem for police officers, however, is that many sex offenders tend to use the hostel community as a base, at least initially, once they are released from prison. Such environments have traditionally been regarded as highly transient in nature, providing the offender with multiple opportunities for mobility and perhaps anonymity if they are to move freely from district to district. Indeed, it is here that the geographical boundaries both within and across jurisdictions become highly problematic. For example, before the Republic of Ireland had a system of registration operationally in place, offenders could quite easily slip across the border from Northern Ireland in order to escape the registration requirement. The Review of the Criminal Justice System in Northern Ireland, in this respect, also highlighted this as a problem area and one particularly suitable for and in need of an element of 'structured co-operation' between the police forces in both parts of the island (Criminal Justice Review Group, 2000). The review recommended that the possibility of co-ordinating an approach to dangerous offender registers should be given careful consideration with a view to information sharing between the authorities in the two jurisdictions (Criminal Justice Review Group, 2000: para 17.53, recommendation 291).

In this respect, the Republic of Ireland made provision, inter alia, for a 'tracking' system for sex offenders through registration and post-release supervision via the Sex Offenders Act 2001. Previously informal initiatives between police forces in Northern Ireland and the Republic of Ireland in terms of information sharing are now becoming more formalised. In the context of England and Wales, the development of the ViSOR database, as mentioned above, and as will also be discussed in the next chapter, will significantly advance cross-jurisdictional initiatives by ensuring that offenders can now be tracked nationally and cannot simply disappear. There has even been some support for a single European-wide system for monitoring sex offenders (Home Office, 2002: para 27), given the mobile nature of these types of offender and the related problems of sex trafficking and offenders committing offences while abroad. The United States, in this respect, has almost since inception maintained its sex offender registry databases at both state and federal level.

However, as outlined at the end of chapter 2, there are a number of problems which remain embedded in the nature of inter-agency working which also have a bearing on cross-jurisdictional co-operation. It was noted there that despite the best efforts of individual agencies at co-operation and effective information sharing about offenders, differences in organisational cultures, priorities and working practices can materially weaken the multi-agency approach (Crawford, 1999) and some offenders may consequently slip through the net. This was evidenced most recently in relation to the significant gaps in information sharing between police forces in England and Wales as highlighted by the Bichard Inquiry into the murder by Ian Huntley of Soham schoolgirls, Holly Wells and Jessica Chapman (Bichard, 2004). All these problems are of course compounded in working to keep track of offenders across not only organisational but geographical boundaries, and perhaps even international ones, where you may have, in essence, separate jurisdictions with disparate legal systems, police forces and organisational practices.

'Grooming Behaviour'

A further difficulty which has only recently arisen in sex offender management discourses is the pervasive use of 'grooming' techniques by would-be offenders (McAlinden, 2006c). This term usually refers to the preparatory stage of sexual abuse whereby an offender will set up opportunities to abuse by gaining the trust of the child in order to prepare them for abuse either directly or, as is the case more recently, through internet chat rooms (Gillespie, 2001, 2004; Gallagher et al, 2003). It has been claimed that 'grooming is a ubiquitous feature of the sexual abuse of children' (Thornton, 2003: 144). Indeed, the sociological process of grooming is highly effective in terms of masking the risk that sex offenders present. Grooming makes it extremely difficult to identify potential offenders and abusive behaviour before it happens. In effect, such techniques help to both facilitate the onset of offending and, at the same time, prevent its discovery.

Lack of Settled Meaning

'Grooming' is not a new concept. The term has been in use for some time by psychologists who have sought to analyse patterns of deviant sexual behaviour. There are widespread uncertainties and misconceptions, however, about what sort of behaviour is covered by the term. As Gillespie (2004) argues, grooming is a transient process that is difficult to capture and virtually impossible to pinpoint when it begins and ends. The lack of settled meaning of this term may be due to a number of interrelated factors:

First, some of the uncertainty is in part attributable to the fact that since only a relatively small amount of research has been carried out, understanding of the area is still fairly rudimentary. Secondly, a related problem is that within the popular imagination[40] and even official discourses[41] grooming is based on concept of 'stranger danger' and is immediately associated with the internet and used mainly

[40] This misconception in the common usage of the term is due largely to media portrayal of the risk of sexual abuse and public education and awareness campaigns on the dangers of chat rooms and safe use of the internet.

[41] Several jurisdictions have recognised the extent of the dangers of 'internet grooming' for some time. For example, Australia, Canada and the United States have various offences to cover online grooming based on either coercion, enticement or luring a child with the intention of having sexual relations. (For Australia's Northern Territory law, see s 201 of the Northern Territory of Australia Criminal Code Act, para 3.4.2; for US federal law, see 18 USC 2422: Coercion and Enticement; for Georgia state law, see Ga. Code Ann. § 16-12-100.2 (1999); for Canada, see s 172.1 of the Criminal Code enacted by the Criminal Amendment Act 2001). However, for the most part, grooming in these jurisdictions remains firmly linked to the internet and legislation has yet to be enacted to cover grooming which takes place off-line. Scotland and New Zealand, however, have also proposed legislation along similar lines to that of the United Kingdom.

to refer to on-line behaviour.[42] Crucially, this is contrary to the reality that children are most likely to be sexually abused by those with whom they have a family relationship (Grubin, 1998), where grooming can also take place and is most often offline. Thirdly, the enactment of recent legislation has not done anything to remove these ambiguities. As will be discussed in chapter 6, Part 2 of the Sexual Offences Act 2003 in the United Kingdom introduced a number of measures to deal with this behaviour.[43] Within the legislation, however, the term 'grooming' is nowhere defined. Moreover, this provision continues to be known as the 'grooming offence,' even though it is not intended to be so. In fact, it is the behaviour following grooming that is to be captured by the offence, and not the grooming process itself. As will also be discussed in chapter 6, these ambiguities surrounding what amounts to sexual grooming also have implications for the criminalisation of such behaviour.

An Abuse of Trust

A key variable in the grooming process is the establishment and subsequent breach of trust. It is the level of trust placed in offenders by children and others which allows them to deliberately suspend suspicion and facilitate the continuum of abuse. In the past two decades, the topic of trust has captured the attention of a number of scholars (Cook and Wall, 1980; Johnson-George and Swap, 1982; Dasgupta, 1988; Luhmann, 1988; Gambetta, 1988; Good, 1988; Coleman, 1990). As Friedrichs points out, although trust is a central cultural concern, there is no single meaning of the term (1996: 11–12). Many of the themes from the general sociological literature on trust, however, in particular the work of Ben-Yehuda (2001) on violations of trust and loyalty—betrayal—can be related specifically to the behaviour of sex offenders in the grooming process.

First, sex offenders actively seek to create and abuse 'trust' in varied social contexts (Luhmann, 1988; Friedrichs, 1996; Kramer et al, 1996; Oliver, 1997). Trust has resonance not only at the micro-level within interpersonal relationships such as those between offenders and children and their carers, but at the macro-level in terms of how relationships operate between offenders and wider society and the institutions within which they may work (Coleman, 1990). Secondly, offenders try to establish intimate and social relationships with those they want to groom. Trust assumes such relationships as loyalty, friendship and belief (Ben-Yehuda, 2001: 11–13). These are the necessary pre-conditions that the offender must construct so that the participants perceive that a genuine, authentic and truthful interaction

---

[42] Grooming was also associated primarily with on-line behaviour in parliamentary debates on the Sexual Offences Act 2003. See eg: Baroness Blatch, *Hansard* HL Deb, vol 644, cols 788–89 (13 February 2003); Lord Alli, *Hansard* HL Deb, vol 644, col 795 (13 February 2003).

[43] Moreover, the dangers of sexual grooming have also been recently recognised by the judiciary. In *Re Attorney General's Reference (No 41 of 2000)* [2001] 1 Cr App R (S) 372 (CA), one of the reasons why the Court of Appeal increased the defendant's original sentence for indecent assault and making indecent photographs of children was because he had sexually groomed a vulnerable child with special needs.

exists (Ben-Yehuda, 2001: 6–7). Thirdly, breach of trust typically involves a range of deception techniques such as secrecy, manipulation, lying, cheating or conceal-ment (Ben-Yehuda, 2001: 6–7). With institutional grooming, in particular, it is the offender's job and related status which provide a ready vehicle for this deception.

In fact, 'grooming' behaviour is much more pervasive than has previously been acknowledged. Current discourses have been largely reactive in nature and neglect other important facets of the sex offender's behavioural pattern. They do not fully consider that sex offenders may also groom not just the child but their family and even the wider community in which they live who may act as the gatekeepers of access. They also ignore the fact that sex offenders may groom criminal justice and other institutions into believing that they present no risk to children.

'Personal Grooming'

Information on grooming has come from the study of offenders in treatment pro-grammes who have frequently acknowledged the process (Budin and Johnson, 1989; Conte et al, 1989; Christiansen and Blake 1990; Elliott et al, 1995; Smallbone and Wortley, 2000) and of victims (Berliner and Conte, 1990, 1995) and from both taken together (Phelan, 1995). The expression 'grooming', first underlined by Salter (1995), is generally used to refer to the process by which a would-be abuser skilfully manipulates a child into a situation where he or she can be more readily sexually abused and is simultaneously less likely to disclose (Van Dam, 2002; Wyre, 2000). Salter alternatively uses the term 'emotional seduction' in this con-text (1995: 74). The grooming process can occur over a short period but more commonly occurs over a longer period to allow the child to feel comfortable. The patience of the offender can also be partly explained by the fact that it is not uncommon for him to be grooming several children at once.[44]

Consistent with Matza's (1964, 1969) 'techniques of neutralisation,' sex offend-ers do not fully internalise any set of sexual or behavioural norms. Rather they have a learnt set of 'definitions favourable to violation.' As noted at the outset, the meaning of grooming in a legal context is uncertain which does seem to reflect something of the phenomenon itself. Personal grooming, however, involves a series of what are, in terms of the literature, fairly well-established stages for manipulating children and normalising deviant sexual relationships (Budin and Johnston, 1989; Conte et al, 1989; Berliner and Conte, 1990, 1995; Elliott et al, 1995; Gallagher, 2000; Ost, 2002).

First, grooming the child can typically include befriending a potential victim by getting to know their interests and being helpful and confiding in order to gain their confidence and trust. Secondly, the offender will cultivate a 'special' friend-ship by bestowing a variety of inducements. This emphasis on the exclusivity of the

---

[44] One commentator has argued that the term 'grooming' is not a wholly appropriate one in light of what children are subjected to and should be replaced with the word 'entrapment' (Gallagher, 1998). Other jurisdictions have proceeded along similar lines. See n 41 above.

relationship helps to 'distance' the child from their parents or others who may represent a source of safety and prevent the abusive behaviour from being discovered. It also enables the offender to control the victim through the giving or withholding of rewards. Thirdly, the offender will often use 'forbidden fruit' type activities such as cursing, telling 'dirty jokes' or showing the child pornography. This latter stage not only begins to normalise sexual behaviour, but may be used to entrap the child further by encouraging feelings of shame and guilt. Finally, the offender will exploit the child's naivety and trust by introducing increasingly intimate physical contact such as play acting, tickling or wrestling and even hugging. The use of touch is important as this determines whether the child is receptive and begins the process of desensitisation—gradually the abuser will escalate boundary violations of the child's body culminating in sexual activity.

The grooming procedure is extremely effective as the vast majority of children do not disclose the abuse. Research shows that fewer than 5 per cent of sex offenders are ever apprehended (Salter, 2003). Estimates also suggest that only 3 per cent of all cases of child sexual abuse (Finkelhor and Dziuba-Leatherman, 1994) and only 12 per cent of rapes involving children (Hanson et al, 1999; Smith et al, 2000) are ever reported to the police. As discussed above, a complex range of emotions all conspire to silence children and inhibit their disclosures of abuse. The process is also significant, for to invoke the much-used phrase 'monsters do not get children, nice men do' (Long and McLachlan, 2002: 6).[45] Contrary to the media-inspired popular belief, a sex offender is not instantly recognisable as the 'dirty old man in the raincoat.' Part of their skill is to ingratiate themselves with children and infiltrate themselves into unsuspecting families, communities and organisations.

'Familial Grooming'

The ambiguities surrounding the grooming process in both legal and sociological terms do not become that much clearer for being extended into the familial and institutional contexts. However, once more, indicators are to be found in the literature. Skilful offenders may also seek to gain access to the child by establishing a friendship with the child's parent or adult caretaker rather than, or in addition to, that with the child. In this respect, adults may be primed and controlled for victimisation in similar ways to children.

In Salter's (2003) more recent work she explains how sex offenders, who often have good social skills, act with careful premeditation and use sophisticated deception techniques to avoid suspicion, sometimes playing double roles in the community. In this respect, the grooming of the child's family or community has a dual purpose: securing the confidence and trust and thus the co-operation of their carers in gaining access to the child; and reducing the likelihood of discovery or disclosure by creating an atmosphere of normality or acceptance.

---

[45] In relation to the gendered nature of offending, as discussed in the introductory chapter, less than 5% of sex offences against children are known to have been committed by women. (See Grubin, 1998; NCIS, 2003). Other American studies place this figure as low as 1–2% (Vandiver and Walker, 2002).

Grooming behaviour, as with the ultimate child victim, is intended to make the victim's guardian's feel comfortable with the offender. This causes parents and others to drop their guard allowing the sex offender easy and recurring access to their children. This has worked to the extent that some offenders have been successful in persuading the child's parents to consent to their child having an unaccompanied outing or an overnight stay with the offender, which provides the abuser with an opportunity to offend with impunity (Salter, 2003: 5).

One of the first stages in the offender's deviant cycle which precludes the onset of sexual abuse is victim identification or selection. Aside from choosing a victim that has general appeal, ease of access and vulnerability play a pivotal role. Sex offenders sometimes plan their assaults around a category of child whom they believe they can safely victimise. This includes children with special needs and learning disabilities (Gallagher, 1998: 807–11). Research also suggests that sex offenders appear to single out and target children and families with obvious vulnerabilities (Conte et al, 1989; Elliott et al, 1995). For instance, they may select a dysfunctional family where the parents are having marital problems (Gruber and Jones, 1983; Finkelhor, 1984), where the mother is ill (Herman, 1981; Finkelhor, 1984) or where the child is being emotionally neglected in some way (Finkelhor, 1984; Bagley and Ramsey, 1986).

Sex offenders will often select single parent families where usually the woman herself is vulnerable either economically or emotionally (Herman, 1981; Bagley and Ramsey, 1986).[46] These include women who may be looking for a 'father-figure' for their children or those who are drug-addicted who will trade their children for drugs (Salter, 1995: 39). One of the easiest ways to make contact with a child is to live with one. Offenders may target single mothers by placing or responding to advertisements in 'lonely hearts' columns in the eventual hope of forming a family relationship—either moving in with or even marrying that person in order to gain access to their children (NCIS, 2003). They may even aspire to find a partner with whom they can have their own children which, in their terms, would provide ready access to victims whom they can abuse.

Aside from the child's family, the community itself can also be primed and controlled through the grooming process. Many offenders tend to adopt a pattern of socially responsible and caring behaviour in public. They endeavour to build a good reputation and to create a strong social perception of themselves as being an upstanding member of the local church or community, as a nice man who is exceptionally kind to children or the type of person who would usually help out when needed (Salter, 2003). Typical access methods also include choosing a career or volunteering for work that will place them in close proximity with children.

---

[46] Several other studies, however, have identified separation from the father as a risk factor. (See eg: Finkelhor, 1984; Russell, 1986).

'Institutional Grooming'

Most of what is known about institutional abuse derives from case studies and official reports. In England and Wales in particular, as noted above, a number of public inquiry reports or official reviews have resulted from the disclosure of institutional physical and sexual abuse in care homes. These inquiries and reviews have highlighted systematic failures to respond to reports of abuse and have concluded that the extent of institutional abuse and the implications for the management of the problem are extensive. All these cases also verify that sex offenders often actively seek situations that bring them into contact with children. It would appear that in common with the internet, which has been used as a ruse to groom children for abuse, certain forms of employment may allow an abuser to gain access to children in a way that would not otherwise be possible.

These occupations relate to a variety of settings (Stanley, 1999). They go beyond the obvious religious work to include also secular paid and voluntary work (Smith, 1993) within schools (La Fontaine and Morris, 1991; Brannan et al, 1993), residential homes (Corby et al, 2001) and a range of community-based childcare settings, including foster care placements (Browne and Lynch, 1999; Waterhouse, 2000) and nursery schools (Finkelhor et al 1988; Hunt, 1994). Indeed, the picture painted by the inquiries and reviews is that the problem of institutional abuse is confined mainly to residential contexts. The reality, however, is that probably every profession or organisation that has contact with children in terms of their care, education or social or leisure activities is vulnerable to infiltration by those who wish to abuse.

Within the institutional context, the relationships created with the child and other adult carers who might protect them are also based on the creation of loyalty and trust and their subsequent violation. As discussed above, a breach of trust typically involves a range of deception techniques that make betrayal possible. In this vein, sex offenders appear to use the special features of the institutional environment to facilitate abuse and prevent disclosure by children and other professionals (Brannan et al, 1993).

Indeed, institutions can create multiple opportunities for the manipulation and abuse of children and can allow the offender to take on a different persona and remain anonymous in terms of their deviant sexual tendencies. The organisational culture itself may be conducive to abuse of power and erosion of the primary functions of care and protection. Childcare institutions appear to be self-protective, secretive and closed by nature. As such they discourage the drawing of attention to any deficiencies in policies and procedures and the signs of abuse (Wescott, 1991: 15–17; Waterhouse, 2000; Sullivan and Beech, 2002: 162). Furthermore, if these organisations are held in high esteem by local agencies or parents, children may experience added difficulties in both resisting and disclosing the abuse (Gallagher, 2000: 810).

Moreover, the particular role which these offenders play within certain institutions may also make the environment more facilitative of abuse. The offender may be in a primary management position with free reign over the institution, with few checks and balances on their behaviour. It is this status or authority that may give them the necessary control over the organisational culture. In short, it may give them 'the power to betray' (Ben-Yehuda, 2001: 28). Indeed, it has been said that it is this facet of the institutional setting which makes the behaviour of the professional offender closely akin to that of the intra-familial offender (Sullivan and Beech, 2002: 164).

As noted above, a system of pre-employment vetting has been introduced for those working with children and young people. It can only ever be effective, however, where there is a clear record of offending and where the identity of the person being vetted is known and assured. The management procedures put in place to date can do little to stop offenders when they are at their most dangerous—when their deviant sexual behaviour and the risk they present remains hidden, and when they have managed to persuade those responsible for children, through grooming, that they are genuine, respectable and worthy of belief.

As will also be discussed in chapter 6, due to the inherent difficulties of early identification of the grooming process prior to actual offending, and in particular in drawing clear boundaries between innocent and more deviant relationships with children, current legal measures may be limited in managing the risk posed by sex offenders in the community. As will also be discussed in chapter 7, given the limitations of the criminal law in response to this pervasive form of deviant sexual behaviour, ultimately concerted efforts must be made to foster social and organisational awareness of how sex offenders operate, in particular how they gain our trust. This has the potential to make children safer on a wider scale, not only within the wider community, but crucially within their own families where they may be most at risk. Indeed, it will be argued that through reintegrative shaming mechanisms like circles of support, vigilant community members may also have a role to play in managing risk and reducing the offender's opportunity for abuse. In the interim, however, it seems that the community for the most part has a negative contribution to make and is often hostile and vocal in its opposition to the placement and management of sex offenders in the local community.

THE COMMUNITY

The community can have a potentially powerful impact on the management and resettlement of sex offenders in the community. The contemporary context of the community's contribution to the sex offender management process was outlined in chapter 2 in relation to media treatment of sexual crime and the resulting 'moral panic' (Cohen 1972/1980) about the presence of sex offenders in the community. It was noted there that media coverage of sexual offences has a number of undesirable effects on the popular imagination such as fostering fear, anger and hostility towards released offenders living in the community (Greer, 2003). One notable example of this was the furore surrounding the *News of the World*'s 'Name and

Shame' campaign in the wake of the murder of Sarah Payne by paedophile Roy Whiting, which was centred on the 'outing' of known and suspected paedophiles (Silverman and Wilson, 2002: 146–66). This ultimately manifested itself in violence and vigilante action in the form of public harassment and attack on such individuals and their properties. There were also several incidents of mistaken identity where the community attacked the wrong person (Ashenden, 2002: 208). In fact, it appears that anyone who is different or arouses suspicion could be singled out as a potential target for intimidation by vigilante groups.

In Northern Ireland, these problems have manifested themselves more starkly in the form of 'punishment beatings' of suspected sex offenders by paramilitary groups (Leggett, 2000; Knox, 2002: 174). These groups, who are purportedly anxious to safeguard society's morals, become involved in the 'informal policing' of sex offenders and others who have displayed inappropriate behaviour. They may play on the fears of the local community concerning the presence of sex offenders and consequently present themselves as protectors and alternative law enforcers in stark contrast to what they see as the failure of the local authorities to adequately deal with the problem. As will be discussed further below, this 'informal policing' of sex offenders by vigilante groups makes the work of the various inter-agency professionals much more difficult in terms of managing sex offenders in the community, particularly in relation to the decision of where to place them on release. As noted in chapter 3, however, community-based restorative justice schemes have been developed as a direct response to the threat of paramilitary violence in Northern Ireland (McEvoy and Mika, 2001, 2002; Mika and McEvoy, 2001).

This section seeks to further examine some of the reasons behind the community's reaction to the presence of sex offenders living in the community, which as we have seen has so far been demonstrated in retributive, punitive and vengeful terms. Communities display a number of general characteristics when faced with the placement of a released sex offender in their area. These may help to explain why they react in an emotive, antagonistic and often even a violent way and consequently undermine effective risk management and offender reintegration:

First, as outlined previously, the knowledge and awareness which communities have about sex offending issues are strongly influenced by the treatment which such issues receive at the hands of the press. Media coverage of high profile cases not only tends to increase fears about sex offenders, but conveys inaccurate information about the nature of sex offending, and in particular about levels of risk. The media explain their sensationalist coverage of sex offender issues and their witch hunt against paedophiles in particular on the basis that they are protecting the community and satisfying the public's appetite for these types of stories. In reality, however, media treatment of particular cases of sexual offending has the opposite effect since it is almost inevitable that once a sex offender has been publicly identified, whatever inter-agency risk management arrangements were being made for the individual, are going to break down. In addition, as will be discussed further below, by highlighting the perceived inadequacies of the authorities in managing offenders, the media help undermine the basic premise that communities must take responsibility for their own protection. As will be discussed in chapter 7 in relation to a future reintegrative response to managing sex offenders in the community, the media could be used quite constructively in helping the community to gain a better perspective of sex offending.

Secondly, members of the community are often complacent and lack responsibility in relation to protection of their children. They believe that it is the responsibility of statutory and voluntary agencies to make the community safe for their children and they do not have a sufficient appreciation of the dangers which children can face, even within their own community. If a sex offender is discovered in a particular locality and is removed from that area, communities may be lulled into a false sense of security that they are now safe. As noted above, there is considerable distortion in the public perception and understanding of the actual nature of sex offending. As outlined throughout this work, the vast bulk of sexual offending occurs in the home where it remains undetected (Grubin, 1998). Moreover, the pervasiveness of 'grooming behaviour' as outlined above, which has the twin effect of allowing sex offenders to gain access to children and preventing their deviant sexual behaviour from being discovered, combined with the hidden and secretive nature of child abuse itself, may mean that the actual number of sex offenders in the community may be considerably greater than is currently publicly acknowledged.

A third and related factor is that the community has failed to understand that the law is somewhat limited in its response to sexual offending and as a result often has unrealistic expectations of statutory and voluntary agencies. As will be discussed in the next two chapters, the methods that exist for managing sex offenders in the community such as registration, civil preventative orders and electronic tagging are replete with practical difficulties which may reduce their effectiveness in aiding law enforcement. In addition, even if these legal measures were totally successful they are, by their nature, only applied to sex offenders who have already been apprehended and adjudicated on. As such, although each of these measures may make a small contribution to keeping communities safe, the law by itself can never hope to adequately deal with the totality of problems posed by managing sex offenders in the community. In short, inter-agency law, policy and practice may facilitate the effective 'management' of the risk posed by sex offenders in the community, but eradication of the full risk is impossible. Communities, however, are slow to recognise and accept these facts. Part of the reason, it seems, is that the community has a great deal more difficulty in dealing with people in the domestic setting. It has also been argued in this respect that the public already accepts that the risk of sexual victimisation by a stranger is slight but is reluctant to visualise the risk in domestic terms (Greer, 2003). They deliberately choose to construct 'sites of danger' as being firmly located within the public space since any alternative undermines the traditional views of the family and home as the given sphere of safety and protection (Saraga, 2001).

A fourth factor which may explain hostile community reaction to the placement and management of sex offenders in the community is colloquially known as the 'Not In My Back Yard' or 'NIMBY' syndrome. That is, the community for the most part is not concerned with where statutory and voluntary agencies place a released sex offender so long as it is not in their local vicinity. Far from effectively managing the risk posed by sex offenders in the community, such an approach on the part of the community can result in crime or 'risk displacement,' or 'crime shuffling' (Pease, 2002: 956), 'deflection' (Barr and Pease, 1990) or 'spill over' (Hakim and Rengert, 1981), as others prefer. By outing an offender from their own community they may be increasing the risk of reoffending if the offender then moves to another community where no one knows them. In effect, the community may succeed in removing the risk from their own immediate vicinity only to place it elsewhere. These terms have only relatively recently been discovered by criminologists and begun to be taken seriously in debates about crime prevention. It is a subject, however, about which ordinary people are very much aware. Members of the public often have an astute and very clear understanding of the effects of displacement. Community residents are often only too keen to move crime out of their area, well aware of the fact that they may not solve the problem but rather shift it on to others, so long as they themselves remain safe (Crawford, 1999: 286).

The community's reaction which is generally to reject sex offenders undoubtedly creates considerable problems for statutory and voluntary agencies in protecting the interests of both individuals and communities, by successfully reintegrating offenders while at the same time securing public safety. As will be discussed further in the next chapter, the above traits displayed by the community have obvious implications for increased community involvement in sex offender issues in terms of possible community notification or public disclosure of information about offenders and their whereabouts. These difficulties, it seems, are especially heightened for those professionals involved in the allocation and provision of housing for sex offenders. Housing authorities face considerable challenges in housing this specific group of ex-offenders (Cowan et al, 1999) and appear to bear the brunt of public dissatisfaction, rather than the police, probation or social services (Cowan et al, 2001: 438). Indeed, it has been argued in this context that social housing has become inextricably linked with the process of crime control, and concerns with public protection in particular, and has become a pivotal criterion in the policing of sex offenders (Cowan et al, 2001).

From a practical standpoint, if an offender is intimidated or hounded out of a particular locality, he may have to be placed in temporary accommodation. As discussed above in relation the problems of 'tracking', the placement of an offender in a hostel may be far from ideal given the fluid and transient nature of both sex offenders and that living environment. Alternatively, in high profile cases, there may be in effect nowhere the offender can be safely moved. Clearly the location of the potential housing features highly in both professional and community agendas. Communities in particular may fear that their estates will become 'dumping grounds' (Stenson and Watt, 1999).[47] In this respect, there have been reports of

[47] In some urban areas, particularly in the United States, the numbers of people being placed in disadvantaged areas on release from prison has promoted social and academic interest in the 'collateral consequences' of imprisonment (Clear et al, 2003; Fagan et al, 2003; Farrall and Sparks, 2006: 7).

attacks by communities on sex offenders and perhaps, as a direct result, evictions of offenders by landlords.[48] Indeed, hostel providers themselves may be reluctant to assist the police and other statutory agencies in this respect if their own premises are subject to attack by the local community due to a perception, well founded or otherwise, that sex offenders are being housed there.

A related difficulty is that sex offenders on release from prison are not currently placed back into the communities in which they offended for fear of vigilante attack. Offenders are therefore removed from the traditional safeguards of their own community where they are recognised and where at least people know who they are and to be on the alert for them. This can be dangerous since, as mentioned previously, isolated offenders who have not successfully reintegrated into the community may go underground and commit crime elsewhere.

In this respect, as will be discussed further in the next two chapters in relation to legislative and judicial 'disintegrative shaming' (Braithwaite, 1989) mechanisms, such as sex offender registration and other control in the community initiatives, negative public attitudes can have a number of damaging and destructive consequences. The consequences for offenders themselves may be that they are constantly living in fear that the local community will find out about their offending identity. The opprobrious popular reaction can effectively stigmatise offenders, isolate them from the rest of the community and ultimately make impossible their effective rehabilitation and reintegration. In particular, offenders who feel that they have failed to readjust to community life as a result of a hostile community reaction to their presence may resort to their previous offending behaviour as a coping mechanism (Maxwell and Morris, 1999; Edwards and Hensley, 2001b; McAlinden, 2005). In effect, and somewhat ironically perhaps, the community in an effort to protect themselves and their children, may actually increase the danger and become the very catalyst which triggers the onset of a new offending profile by the deliberate withholding of social acceptance and support. As Cowan et al argue:

> At heart, the issue is whether crime control processes—the processes of separation and exclusion—are an appropriate tool for the management of 'problem' spaces and populations (1999: 153).

Given these difficulties, communities therefore must also be required to recognise that child protection is everybody's responsibility, that the community has a responsibility to police, should protect themselves and their children as much as statutory agencies, and must consequently contribute to an effective social response to what is clearly a social problem. Indeed, the foregoing discussion highlights the fact that the community needs to be better informed and better educated about the whole nature of sexual offending. It underlines, therefore, the need for a major public education and awareness programme to dispel some of the myths and provide more accurate information to the community about the nature of sex offending and to encourage informed debate and foster community responsibility.

---

[48] 'Jeering Mothers Drive Paedophile Off Council Estate' *The Times*, 11 January 1997.

If we can achieve a society where the community works to protect itself, and statutory agencies such as the police are there to support the community's effort at self-protection, we may achieve a situation where sex offenders can be placed in communities where they will be tolerated, monitored and supervised effectively. As will be discussed in chapter 7, increasing public awareness may in turn facilitate the development of a future 'partnership' where the statutory, voluntary and community sectors work together to formulate a more effective response to the management of the risk posed by sex offenders in the community (Crawford, 1999; Hope, 2001).

Indeed, it may be that the negative feelings and emotions about sex offenders, outlined previously in relation to media treatment of sexual crimes and the public's response to this, can be used more effectively. As will also be discussed in chapter 7, at the opposite end of the spectrum are circles of support and accountability which originated in Canada (Cesaroni, 2001; Silverman and Wilson, 2002: 167–84; Wilson et al, 2002; Petrunik, 2002: 503–5) and have since been piloted successfully in several other jurisdictions, including England and Wales (Quaker Peace and Social Witness, 2005). These restorative social networks of treatment and support, which have been shown to be essential to successful reintegration, represent a much more progressive and forward thinking response to effective offender management. They clearly illustrate the fact that the community, in this respect, can make a positive contribution to the offender's successful rehabilitation and the prevention of future offending. Such schemes, it will be argued, may also have the particular benefit of engaging vigilante groups within the local community and encouraging them to approach the problem of managing sex offenders in the community in a more appropriate and constructive way.

CONCLUSION

Many sex offenders are released from prison each year into the community without the benefit of effective treatment programmes. Moreover, sex offenders are often devious and manipulative by nature and will set up opportunities to reoffend without appropriate levels of vigilance, treatment and support. As such, any future initiatives aimed at better managing the risk posed by sex offenders in the community will have to acknowledge fully the importance of this complex range of factors, in particular the contribution made by the community, and incorporate it into any proposals which are formulated. To paraphrase an old adage, 'if they are part of the problem they must be part of the solution.'

Indeed, this new response can be classified by greater involvement of the community in relation to sex offender issues. It will be tentatively argued in part III of the book that all future efforts aimed at effective risk management and offender reintegration should be targeted towards a restorative or reintegrative approach to justice. Sex offenders on release from custody could be placed back into the communities in which they offended, and where the public can form support groups to assist offenders and the statutory and voluntary agencies in the criminal justice system with their rehabilitation.

As will be discussed in chapter 7, this would not be easily realised in the first instance. Such a response therefore must initially comprise a public education and awareness programme. This could then be followed by the development of community treatment and support initiatives where the community can take an active role in managing, monitoring and reintegrating sex offenders within the community.

5

Sex Offender Registration and Community Notification

CONTEMPORARY POPULAR AND official penal discourses have been marked with a distinct pessimism surrounding rehabilitative philosophies, as outlined in the previous chapter. A lengthy custodial sentence and a prison treatment programme are no longer expected to 'cure' sex offenders but rather to simply help them control their behaviour in order to minimise the risk of future offending (Hudson, 2005: 2). In tandem with this thinking, great emphasis is now being placed on extending the didactics of control from prison into the community for this particular category of offender. Alongside these broader policy developments, as noted in chapter 2, recent years have also been characterised by widespread media and public outcry over crimes committed by convicted sex offenders shortly after their release from prison.

In response to this 'populist punitiveness' (Bottoms, 1995), as will be discussed in this chapter and the next, governments have enacted a whole host of legislative retributive measures which are designed to monitor and manage sex offenders in the community and to control the special risk they are seen to present. One of the most notable of these 'tracking' mechanisms is sex offender registration and community notification. Although registration or notification procedures for sex offenders have been established in a number of jurisdictions, recent schemes are analysed here primarily in the context of 'Megan's Law' in the United States and Part 2 of the Sexual Offences Act 2003 in the United Kingdom.[1] These schemes, which have been premised on the broad aims of specific deterrence and public protection (Home Office, 1996a: para 43),[2] require certain classes of sex offender to register their details with the police. It will be explained, however, that the use of the concept of registration to 'track' sex offenders in the community is not such a recent phenomenon. Such a measure can be traced back at least 50 years in the United States and at least 150 in the United Kingdom.

This chapter explores the general implications and difficulties of sex offender registration as a system of offender reintegration and management. The theoretical debate surrounding the implementation of registration reflects the dichotomy between the rights of victims or potential victims and those of offenders which

---

[1] This Act replaces the registration provisions contained in Part I of the Sex Offenders Act 1997.
[2] See also: United States Congressional Record (139 *Cong. Rec.* H10, 320).

underpins contemporary criminal justice discourses. This points to the difficulty of striking an appropriate balance between the need to protect vulnerable members of society on the one hand, and on the other, the justice of placing a burden and potential stigma on an offender who in many cases will have served his sentence.

In the practical context, two significant lines of critique emerge. First, in common with popular 'name and shame' campaigns, which were discussed in chapter 2, and with signs and public exposure penalties, which will be discussed in the next chapter, registration, and notification procedures in particular, may affect disintegrative shaming with sex offenders. It will be argued that notification schemes may result in public shaming of the offender which can have a number of detrimental consequences. Far from securing the offender's rehabilitation or reintegration into society, this negative labelling of offenders may encourage public outcry and even vigilante justice. It may also serve to stigmatise offenders and heighten their isolation from the law-abiding community which may ultimately lead to a return to offending behaviour (Maxwell and Morris, 1999; Edwards and Hensley, 2001b; McAlinden, 2005).

A second line of critique relates to an array of practical limitations—such as inadequate police resources and the fact that these measures are, by their very nature, targeted only at known sex offenders—which may reduce their overall effectiveness in managing the risk posed by sex offenders in the community. The chapter will also explore whether some of these initial concerns, which surfaced at the time the original legislation was being implemented, have in fact been realised in practice.

THE HISTORY OF REGISTRATION AND COMMUNITY NOTIFICATION

An official history of earlier initiatives to establish registration and notification schemes for sex offenders still has to be written. The ideas embodied in 'Megan's Law' in the United States and the Sexual Offences Act 2003 in the United Kingdom, however, are certainly not new.

Sex offender registration has its origins in the United States, where the development and inception of registration and notification statutes dates back to 1944. At state level, the requirement for convicted offenders to register their names and addresses with the local police has had a chronology of three distinct periods (Earl-Hubbard, 1996). An early period between 1944 and the mid-1960s (Hoover, 1947; Sutherland, 1950); a period of light activity from 1985–90; and a time of intense activity from 1991–96, with nearly 30 states passing legislation in a 2-year period between 1994 and 1996. California enacted a law in 1944, Arizona in 1951 and the next four states between 1957–67 (Florida, Nevada, Ohio and Alabama). No other state registration legislation was enacted until 1984. Indeed, 38 statutes have been passed since 1991, so that since the end of 1996 all states now have a registration requirement (Bedarf, 1995; Thomas and Lieb, 1995; Hebenton and Thomas, 1996b: 436–37).

At federal level, action on registration had its own but related momentum Hebenton and Thomas, 1996b: 437). The Jacob Wetterling Crimes Against Children and Sexually Violent Offender Registration Act, named after the 7-year old boy who was abducted and murdered in Minnesota, was passed as part of the 1994 Federal Violent Crime Control and Law Enforcement Act.[3] The 1994 Act required all states to have registration procedures in place by 1997 in order to retain their share of federal crime-fighting funds and encouraged them to enact community notification laws. The culmination of this regulatory approach came in the summer of 1996 when the federal government passed 'Megan's Law'[4] which amends the 1994 Act to mandate states to disclose information where it is relevant and necessary for public protection. 'Megan's Law,' named after 7-year old Megan Kanka who died at the hands of a paedophile neighbour, came into force early in the summer of 1997. As of January 1996, 47 states had enacted laws requiring sex offenders to register with local police (Glazer, 1996: 28). The three holdouts, Massachusetts, Nebraska and Vermont, have since followed suit. Although some states were independently passing legislation, congress also wanted a national registry of former offenders. To this end, the Pam Lychner Sexual Offender and Tracking Act 1996[5] required the Federal Bureau of Investigation (FBI) to establish a national sex offender registry to collate information from all state registries. Following Zedner's observation that victims are used rhetorically or symbolically 'to lever up punitiveness' (2002: 447),[6] it has been noted that naming legislation after victims of sexual crime in this way appeals to popular emotions such as fear and the desire for vengeance (Simon, 1998). As an interim arrangement, President Clinton ordered a nationwide computer network to track sex offenders in the community.[7] More recently, developments at both federal[8] and state[9] levels have increased, or proposed to increase, registration and reporting requirements.

In the United Kingdom, the spectre of the constantly moving ex-offender has had a longer history (Hebenton and Thomas, 1996a: 98–99; 1996b: 428–30). In the

[3] Pub. L. No. 103–322, 108 Stat. 1796 (codified as 42 USCA § 14071).

[4] See N.J. Stat. Ann. Tit. 2C § 7. Pub. L. No. 104–145, 110 Stat. 1345.

[5] Pub. L. No. 104–236, 110 Stat. 3093 (codified as 42 USCA § 14072).

[6] Ashworth similarly describes this as 'victims in the service of severity' (2000: 186), and Garland as 'the projected, politicized image of the "victim"' (2001: 143).

[7] 'Memorandum on the Development of a National Sexual Offender Registration System' 32 *Weekly Comp. Pres. Doc.* 1137 (25 June, 1996).

[8] The Children's Safety and Violent Crime Reduction Act 2005 (S.4742) requires, for example, quarterly registration in person; expands terms to include juvenile sex crimes and offences covered by the requirements; requires states to notify one another when a sex offender moves between states; and creates a new penalty of a maximum of 20 years' incarceration for those offenders who refuse to comply with the requirements. The Sex Offender Registration and Notification Act (S.1086), currently in bill form, requires sex offenders to register prior to, rather than on release, and to re-register biannually, or every 3 months for a sexually violent predator; increases the duration of registration from 10 to 20 years for first time offenders and to a lifetime requirement for second offenders; and reduces the time for registration of changes of status from 10 to 3 days.

[9] In Florida, the Jessica Lunsford Act 2005 (Chapter 2005–28; House Bill No. 1877), for example, designates failing to register as third, as opposed to fourth, degree felony. The Act has also been enacted in Louisiana and Arizona, with similar legislation being passed in Arkansas, Oregon, Virginia and Washington.

nineteenth century, the perception of a mass of offenders, mobile yet anonymous, fostered an escalating fear of a dangerous criminal class—vast, self-contained, self-perpetuating and largely irreclaimable (Hebenton and Thomas, 1996a: 98). Radzinowicz and Hood (1990) suggest that this new perception was attributable to the abandonment of the transportation of convicts to the colonies, a rapid growth in population mobility and expansion of the 'new police.' Fear of convicts on licence in the community generated the need to 'track' the habitual criminal.

The original aim of compulsory 'after-care' was to impose restrictions on the movement of habitual criminals in the hope that society would be protected from them. The problem of 'tracking' the habitual criminal started as 'ticket-of-leave' with the Penal Servitude Acts 1853 and 1857 whereby ex-convicts were required to report their addresses to the police (Soothill, 1974: 36). However, the granting and revoking of licences proved awkward in practice because of a lack of a central record system (Tobias, 1972; Radzinowicz and Hood, 1990: 250; Hebenton and Thomas, 1993; 1996b: 428–29). When asked by the Home Office in 1883 to report on ticket-of-leave men, the Commissioner of the Metropolis was forced to admit that owing to various subterfuges, such as changes of residence, 'the police could not find or produce a single man of them' (Radzinowicz and Hood, 1990: 249).

The Habitual Criminals Act 1869 proposed a tightening-up of leave conditions and registering of all those convicted of a crime on a national register (Hebenton and Thomas, 1996b: 428–29). The flavour and tenor of the parliamentary debate on the bill has contemporary resonance. The Earl of Kimberley described the aim thus: 'to establish a complete system of communication throughout the country' in order 'to form a complete network of supervision of criminals.'[10] Earl Shaftesbury agreed that:

> The principle is a perfectly legitimate one, that those who have been guilty of repeated offences should, after the expiration of their sentences, for the better security of society, be placed under constant supervision.[11]

Later compulsory after-care was extended to those released from a sentence of preventive detention, imposed by the Prevention of Crime Act 1908. This category of prisoner was required to report to the Central Association for the Aid of Discharged Convicts, which had been set up in 1910 (Soothill and Francis, 1998: 283). As was outlined in the previous chapter in relation to the supervision of offenders in the community generally, while police supervision has continued in various forms over the years, it is the establishment and growth of the criminal record system in England and Wales which has provided a key 'supervisory point' in recent times. As will be discussed further below, the current system of sex offender registration, which was first enacted by Part I of the Sex Offenders Act 1997 and is currently contained in Part 2 of the Sexual Offences Act 2003, was also designed with a key supervisory role in mind.

---

[10] *Hansard* HL Deb, vol CXCIV(194), col 341 (26 February).
[11] *Hansard* HL Deb, vol CXCIV(194), col 697 (5 March).

THE MAIN PROVISIONS

It is proposed to briefly outline the main registration and notification provisions which exist in the United States and the United Kingdom as illustrative of the scope of such measures and their potential for 'disintegrative shaming' (Braithwaite, 1989) which will be discussed further below.

'Megan's Law'

In the United States, as outlined above, in response to the dangers created by repeat sex offenders with regard to children, a package of laws known collectively as 'Megan's Law'[12] were enacted in all 50 states in various forms (Houston, 1994: 734–46; Bedarf, 1995: 886–92; Earl-Hubbard, 1996: 796–814).

All states require sexually violent predators and people convicted of certain crimes against minors to register with local law enforcement authorities, although the register is maintained at state level. Registration applies in most states to convicted offenders, some states apply registration to those found to have committed a sexual offence by judicial decision, and at least one (Minnesota) extends the requirement to those charged with a sexual offence. Typical information obtained includes an offender's name, address, fingerprints, photograph, date of birth, social security number and vehicle registration. Many states are now collecting blood samples for DNA analysis.

The time frame for initial registration currently varies from 'prior to release' or 'immediately' to up to 12 months. The average period is 30 days or less. In most states, the duration is over 10 years, with a growing number of states requiring lifetime registration.[13] In common with most systems of registration, registries are usually only updated when the offender notifies local police that he has changed his address. A person who fails to register shall be guilty of a fourth degree offence (Hebenton and Thomas, 1996a: 106).[14]

Community notification statutes emerged as a means to transform registration legislation into more proactive crime control mechanisms (Hebenton and Thomas, 1996b: 438; Lieb, 1996: 298; Prentky, 1996: 295). Under the requirements of the Federal Crime Control and Law Enforcement Act 1994,[15] states are permitted to consider wider release of information. Bedarf (1995: 903–6), in this respect, points to four basic types of community notification: mandatory self-identification by the offender, discretionary or mandatory police identification, public access to a police book, and public access by telephone.

---

[12] See n 4 above.
[13] Note, however, the forthcoming changes under federal legislation. See n 8 above.
[14] There have, however, been recent amendments in this respect in a number of states. See n 9 above.
[15] See n 3 above.

At least 30 states permit some kind of dissemination of information by police to the public when sex offenders move into the neighbourhood when the release of relevant information is necessary for public protection (Glazer, 1996: 28). Indeed, 18 states (including Washington, Oregon, Alaska, Louisiana, Tennessee and New Jersey) require that local communities are told if a convicted sex offender moves into their area, where the degree of notification depends on the likelihood of reoffending (Oregon Department of Corrections, 1995; Berliner, 1996: 294; Hebenton and Thomas, 1996b: 439; Lieb, 1996: 298). All but 17 states allow public access to the details. More recently, several states including California, Florida (Fischer, 1997), Michigan, Minnesota and Indiana have gone so far as to publish details of known sex offenders on the internet, including their known names, addresses, physical descriptions, photograph, employment history and criminal record. In Indiana, in particular, citizens can search for details of local sex offenders using a map of their area and from April 2006 have even been able to sign up for email notifications of when a sex offender's information has changed in their area.[16] In some of these states, names and addresses of sex offenders are also available for public inspection via CD-ROM databases in local police stations.[17]

The Sexual Offences Act 2003, Part 2

In the United Kingdom, registration was initially provided for by Part I of the Sex Offenders Act 1997. The Act, which applied to the whole of the United Kingdom, required certain categories of sex offender to notify the police of their name and address and any subsequent changes to these details within a specified period.[18] Following the identification of several loopholes in the legislation, as highlighted by academic and parliamentary debate, and attendant calls for reform, the original registration requirements in the 1997 Act were first tightened by Schedule 5 of the Criminal Justice and Courts Services Act 2000. As a result of a joint consultation exercise by the Home Office and the Scottish Executive (Home Office, 2001b), these provisions have since been replaced by Part 2 of the Sexual Offences Act 2003 which has strengthened the legislation further still.[19] There is no tangible register as such. Instead, the offender's details are kept by the local police and fed into the Police National Computer.[20]

[16] 'The Town That Puts Sex Offenders On The Map' *The Sunday Telegraph*, 29 January 2006.

[17] N Riccardi, 'List of Sex Abusers Now On-line' <http://www.legalminds.org/listsaver/noframes/familylaw-1/3052.html> (1997); D Walters, 'Using The Internet For Exposure' < http://www.sacbee.com/voices/sac/walters/walters_aug15.html> (1997).

[18] For an overview of the original registration requirements, see especially: Cobley (1997b, 2000: 323–32) and Thomas (2000: 106–22).

[19] See ss 80–96. For detailed treatment of the registration and notification requirements under the 2003 Act. See especially: Cobley (2005: 361–75) and Thomas (2005: 153–67).

[20] There are several lists of sex offenders maintained by other public bodies all of which predate the 1997 Act including, inter alia, that maintained by the Department for Education ('List 99') which holds details of individuals banned from working with children and which may only be consulted by employers. See Cobley (1997b).

Under the current scheme, which also extends to the whole of the United Kingdom, initial registration, as well as any subsequent registration of changes to the offender's details is now required in person, and not just by post. This must be done within three days of the sentence date or, for those serving a custodial sentence, of their release from prison. This is considerably shorter than the original time frame of 14 days. The police may now also photograph and fingerprint the offender and obtain their national insurance number on each registration for future verification of identity. This recent amendment brings the system of registration in the UK more closely in line with 'Megan's Law' in the United States where, as outlined above, sex offenders are required to provide a much wider range of information to the police. Offenders must confirm their details on an annual basis as well as being required to notify the police of foreign travel or if they spend more than 7 days, also reduced from 14, at an address other than their home address.

The registration requirement has always included those offenders who have been convicted or cautioned for a 'relevant offence,'[21] those found to be under a disability and to have done the act charged, and those found not guilty by reason of insanity. As outlined in chapter 2, the major impetus behind the legislation was the public furore surrounding the presence of paedophiles in the community. The legislation, however, applies to a broad range of sexual offences involving both adult and child victims.

The categories of offender subject to the registration requirement have not changed markedly from the original 1997 Act. The 2003 Act, however, also adds a further category of offender—those who have received a conditional discharge for a 'relevant offence.' In addition, the nature and type of offenders who are subject to registration have also been widened through two further measures—Notification Orders and Foreign Travel Orders—which are also contained in Part 2 of the Act.[22] The former requires offenders who have received convictions for sexual offences abroad to comply with the legislation. As regards the latter, while the legislation generally requires offenders to register their intention of travelling abroad with the police, as noted above, these new orders specifically prevent those offenders with convictions involving children from travelling abroad. The previous registration requirements only applied to those convicted of offences in the United Kingdom. These amendments, therefore, will help to ensure that sex offenders from the United Kingdom do not target children in other countries as a result of the strict regime which is in place here.

The length of time for which an offender is required to register is dependent on the type of offender and the length of the initial sentence imposed. These time frames have also been tightened by the 2003 Act. The registration requirement now ranges from a period of two years, for those who receive a caution for a relevant offence, to a lifetime requirement. The notification periods are halved for

---

[21] What amounts to a 'relevant offence' is set out in sch 3 of the Act.
[22] ss 97–103 and 114–22 respectively.

those offenders under the age of 18, where parents or guardians have the duty of notification. The conditions attached to registration for the offender and, as will be discussed further below, the degree of notification permitted to the community also vary depending on the assessed level of risk (Kemshall and Maguire, 2003). Failure to comply with these requirements is an offence punishable on indictment by a term of imprisonment of up to five years.[23]

ViSOR

Although all work with sex offenders now takes place on an inter-agency basis, as outlined in chapter 2, it is the police who have primary responsibility for maintaining the sex offenders' register. In August 2005, following a number of successful pilot schemes, police forces in England and Wales and Scotland officially launched ViSOR (the Violent and Sex Offender Register) which is to be implemented on a force by force basis. This important development provides the police with a central searchable nationwide database, linked to the Police National Computer, to register, risk assess and manage offenders. At inception, it included details of almost 50,000 sex offenders, violent offenders who have been sentenced for more than 12 months, as well as unmonitored individuals who have been assessed as posing a risk to the public. The register holds a range of detailed information on these individuals such as their known modus operandi, details of convictions or orders in force against them, risk assessments and photographic details.

This new web-based computer system was heralded as a major step forward in public protection and crime detection and prevention.[24] Its aim is clearly to prevent tragedies such as the murders of Holly Wells and Jessica Chapman in 2002 by Soham school caretaker Ian Huntley.[25] The scheme undoubtedly has potential to further strengthen the sex offenders' register and in particular the use made of the information contained within it. Rather than being forced to rely on local unconnected databases or paper files, agencies may now share information easily and keep track of individuals as they move from area to area. It is envisaged that the photographic library of offenders in particular, which will be built up over time, including any distinguishing marks or features, will make it easier to identify

[23] Other jurisdictions have proceeded along similar lines. For example, in the Republic of Ireland, the Sex Offenders Act 2001 provided for a major package of reforms designed to protect the public against sex offenders (McAlinden, 2000). As discussed in chapter 2, this included, inter alia, a new notification procedure or tracking system for all convicted sex offenders which is provided for by Part 2 of that Act.

[24] See, eg: 'Offender Database To Cut Crime' BBC News Online <http://news.bbc.co.uk/1/hi/uk/4163764.stm> (19 August 2005); 'ViSOR: Protecting The Public From Serious Offenders' eGov Monitor <http://www.egovmonitor.com/node/2391> (19 August 2005).

[25] The Bichard Inquiry (2004: para 8) highlighted 'systemic and corporate failures' in the way in which the police managed their intelligence systems and called for police forces to share more information, including that relating to people who have not been convicted of any offence.

offenders and harder for them to change their physical appearance and emerge undetected in another part of the country. As well as having the potential to be an effective offender management and monitoring tool, its search and retrieval capabilities, based on the personal characteristics and features of particular criminals, may also assist police intelligence in the investigation of crime. Northern Ireland has since adopted the system,[26] while the probation and prison services are to be involved as part of the new National Offender Management Service. More agencies are also likely to have access to the database in the future such as the British Transport Police and the National Criminal Intelligence Service.

However, given the range of practical difficulties involved in the operation of the register, which will be discussed further below, it remains to be seen what impact these few changes will actually have in making the operation of the scheme more effective. There may be difficulties, in particular in ensuring that the information held on offenders is complete and up-to-date (Hebenton and Thomas, 1997a). The police, for example, are not required to take photographs and fingerprints, and it is anticipated that it will not be necessary to exercise this power in every case. On the other hand, making the registration requirement and its consequences more onerous, as recent developments seek to do, may also act as a disincentive to registration and ultimately result in lower compliance rates. Some offenders may even leave the jurisdiction in order to escape the obligation to register in the hope that they will be subject to less scrutiny elsewhere. Either way, the information held on offenders may become erratic. This in turn may mean that the effectiveness of the register in achieving the expected aims of reducing reoffending and protecting the public may be limited to the level of symbolism and rhetoric.

Public Disclosure of Information

The most significant difference between the United States and the United Kingdom is the permitted degree of notification given to the local community. The issue of when the community should be notified about the presence of sex offenders living in their area remains controversial in the UK, where there is a much closer restriction on the release of information.

The legislation itself remains silent as to the precise circumstances in which the police may lawfully disclose personal information about offenders. Instead, guidance for the police on the issue of disclosure is governed by a Home Office circular (Home Office, 1997b) which draws on the limited case law in the area.[27] As indicated at the end of chapter 2 in relation to the multi-agency approach,

---

[26] 'Sex Offenders Database Launched' BBC News Online <http://news.bbc.co.uk/2/hi/uk_news/northern_ireland/4618158.stm> (17 January 2006).

[27] The relevant law is scattered across a range of statutes and Common Law. The bulk of the relevant case law is dominated by cases generated in care proceedings. For a comprehensive account of the law governing public authorities' powers to disclose to other public bodies and to private persons, see, eg: Power (2003: 76–86).

currently the police are only entitled to make limited public disclosure of a sex offender's whereabouts. Disclosure is carried out only in exceptional circumstances where there is an immediate danger to the public, which is in itself determined by assessed levels of risk.[28] Calls for the public to have a general right of access to the information notified to the police, a so-called 'Sarah's Law,' following the death of Sarah Payne as discussed in chapter 2, have been repeatedly rejected (Rutherford, 2000; Maguire et al, 2001; Thomas, 2001). It would seem that to date the Government is unwilling to legislate on the use made of information (Silverman and Wilson, 2002: 125–45; Thomas, 2003). The human rights implications of public disclosure of information about offenders (Power, 2003) will be discussed further below in relation to some of the principled objections to the legislation.

Moreover, community notification raises the question of community responsibility with regard to known offenders. It is a fact that most convicted sex offenders will at some point be living in the community on release from custody. Making citizens aware of their presence in a formal way, however, may make matters worse (Boerner, 1992; Berliner, 1996: 296). As will argued below, in relation to the practical problems involved with community notification, it would appear that communities, for the most part, by reacting in hostile ways often forcing offenders to move on, are not ready to receive the kinds of delicate information that statutory and voluntary agencies may share about offenders.

Perhaps the issue of increased community notification can best be addressed as part of an overall initiative aimed at sharing information with the community generally and informing them about the true nature of sexual offending. Such a process must initially involve building public confidence in the work of statutory and voluntary agencies. As will be discussed in chapter 7 in relation to restorative and reintegrative practices with sex offenders, this can only be achieved through the development of a major public education and awareness programme. Ultimately, through the further development of programmes like circles of support and accountability, members of the community may become privy to information about released high-risk sex offenders and may actually participate in the decision-making process regarding risk management and offender reintegration. In this respect, evidence from the United States regarding disclosure to the community indicates that one of the unintended consequences of the dissemination of information to the community is greater public understanding of the supervisory role of agencies and the real risks posed by certain sex offenders (Hebenton and Thomas, 1997a: 44). It may be, therefore, that the issues of public education on contentious sex offender issues and the disclosure of information to the community could in future be part of a two-way process.

---

[28] *R v Chief Constable of North Wales Police, ex parte Thorpe* [1999] QB 396 (CA) is the only case involving disclosure outside child protection proceedings. The Court of Appeal upheld the decision of the Divisional Court and declared that although there should never be a policy of blanket disclosure, the police had a right to notify immediate neighbours that two individuals had moved in with a criminal record of child abuse since there was a specific risk of reoffending.

THE RATIONALE OF REGISTRATION AND NOTIFICATION:
DETERRENCE AND PROTECTION

Before undertaking a discussion of the arguments for and against sex offender registration and community notification, which surfaced at the time the legislation was being implemented and which have been framed largely in terms of the rights of victims versus those of offenders, it is useful to consider the stated official aims behind the formulation of the various statutes.

As outlined in chapter 2, many jurisdictions in recent years have adopted a punitive 'law and order' agenda based on the need to protect the public and manage the risk posed by dangerous offenders more effectively. In this respect, despite the slight nuances and variations in approach to registration, the measures appear to share a number of core aims. These are chiefly to prevent sexual crime, to deter released offenders from committing future crime, to identify and 'track' suspects, and to protect the public, particularly children, from serious harm.

In the United States, the stated intent of registration and notification provisions since their inception has remained to 'deter offenders from committing new offences and to assist police in the investigation and detection of offences' (Hebenton, 1997: 6). The Congressional Record, for example, sets out the reasoning behind the schemes. First, it was hoped that it would enable police quickly to 'track down those who would be the prime suspect.'[29] The register may also help in the fight against crime by creating a list of potential suspects for police to pursue whenever a child was harmed or missing in the offender's area (Hebenton, 1997: 8). Secondly, it was hoped that the existence of a registry would deter released offenders from future crime:

> Registration . . . places a defendant on notice that when subsequent sexual crimes are committed in the area where he lives, he may be subject to investigation. This may well have a prophylactic effect, deterring him from future sexual crimes.[30]

In the United Kingdom, the original Home Office consultative document which proposed the development of a register framed its supposed benefits in terms of 'protecting the public.' It also stated that the register should help the police to identify suspects after a crime has been committed, help to prevent such crimes in the first place, and act as a deterrent to potential reoffenders (Home Office, 1996a: para 43). Essentially, these measures were designed to provide police with information about the whereabouts of known sex offenders, though the main targets were clearly paedophiles. The emphasis, however, was placed not simply on the need for the police to hold this information on a register, but crucially on the use to which this information is put to actively manage the risk posed by offenders (Kemshall and Maguire, 2002). Similarly, in the process of the recent reform of

[29] See n 2 above.
[30] See n 2 above.

the sex offenders' register, the information contained within it was said to be valuable to the police in two ways. First, it helps them monitor sex offenders living in the community. Secondly, it helps in the detection of sexual crime, as the police will immediately know the whereabouts of potential suspects (Home Office, 2002: para 17).

However, as will be argued below, whatever formulation they may take, such laudable twin aims of deterrence and protection have not or will not be realised in practice since there are major obstacles to achieving these goals. As discussed in chapter 2, an abundance of legislation on sex offending was rushed through the legislature of England and Wales in particular within a few short years. This was largely a reactive response to increasing public concern over sex offending and paedophiles in particular. The net result of such law making, as Power notes, is that:

> [T]here is a clear danger that the resultant laws may be drafted without sufficient consideration of the complex issues with which they deal (1999: 4).

THE COMPETING PERSPECTIVES OF THE VICTIM AND THE OFFENDER

At the time the legislation was being implemented in the United States and, particularly the United Kingdom, the tone of the parliamentary and academic debates reflected the competing perspectives of the victim and the offender (McAlinden, 1999, 2000). As mentioned at the outset of this chapter, these principled arguments for and against sex offender registration and community notification point towards a dichotomy which underlies much of contemporary academic criminology and criminal justice policy—the fundamental conflict between the rights of the victim or potential victim and those of the offender (O'Malley, 1996: 25–31; Cobley, 1997a: 101; Cox, 1997).[31] The difficulty lies in reconciling the competing tensions of the need to protect the public, and the justice of placing a potential life-long burden and stigma on individuals.

The Victim

The problems which exist in relation to managing sex offenders in the community on release from custody have been outlined in the previous chapter. The failure of 'the rehabilitative ideal,' the purported high levels of sex offender recidivism and the resulting need to 'track' the offender are largely victim-centred arguments. These have been used to justify the enactment of legislative control in the com-

---

[31] This contemporary view of criminal justice does not hold true, however, if we go back just a couple of decades when rehabilitation and retribution were the dominant form of sentencing paradigm. For 'just deserts' theorists in particular, punishment is justified as the proportional and morally responsible response to crime (von Hirsch, 1976, 1993; von Hirsch and Ashworth, 1998).

munity mechanisms, such as registration, in order to prevent reoffending and manage sex offenders in the community more effectively. In addition, the rights of the child and, as would be expected, the need to protect the public provide further justification for such measures.

The Rights of the Child

The rights of children and the need to protect them from sexual abuse are principles which operate in support of sex offender registration and community notification legislation (Cobley 1997b).[32] Community notification of the whereabouts of known sex offenders may serve to give concerned parents the opportunity to warn their children of the perceived risks in their immediate community (Richards, 1989; Bedarf, 1995: 906; Berliner, 1996: 294; Prentky, 1996: 295; Hebenton and Thomas 1997b). As will be argued below, however, in relation to the practical problems of registration, problems can arise when this information is used as the basis for vigilante witch hunts (Lieb, 1996: 299).

The United Nations Convention on the Rights of the Child (1989) has now been unanimously adopted by 192 countries, with the notable exception of the United States and Somalia who have signalled their intention to formally sign the Convention. The Convention is constructed around the basic premise that the rights of the child and his welfare are paramount and that appropriate legislative measures should be undertaken to ensure this. Articles 3 and 19 in particular emphasise the state's obligation to protect children from all forms of abuse and to make this a primary consideration in all matters affecting children.

In the United States, protecting children and their rights were clear aims behind the formulation of the legislation, as evidenced by the various campaigns which preceded the implementation of the schemes. In Washington, for example, a community initiative known colloquially as 'the tennis shoe brigade' presented children's shoes to the governor asking 'please protect us.' The shoes were to symbolise the feet of those entitled to walk without fear (Hebenton, 1997: 4). Similarly, in Scotland, as discussed in chapter 2, following a number of high profile sexual offences cases involving children, the *Daily Record* newspaper launched a campaign entitled 'Charter for Our Children' (25–29 January 1997), which called for the authorities to notify the local community of the presence of convicted sex offenders living in their area.

Protection

As discussed in the second chapter, in relation to the political and policy-making context, recent years have seen the politicisation of sex offending. It was noted there that sex offender registration and community notification were advanced

---

[32] See also: Sir Lawrence Burton, *Hansard* HC Deb, vol 289, col 65 (27 January 1997); Lord Monson, *Hansard* HL Deb, vol 579, col 552 (14 March 1997).

within an overall retributive framework as part of the current trend in penal policy of incapacitation (Bedarf, 1995: 899). As noted above in relation to the stated official aims of registration and notification, in both the United States and the United Kingdom, these schemes have been framed primarily in terms of protecting persons, particularly children, from attack by convicted sex offenders.

Incapacitative theories of punishment identify particular groups of 'dangerous' and persistent offenders who are likely to do such serious harm that special measures should be taken against them. These measures make them incapable of offending for substantial periods of time and the overarching aim is public protection (Feeley and Simon, 1992; Morris, 1994; Zimring and Hawkins, 1995). It has been argued that registration and notification statutes form part of this darkening criminal justice policy (Rutherford, 1997: 425). They are natural extensions of recent punitive and incapacitative measures which are aimed at dealing with serious and persistent offenders, most notably the 'three strikes and you're out' legislation in the United States, and the range of preventive sentences in the United Kingdom.

However, as also discussed in chapter 2, the enactment of registration and notification statutes constitutes a display of 'populist punitiveness' (Bottoms, 1995), as being 'tough on crime' is a necessary pre-condition of election to political office (Morris and Rothman, 1995: 258). There are similar pieces of legislation which constitute mere political gestures (Soothill and Francis, 1997: 1325) and which have been enacted for their moral force and symbolic significance only, including sex and race discrimination legislation. The criminal law has an important symbolic, denunciatory or educative aspect (Lacey, 2001: 13). Indeed, one of its primary symbolic effects is to define and underpin social assumptions about social morality and sexual deviancy (Lacey, 1988: ch 4; Naffine, 1997: ch 4). However, just as it is impossible to prevent all incidents of sexual or racial discrimination occurring, so too is it impossible to prevent the sexual offender from reoffending by these schemes. Indeed, as will be argued below in relation to the practical difficulties of registration and notification, far from having a meaningful, instrumental, protective or deterrent impact, such substantive legislation may risk relegation to being passive examples of bureaucracy with only limited symbolic value (Hebenton and Thomas, 1997c: 6; Rejtman, 1997).

The Offender

In the United States, sex offender registration appears no longer to be controversial. More contentious has been the rise of community notification schemes (Bedarf, 1995). From the offender's perspective, there are some principled objections to such legislation which have been little considered (Soothill and Francis, 1998: 285–86). As with all incapacitative policies, the legislation appears to treat the offender with only a minimal amount of respect and concern (Lacey, 1988: 33; Broadhurst and Maller, 1992). In essence, as discussed in chapter 2 in relation to the emergence of the 'risk society' (Giddens, 1990; Beck, 1992; Ericson and

Haggerty, 1997), the offender's rights are displaced by a 'knowledge system of rights,' and justice becomes a matter of just knowledge production for efficient risk management in the community (Hebenton and Thomas, 1996a: 109). In this vein, on both sides of the Atlantic, a number of offender-centred critiques have emerged. These relate to the issues surrounding registration as an additional punishment and the civil liberties or human rights implications of the process.

Registration as a Punishment?

The question of whether registration was an extension of 'punishment' was raised by academics at the time the legislation was being implemented. Prior to a fuller operationalisation of the scheme, speculation ranged from the spectre of a police state to a comparatively trivial registration requirement (Lieb, 1996: 299; Soothill and Francis, 1998: 285). Whatever the eventual outcome, it was generally agreed that the balance between freedom and control for many sex offenders would change to some degree. An analysis of the current legislative provisions, outlined at the outset of this chapter, indicates that the nature and effect of the current schemes probably lies somewhere in between. As will be outlined below in relation to the offender's civil rights, it is certainly the case that sex offenders in the relevant categories will have their freedom infringed or their liberty curtailed to some degree. The registration provisions have been tightened considerably by subsequent legislation since their initial inception, to the point where there are now significant requirements placed on sex offenders. In this vein, it does seem difficult to see the legislation other than an extension of the offender's punishment (Bedarf, 1995: 913–39; Soothill and Francis, 1997: 1325).

In this context, the question emerges of 'why punish?' Duff and Garland classify normative theories of punishment as either 'consequentialist' or 'non-consequentialist', or as a mixture of the two (1994: 6–8). In brief, they suggest that a 'consequentialist' holds that the rightness or wrongness of a sanction depends solely on its overall consequences. It is right if its consequences are good and wrong if its consequences are bad (Lacey, 1988: 27–45). In contrast, a 'non-consequentialist' insists that actions may be right or wrong by virtue of their intrinsic character, independently of their consequences (Lacey, 1988: 16–26). This approach is expressed in the retributivist claim that punishment is justified only if it inflicts on the guilty the suffering they deserve (Duff and Garland, 1994: 7).

Certainly, the 'consequentialist' approach has been the official justification for introducing the schemes. It has been amply demonstrated that the legislation was introduced as part of the overall crime control trend in criminal justice policy of incapacitation or public protection. Registration is supposedly justified because sex offenders represent a greater risk to the public than other categories of offender. This rationale, however, as will be discussed below, also presents problems. In relation to the 'non-consequentialist' theory, some will argue that sex offenders deserve all the suffering possible and if the registration requirements cause them further suffering, then so be it.

The argument about who should have access to the information about the where-abouts of released sex offenders, demonstrates that the 'non-consequentialist' approach cannot be dismissed so easily (Soothill and Francis, 1998: 285–86). As will be outlined further below, the dangers of the public finding out the addresses of known sex offenders are well recognised. While some may simply wish to warn their children of the possible dangers, others may decide to continue with vengeful extra-legal punishment (Soothill and Francis, 1998: 290). Thus we are currently wit-nessing a scheme, officially introduced to protect the public, being hijacked by members of the public eager to wreak revenge on known sex offenders irrespective of the consequences (Soothill and Francis, 1998: 286).

It may be difficult, however, to justify registration solely on consequentialist terms. Appropriate responses to the questions of what good may come from such schemes or what harm the system will help to avoid, are less easy to identify (Soothill and Francis, 1998: 286). One also needs to ask whether there is an alter-native approach which could do the job as well at a lower cost. One option, as will be discussed in chapter 7, is a reintegrative community treatment and support programme where the released sex offender admits responsibility for his crime, expresses a willingness to refrain from reoffending, and asks the community's support in achieving this. A restorative community reintegration project such as circles of support and accountability, could help reduce the risk of reoffence by individuals convicted of sexual offences and ease the transition of the offender into the community (Cesaroni, 2001; Petrunik, 2002: 503–5; Silverman and Wilson, 2002: 167–84; Wilson et al, 2002).

More recently, however, the question or whether the registration requirement constitutes a punishment was addressed in a number of European cases. It was held that no breach of Article 7 of the European Convention on Human Rights (ECHR), which provides for 'no punishment without law,' was established in rela-tion to the registration provisions in Part I the Sex Offenders Act 1997.[33] The Commission in *Ibbotson* specifically rejected the argument that this involved a 'retrospective penalty' on the ground that the measure was preventative, not puni-tive, and operated independently of the ordinary sentencing process.[34]

'The Dangerousness Debate'

A related issue surrounding registration as an extension of punishment is that of the so-called 'dangerousness debate.' Indeed, one of the main principled objec-

---

[33] See the decision of the European Commission in *Ibbotson v United Kingdom* [1999] EHRLR 218. A similar decision was reached by the European Court in *Adamson v United Kingdom* (1999) 28 EHRR CD 209. A measure of special police supervision imposed on the applicant in *Raimondo v Italy* (1994) 18 EHRR 237 was also held by the Court to be 'not comparable to a criminal sanction because it is designed to prevent the commission of offences' (para 43).

[34] The British courts have followed a similar approach in relation to sex offender orders (*B v Chief Constable of Avon and Somerset Constabulary* [2001] 1 WLR 340 (DC); *Jones v The Greater Manchester Police Authority* [2001] EWHC Admin 189 (DC)), anti-social behaviour orders (*R (McCann) v Crown Court at Manchester* [2002] UKHL 39 (HL)) and disqualification orders (*R v Field* [2002] EWCA Crim 2913 (CA)).

tions to registration from the offender's perspective, is the fact that sex offenders are being punished not for what they have done, but for what they might do, in the hope of protecting future victims from harm (Bottoms, 1977; Floud and Young, 1981: 235–39; von Hirsch, 1985; Wood, 1988; Grisso and Appelbaum, 1992). This 'new punishment,' based on a perceived likelihood of reoffending, shifts away from punishment of the guilty to punishment based on belonging to a risk category. This is at odds with the notion fundamental to the concept of retributive justice that there should be some degree of proportionality between the crime and the punishment (von Hirsch, 1994; Sampson, 1994: 42–63).

This argument is particularly strong where the successful prediction rate is low. The more difficult question is whether the prediction should be given force if a fairly high prediction rate could be achieved. Some of the empirical issues surrounding incapacitative policies were examined in the Floud Report (1981), which aimed at bringing protective sentencing under statutory control. Indeed, the chief objection to incapacitative policies, it seems, is over prediction (Greenwood, 1982; Menzies et al, 1994; Morris, 1994; Zimring and Hawkins, 1995; Brown, 1996: 32–34; von Hirsch and Ashworth, 1996). The report (1981) and a flurry of debate surrounding it found that clinical predictions of 'dangerousness' tended to be wrong more often than not and that such measures draw into its net more non-dangerous than dangerous offenders, with a 'false positive rate' that has often reached two out of every three (Brody and Tarling, 1981; Monahan, 1981; Bottoms and Brownsword, 1982; Gordon, 1982; Morris and Miller, 1986; Wood, 1988). The concept of dangerousness, and the fallibility of predictive judgments in particular, will be further discussed in chapter 6 in relation to indeterminate sentences as an option of last resort with sex offenders when control in the community fails.

Civil Liberties and Human Rights

A further objection to the legislation which has been advanced on behalf of the offender is that it will contravene his basic civil liberties (Parliament of the Commonwealth of Australia, 1995: paras 4.23–24; Lieb, 1996).[35] It was argued that lifetime registration, in particular, is draconian and marks the ultimate example of infringement of the offender's civil liberties.[36] Civil rights are enshrined in the presumption of innocence, once described as 'the golden thread' running through the web of English criminal law (Roberts, 1995; Ashworth and Blake, 1996).[37] Article 6(2) of the ECHR also provides for the presumption of innocence. It has been argued that to erode this basic building block of our society may be detrimental to the rights of all (Vizard and Hawkes, 1997: 6). As such, the retention and possible

---

[35] See also: John Hutton, *Hansard* HC Deb, vol 289, col 60 (27 January 1997); Lord Monson, *Hansard* HL Deb, vol 579, col 550 (14 March 1997).

[36] David Maclean, *Hansard* HC Deb, vol 289, col 28 (27 January 1997).

[37] *Woolmington v DPP* [1935] AC 462 (HL) 481, *per* Lord Sankey. See also, *Mancini v DPP* [1942] AC 1 (HL) 11.

use of intelligence information on suspect offenders, as presently envisaged under the new ViSOR system, against which no formal adjudication process or determination of guilt has taken place, may be particularly open to challenge on a number of rights-based arguments.

In the main, it has been argued that the registration requirement would curtail the offender's freedom and a possible notification of this information to the local community would breach his right to privacy (Hebenton and Thomas, 1997b). Article 8 of the Convention provides for the right to respect for private and family life. Several areas have been considered by the European Court of Human Rights to form part of 'private life' within the terms of Article 8.[38] One of these is personal information. The collection of personal information by state authorities without consent may amount to a violation of private life.[39] This is most obvious, however, where the collection is surreptitious, by activities such as telephone tapping or interception of post. There is also a prima facie breach of the respect for private life where personal information is collated through fingerprinting and photography by the police,[40] as can now happen on initial registration with the police under the new amendments to the Sex Offenders Act 1997. Proof that the information is used to the detriment of the applicant is unnecessary, so long as the compilation and retention of such a dossier is adequately shown.[41]

The issue of disclosure of information by the police to the community has already been mentioned earlier in this chapter and in chapter 2 in relation to multi-agency risk assessment and management. It was noted there that it has been held in the English domestic courts, both under Article 8 of the ECHR and under English administrative law, that the police were entitled to notify the community about convicted sex offenders living in their area when they reasonably conclude that there is a pressing social need and that this is what is required in order to protect the public or prevent crimes (Power, 2003).[42] It is unclear whether the state has a positive obligation under the ECHR to take steps to control intrusive activities by private bodies, such as the press, when they acquire personal information.[43] However, the Commission has generally taken the view that the range of

---

[38] Note that the Court has repeatedly stressed that the object of Art 8 is essentially that of protecting the individual against arbitrary interference by public authorities (*Marckx v Belgium* (1979) 2 EHRR 330; *X and Y v Netherlands* (1985) 8 EHRR 235; *Kroon v Netherlands* (1994) 19 EHRR 263). This is primarily a negative undertaking. Nevertheless, there may in addition be positive obligations on states that are inherent in a 'respect' for Art 8 rights (*Marckx v Belgium*, para 31; *X and Y v Netherlands*, para 23; *Johnston v Ireland* (1986) 9 EHRR 203, para 55). For a fuller consideration of these arguments, see eg: Power (2003: 87–91).

[39] *Z v Finland* (1997) 25 EHRR 371.

[40] *Murray v United Kingdom* (1994) 19 EHRR 193, para 85; *McVeigh v United Kingdom* (1981) 25 DR 15, 49.

[41] *Hilton v United Kingdom* (1988) 57 DR 108, 117.

[42] See n 28 above.

[43] *A v France* (1993) 17 EHRR 462.1. Recent developments in British courts, however, suggest the possibility of police and probation services being able to make proactive use of injunctions to restrain widespread public disclosure if it is likely to interfere with MAPPP arrangements (*Broadmoor Hospital v Robinson* [2001] 1 WLR 1590 (CA); *Venables & Thompson v NG Newspapers Ltd* [2001] 1 WLR 1038 (CA)), and that this may also be potentially available to sex offenders themselves (Power, 2003: 91–96).

English remedies protecting privacy rights, in particular a claim for breach of confidence, provides sufficient protection for the purposes of Article 8.[44]

The human rights debate also concerns the clash between those traditional civil rights of offenders and the rights of children and others vulnerable to abuse. Indeed, Article 8 rights are not absolute. The potential adverse consequences for the most vulnerable may justify interference with this right on the grounds, inter alia, of 'public safety . . . the prevention of crime and disorder . . . or for the protection of the rights and freedoms of others.'[45] In determining whether a positive obligation to disclose to private bodies exists under Convention jurisprudence, a fair balance must be struck between the general interest of the community and the interests of the individual (Warbrick, 1998; Power, 2003: 87–91)[46]

Braithwaite and Pettit's (1990) political philosophy of 'republicanism' and the related concept of 'dominion' advocate liberty in the form of guaranteed protection from certain kinds of interference. Crimes, especially violent and sexual ones, invade someone else's autonomy. Punishments, therefore, should restore the autonomy of victims, with the least loss of autonomy to the offenders punished. Similarly, Etzioni (1999), an advocate of 'communitarianism' as an organising social principle, argues that community notification has to be considered within the parameters of the 'community equation.' In effect, a balance has to be struck between the sex offender's rights, in particular privacy, and the safety of children, in favour of the child. The task then becomes one of minimising whatever harmful side effects the offender may experience. Indeed, it has been contended that disclosure which might have an impact on an offender's rights, particularly under Articles 2 (right to life), 3 (prohibition on inhuman and degrading treatment) and 8 of the ECHR, should be accompanied by positive state measures which are aimed at ensuring that private third parties do not breach these rights (Power, 2003).[47]

A further challenge to acts of disclosure by the police may also arise under Article 5 of the Convention: the right to liberty and security of person. In this sense it could be argued that public dissemination of the personal information concerning sex offenders by the police, may place offenders at risk of personal harm through violence or vigilante action on the part of the public (Barber, 1998: 22; Mullender, 1998; Power, 1999). As Barber argues, the case law on Article 5 does

---

[44] *Winer v United Kingdom* (1986) 48 DR 154, Ecom HR; *Earl Spencer and Countess Spencer v United Kingdom* (1988) 25 EHRR CD 105.

[45] Art 8(2).

[46] *Cossey v United Kingdom* (1990) 13 EHRR 622: 'the search for which balance is inherent in the whole of the Convention.' In *R (S) v Chief Constable of the South Yorkshire Police* [2004] UKHL 39 (HL), paras 40, 66, 78, 80, 86–88, for example, the retention of fingerprints was held, if an interference with the subject's right under Art 8(1) of the Convention, to be one clearly justified by the strong public interest in preventing crime. Recent cases also imply that agencies may be required to engage in such disclosure in life threatening situations (*LCB v UK* (1998) 27 EHRR 212) and may even be liable for the fatal consequences of a failure to do so (*Osman v UK* (1998) 29 EHRR 245).

[47] Eg: in the case of a sex offender being killed or abused by an angry mob which has been told of his presence, there is a possibility of state liability unless the agency could show that the disclosure was carried out in conformity with information-sharing protocols paying particular attention to the need to obviate risks to the offender (Power, 2003: 90).

not impose a positive duty on the police to protect individual offenders. However, it may prevent the state from deliberately increasing the risk of harm to individuals and from compromising their personal safety. In this vein, it seems that numerous developments in practice have therefore forced restrictions and inroads on traditional rights of privacy, freedom of movement and standardised punishment.

Constitutional Challenge

In the United States, despite the popular acceptance of registration and notification, and the perception that it provides increased protection for people living near a sex offender, it has been met with a number of constitutional challenges. Indeed, deprivation of an offender's rights through registration has become a controversial issue in the US courts (Cohen, 1995: 153). It has been argued that such sweeping legislation is guided by an emotional knee-jerk reaction rather than any rational thought (Laster and O'Malley, 1996). The schemes have been likened to 'wanted' posters in old western days and are said to amount to an 'overkill' (Bean, 1997: 283). It has also been argued that registration being a punishment constitutes 'double jeopardy' if applied retroactively (Berliner, 1996: 294; Feldman, 1997; Young, 1998).

Registration, and more specifically community notification legislation, have been challenged under the US Constitution on a number of grounds, including due process concerns and the prohibition on cruel and unusual punishment under the Fourteenth and Eighth Amendments respectively (Bedarf, 1995; Earl-Hubbard, 1996; Kimball, 1996; Kabat, 1998; Logan, 1999; Van Dujn, 1999).[48] At state and federal levels, both arguments have also been lost in favour of the protection of society argument, and the argument that notification is a form of 'civil regulation' rather than a punishment (Bedarf, 1995: 913–39). At the Supreme Court level, the prevailing legal arguments were based on a 'jurisprudence of prevention' (Richards, 1989), and charges that the legislation was degrading to the offender were also lost under the need to protect the public (Houston, 1994: 746–64; Berliner, 1996: 294; Earl-Hubbard, 1996: 814–49).

FROM RHETORIC TO REALITY

This final section of this chapter will address whether these principled concerns which arose at the time of initial implementation were in fact justified. It will examine, in particular, whether the ostensible commitment to the prevention of reoffending via the official aims of offender deterrence and public protection have been fully realised in practice. In the main, two significant lines of critique emerge. First, it will be argued that registration, and notification in particular, may oper-

---

[48] *State v Noble*, 829, P.2d 1217, at 1218, Ariz. 1992; *State v Ward*, 869, P.2d 1062, at 1065, Wash. 1994; *Doe v Poritz*, Nos. A-170/171–94, N.J. decided 25 July 1995.

ate as a form of public shaming which in turn may have a number of undesirable consequences for the offender which may undermine risk management and reintegration. Secondly, there is also a range of inherent practical difficulties which may limit the scope of this measure in policing sex offenders in the community and in protecting the public.

Notification in Action: Public Shaming of the Offender

Registration of the offender's name and address and notification of this information to the community may result in a social stigma being attached to the offender (Massaro, 1991; Bedarf, 1995: 911–13). Some commentators have argued that community notification is tantamount to putting someone in a public stock, to a brand on the forehead, or in the words of Nathaniel Hawthorne's classic American novel to '*A Scarlet Letter*' (Earl-Hubbard, 1996; Kimball, 1996; Van Dujn, 1999).[49]

The actual means of notifying communities of the presence of a sex offender in their area varies within and between states depending on the classification of risk posed by the offender (Thomas, 2003: 220–21). As discussed at the outset of this chapter, mandatory self-identification is one of the forms of community notification which exists in the United States (Bedarf, 1995: 903–6). In some states released sex offenders are required to wear a scarlet letter 'S' on the front of their clothing to signify to the rest of the community that they are a convicted sex offender. In a few states, offenders must hand out handbills or flyers to their neighbours which contain a picture, physical description and details of their offences, or send notice in writing informing them of their past offending history. In other states still, most notably Louisiana, offenders are required to go door to door within a radius of several blocks personally informing their neighbours that they are a convicted sex offender (Logan, 1999; Petrunik, 2002: 493). In addition, community notification provisions also allow law enforcement officials to take steps to distribute the information about offenders (Van Dujn, 1999: 645). US officials have utilised a variety of means to notify residents of the presence of sex offenders in their community. These include going door to door, front page newspaper advertisements, community meetings, bright coloured fliers and wanted posters and databases of all known local sex offenders which are available via the internet (Thomas, 2003).

An American court in analysing the punitive nature of 'Megan's Law' in response to a constitutional challenge, highlighted the dangers which registration and notification laws may pose for sex offenders. The court used excerpts from *The Scarlet Letter* (Hawthorne, 1994) and *To Kill a Mockingbird* (Lee, 1989) to illustrate the use of devices that 'brand registrants in the eyes of a hostile

---

[49] In this fictional account of seventeenth century Boston, the plight of Hester Prynne, an adulteress forced to wear a scarlet letter 'A' embroidered on the front of her dress to show her crime, embodies what was then Puritan society's use of punishment by humiliation and shame (Hawthorne, 1994).

populace.'[50] Such branding, the court noted, could expose the offenders to 'public humiliation rising to the level of punishment.'[51] Indeed, registration in common with other forms of state-led public punishments are aimed at community safety and are intended to shame offenders into greater respect for the law and create a powerful deterrent to reoffending (Karp, 1998). Such measures, however, as will be discussed further in the next chapter, may carry with them the risk of labelling and stigmatisation which may ultimately have a disintegrative impact on the offender's rehabilitation. Indeed, rather than monitor the offender with the aim of crime prevention, such legislation may make relapse by the offender more likely (Prentky, 1996: 296).[52]

This public shaming of the offender via community notification may also have a number of detrimental effects. First, it may lead to harassment or even vigilante attacks by vengeful members of the community on suspected paedophiles (Parliament of the Commonwealth of Australia, 1995: para 4.27; Berliner, 1996: 292; Prentky, 1996: 296; Soothill and Francis, 1998: 286, 290).[53] In Washington State, for example, shortly after the implementation of the legislation an independent evaluation identified 15 harassment incidents associated with notification. One serious incident involved arson of the offender's future residence (Lieb, 1996: 298). The aftermath of the Sarah Payne case was discussed in chapter 2. Incidents have already come to light in England and Wales, even before the formulation of registration and notification laws, where communities have targeted innocent people (Berliner, 1996: 294).[54]

Secondly, this kind of witch hunt atmosphere is one reminiscent of Arthur Miller's famous play, *The Crucible* (2000), where innocents were accused of witchcraft by their neighbours as a result of old grudges and enmities over land.[55] The play, which is chiefly a study in mass hysteria in which superstition conspires with self-interest to incite a society to self-destruction, has many parallels with the position of sex offenders and the community's reaction to them in contemporary society. An atmosphere of such widespread fear and hatred, which currently surrounds paedophiles in particular, brings with it the associated danger that people will simply use the cry of 'sexual abuse' and 'sex offender' to point the finger at someone against whom they have a grudge or grievance. Someone could falsely

---

[50] *Artway, v Attorney General of New Jersey*, 876 F. Supp. 666 (D.N.J. 1995) at 687.

[51] See n 50 above.

[52] See also: Maxwell and Morris, 1999; Edwards and Hensley, 2001b; McAlinden, 2005.

[53] 'All-Party Witch-Hunt' *The Times*, 24 January 1997; 'Can Sex Offenders Be Left In Peace?' *The Times*, 4 February 1997; 'Paedophile Lists Prompt Mob Attacks' *The Times*, 20 February 1997; 'Trial By Neighbour' *The Times*, 19 August 1997; 'Freed Child Killer Flees From Angry Neighbours' *The Times*, 29 September 1997.' See also: Alun Michael, *Hansard* HC Deb, vol 297, col 751 (7 July 1997).

[54] 'Lock Up The Monsters, But Don't Hound Our Sad Cases' *The Daily* Telegraph, 15 February 1997; 'Child Sex Vigilantes Batter Wrong Man' *The Daily Telegraph*, 23 February 1997; 'Death Of An Accused Teacher' *The Times*, 6 June 1998; 'This Cruel Perversion Of Justice' *The Daily Mail*, 6 December 2000. See also: Peter Thurnham, *Hansard* HC Deb, vol 291, col 221 (25 February 1997).

[55] The play is itself based on two historical examples of mass hysteria and the power of fear; one, the Salem witch trials in the Massachusetts Puritan colony at the end of the seventeenth century; the other, the McCarthy communism trials which gripped 1950s America.

accuse another of being a sex offender or 'cry abuse' because they know that in the atmosphere of hysteria and panic which currently exists they will tend to be believed. In a similar vein, the register if used as an investigative tool may only serve to help the police round-up the 'usual suspects' in a given community producing additional convictions among this group and leading to miscarriages of justice (Houston, 1994: 733).[56]

Indeed, as will be discussed further in the next chapter, this opprobrious reaction of the press and the public to the presence of sex offenders in the community evidenced through disintegrative 'naming and shaming' is clearly at odds with the criminal justice system's calculated knowledge of risk assessment and security. In such a frenzied atmosphere, popular concerns over the management of risk and the expansion of control may in fact end up producing the opposite (Hebenton and Thomas, 1996b: 440–41).

Practical Limitations

While one of the stated objectives of the legislation is to assist law enforcement in the detection and prevention of offences, there has been little substantive research which specifically examines the extent to which this has been achieved (Hebenton and Thomas, 1997a: 44; Plotnikoff and Woolfson, 2000: 50). Nevertheless, at the time when the legislation was being implemented, a number of arguments were raised in relation to the limited potential of these measures in managing sex offenders in the community (McAlinden, 1999, 2000).

The recent changes to registration procedures came about partly as a result of academic commentary which highlighted the weaknesses in the legislation. Questions of how the register would actually operate in practice, however, appear to have been little considered, even in the process of the recent reforms. Failure to address a number of key issues such as adequate policing resources and the scope of offenders who may be subject to the registration requirements, may mean that the legislation is of limited practical effect in managing the risk posed by released sex offenders in the community.

The Police: Powers, Resources and the Efficacy of the Response

There are a number of problems involved in the policing of registration and notification legislation (Soothill and Francis, 1998: 289–90). Most notably these entail resource and efficacy difficulties (Houston, 1994; Bedarf, 1995: 885, 899–903; Parliament of the Commonwealth of Australia, 1995: para 4.23).

As Cobley has suggested (2003: 60–61) the efficacy of the 'register' depends on two factors: the first is offenders' compliance with the notification requirements, and the second is the use made of this information by agencies. In relation to the

---

[56] See also: Lord Monson, *Hansard* HL Deb, vol 579, col 1133 (20 March 1997).

former, evidence from existing registration schemes in the United States has shown that there is limited compliance on the part of sex offenders to register (Lewis, 1988: 2–3, 6, 10; Houston, 1994: 732–73; Bedarf, 1995: 900, 902; Earl-Hubbard, 1996: 852–54), perhaps because the sanction for not registering is not stringent enough. Similar concerns about disparate sentences for breach of the notification requirements have also been expressed by the Home Office where courts are said to have varied considerably in the degree of seriousness attached to non-compliance (Home Office, 2001b: ch 8, para 26).

In many US states, where no aditional resources were forthcoming, registers were initially thought to be up to 25 per cent inaccurate (Bedarf, 1995: 900–3) and only 50 per cent complete.[57] More recent figures, however, have demonstrated that while initial compliance rates were low, these have improved in most states as offenders have become more familiar with the laws (Hebenton and Thomas 1997a: 11). In the United Kingdom, one year after the Sex Offenders Act 1997 came into force, the national rate of compliance with the registration requirement was 94.7 per cent with figures for individual forces ranging between 85.4 and 100 per cent (Plotnikoff and Woolfson, 2000: v). A few years after the implementation of the 1997 Act, the average compliance rate was placed at over 97 per cent (Home Office, 2001b: 5). Over time, some of these offenders will be removed from the register at the expiry of their registration period. However, such a figure is likely to decrease incrementally as registration procedures are tightened and the number of offenders required to register increases as more are released from prison each year. Registers may therefore become dangerously incomplete and result in an unwieldy database with little practical utility (Bedarf, 1995: 901).

In relation to the latter, it was thought that too many sex offenders would potentially be subject to such provisions for them to be realistic policing options. Research conducted in England and Wales prior to the implementation of the 1997 Act showed how potentially large numbers of sex offenders will be involved in registration schemes. Much cited research by Marshall estimated that 125,000 men aged 20 or over in the 1993 population of England and Wales had a conviction for an offence that would have been registrable had the Sex Offenders Act 1997 been in force at that time (Marshall, 1997).[58] In any event, those figures did not take account of cautions so that the real number was thought to be even more (Soothill et al, 1997; Soothill and Francis, 1998: 289). Even these early estimates strongly suggest that the police will tend to face a massive task even if none of the offenders moves addresses (Soothill and Francis, 1997: 1285).

Police, for example, may lack sufficient resources to verify that the addresses recorded for each offender are accurate (Bedarf, 1995: 900–1; Soothill and Francis, 1998: 289–90). Moreover, while the legislation may help police detect when a sex offender has moved without notice, it will not help the police to discover where he

---

[57] 'Sex Offender Registration System Failing' *San Francisco Chronicle*, 4 April 1994.
[58] This number has, however, been doubted by Grubin (1998: 11–12) who distinguishes between incidence (the number of cases over a period of time) and prevalence (the proportion of people in a population who have certain characteristics at any particular time).

has gone. The burden remains on the police to track down the errant sex offender (Bedarf, 1995: 910, 939). Perhaps no amount of money could guarantee the accuracy necessary to administer an effective registration programme. As one American sheriff has noted, 'registration just keeps honest offenders honest' (cited in Bedarf, 1995: 903). The enforcement of the offence of failing to provide the relevant information also depends on the police actually knowing that the offender has withheld information and also knowing where they are. Even though the time frame for registration in the United Kingdom has been reduced from 14 days to 3, in the absence of a requirement mandating immediate registration on sentence or release, the offender still has a head start, however reduced, to escape to a different jurisdiction if he does not want to register.

Aside from compliance rates, as noted above, the effectiveness of registration schemes is largely empirically untested (Bedarf, 1995: 900–3). However, a number of assertions may be made in relation to its potential to aid the investigation, detection or prevention of offences and the overall reduction of sexual crime. Even if registration did produce an accurate database, this may not prevent crime. If a sex offender registers where they live, but is highly mobile searching out targets in distant police jurisdictions, their address does not really matter. Moreover, registration is essentially a reactive tool and only comes into play after a crime has been committed (Bedarf, 1995: 903).[59] The legislation may be of importance if you believe that sex crimes are committed by a limited number of men. Since all the available evidence runs counter to such an assumption, the keeping of registers extends state powers, while offering little potential for making a serious impact on the real extent of the problem of sexual offending (Soothill and Francis, 1997). In the United Kingdom, since the legislation will not be applied retroactively, even with the addition of the new ViSOR system, it will be years before local police forces have a comprehensive register of all known sex offenders, which will be of any use in 'tracking' suspects.[60] In addition, there is little evidence to suggest that the registration scheme 'captures' those more likely to be sexual predators in the future. Research has shown how the reoffending pattern of those subject to the registration requirement and those not is the same, so that the legislation has little practical effect in preventing crime (Lieb, 1996: 298; Marshall, 1997; Soothill and Francis, 1997).

Perhaps, a closing caveat in relation to the efficacy of the legislation could be the danger that concentrating on a few known offenders, will instil a false sense of security into the government, the police and the public, that such measures will be the ultimate tool in combating sex crime (Parliament of the Commonwealth of Australia, 1995: para 4.14; Prentky, 1996: 297–98).[61] Indeed, consistent with Ericson and Haggerty's (1997) model of knowledge-risk-security, outlined in chapter 2, the legislation appeared to be produced, at least in part, from an

[59] David Mellor, *Hansard* HC Deb, vol 281, col 43 (27 January 1997).
[60] Peter Thurnham, *Hansard* HC Deb, vol 281, col 31 (27 January 1997).
[61] Alun Michael, *Hansard* HC Deb, vol 281, col 39 (27 January 1997).

assumption that simply having knowledge about an offender's whereabouts would make the community safe. The legislation failed in particular, however, to develop a clear concept of how this knowledge could actually be used, beyond the transcarceration of the offender through registration, to reduce the risk of future offending and to protect the community.

The Public: Protection, Scope and Abuse in the Home

In relation to the stated official aim of 'protecting the public', there are a number of other practical problems with registration which may undermine the goal of achieving public protection. Labelling the offender via registration and notification may simply serve to create public panic and fear (Bedarf, 1995: 885, 906–9, 939; Winick, 1998: 539). The legislation will not, for instance, ensure that those living in the area know that a resident is a danger (Bedarf, 1995: 906; Thomas, 1997: 11). If children see a public notice of a person labelled as a sex offender, it may make them less wary of other strange and potentially dangerous adults who have not been so labelled (Hebenton and Thomas, 1996c).

As noted in chapter 2, the media have created an image of the paedophile as an 'evil madman' or 'monster' (Soothill and Walby, 1991: 146; Sampson, 1994: 43–44; Ferguson, 1995). Such images can be dangerous since they detract attention from the real abusers (Soothill and Francis, 1997; Wright, 2003). This misconception is significant, for to use the much-used phrase 'monsters do not get children, nice men do' (Sampson, 1994: 46–47, 124–25; Parliament of the Commonwealth of Australia, 1995: paras 2.27–28; Long and McLachlan, 2002: 6). Indeed, despite the media tendency to highlight stranger offences, only a very small minority of these cases actually involve stranger perpetrators. It has been emphasised throughout that the main perpetrators of child sexual abuse are family members or, at the very least, persons well known to the child (Grubin, 1998). Therefore, the fact that a large number of sexual abuse incidents occur in the home, where they often remain hidden, renders knowledge of the offender's whereabouts largely irrelevant.

Indeed, in the United Kingdom, in particular, it has also been argued that the legislation contains many problems of scope which limit its effectiveness. The list of offences which are subject to the registration requirement is both over- and under-inclusive. In one sense it is too wide in that it covers a wide spectrum of sexual offences. Although homosexual offences are no longer included within the new legislative framework, it does cover sex between young people. For example, a young man who has had consensual sex with his underage girlfriend may come within the remit of the legislation and be forced to register as a sex offender. This would seem to broaden the scope of the register beyond what would normally be understood to be a paedophile or even a sex offenders' register. As outlined earlier in relation to policing difficulties, there are already potentially huge numbers involved in registration (Marshall, 1997). Such acts arguably do not qualify as harmful, and it is unlikely that the people concerned will pose a risk to other members of the public

(Soothill and Francis, 1998: 284–85).[62] The obvious problem with this over inclusion is that 'casting the net' too wide may only detract attention and resources from the real dangers and the real problems (Cobley, 1997a: 103).[63]

In another sense, it may be argued that the legislation is too narrow in scope. As Soothill et al (2005b: 40) have pointed out, many offences, including some serious ones, may have a clear sexual motive but may not be recorded as such. Despite recent amendments, the legislation does not include a number of key offences that one would have expected to see included as relevant offences such as burglary with a sexual motive or the murder of a child with a sexual motive. The overriding general limitation of all such legislative measures, which are aimed at managing sexual offenders in the community, however, is that they are focused on those offenders who have already come to the attention of the authorities in some way. Yet, vast numbers of sexual crimes go unreported by the public or undetected by the police. Those offenders who do not appear on official records consequently remain unmonitored in the community, free to re-offend (Sampson, 1994: 23–24, 46–47; Parliament of the Commonwealth of Australia, 1995: paras 2.27–28; Bean, 1997: 284). This is highly significant since research suggests that fewer than five per cent of sex offenders are ever apprehended (Salter, 2003). In effect, therefore, such legislation may be effectively targeting the wrong people (Earl-Hubbard, 1996: 850–52). An unregistered offender may commit a crime and the police may waste valuable hours checking the register while the 'real trail' goes cold (Hebenton and Thomas, 1997c: 6).

A further problem of scope is that those who may require most monitoring and treatment, that is young sexual offenders, are subject to less stringent requirements. On the one hand, early intervention may stem the onset of a sexual offending career. There is a whole body of research to suggest that the onset of a sexual offending career begins in adolescence or even before, and continues into adulthood (Abel et al 1987; Barbaree et al, 1993; Salter, 1995).[64] On the other hand, to register a young person as a sex offender may create a potential label and lifelong stigma. The tension between these two viewpoints in this context has led to a related debate about whether young sex offenders are to be regarded as 'risky children' (James and Jenks, 1996) or 'children at risk' (Coombes, 2003) and as such whether they should more properly be dealt with under the auspices of the child protection rather than the justice system (Sanders and Ladwa-Thomas, 1997; Masson and Morrison, 1999).[65] Indeed, there are problems in responding within

[62] Mr. David Mellor, *Hansard* [HC Debs], 27 January 1997, col 28; Lord Monson, *Hansard* [HL Debs], 20 March 1997, col 1134; Earl Russell, *Hansard* [HL Debs], 20 March 1997, cols 1135–7.

[63] Mr. Alun Michael, *Hansard* [HC Debs], 27 January 1997, col 36.

[64] Grubin (1998: 23), however, has found that while the sexual offending of many adult offenders can be traced to their adolescence, only a minority continue to sexually offend as adults.

[65] There is also a fundamental paradox here within criminal justice policy-making that while young offenders in general are usually initially diverted from formal justice, there is resistance to the idea of diversion for those young people who commit sexual offences. This tension has been attributed to a number of interrelated factors including fears about the progressive nature of sex offending and wider social concerns about sexual offences, particularly where the victims and offenders are children or young people (Brownlie, 2003).

any one framework due to the competing views of welfare and justice and those concerning the best way to manage or control the risks these young offenders present (Brownlie, 2003). These difficulties do at least demonstrate that there is an obvious need for special provision in the case of young offenders who sexually abuse. One such possibility is the use of restorative processes as will be discussed in chapter 7.

CONCLUSION

As outlined in this and the previous chapter, the arguments expounded in favour of registration and notification relate to the wider problems posed by managing sex offenders in the community. These include the supposedly high recidivism among sex offenders, the inadequacy of supervision provisions and the resulting need to 'track' the offender for public protection.

It has been argued, however, that there are a host of ethical questions which relate to registration as a punitive measure which may in turn infringe civil liberties and prevent meaningful imposition. Moreover, public notification of the identity and whereabouts of released sex offenders may amount to a form of 'disintegrative shaming' (Braithwaite, 1989) and have a number of attendant negative consequences for the offender which may prevent their reintegration. In addition, there are a plethora of practical obstacles such as cost and inadequate policing resources, not considered at the time the legislation was being formulated, which may impede its effectiveness in managing the risks posed by sex offenders and reduce it to symbolic significance only. Registration schemes have been heavily criticised as being almost toothless and largely unworkable measures which may potentially allow dangerous sex offenders to slip through the net.

The sum of these difficulties has led two commentators to make the point that the benefits accruing from the containment of sexual crime by control over convicted sex offenders through registration, may in fact be illusory and that the legislation was introduced simply to feed the political agenda of the 'law and order' lobby (Soothill and Francis, 1998). In this respect, given the range of potential difficulties, it is hard to refrain from reaching the conclusion that these retributive measures were enacted in large part to satisfy the concerns of a punitive public in relation to sex offenders and to help instil public confidence that something tangible was being done by the government to control and manage sex offenders in the community more effectively (Simon, 1998).

Particular area of concerns include the fact that the registration requirements did not apply retrospectively but only to those offenders sentenced after 1991, that they do not place any real restrictions on the behaviour of sex offenders and that there are a significant number of unregistered offenders who are therefore beyond the scope of the provisions. Furthermore, it has also been argued that the circumstances in which police may make public disclosure of information about sex offenders remain controversial and are far from being clear cut. As will be discussed in the next chapter, in an attempt to address these criticisms and counteract some of these deficiencies, a number of new civil measures have recently been enacted under the Sexual Offences Act 2003 to further restrict and control the behaviour of sex offenders in the community.

6

Control in the Community

G IVEN THE MYRIAD of problems involved in managing sex offenders
in the community, which were outlined in chapter 4, a number of punitive legislative measures for controlling the behaviour of sex offenders
have been introduced within the last few years. The most notable of these perhaps
has been sex offender registration and community notification, as discussed in the
previous chapter. Following on, this chapter predominantly examines other
mechanisms, within the retributive framework, which have been formulated to
manage the risk posed by sex offenders in the community more effectively.

It begins with an examination of novel probation conditions imposed on sex
offenders by judges in the United States in the form of 'shame penalties.' These measures, in common with popular 'name and shame' campaigns and community notification, discussed earlier in this book, are largely disintegrative in nature. Drawing
specifically on Braithwaite's (1989) dichotomy of reintegrative and disintegrative
shaming, as outlined in chapter 3, it argues that such measures, in particular, have
the potential to result in labelling, stigmatisation and isolation of the offender and
effectively undermine efficient risk management and offender reintegration.

The chapter also critically assesses other recent innovations to control sex
offenders in the community, including the range of new preventive orders enacted
under the Sexual Offences Act 2003 in the United Kingdom and electronic tagging,
which has been piloted or introduced in several jurisdictions. These retributive
measures, however, are also replete with inherent ethical and legal concerns and
practical limitations which may prevent meaningful imposition and ultimately
reduce their effectiveness in securing the management of risk. In addition, in common with punitive coercive measures for offender management, such as registration and notification, they also have the potential to publicly shame and stigmatise
offenders and prevent their reintegration. Finally, the remainder of the chapter
explores the use of chemical castration, secure accommodation and preventive
detention as options of last resort with more persistent offenders.

SHAME PENALTIES

The use of disintegrative shaming mechanisms is not new. History is littered
with examples of the public spectacle of punishment where shaming and public

humiliation were used in order to exact punishment for an offence (Foucault, 1977: 3–72). Public humiliation both enhanced traditional physical punishments and functioned as a punishment by itself (Hibbert, 1963: 28). Punishments such as flogging, hanging, drawing and quartering, the stocks and the pillory, and branding, for example, were carried out publicly and in ceremonial fashion, and were designed to inflict physical suffering in tandem with social disgrace (Ives, 1914: 53; Barnes, 1930: 62–63; Hibbert, 1963: 28).

Branding, a method widely used in the seventeenth century, involved burning a single letter onto the perpetrator's face representing the first letter of the crime committed. These permanent labels which in effect cast the person out of the community were also designed, in part, to prevent the offender from committing similar acts by warning future victims of their criminal tendencies (Ives, 1914: 53). Today, the legislature, the executive and the judiciary, particularly in the United States, have not lost sight of the potential of shame penalties for certain classes of offenders (Brilliant, 1989; Kelley, 1989; McAlinden, 2005).[1]

Signs and Apologies as Public Exposure

In response to the limitations of and the frustrations with the conventional options of prison and parole, a minority of judges in the United States have begun to use shame penalties as part of modern probation conditions, particularly for sex offenders (Kahan, 1996). In practice, there are several types of shaming mechanism, namely signs or public exposure penalties and apologies (Massaro, 1991: 1886–90; Karp, 1998: 281–83).[2]

The sign sanctions are the most obvious illustrations of disintegrative shaming. Well-publicised examples of sign punishments include the requirement that those convicted of drink driving offences affix bumper stickers[3] or distinctive licence plates[4] to their vehicles or that offenders post signs in front of their homes, place advertisements in newspapers or wear t-shirts or signs listing their offences (Kahan, 1996).[5] In one case,[6] the court placed a convicted child molester on pro-

---

[1] 'American Criminals Sentenced To Shame' *The Sunday Times*, 20 April 1997. In the United Kingdom, disintegrative shaming mechanisms have also been used to 'name and shame' certain forms of deviant behaviour. Drug dealers, prostitutes, those soliciting for prostitution and even beggars were to have their names published in newspapers as part of a campaign by the police and the city council in Nottingham to target street crime ('Name and Shame' *The Times*, 7 October 2003).

[2] Note, that the basic typology is that of 'signs' and 'apologies.' Others, however, prefer to divide shame penalties into three categories: public exposure penalties, which are defined by the attempt to communicate the offence and the offender to the public and which correspond roughly to signs; debasement penalties, which are designed specifically to lower the status of the offender through humiliation and embarrassment; and apology penalties, which involve ceremonial or written apologies directed to the court, the victims or the community (Karp, 1998: 281–83).

[3] *Goldschmitt v State*, 490 So.2d 123 (Fla. Dist. Ct. App. 1986).

[4] *People v Letterlough*, 655 N.E.2d 146 (NY 1995).

[5] *Blanton v City of North Las Vegas*, 489 US 538 (1989) (referring to Nev. Rev. Stat. 484.3792 (1)(a)(2) (1987)).

[6] *State v Bateman*, 95 Or. Ct. App. 456, 771 P.2d 314 (1989).

bation for five years subject to a condition, among others, that he place a sign on both sides of his car and on the door of his residence in three-inch lettering which read: 'Dangerous Sex Offender—No Children Allowed' (Brilliant, 1989: 1365–66; Kelley, 1989: 760; Massaro, 1991: 1887–88). Bateman had previously been convicted of sexually abusing a child. The judge was concerned that if she placed Bateman in prison, he would be released without supervision. She justified her requirement that the offender post signs as a response to the lack of community recognition of dangerous people. She hoped that even if the signs did not actually deter individuals like Bateman, they at least would be a warning to parents and children of the danger that such individuals present (Brilliant, 1989: 1366).[7]

The second type of shame sanction is the public apology or confession. This has been used on some first time offenders requiring them to apologise publicly to their victims in face-to-face encounters or write a confessional letter to the local newspaper, announcing the subject of their conviction and apologising to the local community. Other courts have required sex offenders to place ads in the local newspaper publicising their offences or urging others to sex treatment. A Rhode Island Superior Court judge, for example, required an offender to purchase an advertisement in the Providence Journal-Bulletin reading:

> I am Stephen Gererhausen, I am 29 years old . . . I was convicted of child molestation . . . if you are a child molester, get professional help immediately, or you may find your picture and name in the paper and your life under the control of the state (Massaro, 1991: 1880).

The central component of these penalties is public exposure—to bring the crime to the attention of the public so that they may respond with shaming (Karp, 1998: 281). Their primary purpose is not to humiliate or draw public ridicule but rather, as noted above, to protect potential victims by warning them of the danger these offenders pose. Undoubtedly, however, the risk of stigmatisation attaches to those who are subject to such penalties (Kelley, 1989: 775).

Aside from the desired public protection effect, these types of shame penalties may also be attractive to judges and the public because they appear to satisfy the punitive retributive impulse on at least two levels (Karp, 1998: 277–78). On one level, there is the practical imposition of some form of suffering in the threat of stigma and social exclusion. On a second level, they are symbolic of the moral and public condemnation of the offence (Tavuchis, 1991). Not surprisingly, several American commentators have questioned whether this is appropriate terrain for judges. Indeed, these measures like registration and notification measures generally, have been met with both constitutional and non-constitutional challenges (Brilliant, 1989; Kelley, 1989).

---

[7] Other examples of the dramatic use of the 'scarlet letter' approach include Texas, where a judge ordered 14 sex offenders on probation to place bumper stickers or portable plastic placards on their vehicles reading, 'Danger! Registered Sex Offender in Vehicle!' and signs in front of their residences reading, 'Danger! Registered Sex Offender Lives Here!' ('Texas Sex Offenders' *The Ottawa Sun*, 20 May 2001). See also: Petrunik (2002: 493).

The Disintegrative Effects of 'Naming' and 'Shaming'

Contemporary state-led and popular responses to sex offending may have a number of disintegrative effects. Far from achieving the goal of successful social reintegration, measures such as registration and notification and novel probation conditions, in common with popular 'name and shame' campaigns, may only serve to label and stigmatise the offender and isolate them from the rest of the community (Winick, 1998: 539, 556). It was noted in the previous chapter that public notification, in particular, may result in harassment or vigilante attack on suspected sex offenders. This singling out of the offender via shaming sanctions, however, may also have a number of other negative effects, beyond the physical, on at least four interrelated levels:

First, it may impede the successful reintegration of the offender into the community, his ability to get a job or accommodation and therefore ultimately, his rehabilitation (Bedarf, 1995: 885, 910–11; Cobley, 1997a: 103; Soothill and Francis, 1998: 291). Secondly, heightening the offender's sense of isolation may ultimately increase the chance of subsequent delinquent behaviour as a coping mechanism (Maxwell and Morris, 1999; Edwards and Hensley, 2001b; McAlinden, 2005). Through the application of a criminal label, which these measures inevitably entail, the sex offender may find it easier to live out this label than to try to break from it (Winick, 1998: 539, 556). As Becker has said, they 'of necessity develop illegitimate routines' (cited in Tierney, 1996: 143). To return to the language of shame, these measures rebuke both offender and offence (Presser and Gunnison, 1999: 309), which may foster the 'adoption of a delinquent identity' (Braithwaite and Mugford, 1994: 146). Thirdly, from the 'deviancy amplification spiral,'[8] also of the labelling perspective (Wilkins, 1964), the offender who is isolated from 'normal' law abiding society may be forced to associate with similar offenders where they learn more sophisticated techniques. Fourthly, if an offender becomes known or ostracised in the area where he lives he will not be deterred from future crime. The offender may simply go underground where he could be of even greater danger and commit crime elsewhere (Hebenton and Thomas, 1996c: 25; Soothill and Francis, 1998: 288–89). As discussed in chapter 1, people in the immediate vicinity where the offender lives may be protected, but the risk will merely be displaced to another area (Prentky, 1996: 295–96; Soothill and Francis, 1998: 288–89).[9] In sum, as the appellant argued in *State v Bateman* a dual future consequence of such 'name and shame' measures is that 'The defendant will

---

[8] The amplification spiral begins when society becomes less tolerant of particular forms of behaviour. This leads to more acts being defined as deviant, since people are now more conscious of this behaviour. As a result there is more action against criminals who are more severely punished or segregated, and more alienation of deviant groups who now only mix with one another. In turn this generates more crime by deviant groups. The net result is even less tolerance of deviants by conforming society and the process begins all over again. See also: ch 2, n 5.

[9] Sex offenders themselves also affirm that the ostracism they face as a result of deviant stereotypes prevents them from managing their own problems effectively (Hudson, 2005: 160–68, 183).

be at best shunned from society and at worst subjected to physical harassment and abuse.'[10]

Therefore, consistent with Braithwaite's thesis of shaming, far from protecting the public, making the sex offender a public pariah will not stop levels of sexual offending and may even lead to an increase in such crimes (Berliner, 1996: 292; Earl-Hubbard, 1996: 856; Prentky, 1996: 296; Cobley 1997b; Edwards and Hensley, 2001b). Disintegrative shaming practices in the form of coercive criminal justice responses will not deter offenders, protect victims or make significant reductions in recidivism levels, except perhaps in the very short term. Without structured support programmes in the community to assist in offender readjust-ment, to help them desist, and victims to protect themselves, arrest, prosecution and conviction via the criminal justice system may result in more incidents of sex-ual offences in the long term (Finstad, 1990; Braithwaite and Daly, 1994; Hudson, 1998: 237). As will be discussed in chapter 7, however, in relation to restorative and reintegrative shaming practices, shaming can also be used to positive effect in the process of offender management and reintegration.

THE SEXUAL OFFENCES ACT 2003: NEW PREVENTIVE ORDERS

In the United Kingdom, a whole host of other control in the community mechan-isms have recently been added to what has effectively become a legislative melting pot for the management of sex offenders. Part 2 of the Sexual Offences Act 2003, in this respect, introduces two main types of civil preventive order: the sexual offences prevention order and the risk of sexual harm order which have been designed to address predatory sexual behaviour (Shute, 2004).[11] The scope of these measures, in particular the latter which may be invoked whether or not the offender is before the courts for an offence, is in itself highly indicative of the development and expansion of the risk-based approach to the reintegration of sex offenders in recent years (Maruna and LeBel, 2002).

Sexual Offences Prevention Orders

In relation to the first of these, sex offender orders (SOO)[12] and restraining orders (RO),[13] were originally enacted to strengthen the Sex Offenders Act 1997. These measures were a form of civil injunction which could be used to prohibit the

---

[10] Brief for Appellant, *State v Bateman*, see n 6 above at A-2. See also: 'Deadly Result of Naming and Shaming' *The Independent on Sunday*, 20 February 2000.

[11] Note that the third type of order introduced by this Act is the foreign travel order as discussed in the previous chapter in relation to sex offender registration. This allows the courts to impose travel restrictions on sex offenders where they would be at risk of abusing children.

[12] ss 2–3 of the Crime and Disorder Act 1998.

[13] s 66 and sch 5, s 6 of the Criminal Justice and Courts Services Act 2000.

offender from engaging in specified conduct in order to protect the public from serious harm. The overall agreed purpose of the SOO, in particular, was to prevent sex offenders from frequenting places where there are children such as parks and school playgrounds (Home Office, 1999).[14] These orders were also intended to bring previously unregistered sex offenders within the registration requirements of Part I of the Sex Offenders Act 1997, and the multi-agency public protection arrangements, where their conduct indicated that they posed a continuing and serious risk (Power, 1999: 5–11). Both of these orders have now been combined and replaced with a new expanded order—a sexual offences prevention order (SOPO)—under Part 2 of the Sexual Offences Act 2003.[15]

This new order may be made by a court where a person is before it for a violent or sexual offence, or following an application by the police in respect of a person with a conviction for such an offence living in the local community. The court must be satisfied that the defendant's behaviour, since the appropriate date, makes it necessary to make such an order, for the purpose of protecting the public, or any particular members of the public, from serious sexual harm. An important distinction between SOPO and SOO is that the new measure includes acts, behaviour, convictions and findings that occur before the commencement of the Act (Shute, 2004: 426). As with SOO, the new order lasts from at least five years to indefinitely, and while it is in force the offender also remains subject to the registration requirements which are now also contained in Part 2 of the 2003 Act. These new orders also include the use of 'negative conditions' (Kemshall and Maguire, 2002: 14) to restrict and control the behaviour of sex offenders in the community. The restrictions which can be placed on offenders can include, for example, preventing them from contacting their victims, from taking part in activities that involve close contact with children or from living in a household with children under 16.[16] Although applications for a SOPO are a civil procedure,[17] breach of these conditions is a criminal offence where the offender becomes liable on conviction to imprisonment for a term of up to five years. Orders may be varied, renewed, or discharged by the court on application by the police or the offender, who also has a limited right of appeal. This new order like other exclusion based orders is based on the concept of 'spatial separation' (Pease, 1995). It seeks to remove the offender from the circumstances surrounding the offence—from the place, people or community linked to his offending behaviour—in order to reduce criminality. Such measures, however, may give rise to a range of practical difficulties.

[14] Other jurisdictions have enacted similar measures which apply to convicted sex offenders who have acted in such a way as to give reasonable cause for concern that an order is necessary to protect the public from serious harm. See, eg: Part 3 of the Sex Offenders Act 2001 in the Republic of Ireland.

[15] ss 104–13.

[16] See para 216 of the Explanatory Notes to the Act.

[17] As mentioned in the previous chapter, the UK domestic courts have specifically held that applications for SOO were not to be categorised as criminal proceedings and that the measures themselves do not amount to a punishment since these were essentially preventive and not punitive measures (See *B v Chief Constable of Avon and Somerset Constabulary* [2001] 1 WLR 340 (DC); *Jones v The Greater Manchester Police Authority* [2001] EWHC Admin 189 (DC)). See also: ch 5, n 34.

Practical Issues

First, there are problems inherent in the rationale and logic behind these orders. If offenders pose such a high risk that they need this order then perhaps a persuasive argument could be made that they should never have been released from custody into the community in the first place. Secondly, there may also be problems associated with the making of such orders. As with the old SOO, the conduct which could potentially result in the making of an order may in itself be non-criminal (Shute, 2004: 426). In effect, therefore, magistrates are going to have to decide whether otherwise fairly 'innocuous and perfectly lawful' (Power, 1999: 9) behaviour, such as an individual simply hanging around school grounds, constitutes a risk of serious harm to the child. In engaging in these difficult predictions of risk, the only available evidence is likely to be the offender's previous record and any expert reports (Shute, 2004: 432–35). The danger remains therefore that the mere fact of the offender's proximity to children may be sufficient grounds to justify the making of an order (Power, 1999: 9–10). Thirdly, there may also be problems with their application. Research indicates that they will only be used in exceptional circumstances. The power to apply for the original SOO, for example, has not been widely used, with less than 100 orders, all against male sex offenders, being made within the first 28 months following implementation (Knock et al, 2002). However, in the 2-year period following this initial study, a further 172 orders were made, and it is expected that this upward trend will continue with the introduction of the SOPO (Shute, 2004: 452). Action for breach, however, was only taken in respect of approximately 50 per cent of the SOO made (Knock et al, 2002). Moreover, the real figures are likely to be much higher as both the old SOO and the new SOPO must last for a minimum of five years (Shute, 2004: 453).[18] These figures may indicate that such measures are of limited deterrent effect. On the other hand, it may also indicate that they are a useful tool for controlling the behaviour of sex offenders in the community (Cobley, 2003: 61). Fourthly, there may be related difficulties with the monitoring and enforcement of such orders. Effective implementation is dependent on the police or someone else actually seeing the offender exhibiting the prohibited behaviour in direct breach of the order and knowing that the offender has in fact been so prohibited. In other words, enforcement may depend on the local police being not only aware of the offender's status, but being in the right place at the right time. Indeed, some forces in Knock et al's study 'experienced problems' with SOO which were thought to be 'virtually impossible to police' (2002: 27).

As will be discussed further below, these and other such measures are also severely limited by the fact that they are focused on the known risks and not the

---

[18] Furthermore, sentences for breaches of SOO were variable and disparate with offenders often receiving a non-custodial sentence or a short custodial sentence of less than two years (Knock et al, 2002). As Shute argues, the difficulty the courts have when sentencing offenders for breach stems from the task of balancing risk with the fact that the behaviour might, in other circumstances, be relatively harmless (2004: 436–39).

hidden and therefore the most dangerous ones (McAlinden, 2006c). The sum of these practical difficulties, as in the case of sex offender registration, indicates that these are further examples of retributive legislative measures which have been introduced on the basis of community protection and offender deterrence (Shute, 2004: 14), with little consideration being given as to how they were actually going to operate in practice.

Ethical and Legal Concerns

In addition, sexual offences prevention orders may give rise to a number of ethical and legal concerns by the imposition of acute restrictions on the rights and movements of offenders against whom they are obtained (Shute, 2004: 438–39). First, as noted above, the potential width of the provision means that theoretically just about anything could be banned under the order and this could lead to a flurry of cases until the judiciary limits the scope of the provision.[19] Indeed, as with the previous measure, SOO, the indeterminate nature of the provision may lead to inconsistent decisions between magistrates as to the contents of an order and significant variations in the individual demands placed on offenders (Power, 1999: 9). This, as Power notes, is worrying given the offender's limited right of appeal against the making of an order. Secondly, as another situational attempt to control the behaviour of offenders in the community they may be open to challenge, in particular, on the grounds that they violate the right to liberty and security of person under Article 5 of the European Convention on Human Rights (ECHR).[20] These arguments will also be outlined further below in relation to electronic tagging and secure accommodation. Thirdly, it may be possible to argue that there has been a breach of Article 7 of the ECHR, 'no punishment without law,' on the grounds that the terms of the order may be too vague to allow an individual to foresee to a reasonable degree that he is liable to a criminal offence on breach.[21] In the final analysis then, in common with all such measures for managing sex offenders in the community, there are inherent ethical and practical difficulties in striking a delicate balance between the freedom and control of offenders.

---

[19] SOO were challenged on their potential breadth in *B v Chief Constable of Avon and Somerset Constabulary*, see n 17 above, at 347. The order in question prohibited the offender from seeking contact or communicating with a child; from associating with or befriending a child; from residing in a house where children are present; and from undertaking any activity which involves contact with children. In the Queen's Bench Division, Lord Bingham rejected the argument that the terms of this order fell foul of Arts 5(1) (liberty and security of person), 8 (respect for private and family life) and 11 (freedom of peaceful assembly and association with others) of the European Convention since they met the requirements of being 'clear and readily intelligible in its terms, specific as to time and place, and no wider than necessary to restrain the particular harm which it was feared the appellant might cause,' at 355. Since the proceedings have been held to be civil and the measures preventive and not punitive, they are unlikely to breach Arts 6 (right to a fair trial) and 8 respectively.

[20] See n 19 above.

[21] *Kokkinakis v Greece* (1993) 17 EHRR 397, para 52.

Risk of Sexual Harm Orders

The 2003 Act also introduces a second new measure—the risk of sexual harm order (ROSO)—a further civil preventive order which can be used to prohibit specified behaviour, including the 'grooming' of children (Cobley, 2003: 65–69).[22] It may be made by a magistrates' court on application by the police where a person has, on at least two occasions, engaged in sexually explicit conduct or communication with a child, and where this is deemed necessary to protect the child from physical or psychological harm. It is therefore much broader in its remit than that of 'serious harm' as required by the SOPO. The order is similar in many respects to the previous one in that the usual procedures for variation, discharge and appeal and the penalty for breach apply. The order must last for at least two years but may also be made for an indefinite period. The introduction of the ROSO has provoked the most controversy since it is possible for such an order to be made irrespective of whether such a person has previously been convicted of a sexual or other offence. This order, which unlike the SOPO can only be made against persons aged 18 or over, effectively criminalises acts which may be carried out for the purposes of sexual grooming, but only after an individual has been identified as posing a risk to children.

Targeting 'Grooming' Behaviour

Indeed, as discussed in chapter 4 in relation to offender management problems, one of the most recent debates in the area of sexual offences against children has focused on behaviour known as 'grooming'. This phrase, first highlighted by Salter (1995), is used to describe the process by which an offender will seek to gain access to a child to both prepare them for abuse and simultaneously make them less likely to disclose (Gillespie, 2001, 2004; Gallagher et al, 2003). Indeed, as discussed previously, sex offenders can be very inventive in the way in which they obtain access to children, within their own or other families or via the community and even organisations, where the establishment and subsequent breach of trust plays a central role in the grooming process (McAlinden, 2006c).

The term 'grooming' has recently found expression in section 15 of the Sexual Offences Act 2003 which makes it an offence to 'meet a child following sexual grooming.' It covers the behaviour of an offender who meets, or seeks to meet, a child with the intention of committing a sexual assault, if he has met or communicated with that child on at least two earlier occasions. This offence, however, is not restricted to online behaviour. It requires face-to-face meetings to occur or be arranged in order for the offence to be triggered. It is the communication surrounding this meeting which can take place either online or offline. This means that no actual abuse need take place before this offence is invoked. The purpose of

---

[22] ss 123–29.

section 15 is not to act against those who have sexually abused children, but to criminalise the preparatory acts involved in abuse and allow intervention well before actual physical exploitation takes place.

As discussed in chapter 2, in debates about social ordering, the concept of risk increasingly furnishes a discursive framework within which 'responses-to-problems' are being considered (Beck, 1992). Indeed, 'risk penality' which has characterised contemporary criminal justice debates more generally (Feeley and Simon, 1992, 1994; Braithwaite, 2000; Shearing, 2000) has been particularly evident in relation to concerns over the risk posed by sex offenders in the community where assessing, managing and reducing those risks has become a central concern (Parton et al, 1997; Kemshall and Maguire, 2003; Ashenden, 2004)

In tandem with these concerns, the general aim of these new provisions is to prevent or deter contact between children and would-be abusers and, if it does occur, to make it more liable to detection and reporting. Since they will, in effect, empower the police to identify and tackle abusers before they are able to physically abuse a child, they have generally been welcomed as a positive advancement in child protection (Ost, 2004).[23] However, they have also been criticised from a practical standpoint.

Potential Problems

Critics point to the potential difficulties of gaining sufficient evidence and of proving the existence of the requisite *mens rea* of harmful intent (Gillespie, 2002; Ost, 2004; Spencer, 2004). These difficulties stem from the fact that it may be very difficult to make a clear distinction between friendly behaviour towards a child and something that has a more sinister motive, especially in the early stages of the grooming process. Indeed, as noted in chapter 4, there is a dearth of research on grooming and a lack of settled meaning of the term. This could lead to innocent conversations and actions being criminalised, which are outside the ambit of the danger it was intended to address (Gillespie, 2002: 419).[24] Alternatively, it may be impossible to use in practice, particularly in cases where the individual has no prior convictions.

Many sex offenders can now be tracked, to some degree at least, by examining the internet and computer usage of those who may have been reported.[25] As

---

[23] These assumptions about the supposed benefits of the legislation also appear to have underpinned the legislative debates on the 2003 Act. See, eg: Sir Paul Beresford, *Hansard* HC Deb, vol 351, cols 699–700 (12 June 2000); Lord Falconer, *Hansard* HL Deb, vol 646, col 1257 (1 April 2003).

[24] These potential difficulties were also recognised when the legislation was being considered by Parliament. See, eg: Oliver Letwin, *Hansard* HC Deb, vol 394, col 508 (19 November 2002); Baroness Noakes, *Hansard* HL Deb, vol 644, cols 777–78 (13 February 2003); Baroness Gould, *Hansard* HL Deb, vol 644, col 786 (13 February 2003).

[25] Although statistics regarding the extent of online grooming are difficult to establish and evaluate, there have been some surveys of children's experiences online. A US survey found that approximately one in five youths aged between 10 and 17 'received an unwanted sexual solicitation or approach over the internet in the last year' (National Centre for Missing and Exploited Children, *Online Victimisation: A Report of the Nation's Youth* (2000) 14, <http://www.ncmec.org/download/nc62.pdf>). A similar

argued throughout, it is generally accepted, however, that the danger of online solicitation by a predatory stranger is thought to be much lower than offline risk from someone known to the victim (Grubin, 1998). In cases of intra-familial and institutional child abuse, in particular, it is highly unlikely that the police will be able to detect all instances of grooming which occur prior to the actual abuse (Gillespie, 2002; Ost, 2004). These arguments point strongly towards the conclusion that sexual 'grooming' is not easily captured by the criminal law which, as a result, will be somewhat limited in its response to this form of deviant sexual behaviour.

These orders, the ROSO and the SOPO, in common with the other control in the community mechanisms, which have been discussed in this and the previous chapter, have been enacted on the basis of their contribution to public safety and offender deterrence. They are intended to tighten controls on risky individuals and perhaps warn potential victims of the dangers that they may pose. These measures, however, although less overtly premised on 'public shaming,' like their earlier counterparts they may also carry a 'strong stigmatising force' (Shute, 2004: 439) and the associated dangers of ostracism or vigilante abuse. This is said to be particularly the case with any order bearing the prefix 'risk of sexual harm' (Shute, 2004: 439). Moreover, in practical terms the net result of the weaknesses inherent in such measures, as with sex offender registration, is that the worst offending adults will simply find a way around them.

ELECTRONIC TAGGING

Electronic monitoring of offenders, popularly known as tagging, occurs by means of an electronic bracelet attached to the offender's ankle. This usually takes the form of positional tagging which can pinpoint the whereabouts of an offender or curfew tagging which ensures that an offender has returned home by a certain time. The history of tagging is closely linked to the use of home confinement programmes, house arrest and home detention,[26] particularly in the United States and to a lesser extent in the United Kingdom where the measure has had a shorter history.

Tagging Programmes

In the United States, sentences began to appear in the 1980s as a response to burgeoning prison populations. The idea, however, that technology might be used to make such conditions more effective had been around for a long time. The

figure, approximately 20%, has also been produced in the UK (Internet Crime Forum (ICF), *Chat Wise, Street Wise—Children and Internet Chat Services* (2001), <http://www.internetcrimeforum.org.uk/chatwise_streetwise.html>).

[26] Eg: in New Zealand, home detention with electronic monitoring was introduced in October 1999 as an early release option for people sentenced to various lengths of imprisonment (Gibbs, 2003).

concept of electronic tagging was being discussed as early as 1919 (Friel et al, 1987). It took, however, the prison overcrowding crisis (Irwin and Austin, 1994) and the disenchantment with existing community supervision of the early 1980s to bring the practice into the criminal justice field as a sentence of the court, rather than just a short term condition of bail (Whitfield, 1997: 35–37). The first consistent programme to tag offenders started in Florida in 1984. Electronic monitoring has since established itself as a viable community based option in corrections practice in the United States. By 1990, no fewer than 47 states had tagging programmes, with the largest state users being Indiana, Missouri, Ohio, Delaware, Florida and Texas (Whitfield, 1997: 39, 44).

Tagging has been used in the United States and in England and Wales as a means of facilitating among other things, the granting of parole, early release and temporary home leave to prisoners (Nellis, 1991). The range of offences covered for juveniles and adults includes serious traffic offences, drink driving, theft, drug offences, burglary, and serious sexual violence and murder, especially in post-release programmes. More commonly, however, electronic monitoring schemes are used with lower risk offenders (Whitfield, 1997: 46).[27] In recent times, it has been used in the United States to control the movements of sex offenders in some states like Florida where offenders can be 'tracked' via second generation systems known as 'Ground Position by Satellite' (GPS) (Whitfield, 1997: 112–13).[28] The system has pre-programmed rules which control both where and when offenders are permitted to be away from home, so that in addition to the traditional curfew, permitted or prohibited areas can also be specified.

In England and Wales, tagging has been offered as an all-purpose answer to offending to be used as the courts wish—either as a stand-alone option within the range of non-custodial sentences or as a useful means of achieving compliance with specific community penalties. Indeed, a series of legislation has been introduced over recent years to provide for the electronic monitoring of offenders. This has included, most notably, section 13 of the Criminal Justice Act 1991, as amended, which made provision for court ordered curfews that could be monitored electronically (Gibson and Whitfield, 1997; Shaw, 1997).[29] From 1995

---

[27] Parallel schemes are being used in Canada, Sweden (Bishop, 1996), the Netherlands (Boelens, 1996), New Zealand (Gibbs, 2003), Singapore (Schultz, 1995) and Australia (Challinger, 1994), where tagging is used in combination with other community disposals often with a treatment element. Unlike the United States, however, many of these countries expressly exclude sex offenders from the remit of the schemes (Whitfield, 1997: 12, 65–66).

[28] The Jessica Lunsford Act 2005 (Chapter 2005–28; House Bill No 1877), which introduced, inter alia, up to lifetime supervision with electronic monitoring for sex offenders convicted of crimes against children as a condition of release, has also been enacted in Louisiana and Arizona, with similar legislation being passed in Arkansas, Oregon, Virginia and Washington.

[29] Eg: s 12 of the Criminal Justice and Public Order Act 1994 amended the 1991 Act to enable this provision to be piloted in selected areas before being implemented nationally. Section 38 of the Crime (Sentences) Act 1997 amended the 1991 Act so that the offender's consent was not required for electronic monitoring to be carried out. Section 38 of the Powers of Criminal Courts (Sentencing) Act 2000 also provided for the electronic monitoring of curfew orders which require an offender to remain at a specified place.

onwards, electronic monitoring of curfew orders was piloted in various areas of the country to assess its effectiveness and viability (Home Office, 1995, 1996: paras 7.9–7.12; Richardson, 1999). Section 100 of the Crime and Disorder Act 1998 further amended the Criminal Justice Act 1991 to provide for certain categories of prisoner to be released on home detention curfew subject to a risk assessment. On the basis of largely successful trials, Part III of the Criminal Justice and Court Services Act 2000, amended the previous legislation and extended the electronic monitoring of offenders in a number of ways, including making provision for the electronic monitoring of exclusion orders[30]; electronic monitoring as a condition of a community penalty and curfew and/or exclusion requirements to be a condition of a community penalty which could also be monitored electronically[31]; and finally, electronic monitoring of exclusion or curfew requirements as a licence condition.[32] In September 2004, the Home Office established three pilot schemes of satellite tracking of offenders which enables closer monitoring of offender's movements. This was also provided for in the latter piece of legislation but was not commenced until suitable technology to fully support the initiative was available (Nellis, 2005). These measures are generic in that they can apply to a broad range of offenders including, most notably, young offenders.

The Use of Tagging with Sex Offenders

The possible benefits of electronic monitoring for managing sex offenders in the community, as with all such control in the community mechanisms, can be framed largely in terms of deterrence, prevention and control. Electronic tagging could be used as a possible form of controlled supervision of sex offenders. As a licence condition, for example, it would enable the 'tracking' of those offenders released from prison on licence, by electronically monitoring their movements and whereabouts, on a continuous basis, until the expiry of the licence or the removal of the condition, whichever happens first.

Arguably, where electronic tagging would be optimally effective, however, would be its use in combination with other mechanisms, as a means of ensuring compliance with and monitoring the effectiveness of other control in the community mechanisms, such as sexual offences prevention orders. In this way, for example, if a sex offender was electronically tagged within a certain area so that an alarm sounded if he was near a prohibited place such as a school, this would help alert the police to the fact that the order has been breached. It would therefore also help to alleviate some of the problems associated with the effective

---

[30] s 46. An exclusion order is similar in many respects to a 'curfew order.' However, whereas a curfew order requires an offender to remain at a specified place, an exclusion order prohibits an offender from entering a specified place or area for a specified period of not more than a year (three months for a juvenile).

[31] ss 50–51.

[32] s 52.

enforcement and monitoring of such orders, as outlined above. Such a combined measure may also help deter the offender from reoffending. If he knows there is a strong likelihood that breach of the order will lead to apprehension, it may reduce breaches of and increase compliance rates with such orders. In the Sydney Cooke case, for example, discussed in chapter 2, electronic tagging was used as part of an overall management scheme which also comprised probation supervision and accommodation in a secure unit.[33] Indeed, as will be discussed further below, this tentative analysis is supported, at least in part, by the empirical literature. There are, however, a number of potential practical problems associated with tagging. In addition, the adoption of such a measure, while it may be potentially attractive, is also likely to face opposition on human rights grounds.

Practical Issues

In the United States, where the great bulk of experience has been gained, technical problems dominated for a number of years. Transmissions could be blocked or distorted by environmental conditions including proximity to a radio station, lightning storms, water and poor quality telephone lines (Whitfield, 1997: 38). Early 'success' rates of between 50 and 80 per cent were quoted in the first few years. However, patterns of use and effectiveness are still very varied (Schmidt, 1989; Baumer et al, 1993; Travis, 1994). California had the highest technical viola- tion and arrest rates, both running at around 35 per cent after six months (Petersilia and Turner, 1990). In Minnesota, a detailed follow-up study of 300 offenders on an intensive programme, which combined a lengthy period of electronically monitored house detention with traditional supervision, reached cautious results: 'Offenders under the scheme posed no greater risk to public safety than those initially sentenced to prison' (Deschenes et al, 1995). Other researchers also sound a note of caution and point to the relapse pattern after electronic mon- itoring had been completed (Baumer and Mendelsohn, 1990). Studies in Georgia and Arizona, for example, were shown to exacerbate recidivism rates (Irwin, 1990).

In England and Wales, where there is a purported emphasis on an evidence- based approach to criminal justice policy and practice since the onset of the Labour administration in 1997, has seen more encouraging results.[34] During the first year of pilot schemes of curfew with electronic monitoring, provided for by the Criminal Justice and Public Order Act 1994, the successful completion rate was consistently over 80 per cent, although a number of people had breached the order and were allowed to continue (Mair and Mortimer, 1996). Findings from the

---

[33] 'Child Killer To Be Tagged On Release' *The Times*, 4 April 1998; 'Focus: The Evil In Our Midst' *The Sunday Telegraph*, 5 April 1998; 'Search Goes On To House Paedophile' *The Times*, 13 August 1998.

[34] It has also been recently argued in the context of electronic monitoring, that evidence-based policy remains at the level of rhetoric since the consistent messages produced by government commis- sioned research do not appear to have been acted on (Mair, 2005).

second year of trials produced similar results, although completion rates also varied by the main offence. Theft and violence were the most common categories for which individuals were reconvicted within two years (Mortimer and May, 1998; Mortimer et al, 1999) where rates ran as high as 73 per cent (Sugg et al, 2001). Another study covering the first 16 months of the home detention curfew scheme produced more cautious results. Although the scheme was deemed to be operating relatively smoothly and had gone some way to achieving its central aim of easing the transition from custody to the community, in comparison with other community penalties, it was found to have a broadly neutral impact on reoffending (Dodgson et al, 2001).[35]

The principle that tagging works best alongside community penalties as an enhancement to and as a component part of an intensive supervision programme, typically post-release, is well supported (Baumer et al, 1993; English et al, 1994; Bonta et al, 1999; Walter et al, 2001), where attention can be paid to setting up a framework of control and preparing offenders for the transition to unsupervised living (Baumer and Mendelsohn, 1990). Indeed, as noted above, the general feeling among American researchers is that tagging had no discernible impact on reoffending. It had some value as a punishment and as a short-term control, but longer lasting change was far more likely to come from programmes which address the underlying causes of offending (Friel et al, 1987; Gowen, 1995; Whitfield, 1997).

Perhaps the major drawback for electronic tagging schemes, however, is the projected costs involved with leasing or purchasing equipment and the management costs in maintaining dedicated staff units (Whitfield, 1997: 104–6). In addition, high breach rates may simply increase prison costs. Indeed, in the United States where the majority of schemes have been found to increase correctional costs due to net widening, 'electronic monitoring has simply become an expensive trip wire into custody' (Whitfield, 1997: 106). The question of net widening and the need to target resources more effectively are issues which ensure that tagging remains a controversial topic (Whitfield, 1997: 51). In England and Wales, however, early indications are that costs will be offset by the potential savings per annum in terms of the net reduction in the prison population (Dodgson et al, 2001).

Aside from compliance rates and the financial implications, electronic tagging has significant limitations which may reduce its effectiveness in controlling future offending and ultimately in protecting children. It can only ever tell the police or probation services where the offender is at a given time and not what he is doing. In common with registration, the worst offenders, who may not worry about the prospect of apprehension as long as they are able to commit a further offence, will find a way around the schemes. In the cases of drug or sexual offences, for

---

[35] Research on the Scottish experience is also less optimistic. Results from pilot schemes found that it was rare for orders to be completed without at least some breach of their requirements. This was particularly so in the case of young offenders and those with serious criminal records (Bromfield Smith, 2001).

example, electronic monitoring may be able to prevent an offender from committing these offences on the street, but it cannot keep offenders from committing such acts in their own homes (Thomas, 1989). There is the added problem that the offender will simply remove the tracking device, rendering the entire scheme virtually useless.

In addition, there are particular dangers in using tagging exclusively or mainly for sex offenders (Walter et al, 2001). The tagging device, if clearly visible, could lead the public to immediately identify someone as a sex offender, perhaps mistakenly, and could lead to community hostility and attacks on suspected sex offenders. In this vein, the use of this device may bring with it the unwanted problems of stigmatisation and disintegrative public shaming which have been more clearly associated with sex offender registration and shame penalties as outlined at the outset of this and in the previous chapter.

Ethical and Legal Concerns

Electronic monitoring also raises a number of difficult issues such as the ethics of this type of coercive surveillance, the extension of social control, the intrusiveness of equipment and whether its embarrassing and degrading aspects amount to an infringement of basic civil liberties (Whitfield, 1997: 79). Home detention schemes, in particular, may have a negative impact on the offender's family (Gibbs, 2003). Enforced curfew hours may mean that domestic and family pressures increase and that lifestyles change. This may drive some offenders to sedentary and escapist activities at home, including domestic violence (Walter et al, 2001).

The constitutionality of electronic monitoring has never been successfully challenged in the United States where the courts have generally viewed the measure as an enhancement of supervision. Arguments that it might be an infringement of an offender's right to privacy, as well as guarantees against self-incrimination, unlawful search and seizure and cruel and unusual punishment, are all undermined by the consensual nature of taggling. It may be argued, as is the case with chemical castration, that an offender can never truly give consent to the order since it rests on his perception that any alternative, such as prison, is likely to be worse. Nevertheless, the offender's consent forms the basis for allowing the operating authority to intrude into the offender's life and home.

The measure, however, may also be susceptible to challenge under Article 5 of the European Convention on Human Rights, as outlined above and below in relation to sexual offences prevention orders and secure accommodation respectively. This provides that no one shall be deprived of the right to liberty and security of person except in a limited range of circumstances[36] and in accordance with a procedure prescribed by law.[37] In fact, at the time of the enactment of the original

---

[36] Art 5(1)(a)–(f).

[37] The emphasis in Art 5 on due process of law in relation to the deprivation of liberty overlaps with the more general and comprehensive protection for procedural due process granted by Art 6.

sex offender orders, such human rights considerations prompted the Government to resist a further opposition amendment which would have enabled magistrates to impose positive obligations on sex offenders, namely electronic tagging and a requirement that the offender is forced to remain in a given place for a specified period.[38] However, the European Court of Human Rights has held that a person placed under police supervision, including a curfew, suffered only a 'restriction of liberty.'[39] The Commission has also taken the view that an individual who is prevented from leaving a particular area by a curfew or order has not been deprived of his liberty.[40] It may be, however, that there is a fine dividing line between deprivation of liberty, as specifically prohibited by Article 5, and restrictions on freedom of movement.[41] The distinction, in fact, is by no means clear-cut and remains one of degree and not one of nature or substance (Murdoch, 1993: 495; Harris et al, 1995: 97–99).[42] Whether a deprivation of liberty has occurred in a particular case within the scope of Article 5, as opposed to a mere restriction on freedom of movement, will depend on the individual situation of the person as well as on the circumstances in which he has been placed, including the type, duration, effects and manner of implementation of the measure in question.[43]

Public attitudes to tagging, however, remain cautiously positive. Support for tagging in one American study was described as 'strong but conditional,' where conditions were related to how and why it was used, offence seriousness and the actual extent to which offenders are monitored (Brown and Elrod, 1995). In a more recent New Zealand study, home detention was also viewed positively and there was a broad acceptance of electronic monitoring and a high level of tolerance for such coercive private surveillance (Gibbs, 2003). Indeed, electronic monitoring has arrived at a time when the pressure to become tougher, more controlling and more restrictive has affected the whole of the criminal justice system (Whitfield, 1997: 54), not least in relation to sex offenders. Until this changes, tagging could have an integral and significant role to play in the management of sex offenders in the community. Tagging has both punishment and control features— the significance of the tag lies in its ability to act, not only as a constraint on patterns of behaviour in the community, but to reinforce the consequences of

[38] See, eg: Alun Michael, HC *Standing Committee on the Crime and Disorder Bill*, 5 May 1998.
[39] *Raimondo v Italy* (1994) 18 EHRR 237.
[40] *Greek Case* (1969) 12 YB 1.
[41] The deprivation of liberty can generally be distinguished from the 'right to liberty of movement' which is governed by Art 2 of Protocol 4 to the Convention. Restrictions on movement may take the form of limitation of residence to a particular town or district, or prohibition of visits to or residence in certain places, or of journeys for certain purposes. This Article has not been enacted as a Convention right under the Human Rights Act 1998.
[42] *Guzzardi v Italy* (1980) 3 EHRR 333, para 33; *Ashingdane v United Kingdom* (1985) 7 EHRR 528, para 19. Note, however, that Treschel (1980) argues that Art 5 does not protect against mere restrictions on the liberty of movement on the basis that the Fourth Protocol to the Convention was added specifically to do just that, and would have been unnecessary if Art 5 had been considered to cover restrictions on the liberty of movements.
[43] *Guzzardi v Italy*, see n 42 above, para 92, adopting the language of *Engel and others v Netherlands (No 1)* (1976) 1 EHRR 647, para 59.

particular actions—and the two can never be completely separated. In common with the shame penalties outlined at the outset of this chapter, it is this punitive element, in particular, which may give the measure populist appeal.

Despite the plethora of legislation which exists to facilitate the effective management of sex offenders in the community, further reform and expansion of the legislative framework seem inevitable. As noted in chapter 4, in the wake of the 'Soham Murders' and the subsequent revelations that Ian Huntley was previously known to the police for sexual offences, the resulting report of the Bichard Inquiry (Bichard, 2004) made a number of recommendations concerning improved information and intelligence systems, most of which have yet to be implemented. As also noted in chapter 4, the more recent 'sex offenders in school row,' also indicate that in the United Kingdom at least we are likely to see the enactment of further legislation to control the activities of both known and suspected sex offenders.

As argued at the outset of the book, given the wide variation of measures used to control sex offenders in the community, the current focus of criminal justice policy and practice is arguably on a 'what works' approach. When it comes to sexual offences, however, particularly those against children, the traditional regulatory framework does not seem to be working. This is evidenced by a number of factors—by statistical evidence showing the increase in sexual offences generally[44]; by media coverage of high profile cases; and by the acknowledged weaknesses inherent in much of the legislation. The failings of current control in the community mechanisms, as outlined in this and the previous chapter, point to the need to think more constructively about alternative responses to the problem of sex offender risk management and reintegration. In the interim, a natural question is what can be done with more persistent offenders who remain resistant to traditional methods of community control.

WHAT HAPPENS WHEN CONTROL IN THE COMMUNITY FAILS?

There are also a number of other more stringent measures which are generally regarded as options of last resort where the mainstream legislative mechanisms have failed. Such measures can potentially be used with the small number of serious sex offenders who are thought to represent such a high-risk of reoffending that these additional measures are justified. It has been argued that when the taboos of childhood sexuality are violated:

> [P]unishments that we accept in almost no other circumstance—physical mutilation, hormonal alteration and total ostracism from society—are readily dreamt up and effected (Kleinhams, 2002: 233).

---

[44] As noted in ch 1, recorded crime statistics show that the total number of recorded sexual offences has increased by 9.6% in the period 1999/2000 to 2001/2002 and by 94.4% in the last 25 years ('Recorded Crime Statistics: 1898–2001/02', <http://www.homeoffice.gov.uk/rds/pdfs/100years.xls>). Moreover, Home Office research reveals that actual recidivism rates for sexual offenders are 5.3 times the official reconviction rate (Falshaw et al, 2003).

Such criminal justice approaches to the 'punishment' of paedophilic sex offenders include chemical castration, secure accommodation and indeterminate detention. Closer examination of these measures, however, indicates that they also face important ethical or legal questions and serious practical limitations.

Chemical Castration

Although chemical castration is in use in the United States and several European countries, it has not been implemented on a widespread basis anywhere in the United Kingdom, and there are no plans yet to introduce it. However, since it provides another means of managing sex offenders in the community, there is merit in exploring its meaning, origins, and application in other jurisdictions.

What is Castration and Who is it Suitable For?

Castration may be performed in one of two ways. One is through the use of a surgical procedure. The other is through the administration of pharmacological treatments. Surgical castration, or 'orchiectomy', involves the removal of the male testes to diminish sex drive (Vanderzyl, 1994: 115–16).[45] Compulsory physical castration has been widely practised for thousands of years as a method of punishment for sexual crime[46] and as a form of compulsory sterilisation to prevent undesirable procreation.[47] Surgical castration, however, is an extreme and permanent procedure which makes it an unlikely alternative to prison on humanitarian and civil liberty grounds (Loveland, 1996: 744).

'Chemical castration' on the other hand, first tested in the early 1960s at Johns Hopkins University (Money, 1970: 165), is a non-surgical, reversible procedure. Essentially, it involves the offender being given anti-androgens, in tablet or injection form, to suppress hormonal and sexual activity (Melella et al, 1989: 225; Stadler, 1997: 1289–94). Today, the most common treatment involves the administration of medroxyprogesterone acetate (MPA), a synthetic progesterone manufactured under the trade name 'Depo-Provera.'[48] Offenders typically receive 300–400 milligram doses every 7–10 days (Bradford, 1983; Fitzgerald, 1990: 6).

[45] It can also mean the removal of a woman's ovaries.

[46] In the Middle Ages, individuals were castrated as a punishment for rape or adultery according to the *lex talionis*, the primitive law embodied in the phrase 'an eye for an eye, a tooth for a tooth' (Heim and Hursch, 1979: 281–82). In the US, castration of prisoners began from the mid-nineteenth century (Baker, 1984: 375–79). By virtue of a law enacted in 1855, black men in Kansas who raped, attempted to rape, or tried to force marriage on white women were punished by castration.

[47] Compulsory sterilisation gained popularity in the late nineteenth century as part of the eugenics movement. Legislation was first enacted in the US in 1905 and by 1942 a total of 32 states had enacted compulsory sterilisation measures. However, after the revelation of the horrors of Hitler's attempt to create a 'Master Aryan Race,' compulsory sterilisation was virtually discarded by civilised society. There are currently only 10 US states with such statutes (Floyd, 1990; Ghent, 1990; Adler, 1996: 1335–42; Stadler, 1997: 1306–11).

[48] *American Medical Association, Physicians Desk Reference,* 2263 (52nd ed, 1998).

With this treatment the uncertainties posed by experimental surgery are eliminated. It reduces an offender's impulses to sexually assault others without the negative connotations associated with surgical castration.

The drug inhibits the sex drive and sexually dangerous behaviour by reducing the production of testosterone and lowering androgen levels in the bloodstream (Berlin and Meinecke, 1981; Bradford, 1983; Fitzgerald, 1990). Clinically, Depo-Provera diminishes the frequency and intensity of compulsive erotic fantasy (Gagne, 1981: 645–46; Bradford, 1983: 163–64), and reduces aggressive behaviour generally (Fitzgerald, 1990: 2–3). This produces what researchers call a 'sexual calm,' which is believed to reduce the occurrence of repeat offences (Carpenter, 1998: 440). Various side effects, however, have been reported. Some suggest that the side effects are medically significant and harmful, requiring sparing use of the drug (Freeman-Longo and Wall, 1986: 58). The few documented side effects, however, are believed to be fully reversible with termination of treatment (Fitzgerald, 1990: 7; Icenogle, 1994: 298).

In order to target resources effectively, comprehensive psychological pre-screening is an essential prerequisite of the process (Berlin and Meinecke, 1981: 601–2). The pivotal criterion in calculating the treatability of a sex offender is his acknowledgement that his conduct is intolerable and beyond his control. An offender who feels remorse or guilt, but who is unable to 'control' his behaviour is more likely to respond to Depo-Provera treatment than the individual with little regard for the damage he has done (Peters, 1993: 313). Accordingly, therapists have found that paraphiliacs,[49] who demonstrate a pattern of sexual arousal accompanied by a distinctive fantasy or its achievement, are excellent candidates for this treatment.[50]

Today, several countries have some form of legislation that provides for castration of habitual sex offenders (Russell, 1997; Carpenter, 1998). The use of surgical castration as a treatment for sex offenders to stop them from reoffending has been statutorily regulated in several European countries since the late nineteenth century (Heim and Hursch, 1979; Russell, 1997: 440–45). Chemical castration also remains popular in countries such as Sweden, Denmark, Germany, Norway, Finland and Czechoslovakia. In the United States, legislation providing for mandatory chemical castration of paraphiliac child sex offenders, often as a condition of probation and in combination with counselling as part of an overall

---

[49] A paraphilia is a sexual deviation disorder. Recognised paraphilias include voyeurism, exhibitism, fetishism, erotic sadism, sexual masochism and paedophilia (sexual attraction to children) (Berlin and Meineke, 1981: 601).

[50] American experts have classified sex offenders into three other types, which are not mutually exclusive (Fitzgerald, 1990: 4–5; Stadler, 1997: 1288–94): Type I offenders deny the perpetration of the crimes; Type II admit to the offence, but blame their criminal behaviour on non-sexual or non-personal forces, eg, drugs or alcohol; Type III are violent and appear to be prompted by non-sexual reasons, eg, anger, power or violence. As they are generally acting out of other criminal impulses, it is thought that therapy which concentrates on the diminution of one's sex drive holds little promise for these groups.

treatment programme,[51] was enacted first in California[52] (Stadler, 1997) and Montana[53] and then in several other states[54] (Peters, 1993: 313–15; Lombardo, 1997; Murray, 1998). In the United Kingdom, the use of chemical castration has been confined to a small number of difficult cases where offenders actually requested the procedure (Vanderzyl, 1994: 107–8; Russell, 1997: 431–32; Carpenter, 1998: 444).[55] With the exception of California, all the above mentioned laws contemplate castration on a voluntary basis.

As will be outlined further below, however, in the United States in particular castration has not met with a favourable reception. Public policy arguments continue to rage over the use of castration as a punishment, or a treatment, for repeat sex offenders. Legislative proponents have seized on recidivism research which demonstrates the prison system's ineffective deterrence and the diminished likelihood of reoffending following the chemical treatment (Stadler, 1997: 1294–99; Carpenter, 1998). Others, however, believe that castration in whatever form is a barbaric form of punishment and advocate its absolute prohibition (Peters, 1993: 309–10).

Practical Issues

Statistics with regard to the effects of surgical castration are generally favourable. Older European studies found that recidivism rates were dramatically lowered (ranging from 1.3 to 7.44 per cent) when compared with a control group (which could range from 50 to 84 per cent) (Bremer, 1959; Heim and Hursch, 1979; Ortmann, cited in Baker, 1984: 385; Berlin and Krout, 1986).[56] Opinions regarding the effectiveness of chemical castration, however, are varied and controversial. Proponents of the chemical treatment contend that it has virtually the same effect on testosterone levels as surgical castration (Murray, 1998: 735). Indeed, the majority of studies assert that Depo-Provera treatment has proven highly effective for paraphiliacs, in reducing recidivism levels and controlling deviant sexual

[51] Eg: in response to the outcry over sexual abuse, the Roman Catholic Church in the US began a programme for paedophile priests in 1985 at the St Luke Institute using a combination of counselling and chemical treatment (Russell, 1997: 432).

[52] Act of 17 Sept 1996, Ch.596, 1996 Cal. Legis. Serv. 2711–12 (West). Codified at *Cal. Penal Code* § 645 (West Supp. 1996).

[53] *Mont. Stat. Ann.* § 45-5-512 (1997).

[54] Eg: following this lead, Florida (Act of 30 May 1997, *1997 Fla. Sess. Law Serv.*, Ch.97–184 (West 1997)) and Georgia (1997 *Ga. Laws* 484 (West 1997) have enacted similar legislation aimed at sex offenders. Texas became the first state to offer sex offenders surgical castration in prison ('Texas Sex Offenders Offered Castration' *The Times*, 22 May 1997).

[55] See, eg: the cases of Mark Whitman ('Sex Offender Sues Mental Health Act Commission On Drug Withdrawal' *The Guardian*, 4 December 1990; 'Paedophile Cannot Sue Watchdog Over Veto On Chemical Castration' *The Guardian*, 12 July 1991); and a second offender known only as Tom ('Castration Was My Cure' *The Sunday Telegraph*, 24 July 1994).

[56] Other studies have produced less positive results, eg, a German study of 39 sex offenders who agreed to voluntary surgical castration while imprisoned, found that the sexual responsiveness of castrated males varied considerably and that the effect of castration on male sexuality is not predictable with any certainty (Heim, 1981).

behaviour (Berlin and Meinecke, 1981). A leading study, conducted by Dr Fred Berlin at John Hopkins University (Berlin and Malin, 1991), found that recidivism rates among 600 paraphiliacs after treatment with a testosterone reducing chemical ranged from less than 3 to 10 per cent. Other studies have produced similar results: lower recidivism rates in paedophiles of as little as 5 per cent (Besharov and Vachhs, 1992); one relapse in six months out of 22 treated paraphiliacs in a US study (Kravitz et al, 1995); and one new offence in four years among 26 Danish subjects at the Herstedvester Penal Institute.[57] In most of these studies, chemical castration was administered in conjunction with some form of therapy or counselling. Indeed, many experts insist that offenders are more responsive to individual and group psychotherapy when this is combined with chemical treatment (Fitzgerald, 1990: 8–9; Icenogle, 1994: 284–85).[58]

These generally positive results, however, are subject to a number of obvious caveats which may undermine the overall effectiveness of chemical castration as a response to sexual offending. First, chemical castration is only a short-term temporary solution. Most treatments will merely suspend the offender's hormonal activity so that full sexual inclination will return after the cessation of treatment (Fitzgerald, 1990: 7; Icenogle, 1994: 298). Secondly, as noted above, the treatment is limited in its applicability to certain types of offender, most notably 'paraphiliacs' (Fitzgerald, 1990: 4–5; Stadler, 1997: 1288–94). As such, since it is aimed at decreasing sex drive, it may not be an effective solution for many sex offenders. Thirdly, experts agree that willing co-operation is an important element in the process, since chemical castration, like treatment generally, is most effective on subjects who have participated voluntarily and genuinely want to change their behaviour (Fitzgerald, 1990: 4–5; Stadler, 1997: 1294). However, given the offender's limited options, the question also arises as to whether consent can ever truly be given due to the 'inherently coercive nature' (Vanderzyl, 1994: 121–22) of the choice between treatment and the total deprivation of liberty (Green, 1986: 16; Peters, 1993). Fourthly, there are no definitive and reliable instruments of measurement for determining the treatment's effectiveness. In some studies, it may be difficult to assert definitively that improvement in the reoffending rate is due to the chemical drug, psychotherapy or other factors related to treatment (Stadler, 1997: 1293). Many studies have simply relied on offenders to self-report truthfully all their deviant sexual behaviour.[59] Fifthly, much of the debate to date appears to have focused exclusively on male sexual offenders. Indeed, both the surgical and chemical procedures have largely been developed with men in mind. If injected into females, Depo-Provera has no effect on the sex drive but only prevents

[57] 'Danes Favour Chemical Castration' *Tulsa World*, 1 September 1996.

[58] However, the reliability of these studies has been questioned. Some commentators have noted that research design flaws taint the results of both chemical and surgical castration studies (Heim, 1981: 18; Baker, 1984: 386; Green, 1986: 7).

[59] While self-reporting is an acknowledged weakness of recidivism studies in general (Abel et al, 1987), the results of the castration studies may be even more skewed where the subjects are prisoners released on parole or on licence who may be less willing to report their sexual offences or fantasies accurately out of fear of being returned to prison (Kiersch, 1990; Brody and Green, 1994: 352).

procreation. This may be a significant failing since increasing numbers of female paedophiles are being discovered every year (Loveland, 1996: 744). Sixthly, cost and the need for an appropriate infrastructure in terms of resources and suitably qualified medical personnel are further factors which may make the whole process prohibitive. One such projection indicated that the cost of administering Depo-Provera to offenders released in a given year would be $166, 600.[60] Finally, state officials and doctors, particularly in the United States, may be reluctant to perform the procedures because of the spectre of liability (Russell, 1997: 457). One possible reservation for doctors surrounds the blurring of the line between punishment and treatment associated with castration.

Ethical and Legal Concerns

Even as society abhors the sexual abuse of children, people hold individual and conflicting views with regard to the best way to eradicate sexual violence without infringing on the rights of the offender. While critics are concerned primarily with the civil and human rights implications of chemical castration (Fitzgerald, 1990: 39–44; Cohen, 1995), voluntary castration appears to jump these hurdles.[61] Indeed, the context in which Depo-Provera treatment is given is critical to both its legality and its ethical usage in treating sex offenders (Berlin, 1989; Peters, 1993: 315).

The main civil rights issues surrounding chemical castration in the United States have arisen through a number of constitutional challenges all of which involve the common theme of individual freedom: First, that the drug's interference with an offender's sexual fantasies implicates the right to mental autonomy, a subset of the freedom of speech protected by the First Amendment.[62] Secondly, that chemical castration breaches the Eighth Amendment's prohibition on cruel and unusual punishment.[63] Thirdly, that chemical castration raises both substantive due process and equal protection concerns[64] under the Fourteenth Amendment. It temporarily sterilises women, thereby implicating the fundamental right to procreate, and temporarily sterilises women but not men, thereby implicating the Equal Protection Clause. Fourthly, it contravenes the right to privacy[65] and bodily integrity which encompasses the right to procreative freedom[66] by its effect on the male sex drive and the right to refuse medical treatment.[67] The

---

[60] *Cal. Senate Rules Committee, Analysis Of Senate Floor Bill No 3339* (15 August 1996).

[61] Such considerations have arisen especially in the context of the US where probation generally cannot be imposed unless the offender knowingly and voluntarily accepts it (Green, 1986: 15; Fitzgerald, 1990: 17–18; Ginzberg, 1992).

[62] *Rennie v Klein* (462 F Supp. 1131, DNJ (1978)).

[63] See n 62 above.

[64] *Skinner v Oklahoma* (316, US 535 (1942)).

[65] *Griswold v Connecticut* (381 US 479 (1965)).

[66] See n 62 above.

[67] *Rennie v Klein*, see n 62 above; *Rogers v Okin* (478 F Supp 1342 (D Mass 1979)); *Washington v Harper* (494 US 210 (1990)); *Cruzan v Harper* (497 US 261 (1990)).

greater number of these challenges have been levelled against the California legislation (Symonds, 1980; Green, 1986: 18–25. Melella et al, 1989; Lombardo, 1997; Stadler, 1997; Murray, 1998).[68]

For the majority of American commentators, however, Depo-Provera treatment does not violate any of the offender's constitutional rights (Rainear, 1984: 199–223; Fitzgerald, 1990: 31–52; Fromson, 1994: 326–29; Peters, 1993: 318–25). Autonomy and integrity remain intact, as the treatment is not so intrusive as to infringe on one's thoughts or ideas. Nor does treatment violate the Eighth Amendment when used for a legitimate medical purpose. Furthermore, given that the offender is usually presented with a choice, the offender's right to privacy remains inviolate.

Similar issues arise through an examination of human rights issues under the European Convention on Human Rights. Potential challenges to chemical castration could be raised primarily under Articles 3 and 8 which provide for the prohibition on torture, inhuman and degrading treatment and the respect for private and family life respectively. The European Court has made it clear that Article 3 enshrines one of the most fundamental values of a democratic society.[69] The prohibition is in absolute terms and derogation is never justifiable for any reason, even that of the highest public interest.[70] It appears that free and informed consent, however, will be a defence to a claim of violation in the case of medical treatment.[71]

Indeed, it is argued that chemical castration is a legitimate form of treatment and not punishment. When administered on a voluntary basis it does not amount to inhuman or degrading treatment, and as such is entirely compatible with civil and human rights (Peters, 1993: 319–23).[72] In fact there are tangible benefits for society as well as the offender which may negative such concerns. It offers considerable rehabilitative value in treating paraphiliac sex offenders when used as part of an ongoing therapeutic programme (Melella et al, 1989: 225; Icenogle, 1994: 285), and is no longer considered experimental (Berlin, 1989: 235; Peters, 1993: 319). It makes the offender more amenable to therapy and if the treatment results in lower recidivism rates, it can be argued that the benefits of Depo-Provera far outweigh any short-term adverse side effects. Opponents argue that imprisonment would be a less restrictive and intrusive alternative. On the other hand, offenders undergoing this treatment, together with therapy are more likely to be rehabilitated and less likely to repeat the crime and will thus be spared the

---

[68] See n 52 above.

[69] *Soering v United Kingdom* (1989) 11 EHRR 439, para 88; *Chabal v United Kingdom* (1966) 23 EHRR 413, para 79.

[70] *D v United Kingdom* (1997) 24 EHRR 423.

[71] *X v Denmark* (1983) 32 Dr 282, Em HR.

[72] In the United States, federal court decisions, however, have virtually eliminated any distinction between treatment and punishment for the purpose of Eighth Amendment analysis (Peters, 1993: 319). For example, *Knecht v Gillman* (488 F2d 1136 at 1139–40 (8th Cir 1973)) established that it was cruel and unusual punishment when a behavioural modification programme at a medical facility for the criminally insane used a drug which induced vomiting, since, because it is a painful and debilitating experience, the drug had no therapeutic value.

debilitating effects of incarceration (Peters, 1993: 315–16; Icenogle, 1994: 300; Murray, 1998: 751). This in turn not only provides long-term public safety but increased freedom for the offender. Offenders will receive help to control their behaviour and can return to the community under supervision where they can maintain social and family ties. As outlined throughout this work in relation to 'reintegrative shaming' (Braithwaite, 1989), these social bonds may themselves contribute to offender integration by helping them to readjust to society. Indeed, as will be argued in chapter 7, chemical castration may have a practical role to play in reintegrative shaming practices in helping the offender to desist as part of a comprehensive community treatment and support programme.

A case under Article 3 may also raise issues in connection with Article 8, where the emphasis has been placed primarily on the Article 8 claim.[73] The European Court has also stressed that the right to physical and moral integrity, guaranteed by Article 8, comes into play even though it is not so severe as to amount to inhuman treatment under Article 3.[74] As discussed in the previous chapter, several areas have been considered by the Court to form part of 'private life' for Article 8 purposes. 'Private life' covers the physical and moral integrity of the person. It therefore includes physical or sexual assault,[75] corporal punishment[76] and a compulsory blood[77] and urine test.[78]

However, as outlined previously, Article 8 rights are qualified rather than absolute. Derogation is permitted in a number of circumstances, including 'public safety . . . and the protection of rights and freedoms of others.' Given the tangible benefits which Depo-Provera treatment has for the offender in helping him to desist, it is argued that interference with or restriction of privacy rights by the state would be justified as being in accordance with the law and necessary in a democratic society in support of one of these legitimate aims. These could include the state's interest in rehabilitating sex offenders thereby preventing sexual crime, ensuring public safety and protecting the rights and freedoms of not only the public, but those of the offender as well. In any case, once more, it is argued that Depo-Provera treatment does not infringe the offender's rights when they self-elect for the procedure (Peters, 1993: 322–23).[79]

Secure Accommodation

The option of secure accommodation for sex offenders, as the name suggests, involves the use of a secure residential facility, often with a treatment remit. There

---

[73] *Marco v Belgium* (1979) 2 EHRR 330; *X and Y v Netherlands* (1985) 8 EHRR 235.
[74] *Raninen v Finland* (1997) 26 EHRR 563.
[75] *X and Y v Netherlands*, see n 73 above.
[76] *Costello-Roberts v United Kingdom* (1993) 19 EHRR 112, Com Rep, para 49.
[77] *X v Austria* (1979) 18 DR 154, Ecomm HR.
[78] *Peters v Netherlands* (1994) 77-A DR Em HR.
[79] If there is no infringement of Art 8, however, it is unlikely that there will be a breach of Art 3 (*Oslo v Sweden (No 1)* (1988) 11 EHRR 259; *Hendricks v Netherlands* (1983) 5 EHRR 223).

are a number of such secure units in use in England and Wales. This measure represents a sort of 'half-way house' between prison and the community. Long-term preventive detention in prison, as will be discussed further below, in the absence of the commission of further offences, may not be a morally defensible option. Equally, an open hostel environment without a sustained form of intensive supervision and control of the offender's movements and activities would fail to appropriately manage the risk sex offenders are seen as presenting and may ultimately jeopardise public safety. Such a measure, it is generally believed, should not be of blanket use with all sex offenders, but only with the small number of dangerous sex offenders who pose a long-term risk and for whom reintegration is virtually impossible. Indeed, it may be necessary to impose such a measure for those offenders who have failed to address their offending behaviour and cognitive distortions while in prison.

The option of placing the sex offender in secure accommodation on release from custody has dual benefits in providing effective protection for both the offender and the community. It may protect the offender from harassment and abuse until such hysteria dies down, while at the same time it may also help him to adjust to the demands of living on the outside. Indeed, consideration of the measure in England and Wales has arisen mainly due to problems of vigilante attack on known or suspected paedophiles. Following his release from prison, the high profile sex offender Sydney Cooke, whose case was discussed above, was placed in such a facility as much for his own as society's protection.[80] Many sex offenders themselves, it seems, also realise that they are vulnerable to assault when released (Crawley and Sparks, 2006).

However, the segregation of high-risk or high profile sex offenders post-release in these specialist units, after the completion of their sentences, reinforces their social exclusion. By setting their living space apart from the rest of the community it underlines the idea that they are 'transinstitutionalized, from one site of social exclusion to the other' (Cowan et al, 2001; See also, Cowan and Gilroy, 1999). These are the unfortunate precursors to Braithwaite's (1989) 'disintegrative shaming' little or no effort is made to forgive offenders or affirm the basic goodness of their character and thus reinforce their membership in the community of law-abiding citizens. The significance of this symbolic or literal exile from the community is that the communal rejection of offenders and the treating of them as outcasts may ultimately provoke a rebellious and criminal reaction from them (Maxwell and Morris, 1999; Edwards and Hensley, 2001b; McAlinden, 2005).

Indeed, the widespread adoption of such a measure would also be likely to face opposition on both practical and civil liberties grounds. First, from a practical standpoint, as outlined in chapter 4, reassuring communities concerning the housing of sex offenders is almost impossible in the atmosphere of fear, panic, anger and anxiety which exists in relation to child sexual abusers. As such the establishment of a secure unit, which by its nature would be likely to house the

---

[80] 'Search Goes On To House Paedophile' *The Times,* 13 August 1998.

most difficult to manage if not the most dangerous sex offenders, would be likely to cause uproar in the local community. Community backlash could result from the belief that their estates are to become 'dumping grounds' for sex offenders (Cowan et al, 1999: 452; Stenson and Watt, 1999). Careful planning would therefore be needed to deal with community antagonism when its proposed existence became public. As will be discussed in chapter 8 in relation to potential problems with restorative or reintegrative justice, care would also have to be taken not to tip an estate into a downward spiral which would result in a given area being regarded as 'problem' by placing unwanted individuals in their area (Cowan et al, 2001: 452; Bottoms and Wiles, 2002: 644–51).

Secondly, in common with all these measures used to control or manage sex offenders in the community on release from custody, including sex offender registration outlined in the previous chapter, secure accommodation may amount to double jeopardy. Indeed, the measure may meet many of the objections countered against any form of preventive detention which will be discussed in the next section. In the main, there is a fundamental ethical dilemma as to whether an offender who has served his prison sentence should be further detained in this way. In this respect, Article 5 of the European Convention, as outlined above in relation to electronic tagging, again becomes relevant. This Article guarantees the fundamental right to liberty[81] and the security of the person which is at the heart of all political systems that abide by the rule of law.[82] The purpose of the Article is to protect the individual from arbitrary arrest and detention.[83] A person detained has the right to information as to reasons for detention,[84] to challenge the lawfulness of his detention,[85] and if successful, to obtain compensation for wrongful detention.[86]

The right to physical liberty, however, as also noted above, is not absolute. It must give way where vital community interests are at stake. A prescribed exception is the detention of persons in special circumstances. Article 5(1)(e) permits the deprivation of liberty of, inter alia, persons of *unsound* mind. The detention must be lawful on substantive and procedural grounds and must not be arbitrary.[87] It has been said that the Convention allows the detention of persons in these categories, not only because they are considered as potentially dangerous for public safety, but because their own interests may necessitate their detention.[88] Indeed, this is a twin aim of secure accommodation as outlined above. However,

---

[81] By 'liberty' is meant physical liberty: see *Engel and others v Netherlands*, see note 43 above, para 58; Treschel (1980); Fawcett (1987: 69). 'Security' is also to be understood in the context of physical liberty: *East African Asians v United Kingdom* (1981) 3 EHRR 76, 89.

[82] *Winterwerp v Netherlands* (1979) 2 EHRR 387, para 37; *Brogan v United Kingdom* (1988) 11 EHRR 17, para 58.

[83] *Engel and others v Netherlands* see note 43 above, para 58; *Bozano v France* (1986) 9 EHRR 297, para 54.

[84] Art 5(2).

[85] Art 5(4).

[86] Art 5(5).

[87] *Winterwerp v Netherlands*, see n 82 above, para 39.

[88] *Guzzardi v Italy* (1980), see n 42 above, para 98.

this latter reason is difficult to justify unless the person in question is mentally incompetent to make decisions on his own behalf. The provision has been applied in cases dealing with the detention of psychiatric patients.[89] Where the person to be detained is competent and of *sound* mind it is likely that, in the absence of consent, the use of secure accommodation with sex offenders would violate Article 5 of the Convention.

Indeterminate Detention

In the United States and the United Kingdom, indeterminate detention has been developed as a further legislative response to deal with high-risk violent and sexual offenders who have proven themselves to be resistant to the constraints traditionally imposed by the criminal justice system. The need for some form of protective sentencing arises because normally sex offenders serving custodial prison sentences cannot be detained after the expiry of their sentences. Such offenders, however, without the benefit of effective treatment programmes may emerge just as dangerous as when they went in.

A subcategory of this wider group is that of the sexual or violent offender who has some form of serious mental disorder or severe personality disorder which may be untreatable.[90] These offenders are not easily placed within either of the traditional categories of confinement—the mental health and criminal justice systems—they may have an illness which is not susceptible to effective treatment, while at the same time they may have committed no further offence. Indeed, as noted in chapter 4, there is a related debate as to whether sex offending is properly to be regarded as a crime requiring punishment or an illness requiring treatment in recognition of the fact that sex offenders will usually have some form of cognitive distortion. To use the crude terminology, sex offenders may not be easily classified as either 'mad' or 'bad'—in fact, they may be both. While these jurisdictions have both recognised these problems there are significant differences in approach.

Civil Commitment

The American response has been to develop a form of civil commitment for dangerous sex offenders within the mental health system after they have served their time in penal institutions (Alexander, 1995; Lieb et al, 1998). In the 1930s, several US states enacted statutes which provided for the civil commitment of certain classes of sex offender. Many of these statutes were repealed in the 1960s following campaigns by civil libertarians, but were later re-enacted in the 1980s in response

---

[89] See n 87 above.

[90] Psychiatrists are often split over the treatment of people with personality disorder where there is a lack of consensus in particular about treatability (Collins, 1991; Cope, 1993; Benjamin, 1997; Sanislow and McGlashan, 1998) and the most appropriate setting (Links, 1996, 1998; Melia, 1999; Norton and Hinshelwood, 1996).

to burgeoning public concern over recidivism rates. In the interim period, several states such as Washington[91] (La Fond, 1992; Scheingold et al, 1992) and Minnesota[92] (Blakey, 1996), kept these laws on their statute books although they were utilised somewhat sporadically (Erlinder, 1993).

The control of sex offenders has therefore been extended beyond the criminal and into the civil context. The principal concern with such measures, however, is the use of the mental health as opposed to the traditional justice system to manage offending behaviour (Alexander, 1995). It is this punitive element in a system which is otherwise premised on treatment and therapeutic principles which gives rise to civil liberties and human rights concerns (Lafond, 1992). Indeed, in the United States such measures have been constitutionally challenged on equal protection and due process grounds where it has been argued unsuccessfully that they were incompatible with the ethos of care (Fujimoto, 1992; Blakey, 1996).[93] These measures, therefore, also appear to single sex offenders out as being different from other types of offender, the justification once more being the special risk that they are seen to present. As will be discussed further below, they are based very clearly on the sentencing philosophy of incapacitation with clear aims of public protection and harm prevention, where the concept of dangerousness is used to assess, manage and minimise future risk.

Protective Sentencing

In the United Kingdom, the need for some form of protective sentencing for dangerous offenders has been recognised for a longer time. Persistent dangerous recidivists have been an intractable problem for almost a century. Legislative attempts to target dangerous people, however, tend either not to work at all or to impact on the wrong type of offender (Ashworth, 1983: 237; Kinzig, 1997: 25–27).

In 1908 a 'double track' system was introduced by the Prevention of Crime Act (Kinzig, 1997: 48–49). Habitual offenders could be sentenced to between 5 and 10 years preventive detention immediately following a prison sentence. This double track system survived for only 40 years. This was followed by the return of the 'single track' system of the Criminal Justice Act 1948. The system provided preventive detention for dangerous recidivists with a duration fixed between 5 and 14 years as a substitute to an ordinary prison sentence. The courts were also more than hesitant in applying this provision (Kinzig, 1997: 48–49)[94] and preventive detention was revoked by the Criminal Justice Act 1967. Until the Criminal Justice Act 1991

---

[91] Washington Revised Code Ann § 71.05.020, 71.09.020 & 71.09.060 (1992 & Supp 1995).

[92] Minnesota Stat Ann § 253B.02 (1994 & Supp 1995).

[93] See especially: *In re Young*, 122 Wash 2d 1, 857 P2d 989 (Wash 1993); *In re Blodgett*, 510 NW2d 910 (Minn 1994); *In re matter of Linehan*, 518 NW2d 609 (Minn 1994); *In re matter of Rickmeyer*, 519 NW2d 188 (Minn 1994).

[94] There is a fundamental tension here between the role of the legislature and the judiciary where there is often a marked judicial reluctance to fully implement legislation which provides for longer than commensurate sentences. For a discussion of these arguments in the UK context, see, eg: Henham (2001, 2003); for the New Zealand context, see, eg: Richardson and Freiberg (2001).

society's need for protection against dangerous recidivists[95] was addressed by so-called 'extended sentences' and life imprisonment (Padfield, 1996). The extended sentence, provided for by section 28 of the Power of Criminal Courts Act 1973, required at least three prior convictions and extended the tariff for offences by between 5 and 10 years. The main preoccupation was to prevent the offender from relapsing by providing appropriate treatment. Once released from an extended sentence the offender would be subjected to a much longer period of probation (Walker, 1985: 357; Kinzig, 1997: 49–50). However, the extension of the tariff was rarely used as judges had an aversion to this type of sanction since it resembled double punishment (Stockdale and Devlin, 1987: 162; Wasik and Taylor, 1991: 38; Kinzig, 1997: 50). Extended sentences were finally abolished by the 'twin track' approach of the Criminal Justice Act 1991. The life sentence was used from the 1960s onwards to confine dangerous people for an indefinite period if they had committed one of a list of offences[96] and it thus took over the role played by preventive detention (Kinzig, 1997: 53).

A number of documents, however, helped to revive the phenomenon of indeterminate sentencing for dangerous offenders. The Butler Committee recommended that indeterminate reviewable sentences should be introduced for dangerous offenders (Home Office et al, 1975). The Floud Committee (Floud and Young, 1981), which aimed at bringing protective sentencing under statutory control, also considered the issue of dangerousness. More recently, the report of the Fallon Inquiry into disturbances at Ashworth special hospital reopened the debate on how best to treat people with personality disorder (Fallon et al, 1999). Following the implementation of the 'twin track' approach of the Criminal Justice Act 1991, and the onset of a strong crime control 'law and order' ideology of incapacitation, a number of successive legislative amendments provided for some form of protective sentencing. These have included extending the 'normal sentence' for serious violent or sexual offenders[97]; automatic life sentences on conviction of a second serious offence[98]; and the re-enactment of extended sentences[99] and discretionary life sentences (Thomas, 1998; Henham, 2001).

The recent approach to the treatment and management of dangerous offenders, however, is a fluid one and is much more multifaceted in nature. In effect, there have been several recent changes to the sentencing framework and proposed amendments to the mental health legislation. Following a joint public consultation exercise (Home Office and Department of Health, 1999), the Dangerous

---

[95] English criminal law has rarely used the word 'dangerous', but rather the formulation 'persistent offender,' which is much closer to the American concept of 'habitual offender.' In contrast, Ashworth (1983: 230) prefers the three classifications of 'dangerous offenders,' 'professional criminals' and 'petty persistent offenders.'

[96] The discretionary life sentence may be imposed for a variety of offences, eg, sexual offences, armed offences, or offences against the person.

[97] s 80(2)(b) Powers of Criminal Courts (Sentencing) Act 2000 (formerly, s 2(2)(b) Criminal Justice Act 1991).

[98] s 109 of 2000 Act (formerly, s 2 Crime (Sentences) Act 1997).

[99] s 85 of 2000 Act (formerly, s 58 Crime and Disorder Act 1998).

People with Severe Personality Disorder Bill 2000, proposed the introduction of an indeterminate sentence for those with a dangerous severe personality disorder (DSPD). These proposals, which were heavily criticised on procedural and substantive grounds (McAlinden, 2001), were shelved to await a comprehensive review of the mental health legislation,[100] the outcome of which is still pending (Department of Health and Home Office, 2000; Fennell, 2001; Prins, 2001).

In the interim, Chapter 5 of Part 12 of the Criminal Justice Act 2003 has introduced a new sentence for dangerous offenders—an indeterminate sentence of imprisonment for public protection purposes[101]—for those who present a significant risk of serious harm to the public. This sentence replaces the automatic life sentence for a second serious offence whereby offenders would be detained indefinitely until it is considered that the risk of reoffending has sufficiently diminished (Henham, 2003; Padfield, 2003). Alongside these broader legislative and policy developments, the Government has pledged to provide at least 300 new DSPD places for such individuals (Home Office et al, 2005). Such preventive measures, however, whatever form they may take, raise a number of common practical questions and ethical and legal concerns (McAlinden, 2001).

Practical Issues

The first main issue arising is the fact that no comprehensive definition of dangerousness exists. Even the new legislation which attempts to make provision for 'the assessment of dangerousness'[102] simply says that the court will usually determine the degree of danger to the public on the basis of the nature and circumstances of the offence, an offender's criminal record and any other information about the offender (Murphy, 1995: 126; Thomas, 2004: 710). An examination of case law, however, shows that these criteria appear vague and elusive and the courts have failed to grasp the central issue, the assessment of the future risk of serious harm (Clarkson, 1997; Dingwall, 1998; Henham, 2001).[103] As one commentator put it:

> [T]he law does not provide a clear and certain definition of the 'magic ingredient' which transforms the ordinary wicked offender into a prisoner against whom the public must be given special protection (Baker, 1993: 540).

The principal danger arising from this situation is the arbitrary determination of dangerousness.

Research findings show that predictions of dangerousness are prone to overprediction. In the United States, five major investigations of the validity of clinical assessments of dangerousness have all highlighted the weaknesses in predictive

---

[100] See the Draft Mental Health Bill 2004.

[101] ss 225–26.

[102] s 229.

[103] See, eg: *R v Parole Board ex parte* Bradley [1990] 3 All ER 828 (DC); *R v Blackburn* (1979) 1 Cr App R (S) 205 (CA). Part of the difficulty, it seems, stems from requiring judges to weigh complex medical evidence alongside traditional legal criteria in the form of aggravating and mitigating factors (Henham, 2001: 709).

judgments. The *Baxtrom*[104] case is often cited as providing the most striking evidence of the gross inaccuracy of clinical predictions of dangerousness (Steadman and Cocozza, 1974). In an investigation of the behaviour of 246 insane criminals over a period of four years after their transfer to a civil hospital or discharge from custody, only 26 exhibited sufficiently violent behaviour to justify their return to secure hospitals, and of the 98 who were actually released into the community only two committed further serious crimes of violence. In the *Dixon*[105] case, only 14 per cent of former patients 'engaged in behaviour injurious to another person' within four years of their release (Thornberry and Jacoby, 1979). The third study examined reports made to the court by two psychiatrists in respect of a sample of defendants who were found incompetent to stand trial and assessed for dangerousness. The study found that those evaluated as dangerous were no more so than those evaluated as safe and that there was no significant difference between the two groups on any of the measures of violent behaviour that were examined (Cocozza and Steadman, 1976). In the remaining two studies the risk of unnecessary detention imposed on offenders by a protective sentence was shown to be considerable. Between half and two-thirds of the judgments of dangerousness that were put to the test were not borne out by subsequent harmful behaviour within the period of the investigations (Kozol et al, 1972; US State of Maryland, Department of Public Safety and Correctional Services, 1973).

In the United Kingdom, the Floud Committee found that clinical predictions of 'dangerousness' tended to be wrong more often than not, and that indeterminate sentences draw into the net more non-dangerous than dangerous offenders with a 'false positive rate' that has often reached two out of every three (Floud and Young, 1981; Wood, 1988; Morris, 1994). A largescale Home Office study by Brody and Tarling (1981) found that only 17 per cent of the dangerous offenders who had been released committed a further dangerous offence within five years. An extensive range of British and American studies confirm the problem of over-prediction (Bottoms and. Brownsword, 1982; Monahan, 1981; Greenwood, 1982; von Hirsch and Ashworth, 1996).[106] A comparative study of incapacitation policies in New Zealand, the United States and the United Kingdom revealed that the approach draws in vastly more offenders than ever go on to commit serious offences and yet paradoxically fails to identify correctly the small number of offenders who pose a genuine threat to the community (Brown, 1996). In a similar vein, a more recent Home Office study examined reconviction rates of serious sex offenders four and six years after they were released from long determinate sentences of imprisonment in comparison with those identified as 'high-risk' by their parole board (Hood et al, 2002). The proportion reconvicted for another sexual offence was relatively low:

---

[104] *Baxtrom v Herald* (1966), 388 US 107.

[105] *Dixon v Attorney General of Commonwealth of Pennsylvania* (1971), 225 F. Supp., 966.

[106] Note, however, that some studies have been criticised as having serious methodological weaknesses. The thrust of the criticism is that, although still of significant inaccuracy, assessments of dangerousness may be more accurate than the studies appear to suggest. See generally: Monahan (1973) and Prins (1990).

less than 10 per cent, even among those followed for six years. There was only one 'false negative,' but a significant number of 'false positives': 9 out of 10 of those thought to pose a 'high-risk' were not reconvicted of a sexual offence within four years of their release. Particularly prominent among them were offenders against children within their own family, suggesting that perhaps this category offender will not reoffend given appropriate levels of treatment and support.

Moreover, incarcerating a modest number of the most dangerous offenders appears to have had little effect on violent crime rates (Brody and Tarling, 1981; Zimring and Hawkins, 1995). Home Office Research calculates that a 25 per cent increase in imprisonment is necessary to reduce crime by 1 per cent (Home Office, 1986). On a long-term view, the utilitarian calculation may well go the other way due to the criminogenic effects of imprisonment (Greenwood, 1982; Blumstein et al, 1983).

There are also implications for the management of prisons. Incapacitative sentences will increase an already strained prison population and require the allocation of expensive prison space to offenders who are well past their peak ages of criminality (Tonry, 1988; Zimring and Hawkins, 1995). Aside from the fiscal costs, there is a wide range of literature on the effects of imprisonment on the individual where the psychological costs are deemed incalculable (Cohen and Taylor, 1981; Porporino and Zamble, 1984; Walker, 1987; Liebling, 1992; Flannagan, 1995). Inmates who face either a very long sentence or no possibility of release will find 'locations of resistance' (Mathieson, 1965) and have no incentive to conform to the disciplinary regime. As these inmates age there is also a need for increased medical services for an elderly inmate population.

Ethical and Legal Concerns

As noted in chapter 5, the main principled objection to incapacitation is that individuals are being punished not for what they have done but for what they might do in the hope of protecting future victims from harm (Wood, 1988: 424–33; Walker, 1996). This objection is particularly strong where the successful prediction rate is low. The more difficult question is whether the prediction should be given force if a fairly high prediction rate could be achieved. The Floud Committee thought that a 'just distribution of risk should result in the prolonged detention of high-risk offenders rather than an increased danger to victims (Floud and Young, 1981: 233–35). Wood (1988) has put the case for transfer to a form of civil detention if disproportionately long criminal sentences are thought inappropriate. This, as outlined above, is effectively what occurs in the United States in the case of sex offenders. In addition, as argued above, selective incapacitation has increasingly involved the unduly harsh sentencing of habitual offenders who commit non-violent crimes (von Hirsch, 1985; Ashworth, 1995: 167).

To the totality of principled objections to incapacitation generally must be added an array of specific ethical objections to the proposed measures. Such measures must be based on strong and tested evidence and sufficiently high and tightly defined definitions of dangerousness to justify the loss of liberty when set against personal or public safety. However, as outlined above, assessments of risk and dangerousness are in themselves highly difficult and uncertain processes. As the then Home Secretary acknowledged in relation to the original DSPD proposals, it is not 'a counsel of perfection'[107] and some people will undoubtedly slip through the net.

A further concern is that we could have a situation where an individual's civil rights were overlooked and where people were incarcerated and forgotten in the long term. The measures, therefore, must be subject to rigorous judicial procedures to ensure that people are not detained unnecessarily or in an arbitrary manner and to prevent miscarriages of justice occurring in their implementation. In this respect, these new measures may not comply with the European Convention on Human Rights. The fact that the sentence is not fixed by law and that there is no specific minimum review period may contravene Article 5 as the European Court has held that a period of eight weeks was too long to satisfy Article 5(4) which requires a 'speedy determination of lawfulness of detention.'[108] The Government has recognised that detaining people indefinitely on the basis that they pose a danger to society is a serious step. As such, they aim to ensure that the system will involve a robust system of checks and balances covering both legal and clinical issues. However, it seems impossible to envisage a situation in which the measures will be executed with 100 per cent accuracy and with no errors arising in their enforcement.

As acknowledged at the outset of this section, there undoubtedly is a small number of sex offenders for whom these additional measures may be justified. For the most part, however, it is argued that the wholehearted pursuit of such policies, which are used when the traditional justice mechanisms of control have failed, should be resisted. They will ultimately take us further down the undesirable road of harsh punitive retributive sanctions for sex offenders. Moreover, they reinforce the current populist thinking, which has in turn been reflected in the risk-based managerialist legislative and policy agenda, that concerns over sex offenders are best placed within the context of removing them from society or coercively restricting their behaviour rather than reintegrating or reforming them (Simon, 1998). For the vast majority of offenders, however, what is needed, as the next part of the book will argue, are reintegrative initiatives which will attempt to address the underlying causes of individual offending behaviour and engage offenders in the rehabilitation process at an early stage in their offending profile.

CONCLUSION

It has been argued that there are too many offenders subject to legislative control in the community mechanisms, via registration requirements for example, for

---

[107] Jack Straw, *Hansard* HC Deb, vol 325, cols 601–3 (15 February 1999).
[108] *E v Norway* (1994) 17 EHRR 30, para 66.

these measures to be serious policing options. At the same time, all such measures which focus attention almost exclusively on known sex offenders can hope to have little impact on the real problem and extent of child sexual abuse. Moreover, it has also been argued that the stigmatising effect of retributive measures, designed to control the whereabouts of sex offenders in the community, may impede their successful reintegration and lead ultimately to a return to offending behaviour. The sum of these difficulties then points toward the need to think more constructively and devise a more progressive and ultimately more effective response to the problem.

The aims of the criminal justice system vis-à-vis sex offenders are to prevent reoffending as well as punish the offender, yet the first objective is somewhat negated by the second (Geiran, 1996a: 153). Punishment of the sex offender by imprisonment, or the additional punishment of registration, notification or tagging, is only the first step (Finstad, 1990: 171; Vizard and Hawkes, 1997a: 7). Programmes must also be developed to treat and support the sex offender in the community, in order to prevent future offending.

Situational attempts to control sex offenders in the community, as discussed in this and the previous chapter, may make a contribution to the risk management process, but none of them is a panacea. What is needed is a real attempt to monitor the actual behaviour of sexual offenders in the community and not just their whereabouts. As will be discussed in the next chapter, a number of jurisdictions have adopted innovative reintegrative shaming practices with sex offenders with the broad aims of reducing the incidence of child sexual abuse, preventing future offending and reintegrating the offender back into society.

In this respect, Cohen's (1985) distinction between inclusionary and exclusionary visions of social control can be applied to the current state-led and, indeed, popular response to sex offenders. His exclusionary vision is based on 'the impulse to classify, separate, segregate and exclude' (1985: 225–26). Using this distinction, Cowan et al rightly argue that these processes of classification, separation, segregation and exclusion begin as soon as the sex offender enters the criminal justice system through, for example, segregation in prison and subsequent risk assessment and management procedures (2001: 451). In their view, as has also been discussed in this and previous chapters, these processes continue post-release, via control in the community measures such as sex offender registration, sexual offences prevention orders and risk of sexual harm orders and the segregation of offenders into social housing (Cowan et al, 1999, 2001), and also via the general ostracism by the local community. As Edwards and Henley argue:

> [T]he new penology has disjoined the sexual offender from every other type of criminal, while having ceremoniously and symbolically bestowed on him or her a permanent indelible and unforgivable stain that precludes any hope of redemption and transformation (2001a: 650).

The inclusionary vision, on the other hand, refers to forms of social control that are 'dispersed throughout the social body' usually by 'the more sophisticated method of "technological incapacitation"' (Cohen, 1985: 220, 222). It is this vision which is also encapsulated by Braithwaite's (1989) notion of 'reintegrative shaming.' As will be argued in the next and final part of the book, communitarian societies are better able to provide a more effective mechanism for sanctioning deviance and informally controlling sex offenders rather than the 'stigmatising shaming' (Braithwaite, 1989) of harsh formal penal responses, 'which both the formal justice system and wider society too readily perform' (Kirkegaard and Northey, 2000: 72).

PART III:
TOWARDS A RESTORATIVE OR REINTEGRATIVE APPROACH

7

Reintegrative Shaming Practices

T HIS CHAPTER OUTLINES some examples of reintegrative shaming practices with sex offenders. Although restorative or reintegrative practices for sex offenders are in short supply, a few have been developed, principally in Canada and parts of the United States, which emphasise both rehabilitative and reintegrative principles. These schemes have grown out of the shared association with the principles and practices of restorative community justice and reintegrative shaming in particular. Early evaluations of the effectiveness of the schemes, in terms of reducing sex offender recidivism and promoting both offender and community accountability and engagement with the reintegrative process, are also examined.

The chapter then examines how we could usefully move from theory to practice in implementing reintegrative shaming practices with sex offenders on a more widespread and holistic basis. This latter analysis addresses a number of key theoretical and practical issues: should schemes operate as an additional or an alternative form of justice and what would be the role of the formal criminal law in such processes?; how may the public be persuaded that this is an effective way of managing sex offenders in the community?; and how could the community play a more constructive role in helping statutory and voluntary agencies in the successful reintegration of the offender?

'STOP IT NOW!'

In the United States, several states have developed dynamic ways of treating and managing sex offenders in the community (Knopp, 1991: 191; Zehr, 1995: 208). There a number of well-known schemes such as 'The Safer Society Foundation'[1] (Knopp, 1991). The most widespread and developed, however, is perhaps 'The Stop It Now!' programme.[2]

---

[1] The Safer Society Foundation, sponsored by an association of churches, offers treatment programmes, for juvenile and adult sex offenders, which often take place in a residential setting. It calls for offender-specific interventions in the post-conviction phase, including education and training (Knopp, 1984, 1991). The scheme is based on the premise of 'restraint of the few very serious sex offenders' where the restraint used should be the least restrictive and most humane option for the shortest period of time in the most remedial and restorative environment (Knopp, 1991: 185–86).

[2] See: <http://www.stopitnow.com>.

This restorative outreach scheme for sex offenders was first established in Vermont by Fran Henry, a survivor of sexual abuse, but has since been developed in other areas of the country, including Georgia, Minnesota and Philadelphia. It is essentially a prevention programme which aims to educate the public about child sexual abuse and change attitudes and behaviour so that people are more open about abuse and can take appropriate steps to prevent it. It seeks to stop child sexual abuse by encouraging abusers and potential abusers to recognise their behaviour as abusive and to seek help, and by giving adults the necessary information to recognise the signs of abuse and about how to protect children effectively. As well as raising general awareness about sexual abuse, the programme therefore is targeted at a number of specific groups: adults who have abused or are thinking about abusing a child; parents of children and young people with worrying sexual behaviour; and family and friends of abusers to encourage them to support abusers and empower them to confront them when they exhibit inappropriate behaviour.

The campaign is based on the following core values which are fundamental to a reintegrative approach to managing the risk posed by sex offenders in the community and which lie at the heart of this book: (1) protecting children—by raising awareness and understanding of the nature and scale of sexual abuse and the ways in which abusers operate; (2) balancing understanding with accountability—by recognising that sex offenders are human beings, and not the monsters of popular imagination, who can be helped to stop their abusive behaviour, while at the same time holding them responsible for the harmful consequences of their actions; (3) developing a public health approach—acknowledging the scale of the problem of child sexual abuse requires a large-scale systematic social approach to prevention; and (4) working together—by building partnerships between statutory and voluntary agencies in the fields of child protection, criminal justice and health (including the courts, police, probation, social services, and housing) and also in developing links with the local community in specific project areas.

At a practical level, these aims and values are delivered through a number of projects which are tailored to the needs of the local community. Key elements include the following: (1) media campaigns to destroy some of the stigmas associated with abuse, educate adults about the nature of sexual abuse and the ways families and communities can stop it, and increase public awareness of the trauma of abuse; (2) public information leaflets explaining the nature of child sexual abuse, how to recognise it and seek help[3]; (3) training for professionals; (4) public meetings to promote discussion about child protection and the potential role of individuals and the community; and (5) a telephone helpline offering advice and support to people who suspect that someone they know presents a risk to a child and to those abusers seeking help to desist.

In addition to these local initiatives, a free confidential national helpline has also been set up. The trained helpline staff aim to encourage offenders to take respon-

---

[3] See, eg: < http://www.stopitnow.com/warnings.html>; <http://www.stopitnow.org.uk/publications.htm>.

sibility for their behaviour and to come forward and be assessed to see if they are suitable to undergo treatment. As well as offering confidential advice to callers, the project also helps them make contact with local child protection agencies and treatment resources. The programme, however, does not offer amnesty. It offers a way for the abuser to learn about treatment and have the support needed to stop the abuse through the current legal system.

Several studies have examined the effectiveness of this child sexual abuse prevention programme (Tabachnik and Chasan-Taber, 1999; Henry and Tabachnick, 2002; Klein and Tabachnik, 2002). One such study, for example, examined the numbers of offenders who self-elected or were nominated by others for the programme during the two year period from 1995–97. In Vermont, treatment providers reported that 50 persons reported for treatment. Of these, 11 were adults who self-reported and 39 were adolescents who entered treatment as a result of a parent or guardian soliciting help (Tabachnik et al, 2001). An earlier study in Vermont examined the extent to which those offenders who did enter the programme reoffended. This study found that without the appropriate treatment and support, 38 per cent of abusers returning to the streets abused again. With these initiatives in place, however, the incidence of reoffending dropped to 6 per cent.[4] As Pam Gatos, state-wide co-ordinator of the programme said at a conference held by Stop It Now!, which reiterates one of the central points made in this book:

> With the majority of these people, even if they go to prison, they will be released into the community. . . . To ensure community safety, we need to be able to support them . . . a sex abuser who is isolated and driven underground is much more likely to reoffend than one who has support in place in the community.[5]

The Stop It Now! programme has now been extended throughout the United States and further afield to the United Kingdom and Ireland. 'Stop it Now! UK & Ireland' is a major national and local campaign which, like its American counterpart, is also based on the primary aims of protection and prevention. A network of local projects have been developed in Surrey, Derbyshire Thames Valley, the Black Country and Northern Ireland. Projects are also in the developmental stage in Hampshire and the Isle of Wight, South West England and Essex, with the possibility of further expansion. The Stop It Now! UK helpline, for example, has been operating since June 2002. It has received a total of 3496 calls of which 47 per cent are from persons worried about their own behaviour or predisposition to sexually abuse children (Quaker, Peace and Social Witness, 2005).

Many of the core elements of the Stop It Now! programme, in particular media and information campaigns and organised community forums, have strong restorative or reintegrative potential. In the main, these schemes represent a very positive social response to child sexual abuse and the problem of managing the risk posed by sex offenders in the community. They promote understanding about

[4] See: <http:///www.stopitnow.com/about.htm>.
[5] 'Dealing With Child Sexual Abuse When A Loved One Is The Abuser' *Valley News*, (30 July 1999).

child sexual abuse and abusers and encourage responsible action on the part of the local community in tandem with key statutory and voluntary agencies who work to manage offenders and protect children. At the same time, however, they also offer a means of challenging abusers or potential abusers about their offending behaviour and providing them with support in their effort to change. These benefits will also be discussed further below, in relation to circles of support and accountability and how such schemes as a whole meet the aims of restorative justice, and reintegrative shaming in particular, and also in relation to how the use of such schemes may be further extended.

CIRCLES OF SUPPORT AND ACCOUNTABILITY

Perhaps one of the best known restorative based reintegrative schemes for sex offenders are circles of support and accountability which originated in Canada but have since been piloted in a number of other jurisdictions. The scheme involves carefully recruited and trained volunteers, mostly from the faith community, in co-operation with family members, self-help groups, educators, the police and treatment professionals. These volunteers form support groups or circles of support with selected high-risk and potentially high profile sex offenders who are re-entering the community at warrant expiry[6] from prison (Kirkegaard and Northey, 2000; Cesaroni, 2001; Petrunik, 2002: 503–5; Silverman and Wilson, 2002: 167–84; Wilson et al, 2002). As the name suggests, circles aim to hold offenders accountable through the provision of practical and emotional support.

This scheme, which had its origins in the restorative work of the Canadian Mennonite Church in 1994, was conceived initially as a community faith response to an immediate need based on a perceived fear held by a particular community. Circles have since developed over the last ten years and are currently supported by the Correctional Service of Canada as the 'Community Reintegration Project.' They are based on the twin philosophies of safety and support—they operate as a means of addressing public concerns surrounding the reintegration of sex offenders and also of easing the offender's transition into the community. Circle members have a dual responsibility to be caring for the offender often in the midst of wider public hostility, and at the same time to be concerned that community safety is not compromised.

This intensive and individualised project endeavours to use a decentralised model that allows circles to be established with statutory support in selected communities within which the offender chooses to live after release from custody. A key concept which underpins this process, and one which has been outlined earlier in this book, is that the community must accept responsibility for its own members and for addressing the problem of sexual abuse. In this vein, the central

---

[6] 'Warrant expiry' is the term used to refer to the end of a sentence. This is the last day that the Correctional Service of Canada has jurisdiction over an offender.

philosophy of the support circle, which reflects one of the basic principles of restorative justice (McCold, 1996: 90–96), is encapsulated in the following phrase:

It is essential to the life of the community that it reclaim its role in dealing with criminal conflict, with victims and offenders.[7]

Since individual sex offenders will have different needs and represent different levels of risk, the structure, dynamics and experience of each circle that develops is necessarily different, but there are some common features. As will be discussed further below, circles are centrally concerned with the needs of the offenders, victims and communities and with providing an alternative yet complementary approach to the traditional justice system. In this respect, it is proposed to thematically discuss circles as an illustration of how such schemes as a whole meet the aims of restorative justice, reintegrative shaming in particular, and resettlement processes, which were outlined in chapter 3.

Are Circles Truly Restorative?

Restorative or reintegrative justice processes have a number of common aims which are evident in the work of circles with sex offenders. These include changing the focus of justice intervention from retribution to reparation; altering the justice process to bring informal justice processes closer to local communities and increase citizen involvement in the process of restoration (and reintegration); considering the impact on victims and significant others; and empowering victims and offenders (Zehr, 1990, 1995; Van Ness, 1993; Bazemore and Umbreit, 1995). In addition, circles share many of the key values which are said to underpin restorative processes (Dignan and Lowey, 1999; Crawford and Goodey, 2000). These include: (1) the principle of 'inclusivity'—restorative approaches extend the range of those who are entitled to participate in the process of dealing with the offence and the range of potential outcomes to include restoration for the victim and reintegration of the offender back into the community; (2) the balance of interests—restorative approaches recognise the need to strike an appropriate balance between the various interests at stake, including that of the offender, the community and the state, with mutual respect for and empowerment of all parties involved in the process; and (3) problem-solving orientation—the approach is forward looking and aims to prevent future offending which goes beyond dealing with the aftermath of the particular crime to reintegrating offenders back into the community.

From a purist point of view, there are those who may argue that using circles in conjunction with formal criminal justice, after prison, is not really restorative justice as it cannot be legitimately considered part of the process of sanctioning or censure or 'doing justice' (Zehr, 1990, 1995; Bazemore, 1996; Walgrave, 2000,

---

[7] See: <http://www.csc.scc.gc.ca/text/pblct/interactive/ia1296e.shtml>.

2001). According to this view, the use of circles with sex offenders on release may be more properly regarded as a form of 'restorative therapy' or as 'informal treatment.' Traditionally, justice systems have been expected, inter alia, to address the need to sanction crime and offenders—to publicly denounce harmful behaviour and to provide consequences for offenders—as well as enhance public safety and rehabilitate offenders (Bazemore, 1996: 49–56). The restorative paradigm, however, addresses these objectives, albeit in a different often more informal way, that tends to balance and merge, rather than compartmentalise these functions (Bazemore and Umbreit, 1995; Braithwaite and Braithwaite, 2001: 35–38; Braithwaite, 2002b; Willemsens, 2003). Indeed, as outlined at the outset of this book, and as will be explained more fully below, the type of restorative approach to sex offender risk management and reintegration envisaged here is an integrated model which combines options for restorative justice via circles with more formal sanctions. Moreover, central to this proposed model is the presentation of restorative justice as treatment or management in a new guise, involving both the state and the community, where it has the capacity to transform formal institutions and working practices related to sex offender reintegration.

Several authors, in this respect, have underlined the transformative potential of restorative justice (Morris, 1994; Wright, 1996; Van Ness and Strong, 1997/2002; Sullivan and Tifft, 2000, 2001: ch 9; Walgrave, 2001; Blad, 2006). The work of O'Connell in particular, envisages a much broader role for restorative justice and suggests that the restorative paradigm can create more responsive environments and make a considerable contribution to civil society through bureaucratic reform (O'Connell, 2000; Ritchie and O'Connell, 2001). Some of the themes raised by this work can usefully be related to the restorative and transformative potential of circles in the field of sex offender management.

A central argument is that restorative justice may have a role which extends beyond reactive and situational arrangements to embrace a framework supported by a coherent management philosophy and an effective implementation plan that is both preventive and strategic (Ritchie and O'Connell, 2001: 150). It has been argued throughout this book that measures such as circles of support present an opportunity to move away from the further enactment of situational legislative and policy responses to sex offender management, such as sexual offences prevention orders and registration, which are often implemented after specific cases occur. Instead, restorative justice offers the possibility of transforming multi-agency procedures to become more effective risk management strategies which are not simply reactive responses to sexual offending but are also focused on their preventive potential.

The authors argue that promoting responsiveness involves at least three core elements: maximising participation, shifting emphasis from formal to social controls and employing tensions creatively (Ritchie and O'Connell, 2001: 154–56). In relation to the first of these, circles open up the work of statutory and voluntary agencies and include the local community more fully in the process of sex offender reintegration. They move 'responsibility and authority back to community members' (Pranis, 1998: 48) and offer the opportunity for effective processes of engagement with community problems. In relation to the second of these, a social control system is concerned with 'treatment, a sense of collective worth, and communal expectations' (Ritchie and O'Connell, 2001: 154). The cornerstone of such a system also encapsulates the philosophy of circles—that of support, reflection, repair, reassurance, flexible application, and employing a relational focus to (re)build confidence about behavioural norms. By employing these devices, the number of potential victims and offenders can be reduced substantially. Finally, whereas systems of formal control seek the minimisation of friction, the promotion of top-down initiatives and compliance through the enforcement of rules, circles tap into the values of responsiveness, inclusion and reflection. This allows for the development of more rational and considered community responses to sex offender reintegration than we have witnessed in the past, where 'conflicts are nurtured and made visible' and where 'professionals do not monopolize the handling of them' (Christie, 1977: 4).

Having tested their theory positively in the multiple institutional settings of education, policing and corrections, they conclude that 'the relational wins out over the institutional' (Ritchie and O'Connell, 2001: 153). These case studies demonstrate the capacity of voluntary compliance and an emphasis on relationship and the consequences of inappropriate behaviours to inform and guide professional practice and transform inter-agency processes which would reduce costs, improve services and deliver more agreeable working practices (Ritchie and O'Connell, 2001: 156–62). They conclude that: 'A healthy and more productive alignment between the relational and institutional paradigms can be achieved using restorative justice practices' (Ritchie and O'Connell, 2001: 156). In terms of the work of circles, an increased depth of understanding and improved levels of empathy between state agencies and the community can also deliver systems and practice improvements. Restorative processes and sound management principles can together provide a means of establishing trust where previously confusion and system atrophy has prevailed. An improved relational focus, using restorative principles, provides a foundation for organic change. It could tangibly improve and minimise dissonance between the formal state institutional perspective and that of the community in relation to the reintegration of sex offenders (Ritchie and O'Connell, 2001: 161, 163).

Reintegrative Shaming

Circles of support are tailored, in particular, to the central facets of reintegrative shaming theory (McAlinden, 2005). First, circles of support are accompanied by one of the principal hallmarks of reintegrative shame cultures—the aim is to control wrong doers within a communitarian society and informally sanction deviance by reintegration into cohesive networks, rather than by formal restraint (Braithwaite, 1989: 84–85). The circle is focused on the development of a network of support and treatment built around the offender, the core member, involving the wider community in tandem with state and voluntary agencies. The offender is involved from the beginning and included in all decision-making. Circles of support seek to create a strong identification between the shamed offender and other members of the community where there is a clear emphasis on intimate face-to-face associations, interdependence and co-operation. Circle members, in this way, provide a stepping stone between the formal support of agencies and the informal support of family and friends (Quaker Peace and Social Witness, 2005: 16).

Unlike legislative and judicial shame penalties which prescribe the sanction but leave the shaming to the community at large, reintegrative shaming mechanisms bring relevant community members together in an organised forum that evokes shame in the offender and promotes reintegration. In this vein, it is argued that circles provide a much more effective forum for the management of the risk posed by sex offenders in the community than supervision or registration or notification provisions because of 'the unique insights into the detail of core members' behaviours and lifestyles' (Bates, cited in Quaker Peace and Social Witness, 2005: 7). In addition, as will be discussed further below, the input and involvement of the local community in this way represents a better compromise on the demand for community notification via a 'Sarah's Law' and its associated dangers which have been outlined previously. The community are no longer dependent on statutory or voluntary agencies to notify them of any impending risk but instead become themselves a powerful resource in the risk management process.

Once the circle is established, members are involved in assisting offenders with reintegration in a number of ways, from helping them find housing and employment to helping them change their attitudes and behaviour and avoid situations that might lead to reoffending (Petrunik, 2002: 504). The offender and other members of the circle enter into a signed covenant which operates as a reintegrative plan of action and specifies each member's area of assistance. Members are trained to recognise inappropriate pro-offending behaviour. The covenant also indicates what process will be followed should an emergency situation arise. The offender agrees to relate to the circle of support and accept its help and advice, to pursue a predetermined course of treatment and to act responsibly in the community. As discussed in chapter 4, prison treatment programmes in particular have failed to fully engage with offenders and adequately prepare them for life on release. Circles work towards redressing this imbalance. Offenders are thus more likely to experience shame in an intimate small group setting like circles of support than in an undifferentiated mass society where shame penalties may miss the mark by failing to create an appropriate and conducive context for shaming (Karp, 1998: 290).

Secondly, circles of support also meet both facets of reintegrative shaming: (1) the overt disapproval of the delinquent act (shaming) by socially significant members; and (2) the ongoing inclusion of the offender within an interdependent relationship (reintegration) (Zhang, 1995: 251). In relation to the first of these elements, circles usually consist of between 4 and 7 members drawn from the local community, usually members of a church or religious faith group (Petrunik, 2002:

504). This inner circle may also be supplemented by an outer circle consisting of police, social workers, and significant others such as family and friends who sit in occasionally as needed (Petrunik, 2002: 504). The ideal size of each circle is between 6 and 8 members with a maximum of 12 in order to optimise trust and communication. In relation to the second of these elements, a key premise is that by forging 'social bonds' (Freiburg, 2001) and 'inclusive' relationships and the sense of 'belonging to a family,' the core member will be deterred from reoffending (Silverman and Wilson, 2002: 173, 178). The offender has contact with someone from the circle each day in the high-risk phase just after release. All members meet weekly to discuss any issues which may have arisen and need to be addressed. The life of a circle extends as long as the risk to the community and the offender are above average. Normally, a minimum commitment of one year is expected from all circle members. The intensity, however, with which members are involved in the life of the offender will hopefully diminish.

Thirdly, reintegrative shaming is accomplished when four conditions are fulfilled (Braithwaite, 1989: 100–1). These are also evident in the work of circles of support and accountability: (1) *the shaming maintains bonds of love or respect between the person being shamed and the person doing the shaming*—this is demonstrated by the dual commitment on the part of the offender and the other circle members which is encapsulated in the signed covenant; (2) *is directed at the evil of the act rather than the evil of the person*—the circle confronts and challenges offenders about their deviant attitudes and behaviour and holds them accountable to the community and their commitment not to reoffend; (3) *is delivered in a context of general social approval*—the scheme provides intensive support, guidance and supervision for the offender, mediating between the police, media and the general community to minimise risk and assist in reintegration; and finally (4) *is terminated with gestures or ceremonies of acceptance and forgiveness*—the net result is that sex offenders receive sympathy and help in reintegration, and not just hostility, from at least some members of the community. In the words of Petrunik (2002: 506):

> Rather than being driven from neighborhood to neighborhood like some tormented Frankenstein and perhaps re-offending in despair that he can never be any different, the sex offender is given a chance to redeem himself under the caring but ever so watchful eyes of a concerned community.

Resettlement

It has already been outlined in chapter 3, in relation to the literature on offender resettlement and desistance from crime, that the social context can have a significant effect on offender rehabilitation (Rutter and Giller, 1983; Sampson and Laub, 1994; Hagan, 1997; Hope, 2001; Farrall, 2002: 145–92). This literature also highlights the contribution of the community to offender rehabilitation and links, in particular, to Braithwaite's (1989) thesis of 'reintegrative shaming.'

By helping the offender establish a 'reconnection with' the local community, circles play an important part of the process by which offenders put their 'pasts behind them' (Farrall and Sparks, 2006: 8). Circles can provide the offender with many of the 'benevolent' (Farrall and Sparks, 2006: 12) factors that underlie 'trajectories of change' (Laub et al, 1998) and a suitable social space in which offenders can publicly affirm to themselves and others their commitment to a future non-offending identity. In short, they may provide both a symbolic and actual means of hope of offender desistance and reintegration by supporting the ex-perpetrator in his efforts to change (Burnett and Maruna, 2004; Farrall and Calverley, 2005).

Reintegrative shaming processes combine elements of both the structural and the individual in creating vivid 'connections between action and local context' (Farrall and Sparks, 2006: 14). By developing appropriate 'social and interactional processes' (Maruna, 2001: 13), via role affirming empowering relationships and local infrastructures, circles can provide the support and stability for offenders, which are known to be essential to their reintegration and therefore their efforts not to reoffend. This 'strengths-based' approach to offender resettlement is characterised by the themes of repair, reconciliation and community partnership (Farrant and Levenson, 2002; Burnett and Maruna, 2006: 84). Genuine offender reintegration involves ' "earning" one's place back in the moral community' and developing pro-social concepts of self (Burnett and Maruna, 2006: 84).

Circles are therefore based on the premise that effective resettlement is more likely to occur if the offender is released into a community of care and support rather than one of hatred and fear. Indeed, in tandem with this broad premise, it is contended that the public anxiety and hostility surrounding sex offenders can best be managed by recognising public anxiety and demonstrating that by providing appropriate opportunities for treatment and support, the offender can be reintegrated into society where the community accepts the offender in their midst with a greater awareness of the risks involved. As argued in chapter 3:

> [S]uch rituals, if they were to be institutionalized as part of reintegration practice, might improve efforts to reintegrate ex-offenders into society (Maruna, 2001: 13).

Extending the Use of Circles

Circles have been used in several Canadian provinces and some US states, such as Minnesota. Between its origins in 1994 and 2000, the Community Reintegration Project has set up 30 circles in Toronto and another 12 in other parts of Canada. Most of the circles have been in operation for 18–24 months and the longest has been in place for more than six years (Petrunik, 2002: 501). It is also worth noting that in tandem with this initiative, the Correctional Service of Canada has a web page dedicated to public education and awareness where extensive material is provided, including statistics on sexual offences, information about prisons and conditional release, and the most common myths and misconceptions as well as the 'real' situation based on current facts and statistics.[8] Indeed, as will be discussed at the end of this chapter, public education is an essential component to the further implementation of such schemes.

Several other jurisdictions, in this respect, are exploring the possibility of introducing circles with sex offenders. The Quaker Community was instrumental in bringing the idea to England and Wales. However, the cultural and statutory context in which circles have developed in the latter jurisdiction differs from the Canadian context. As mentioned above, circles developed there as a particular community response to a local sex offender problem, although the initiative is now supported by the Correctional Service. In England and Wales, however, circles were replicated as a series of 3-year pilot projects funded by the Home Office and managed by the Quakers in conjunction with statutory agencies, primarily the Police, Probation and Prison services. Circles have been adapted and developed in Thames Valley, the Hampton Trust and the Lucy Faithful Foundation to support statutory agencies in the effective management of high-risk sex offenders released into the community. For example, circles can report areas of concern back to the Multi-Agency Public Protection Panels (MAPPPs), which were outlined in chapter 2. This has enabled agencies to tighten control of the offender through, for example, targeted surveillance (Quaker Peace and Social Witness, 2005: 14). It has been argued, in this vein, that while the Canadian model is organic, the model which exists in England and Wales is rather more systemic (Quaker Peace and Social Witness, 2005: 6).

The Thames Valley project developed three key principles as a reference point for the work of circles with sex offenders. These were supporting, monitoring and maintaining sex offenders in their efforts to reduce reoffending behaviour. Sex offenders are supported by circle members reducing their isolation and emotional loneliness, by modelling appropriate relationships and by demonstrating care and humanity. They are monitored in the community which in turn enhances public protection by creating safer communities and helping to support the work of statutory agencies in the MAPPPs. Finally, sex offenders are maintained in their efforts not to reoffend by being held accountable for their behaviour and by establishing a relationship of trust with other circle members who reinforce treatment objectives (Quaker Peace and Social Witness, 2005: 24). These principles map almost exactly on to the twin philosophies of safety and support and the principles of reintegrative shaming which underpin the Canadian model.

Like their Canadian counterpart, circles in England and Wales aim to secure a wide representation of the local community. Members are carefully recruited and selected and have been comprised of professionals, including those with a background in criminal justice, those from faith communities, survivors of abuse, students and parents. These circle members receive training in what their roles and responsibilities will be as volunteers across a range of areas such as, inter alia, housing and employment issues, questioning styles and techniques, and substance

---

[8] See: <http://www.csc.scc.gc.ca/text/pub-ed_e.shtml>.

misuse. As will be discussed further below, if this approach is to have more widespread support and utility, a range of volunteers from a variety of community settings is required (Brown, 2005: 246).

Thames Valley, for example, established 15 circles and worked in total with 20 high-risk sex offenders over a 3-year period. For two out of the three pilot projects, the initial 3-year period has now been extended to a fourth year. At the time of writing, a further five projects are also up and running with another three about to start (Quaker Peace and Social Witness, 2005: 6). In keeping with the partnership approach between the public and professional agencies, the Hampshire scheme has also piloted lay representation on the MAPPPs, where once risk assessment is complete, action plans are put in place to lower and minimise risk (Quaker Peace and Social Witness, 2005: 6). As will be discussed at the end of this chapter, it is a central contention of this book that such piecemeal initiatives need to be adopted on a much more widespread and holistic basis.[9]

Indeed, with regard to the future development of circles, it is hoped that the small nucleus of projects, which have so far developed on a piecemeal and ad hoc basis and are currently confined to only a handful of jurisdictions, will continue to diffuse profusely and expand rapidly in influence and numbers both within and across jurisdictions. As will also be discussed at the end of this chapter, if the widespread extension of these projects consistently occurs, ultimately this could mean that circles would become an integral and standard part of multi-agency reintegration and management procedures for sex offenders. A strong network of local circle projects would mean that, in as many areas as possible, the sex offender problem can be responded to in a much more all-encompassing way taking into account the needs and rights of local citizens as well as the offender.

As discussed in chapter 4, the organisational and policy framework for managing sex offenders in the community in England and Wales has recently gone through a major reorganisation with the National Offender Management Service (NOMS) bringing together the Prison Service and Probation Service as 'end to end' offender management. The broad aims of this new holistic approach to offender management are based on a personal relationship approach rather than an administrative or bureaucratic one in which the offender will take an active part.[10] Moreover, the new NOMS model has another core value of involving the local community in offender management through improving communication with local people, fostering greater organisational awareness of public concerns and encouraging the active participation of the community in local projects. These core values and aims would appear to be highly consistent with the community-based restorative approach which lies at the heart of the work undertaken by

---

[9] This unique form of addressing the needs of sex offenders and of communities is also being piloted or considered in a number of jurisdictions such as Scotland, Northern Ireland and the Republic of Ireland.

[10] See: <http://www.noms.homeoffice.gov.uk/>.

circles of support and accountability with sex offenders (Quaker Peace and Social Witness, 2005: 17).[11]

Some may dismiss this ideal vision of offender reintegration and management as somewhat Utopian and no doubt there will be opposition, resistance and even failures along the way. However, as the evidence increasingly shows that circles may help change public perceptions about sex offenders, and above all reduce offending behaviour, opposition will become harder to sustain (Quaker Peace and Social Witness, 2005: 46). As will be argued further below, there are a number of prerequisites which are necessary for the widespread adoption of such an approach. In the interim, questions inevitably arise as to the perceived success or advantages of this model where comparisons are usually made with the traditional justice response to sex offending. As Hudson has argued, restorative justice must be seen as 'effective justice,' and not simply diversion, in terms of being able to reduce reoffending, and as 'expressive justice' (Garland, 2001) in the symbolic sense of 'occasioning strong censure' (2002: 626).

THE EFFECTIVENESS OF REINTEGRATIVE JUSTICE

In relation to the effectiveness of restorative justice programmes generally, proponents contend that it is more likely than retributive justice to reduce the incidence of crime because of its concern for the safety of victims. It addresses crime at the macro level as well at the micro level—it recognises the need for building safe communities as well as the need to resolve specific crime problems (Van Ness, 1993: 258).

Despite the proliferation of restorative and community justice programmes, there is a general paucity of evaluation research. Most of the empirical research which has been carried out on restorative justice programmes has been concentrated on the two main restorative models: victim-offender mediation and family group conferencing (Miers et al, 2001; Kurki, 2003; Schiff, 2003). It also seems that there is little to choose between these models as regards the extent to which they achieve their goals. As outlined in chapter 3, however, the conferencing model provides a forum in which a much broader range of interests can be represented.

Victim-Offender Mediation and Family Group Conferencing

Data from the United Kingdom, Australia and New Zealand suggests that these models can have a reductive effect in certain cases and can change the behaviour

---

[11] There are a few other examples of restorative innovations with sex offenders. Some victim-offender mediation programmes in Canada and England arrange for surrogate victims to meet sex offenders so that certain benefits of encounter are realised without added trauma to victims (Zehr, 1995: 208). There are also a few examples of non-profit, privately owned initiatives. In the US, a house in Minnesota is devoted exclusively to the intensive treatment of sex offenders, to work with the whole family, with a gradual monitored easing of the offender back into the community (Knopp, 1984; Knopp, 1991: 191). See also: ch 3.

of some offenders (Hoyle and Young, 2002: 538). Generally, however, there is more evidence that restorative justice is effective in reducing either the frequency or severity of reoffending for juveniles than in the case of adult offenders (Sherman et al, 2000; Strang, 2001). Maxwell and Morris (2001), for example, in their evaluation of family group conferencing in New Zealand suggested that what happens during a family group conference can have a predictive influence over the likelihood of subsequent reoffending. They concluded that when the restorative process is implemented successfully and consistent with restorative values and outcomes, there was evidence of a reduction in the reoffending rates of young offenders. Studies also confirm that it is what actually happens at the conference that affects reoffending (Maxwell and Morris, 2000, 2001; Daly, 2002b). In this respect, there are two internal dynamics of the conference process which are associated with subsequent offending—the offender's expression of remorse and agreeing the outcome by genuine consensus. In the former study, these elements distinguished those young people who were not 'persistently reconvicted' during a six and a half year follow-up period (Maxwell and Morris, 2000). As will be discussed further in the next chapter, it is also these factors in the work of restorative processes with sex offenders which may ultimately have an impact on their future rehabilitation and reintegration.

In the United Kingdom, there have been successive evaluative studies on the impact of restorative police cautioning in Thames Valley in particular. Hoyle et al's (2002) study, based on an in-depth analysis of 56 cautions and conferences involving 67 offenders, found that around one-quarter of offenders reported that they had either desisted from crime or reduced their offending behaviour at least in part because of the restorative caution. They also reported other benefits of this initiative for both victims and offenders respectively in terms of formal reparation agreements and understanding the effects of their offending. A follow-up study, however, which examined the impact of restorative cautioning on resanctioning rates (which included cautions, final warnings and reprimands, as well as convictions) produced less positive results. It concluded that there was insufficient evidence to suggest that restorative cautioning was more effective than traditional cautioning in reducing resanctioning rates or the seriousness and frequency of subsequent offending (Wilcox et al, 2004).

Other studies have given increased grounds for optimism. One possible criticism of some of these previous studies is that perhaps these conferences were only effective because the offenders involved were predisposed to be co-operative and to show remorse so that they would have reduced their offending behaviour anyway (Hoyle and Young, 2002: 538). In order to surmount this difficulty, the Reintegrative Shaming Experiment (RISE) evaluation in Canberra, Australia, randomly allocated offenders willing to meet their victims into either a restorative or non-restorative process and then examined which group offended at the higher rate following the intervention (Sherman et al, 2000; Strang, 2001). The study found that a diversionary conference caused a significant drop in recidivism rates by violent offenders, a small increase by drink drivers and no discernible difference with juvenile property offenders. It has been noted that although these results are disappointing on the one hand, in that the majority of criminal offences are property offences, on the other, the results are also encouraging since, as noted in chapter 2, contemporary popular and official discourses are more concerned with the danger posed by violent or sexual offences (Hoyle and Young, 2002: 538).

In addition to measurement of the instrumental effect of restorative measures on subsequent reoffending, other studies have evaluated the impact of schemes within the context of other intrinsic outcomes (Miers, 2004: 31–32). European (Miers et al, 2001) and Australian studies (Strang et al, 1999; Daly, 2001, 2002b), in particular, demonstrate very high levels of procedural justice—that is parti-cipation and satisfaction on the part of both victims (Umbreit et al, 2001) and offenders with the process and outcomes. However, such positive findings are not universal (Dignan, 2001). Maxwell and Morris (1993), for example, in their early research from New Zealand found that conferences tended to be largely offender-centred events with low levels of victim attendance and satisfaction. Newburn et al (2002: 41) in their study of referral order pilot schemes in England and Wales found very low rates of victim attendance in young offender panels, of as little as 13 per cent. Moreover, some victims also appear to view the process as a 'soft option' and are unsure about the impact of the intervention on the offender (Newburn et al, 2002: 46; Miers, 2004: 32). In relation to offenders, some can also feel pressurised into taking part (Hoyle et al, 2002: table 7) and find the experience of meeting their victim embarrassing, upsetting and even threatening (Sawyer, 2000).

These studies as a whole also report mixed levels of 'restorativeness.' The RISE project found high levels of restorative as well as procedural justice (Sherman et al, 2000; Strang, 2001). More recently, however, the South Australia Juvenile Justice (SAJJ) Research on Conferencing Project found high levels of procedural justice, but relatively less evidence of restoration (Daly, 2002b: 69). This was measured by relational variables such as the degree to which offenders and victims recognised and were affected by each other, the degree to which there was positive movement between the offender and the victim and their supporters, and offender and victim perceptions of genuine apologies.[12] On the other hand, there is considerable evid-ence that meeting offenders in either the mediation (Umbreit et al, 2001) or con-ference (Daly, 2002b: 70–71) process can have a beneficial impact on victims—it reduces victims' anger and fear of offenders and it helps them to gain a sense of closure and recover from the offence, although this is usually influenced by a num-ber of factors including support from family and friends and personal resources (Daly, 2002b: 70–71). In sum, as Daly argues, 'Overall, the real story of restorative justice has many positives and has much to commend, but the evidence is mixed' (2002b: 72). As will be discussed further below, however, early indications of the

---

[12] Note, however, that it has also been argued that the measures of restoration used by Daly seem closer to reconciliation than restoration. It has been further argued in this context that the expectation of reconciliation, where much lower levels would be expected, saddles restorative justice processes with unrealistic expectations (Harris, 2003b).

effectiveness of circles, in terms of promoting both offender and community accountability, appear to have produced more positive results.

There is of course the usual corollary that most of these studies have been carried out within the context of young offenders and less serious offences. Although some studies have demonstrated slight reductions in reoffending and in the seriousness of offences subsequently committed, it is perhaps too early therefore to draw conclusions on the effect of restorative processes as a whole on reoffending rates (Dignan and Lowey, 1999). In any case, it has also been suggested that given the range of complex factors that generate and sustain criminal behaviour, it is unrealistic to assume that restorative justice will have a major impact on reoffending and even less on overall crime rates (Hoyle and Young, 2002: 529). Most offences go undetected, as is certainly the case with sexual offences, and most offenders desist anyway by a certain age when they are replaced by new offenders (Zimring and Hawkins, 1995). Such a critique, however, is equally applicable to state sanctions such as court processes and prisons.

Maxwell and Morris (1999) emphasise that while both victim-offender mediation and family group conferencing have been reasonably intensely evaluated, including the process itself, implementation and reconviction so far, the evaluations have not yet examined the cost effectiveness of the models in comparison with conventional criminal justice processes, nor their preventive potential. As will be discussed below, these are elements which will need to be addressed. As the authors suggest therefore further research is perhaps needed to pinpoint exactly what it is about restorative justice that 'works' in reducing reoffending (Morris and Maxwell, 2001).

Such an argument may bring us back to the debate on the importance of shame in restorative processes and how it might affect the psychological recovery of both victims and offenders (Scheff and Retzinger, 1991; Moore, 1993; Ahmed, 2001; Harris, 2001; Zehr, 2002), as outlined briefly in chapter 3. It was noted there, however, that for some scholars, and Maxwell and Morris in particular (Maxwell and Morris, 2002, 2004; Morris, 2002b), empathy and remorse are recognised as more important elements in achieving these restorative outcomes (Karstedt, 2002; Taylor, 2002; van Stokkom, 2002; Sherman, 2003). In any event more qualitative data, including participant observation, may be needed to supplement the existing quantitative data on what have mostly been process outcomes (Harris et al, 2004: 205).

Circles of Support

As regards the other main restorative justice model, there is little quantitative analysis available on circles given the relative newness of the concept. Critics argue that this lack of empirical analyses means that there is no basis for determining whether these initiatives have been successful in achieving their stated objectives (La Prairie, 1994). It is hoped that this will change over time, however, as programmes and practices become more established.

The limited number of empirical studies to date have focused on the extent to which circles reduce recidivism rates among sex offenders processed through the circles. This research evidence strongly suggests that circles have been used successfully with high-risk sex offenders. In the first two years, the project claimed not a single relapse (John Howard Society, 1997, cited in Nash, 1999). A more recent evaluation of circles in Ontario, for example, found offenders receiving assistance via a circle reoffended at a lower rate incrementally in comparison with a matched control sample (Wilson et al, 2002). Only 3 from the 30 high-risk sex offenders, who were at risk in the community for an average of 30 months, ranging from 16 months to six and a half years, were known to have reoffended. In comparing the expected recidivism rate, using risk assessment scales, with the observed rate, sexual recidivism was reduced by more than 50 per cent (Wilson et al, 2002: 378). Furthermore, from a harm reduction perspective, each incident of sexual recidivism was categorically less invasive and severe than the offence for which the offender had most recently been imprisoned (Wilson et al, 2002: 378).[13]

Recent evaluations have also been carried out on the pilot projects in England and Wales over the last three years. Initially, as might be expected, the difficulties of successfully establishing circles of support and accountability were compounded by the media. In Thames Valley, for example, circles were first operationalised in April 2002. Four months later, Holly Wells and Jessica Chapman were murdered by Ian Huntley, who was previously known to the police for sex offences against both women and children, in Soham, Cambridgeshire. The first introduction of circles to the wider public was thereby heralded through national headlines such as 'What a Waste of Our Cash' (Quaker Peace and Social Witness, 2005: 16). Similarly, the pilot site in Hampshire, set up by the Hampton Trust, also had to establish itself within the context of riots in Portsmouth following the *News of the World*'s 'Name and Shame' campaign and the kidnapping and murder of Sarah Payne. However, as will be discussed further below, despite these tentative beginnings, early indications are that communities are willing to play a constructive, supportive and positive role in the process of offender management and reintegration.

In England and Wales, circles have also worked effectively with sex offenders and have successfully contributed to their management in the community (Quaker Peace and Social Witness, 2005: 5). The most recent evaluation concluded that in the Thames Valley, expected rates of recidivism amongst a group of high-risk sex offenders was reduced. As indicated in chapter 4 in relation to treatment and recidivism studies, it is generally well accepted that the use of formal reconviction rates is a very blunt instrument in the evaluation of programmes and does not always provide a true reflection of actual deviant behaviour following intervention (Marshall and Barbaree, 1988; Marques et al, 1994; Friendship et al, 2001, Friendship, Beech et al, 2001; Friendship and Thornton, 2001; Francis et al,

---

[13] The offences that resulted in charges were an indecent telephone call, a sexual offence against a female adult and a sexual offence against a child.

2002). The sex offender treatment literature also refers to pro-offending or offence related behaviour which might indicate an eventual decline into reoffending as recidivism (Falshaw et al, 2003). Recent research also suggests that this 'soft data', which is routinely held by circles, is highly significant in evaluating the effectiveness of interventions through the identification of a possible return to offending behaviour (Bates et al, 2004; Quaker Peace and Social Witness, 2005: 18).

In this vein, only eight core members out of a total of 20 were identified as displaying problem or early recidivist behaviour. Such behaviour included drinking more heavily than reported to the circle; grooming girls under 16 via internet chatrooms or grooming families in order to get access to a child by developing a relationship with a vulnerable single mother with a number of children under 16; possession of inappropriate pornographic videos or photographs; and carrying out activities which were known to be part of the modus operandi of previous offences (for example, attempted burglary to access female adult victims and buying a car for the purposes of abducting a child).

Of these offenders, only three men were recalled on licence, none of whom had committed or been reconvicted of further sexual offences. One core member, however, was reconvicted for breaching a sexual offences prevention order, which were outlined in the previous chapter (Quaker Peace and Social Witness, 2005: 6, 21). These numbers broadly equate with the experience of the Canadian circles which were evaluated, albeit, over a longer period. Moreover, these recalls were also perceived in a positive light. It should be emphasised that these were very high-risk sex offenders with long entrenched deviant sexual tendencies. In each case, however, the recall was facilitated by vital information passed to the professional agencies in the MAPPPS by circle volunteers who had identified the recidivist type behaviour in the core member which gave them cause for concern. Without the intervention of the circle at such an early stage, progression to reoffence and subsequent reconviction may well have occurred (Quaker Peace and Social Witness, 2005: 22).

These findings are highly indicative of the accountability aspect of the work of circles and demonstrate effectively the critical role that they may have in managing the risk posed by dangerous sex offenders in the community from both a resettlement and a public protection perspective—the development of these wider networks have supported offenders in their efforts to make the transition from offending to being responsible and resettled members of the community while at the same time they have acted as a form of preventative governance in thwarting further acts of abuse. Moreover, they also highlight that the circle model potentially offers professional agencies in working towards offender integration, a clear means of actively and positively engaging with the local community on contentious sex offender issues (Quaker Peace and Social Witness, 2005: 18). As noted above, circles have opened up the work of statutory agencies by providing an opportunity for the general public to contribute to the management of individual offenders. A small nucleus of community members may offer a practical means of addressing the concerns of the rest of the community. In this way, trained circle volunteers may be able to counteract the growth of mis-information about sex offenders which exists in the wider community. By providing accurate information, volunteers can counterbalance the distorted perceptions and sceptical and mistrustful attitudes of the local community concerning sex offenders and the work that takes place with them and in turn increase public confidence in the work of statutory and voluntary agencies. In short, these findings clearly challenge some of the traditional and oversimplified views concerning the legitimate role of the community that contribute to the debate about what should be done with released sex offenders (Hudson, 2005: 49).

As will be discussed further below, provision of effective programmes, responsive to the needs of particular individuals, to which people can be referred, will be crucial to any system put in place. If restorative approaches are to be integrated into the criminal justice system it will be important to have full evaluations carried out. At the same time, however, many restorative and community justice initiatives have objectives which are much more holistic than traditional regulatory responses which typically use recidivism rates as the key outcome measure of crime control. As noted above, Morris and Maxwell (2001), and others (Miers, 2004: 34–37), have suggested that in implementing restorative justice, we need to ask the question, 'what do we mean by "what works"?'

Aside from rates of reoffending or reconviction, and consistent with the restorative ideal, there are other equally important measures of outcome. Any future evaluative framework for these approaches would therefore also have to include measurable criteria to assess outcomes such as cost effectiveness; overall contribution to community safety; victim, offender and community involvement; responses to the needs of victims and satisfaction rates with the process; offender shaming and reintegration; improvement in the relationships of offenders with their families and the local community; and reparation to victims and the wider community, as well as reductions or changes in offending behaviour (Christie, 1977; Maxwell and Morris, 1999, 2002; Bazemore and Griffiths, 2003).

Indeed, it has also been argued that any reductions in offending behaviour that may be achieved through the use of restorative justice should be best regarded as a bonus rather than as a prerequisite for success (Hoyle and Young, 2002: 529). As will be outlined in the next chapter, where restorative justice could have a real impact is in improving the safety of victims, providing relief for communities, and reintegrating offenders back into society. It is only by achieving widespread acceptance that restorative justice can be an effective practice with serious forms of offending like sexual crime, that it will have the potential to become a standard element of reintegrating sex offenders into communities over the next decade.

FROM THEORY TO PRACTICE: IMPLEMENTING REINTEGRATIVE
SHAMING PRACTICES

Implementing reintegrative shaming practices with sex offenders on a more wide-spread basis involves an examination of a number of key issues. These include whether such schemes should operate as an addition to the formal retributive framework or as alternative to it?; the need for public education and awareness programmes; and ultimately a partnership approach to justice (McAlinden, 2005).

An Additional or Alternative Form of Justice?

The nuances of the relationship between formal criminal law and restorative just-ice were examined at the end of chapter 3. It was argued there that there are poten-tial conflicts between these justice paradigms on a number of inter-related levels—principally, in academic debates; in criminal justice policy-making; and in the use which has so far been made of restorative justice within the current retributive system in dealing with offending behaviour. The common thread perhaps, which lies at the heart of these debates, is how far the paradigms can be reconciled. This in itself involves a determination of a key question for the justice debate—should reintegrative shaming practices operate as an additional or an alternative form of justice?

In terms of how such reintegrative shaming practices with sex offenders could actually operate with respect to the present regulatory framework, there are two main possibilities. One is as an avenue to diversionary treatment. As an alternative to the traditional criminal justice system, sex offenders would forego criminal prosecution in exchange for undergoing a treatment and support programme. The other main possibility is to prosecute all but the most minor sexual offences and then put this new system into operational effect after the convicted offender is released from prison. In this instance, it would operate as an addition rather than as an alternative to custody.

As outlined in chapter 3, restorative approaches advocate that the opinions of victims and their families should be taken into account. There are two competing views which victims may have, however, which are difficult to reconcile in any sys-tem of justice. On the one hand, some victims of intra-familial abuse (Sauzier, 1989; Berliner and Conte, 1995) in common with domestic abuse victims (Carbonatto, 1995, 1998; Hoyle, 1998) may want to see the offender punished or vilified but more commonly they simply want the abuse to stop. On the other hand, for many other victims, particularly those who have been abused or assaulted by strangers, the victims of extra-familial abuse, the expressive functions of punishment in public and state condemnation of the offence are an important part of the healing and vindication process (Morris and Gelsthorpe, 2000a: 412; Hudson, 2002: 622; Wright, 2002: 664). In the latter instance, a diversionary scheme may unjustly release the offender from criminal prosecution.[14] In the former instance, it may act as a powerful incentive to both victims and offenders coming forward to seek help.

In this respect, it is submitted that restorative schemes could be integrated within the current regulatory framework, in a sophisticated way, making provision for the necessary safeguards. Restorative schemes that are locally based or designed to deal with specific crime problems could be encouraged to develop in a way that is complementary, but not as a complete alternative to, the formal criminal justice system. Such a system would be akin to Braithwaite's (1999, 2002b: especially ch 2) notion of responsive regulation where essentially restorative justice is at the base of an enforcement pyramid, backed-up with explicit deterrent and incapacitative sanctions.[15]

The essential argument behind this 'presumptive pyramid of strategies' (Braithwaite and Braithwaite, 2001: 36) is that calibrated punishment is less arbitrary and therefore less stigmatising. Retributive punishment and stigmatisation are normally 'overkill' and can have some terrible effects on the individuals who suffer it. In this 'restorative theory of censure' (Braithwaite and Braithwaite, 2001: 35–38), the preference is for the 'reasoned dialogue of restorative justice' (Braithwaite and Braithwaite, 2001: 36) as a first response to wrongdoing, and as a second and third, until it becomes clear that restoration has no prospect of working in a particular case. Only then should the response escalate to punishment. According to Braithwaite, deterrence, rather than retribution, would then be attempted and it is only where this fails would incapacitative punishment be tried. Indeed, as will be discussed further below, there are rare cases where the community need direct protection from an offender, and where imprisonment can offer such a protective form of punishment.

As will be discussed further in the final chapter, following Soothill et al's (Soothill 2005, Soothill et al 2005a, 2005b) typology of offenders, offenders could be dealt with in various ways based on perceived categories of risk. 'Known and high-risk' offenders could continue to be prosecuted in the normal way through the criminal justice system initially, despite its failings. If convicted, they could be reintegrated into the community via circles of support on release. As outlined

---

[14] An example of a diversionary scheme is the 'Confidential Doctor' system in Holland (Jay and Doganis, 1987: ch 9) where the primary concern is not the prosecution or punishment of the offender but the protection and well-being of the child. If a sex offender openly admits to their offending behaviour they can be diverted out of the criminal justice system and placed on a treatment programme. In the case of intra-familial abuse, the child is taken from the family home by the authorities to an appropriate safe place until the offending adult removes themselves. The child can then return home while the offender undergoes treatment. If the offender refuses, the response board reports them to the Child Protection Board and the Central Police.

[15] Desert theorists, however, traditionally raise two objections to such an approach: (1) purely incapacitative sentences for recidivists may lead to disproportionately severe sentences (von Hirsch, 1985: ch 11; Dignan, 2003); and (2) the threat of deterrent or incapacitative sentences may mean that offenders will feel compelled to participate in restorative justice processes and this will consequently undermine the integrity of the 'making-amends' process (von Hirsch et al, 2003: 36). Indeed, an intractable problem for retributivist theory is how to maintain moderate and proportionate sentences for recidivists.

above, for these offenders, the risk of reoffending is so high that the preumption of starting at the base of the pyramid is overridden and we must move straight to incapacitation (Braithwaite and Braithwaite, 2001: 37). For 'known and low or low-middle risk' offenders, circles could be used as an effective alternative to the formal state sanctioning process. Much in the same way as happens in the youth justice system in England and Wales, the legal framework and more punitive sanctions, however, can be retained as a backdrop or as an option of last resort with more persistent offenders. Moreover, it will also be argued that by encouraging more perpetrators and victims to voluntarily come forward, mainly by reducing the public villification of offenders, it may also offer an important way of probing and managing 'unknown risks' where offenders may be strongly suspected of sexual offences by the authorities but have not actually been prosecuted.

Such schemes could also be potentially used as an effective first response to young sex offenders in particular since, as outlined in chapter 5, there is broad agreement that the current retributive framework does not adequately address the specialist needs posed by this group of offenders (Brownlie, 2003). The use of restorative schemes may help to provide a plausible answer to the long-standing question of diversion or prosecution for these offenders which is inherent in the current choice between the child protection and justice systems (Daly, 2006) and which in turn echoes the confusion about whether these young people are victims or offenders (Sanders and Ladwa-Thomas, 1997; Masson and Morrison, 1999). This, indeed, as outlined in chapter 3, is what currently happens in South Australia, where young people charged with sexual offences, who have acknowledged their behaviour, are diverted from court processes and instead participate in a restorative conference (Daly, 2002a; 2006). An archival study examined nearly 400 such cases of youth sexual assault, which were finalised in court and by conference or formal caution over a six and a half year period. This showed that the conference process may be less victimizing than the court process and that its 'penalty regime' may ultimately produce more beneficial outcomes, particularly in terms of a greater degree of disclosure of sex offending and victimisation and more effective forms of counselling or treatment (Daly, 2006).

Since the myriad of alternative justice practices are relatively new, schemes may be expected to continue to evolve as they are adapted to local circumstances (Bazemore and Griffiths, 2003). As discussed above, there is, however, a need for broadly based community support and the development of sufficiently varied and local programmes to allow restorative packages to be developed. The model of circles outlined at the beginning of this chapter clearly allows for such flexibility in community-based approaches. Although development would undoubtedly continue to be piecemeal at the outset, schemes should be available throughout the United Kingdom.

However, a number of initial suggestions can be made. Restorative programmes of support and treatment in the community could operate on the basis of a referral by a statutory criminal justice agency, with key agencies in the inter-agency approach being informed of all referrals. Ultimately, it is contended that there should be a statutory basis for the process, as the research evidence indicates that in jurisdictions where there is no statutory basis or discretionary use of the restorative process, referrals tend to occur haphazardly and arbitrarily (Morris and Maxwell, 2001). A dedicated statutory agency, such as probation, could be responsible for the operation of such schemes and could act as a co-ordinator of the projects. Perhaps such schemes could be integrated into existing inter-agency risk assessment and management procedures where recommendations could be made about how to process an individual case and where the various agencies would agree a restorative response. Schemes could also be developed as part of the offender's programme of supervision or treatment in the community and, in common with current arrangements, would address all aspects of the offender's life necessary for successful reintegration, including finding suitable accommodation and employment, and not just his abusive behaviour.

All those involved in delivering restorative justice programmes should receive substantial human rights training in addition to specialist training in approaches such as mediation and dispute resolution through accredited and specifically designed training programmes (Ashworth, 2002; Braithwaite, 2002a; Wright, 2002). To safeguard the rights of individuals and to ensure, in particular, that victims and offenders would not be coerced into participating, restorative justice schemes should be subject to explicit codes of conduct, based on domestic law and international human rights standards, to ensure that they operated in a fair and lawful way respecting the rights of all participants. Where children are concerned, there is a need for agencies in the inter-agency approach to draw up an explicit child protection policy. Finally, restorative approaches should be subject to regular, rigorous and independent inspection to ensure that standards are being met. Schemes should be evaluated and inspection and evaluation reports published.

Voluntary participation of the key stakeholders—victims and offenders in particular—must also be a cornerstone of the process and either party should have the right to opt out at any stage. As will be discussed in the next chapter in relation to the critiques of restorative justice as applied to sexual offences, to force victims to participate could lead to further victimisation and disempowerment. Moreover, to force offenders to participate in programmes may be futile since, as indicated in chapter 4, the research evidence suggests that the effectiveness of interventions is often increased when offenders become involved voluntarily (McIvor, 1992; McLaren, 1992; McGuire, 1995).[16]

---

[16] As outlined in ch 3, although non-coercive practice is often cited as one of the key principles which underpin restorative practices, there is an increasing honesty within restorative thinking that coercion is never truly absent from restorative processes. If an offender in particular is given the choice between a sentence of imprisonment or engagement in a restorative programme, it is a fallacy to say that this does not involve at least some element of latent coercion (Hoyle and Young, 2002: 527).

Public Education and Awareness

A prerequisite to developing a restorative or communitarian response to managing the problems and risks posed by sex offenders in the community and extending the use of circles within communities is the need to foster public education and awareness. The momentous contribution which the community makes to the successful placement and management of sex offenders in the community has been discussed at length in chapter 4, and again in chapter 5, in relation to the problems posed by community notification. It was noted there that communities often fail to co-operate with statutory and voluntary agencies and make their task of reintegrating and managing sex offenders in the community extremely difficult. One of the greatest challenges facing statutory and voluntary agencies is low public awareness and understanding of the various issues surrounding 'risk' and the management of sex offenders. Myths and misconceptions about sexual offending shape and colour public attitudes, impeding meaningful discussion of policies and programmes.

This underlines the necessity of a rigorous public education and awareness programme, driven by government, designed to provide accurate information and dispel the popular misconceptions about sexual offending (Grubin, 1998; Silverman and Wilson, 2002: 54–59).[17] It is increasingly evident that public education and awareness has much to contribute to a 'culture of safety' (Busch, 2002: 223)—to both the effective prevention of sex offending and the successful reintegration and rehabilitation of offenders. As Wright (2003: 102) argues, 'It is critical to place the fear of . . . sex offenders in a political and normative context.' This would hopefully challenge some of the oversimplified views regarding sex offenders, shift cultural attitudes, and help to promote a culture of social inclusion.

One of the most recent texts on this theme is Salter's (2003) book, *Predators, Pedophiles, Rapists and Other Sex Offenders.* However, it is the subtitle which is the most illuminating: *Who They Are, How They Operate, and How We Can Protect Ourselves and Our Children.* Salter argues that it is our misconceptions about sex offenders, in large part generated by the media (Silverman and Wilson, 2002; Greer, 2003), that make us so vulnerable to them. Sex offenders rely on these misassumptions to carefully gain access to children. It is only by dispelling the myths surrounding sex offenders—including how they deceive their victims and manipulate them in order to gain their trust—can we effectively deflect sex offenders and protect children.

While it is wholeheartedly recognised that the enormity of this task cannot be underestimated some tentative suggestions can be made. In this respect, Home Office research entitled *Sex Offending Against Children: Understanding the Risk*

---

[17] Many bodies and individuals have long since highlighted the need to develop an effective information policy as a primary prevention initiative. These include The 1994 National Commission of Enquiry into the Prevention of Child Abuse Report (NOTA, 1995); The Inter-Departmental Group on Child Abuse 1992 (cited in Voluntary Sector Sex Offender Working Group, 1997a: 12); and the Voluntary Sector Sex Offender Working Group (1997a: 19).

(Grubin, 1998) suggests that there are a number of issues which the community could usefully be educated about including: (1) that contrary to media portrayal and popular belief, the abuser is rarely the 'dirty old man' in the raincoat which we imagine lurking in the corner of the local playground or park—the vast majority of sexual abuse, approximately 80 per cent, is perpetrated by people known to the child rather than a predatory stranger, with these offences taking place in the home of either the offender or the victim; (2) not all sex offenders are paedophiles—in only about 25 to 40 per cent of offenders is there a recurrent and intense sexual attraction to children that would attract a level of 'paedophilia'; (3) that sexual abusers are men and women and, in a growing number of cases, adolescents or children; (4) that there are different levels of risk and that not all sexual offenders pose the same degree of high-risk; and that in tandem with this, recidivism research has shown that most sex offenders will not reoffend given appropriate treatment and support.

Taken together these findings point to the need to educate the public that sex offenders are a heterogeneous population, some of whom may benefit from treatment (Hudson, 2005: 168, 183). As highlighted previously, most perpetrators assault children known to them, with these offences taking place in the home of either the offender or the victim.[18] In view of this stark reality, it is essential that children and all those responsible for them are also made aware that the danger often may not lie with strangers but with those closest to them. In this way, vigilance would be increased and risk and the opportunity for offending reduced.

In addition, as noted above, circles have opened up the work of statutory and voluntary agencies in allowing the local community an insight into how high-risk and high need sex offenders are treated and managed. However, 'The public educative function of the restorative justice process is the least often mentioned responsibility of the community' (McCold, 1996: 95). Circle members may also be able to provide a means of outreach to the wider community by including 'a community education component that emphasises an alternative paradigm of justice' (Mika, 1992: 565) and by serving 'as a model for peaceful resolution processes' (McCold, 1996: 96). The wider community could usefully be provided with general information about the treatment and management programmes which are available for sex offenders, including the work of circles, and the general mandate of those who work to secure the offender's reintegration. This may provide a measure of reassurance and foster community confidence that sex offenders are not just released onto an unsuspecting public with little attention to their post-custody behaviour or whereabouts.

The theoretical logic behind such an approach is well grounded in the wider debates about risk and governance, as outlined principally in chapter 2. Ericson and Haggerty's (1997) model of 'Knowledge-risk-security', in particular,

---

[18] A further interesting study in this respect is another prepared for the Home Office which looked at 94 cases of physical and sexual abuse (Davis et al, 1999). All but one of the complainants knew their alleged abusers, of whom 48% were family members or relations, 20% were family friends or neighbours, 15% were professionals (youth workers, teachers, doctors), and six% were acquaintances.

emphasises the proactive 'management' of knowledge about offenders and the production of compensatory measures against risk (Hebenton and Thomas, 1996b). In line with this model, the public, through community education and awareness programmes, would be admitted as consumers of this knowledge (Reiss, 1989). This information will increase community understanding of the problems posed by sex offenders in the community to the point where people are aware not of individuals but of situations. Whereas legal responses to managing sex offenders in the community focus on knowledge of the whereabouts of known 'risky' *individuals*, such social responses would be based on knowledge of 'risky' *behaviour or methods*, which could also encompass previously unknown offenders. Such social knowledge, therefore, could add a further layer of protection between children and abusers.

At a practical level, the purpose behind this approach is much more fundamental. This 'opening up' of knowledge and awareness on the part of the community is especially important when one considers the grooming process—that many sex offenders are manipulative and devious by nature and will seek to infiltrate unsuspecting families for sexual purposes. Criminal justice interventions can do little to prevent this unless the offender has already come to their attention. Communities can, however, by arranging networks of support and control where necessary (McAlinden, 2005: 388). Braithwaite (1999), for instance, uses the example of 'Uncle Harry' as a 'significant other' of the offender, and says that 'Uncle Harrys' have a much more plural range of incapacitative keys that they can turn than a prison guard who can turn just one key.

Through the dissemination and digestion of this information, communities in possession of the full facts about the nature of sexual offending and sex offenders will feel empowered to take responsibility for the protection of their children. They will eventually feel more able to handle this problem as it occurs in a considered and responsible manner. By responding to the problem of managing sex offenders in the community in a more constructive way, they should also be a help rather than a hindrance to statutory and voluntary agencies in the successful reintegration of sexual offenders into the community and the effective management of risk.

Challenging the media's image that sex offences are committed exclusively by strangers, however, raises a number of difficult issues. As noted in chapter two, sexual offending against children has become the subject of a 'moral panic' (Cohen, 1972/1980; Hall et al, 1978) in the media and amongst polticians and the recent legislation, common to many jurisdictions, is in part a reflection of this. In extending the public understanding of sexual offending to familial contexts in particular, there is a danger of simply increasing levels of suspiscion, mistrust and surveillance (Foucault, 1977). If society is encouraged to look very closely for abuse, there might be an associated danger of undermining trust rather than seeking to safeguard it. This might further heighten the moral panic surrounding sexual crime creating a society where no one trusts anyone (Hudson, 2005: 183). Furthermore, it has already been argued that the public already accepts that the risk of sexual victimisation by a stranger is small but is unwilling to perceive risk in domestic terms (Saraga, 2001; Greer, 2003). Care will need to be taken, therefore, to deliver this information in a sensitive and responsible way so as to avoid a compounding of current problems and, above all, to make sure that one panic about sex offending is not simply replaced by another.

Once public awareness of practices and processes surrounding offenders grows, a partnership approach may begin to be developed between statutory and voluntary agencies and local communities. Each of these relevant constituencies could come to recognise the legitimacy of each other's concerns and work together to better manage sex offenders in the community and to deliver reintegrative treatment and support programmes within an overall statutory framework.

A 'Partnership' Approach to Justice

The final element to be considered in the implementation of reintegrative shaming practices with sex offenders is the need to develop a 'partnership' approach to justice, between state agencies and the community, on a more widespread basis. There have been encouraging initiatives in this area thus far, but these efforts have only been incremental. The evaluation of circle programmes has shown that the community can take a more proactive and effective role in securing offender reintegration than at present. In the composition of circles, traditional community and state roles have been reformulated so that the community is now a critical dimension to the effective reintegration of sex offenders and, moreover, has gained the trust of the relevant agencies to work in this way (Quaker Peace and Social Witness, 2005: 3). The opportunity should be taken, therefore, to develop these partnerships further in the hope of developing more meaningful strategies to manage the risk posed by sex offenders in the community.

As discussed in chapter two, contemporary governments have sought to redefine their responsibilities in relation to crime prevention and control by shifting these obligations beyond state agencies 'to organisations, institutions and individuals of civil society' (Garland, 1996: 451). Crawford argues that a number of metaphors in social and political theory, which describe a series of processes which unfolded across diverse areas of social life at the end of the twentieth century, are linked to the shift in the governance of crime control towards 'community partnership' (1999: 6, 14–62, 63–93, 202–33). These include, 'governing without government' (Rhodes, 1995: 3), the 'death of the social' (Rose, 1996), the 'hollowing out of the national state' (Jessop, 1993: 10), the emergence of the 'risk society' (Beck, 1992; Ericson, 1996) and 'less government, but more governance' (Osborne and Gaebler, 1992). As Crawford argues, these are used to describe:

> A pattern of shifting relations between, the state, the market, and civil society; a move from "the social" to "community"; greater individual and group responsibility for the management of local risks and security; and the emergence of new forms of management of public services and structures for policy formation and implementation (1999: 6).

The Crime and Disorder Act 1998 in England and Wales, for example, by creating a swathe of new powers and duties to promote 'community crime prevention', 'community safety' and 'multi-agency partnerships', served to highlight the centrality of these components to criminal justice discourses and discussions about the local governance of crime in particular (Hope, 2001).[19] The interest and fascination with 'community policing' (Cordner, 1988; Goldstein, 1990; Fielding, 1995), is perhaps one of the most obvious and well-documented expressions of this recent appeal to 'community' in the field of criminal justice. It will be argued that all future efforts at sex offender reintegration should be targeted towards a form of community or problem-oriented policing (McCold and Wachtel, 1998; Weitekamp et al, 2003), where offenders are placed back into the communities in which they offended and where the public can form support groups to assist them and statutory and voluntary agencies with their rehabilitation.

What all the interventions to deal effectively with sexual crime, outlined at the outset of this chapter, have in common, is a practical agenda for meeting the needs of victims, offenders and communities, often using community resources (Presser and Gunnison, 1999: 312). Much of the traditional debate on the value of restorative or reintegrative justice has centred on the perspectives of victims and offenders, as will be outlined in detail in the next chapter. However, the community can also bring benefits to and can itself benefit from the reintegrative shaming process. Indeed, without the community, restorative justice is reduced to the competing perspectives of the victim and the offender, and there is no social group with reference to whom the offender can experience either shame or reintegration (Hudson, 1998: 251–2).

As outlined earlier in this chapter in relation to circles of support and accountability in particular, the community has potentially a very important role to play in the management of sex offenders in the community. Communities can offer support and encouragement, protect the offender from vengeance, and promote change and accountability in the community to prevent similar harms from reoccurring. They can create favourable conditions for restoration, support victims and their needs and can provide a safe place where inappropriate behaviour can be challenged (McCold, 1996: 92–96). By ensuring a more rational response on the part of the community to the placement and management of sex offenders in their area, the fuller implementation of such community initiatives could have many positive benefits for the offender, the wider community and those professionals in the multi-agency approach. If the management of sex offenders in the community is focused on both public protection as well as offender reintegration, then a synergy is achieved (Quaker Peace and Social Witness, 2005: 14). By successful reintegration the level of public protection is increased, while at the same time, the risk of reoffending is lowered.

---

[19] Responses to crime based on prevention, the promotion of community safety and the partnership approach are well established in a number of other jurisdictions such as Scotland, the Republic of Ireland, France, the Netherlands, New Zealand and South Africa (Crawford and Blair, 1999; Crawford and Matassa, 1999).

In relation to the offender, such initiatives will clearly stop or at least reduce the number of incidents of vigilante attacks by members of the public on known or suspected paedophiles. Sexual offenders could be rehabilitated and reintegrated into their local neighbourhood by remaining at restricted liberty while ensuring that any social factors, which may have been associated with offending, are addressed and not sidelined. By adopting such an approach the community itself has an involvement, thus reducing the social exclusion and stigmatisation of offenders that can lead to further offending. Moreover, there is also less chance that the offender will go underground where risk is not effectively managed but simply displaced to another community.

Encouraging community responsibility will also facilitate increased co-operation and the development of more cohesive and effective partnerships between the statutory, voluntary and community sectors in relation to child protection and sexual offender issues. It will allow for the development of restorative community treatment and support networks in addition to more formal statutory systems. In 'a balanced restorative justice model' (Weitekamp et al, 2003: 321), based on 'consensus' and 'active participation of the key stakeholders' (Uekert, 2003: 133), the community are involved with statutory and voluntary agencies in local community schemes with clear lines of responsibility. This would facilitate 'a climate of confidence between the partners' (Aersten, 2006: 89), co-operation, and a shared understanding of the multiple interests in the problem (Goldstein, 1990: 40–41). It would also strengthen the decision-making process of the statutory and voluntary sectors in relation to offender resettlement and help to improve the accountability of all three sectors (Goldstein, 1990: 47–49).

A 'community-system' partnership (Crawford, 1999; Bazemore and Griffiths, 2003: 78) would represent 'a positive, developmental approach' (Weitekamp et al, 2003: 321) to reintegration and would, therefore, serve to alleviate the problems experienced by statutory and voluntary agencies in effectively managing sex offenders in the community. The local community may be able to assist in the determination of what is the most appropriate action to be taken in addressing the needs of the victim and the community, as well as the needs of the offender in terms of his reintegration. Local facilities and resources are utilised while relevant agencies and voluntary groups are enlisted to provide support and expertise (McCold, 1996: 96–98). This will also allow for sex offenders to be placed back into the community, where people at least know who they are and know of their offending history, and can take appropriate steps to supervise the individual and to protect themselves and their children from harm.

In the main, there will be a better balance between a proactive response to the problem of managing sex offenders in the community generally rather than a reactive response after specific problems occur (Goldstein, 1990: 32, 45–47). By focusing on the substantive problem in this way, responses will be tailor made to the needs of the community and individuals (Goldstein, 1990: 43–45) with effective and efficient risk management posed as the ultimate goal (Goldstein, 1990: 35–36). This would constitute a positive dynamic approach to offender reintegtation which would 'make obsolete the negative, punishment-orientated policies' (Weitekamp et al, 2003: 321) which characterise contemporary criminal justice policy and practice in relation to sex offenders.

Moreover, a 'co-ordinated community response' (Uekert, 2003) would enable the intertwining of the formal criminal justice system with informal and community-oriented ways of conflict handling and allow restorative justice to interact with criminal justice procedures in a more explicit way (Aersten, 2006: 89). 'Developing such an organizational model in the form of a partnership might finally underpin the institutionalization of restorative justice' (Aersten, 2006: 89). As will be discussed in the next chapter, however, in relation to the critiques of restorative or reintegrative justice, there are potential difficulties in promoting social inclusion. There may also be associated problems in both identifying and securing the relevant 'community' in order to form these local community-agency partnerships.

CONCLUSION

The benefits of reintegrative shaming practices for sex offenders, which can be used to support offenders undergoing treatment and assist their reintegration, underline the need to involve the community in offender monitoring. As Eldridge and Wyre argue:

> In order for relapse prevention to be effective, sexual offenders need to be able to engage in a social life that is safe in the context of their individual pattern of offending. This requires an aware culture in which the offender is not an outcast but neither is he the subject of naïve trust (1998: 91).

The wholesale adoption of such an approach may be initially hard to reconcile with the 'populist punitiveness' discussed above. The particular position of sex offenders within popular discourses as the ultimate demon and the current 'law and order' ideology of crime control, incapacitation and risk management, common to many jurisdictions, may not rest easily with the advocacy of a restorative therapeutic response (Crawford, 2006; Tonry, 2006). On the other hand, it has also been argued that a further unwanted consequence of disintegrative shaming is that sexual offending behaviour may be increased if the offender feels socially isolated. Support and treatment for the offender in the community via reintegrative schemes, perhaps in a type of secure accommodation, could have the double benefit of protecting the offender from vigilante attack and also helping him or her to adjust to the demands of living on the outside. Furthermore, as outlined in chapter 6, chemical castration has been shown to be effective with some sex offenders on a voluntary basis. This may also have a role to play here in helping sex offenders to control their offending behaviour at an early stage in these programmes. Moreover, a form of community treatment programme which could deliver some tangible benefit in the form of reducing future offending behaviour may persuade the public that this is an ultimately more effective way to protect their children from the risk they feel the offender poses.

Before outlining the possible benefits which such schemes could have in terms of the effective management of sex offenders in the community, there are a number of obvious caveats: Firstly, as indicated above, as yet, there are no longitudinal studies available to establish with any certainty how effective these schemes are in terms of recidivism rates following participation in a programme. Secondly, there are the logistical problems of ensuring sufficient resources in terms of the availability of programmes with suitably qualified staff, and the monitoring and evaluation of programmes which ensure genuine engagement on the part of the offender. As will be discussed in the next chapter, the overwhelming positive aspect of these schemes, however, is the fact that they encourage and facilitate the treatment and reintegration of the offender and provide some level of engagement and truth for the parties about what has happened.

8

Reintegrative Justice: Addressing the Critics

THIS CHAPTER SEEKS to address the key concerns put forward by critics of restorative or reintegrative justice. It initially outlines some of the general critiques raised by opponents of restorative justice as a whole. Following this, it then addresses the major criticisms of restorative justice as applied to child sexual offences, before turning attention to the potential problems associated with shaming mechanisms in particular.

CONTEXTUALISING THE DEBATES

While differences and debates continue among proponents and practitioners of restorative or reintegrative justice as a whole, its general principles of providing restitution to victims and communities, promoting offender reintegration and repairing relationships between victims, offenders and communities are well understood and increasingly accepted (Johnstone, 2001; Sullivan and Tifft, 2001; Braithwaite, 2002b; McEvoy et al, 2002).

Much of the traditional debate has centred on the advantages of informal justice over litigation in terms of reducing the hostile and adversarial nature of that process and the benefits to the parties of co-operation rather than coercion (Folberg and Taylor, 1984; Semple, 1994). These advantages can be grouped under three broad headings: The first benefit is the informality and flexibility of the process which is conducive to a more responsive approach to dealing with disputes. The second is its emphasis on a 'future-focus' which aims to encourage parties to avoid becoming entrenched in apportioning blame for past conduct. The third is its capacity to 'empower' the parties by requiring them to define the dispute, state their respective desired outcomes, participate more actively in their own negotiations and achieve an agreed outcome of their dispute (Raitt, 1997: 78). For feminism, too, informal justice has been seen as holding out a hope of escaping the problems of formal procedures (Harris, 2003). The advantages of informal mechanisms for coping with family disputes are said to be that they are 'personalised, voluntary, consensus-oriented and therapeutic, and that, unlike formal methods, they empower the participants' (O'Donovan, 1985: 195).[1]

However, the framework of restorative justice has not been without its critics. Opponents of restorative justice have pointed out the dangers inherent in a communitarian approach to justice generally, principally the need to ensure legitimacy (Paternoster et al, 1997), accountability (Roche, 2003) and adequate safeguards (Van Ness, 1998; Braithwaite, 1999; Ashworth, 2002; Hudson, 2002; Wright, 2002). Paternoster et al (1997) identify several elements which provide legitimacy. These include: representation, in the sense of playing a part in decision making; consistency; impartiality; accuracy; the competency of the legal authority; correctability, as the scope for appeal; and ethicality, treating people with dignity and respect.

Restorative justice embodies some of these elements, particularly with regard to representation of and respect for victims and offenders. It does not meet others since they relate primarily to expectations of 'legal authority' derived principally from conventional justice values (Morris and Gelsthorpe, 2000a: 421). Restorative justice involves somewhat different values and its legitimacy must derive from these. As will be discussed below, important elements in providing the legitimacy of restorative justice are the inclusion of the key parties, and increased understanding of the offence and its consequences (Morris and Gelsthorpe, 2000a: 421).

Critics also argue that the lack of procedural rules and structure and the absence of recorded precedent make the mode of operation and the decision-making arbitrary and uncertain. There may be a thin line between voluntarily agreed measures and community-based schemes which, while they do not determine guilt, may nonetheless impose sanctions. There are also concerns about double jeopardy if individuals find themselves involved in a community-based scheme and yet also face simultaneous or subsequent action through the formal criminal justice system. In addition, it may be difficult to ensure that the alleged offender is able to receive professional advice about his rights. The majority of these objections have been founded on the basic premise that restorative justice aims to replace the formal administration of state justice and the consequent dangers associated with a non-legal community response (Ashworth, 2002). Schemes, however, which work in partnership with, take referrals from, and are subject to accreditation and monitoring by the criminal justice system, as outlined in the previous chapter, may negate such concerns.

Opinions also differ on the types of offences for which restorative processes should be used and the circumstances in which they should be used. While some scholars accept the usefulness and viability of restorative justice in dealing with low level crime that most commonly concerns local communities such as joyriding or vandalism, or with first time and young offenders, they are usually more

---

[1] A broader feminist rhetoric has linked all such formal processes with patriarchal masculinities, and hence informality with an ideal of female non-aggression and directness of address (Griffiths, 1986; MacKinnon, 1987).

reticent to extend this paradigm to serious and persistent forms of offending (Johnstone, 2003). Indeed, for the most part, 'sexual offences have been excluded from the RJ agenda' (Daly, 2006: 334) by the many writers who have traditionally highlighted the particular unsuitability of restorative programmes in the domain of sexual or domestic violence (Stubbs, 1997, 2002; Coker, 1999; Koss, 2000; Presser and Gaarder, 2000; Lewis et al, 2001; Busch, 2002). Too often, however, critics blithely reject any suggestions of using restorative justice for cases of inter-personal sexual violence without offering a well-thought out explanation of why it is unsuitable. Occasionally, a vague reference to 'power-imbalances' or 'vulnera-ble victims' is thrown out without any attempt to consider that the criminal just-ice process has to deal with such problems, and without serious thought to how these sensitive matters could be dealt with in a restorative process.

More recently, however, there has been increased feminist engagement with new forms of justice (Daly and Stubbs, 2006) and a growing recognition that restorative justice initiatives may have a role to play in dealing with intimate vio-lence and abuse (Mills, 2003; Cameron, 2006; Coker, 2006). The appropriateness of restorative justice in cases of domestic and family violence, however, is far from being uncontroversial (Cook, 2006), particularly among survivors of historical child sexual abuse (Jülich, 2006). The adult survivors in Jülich's study (18 women and 3 men) spoke of justice in ways that reflected restorative goals, yet paradox-ically were reluctant to endorse restorative justice as a paradigm within which they would pursue justice. These survivors shared many of the common concerns of critics, such as fears about power, manipulation and offender-centred processes, which will be addressed further below.

The potential of combining elements of restoration with the traditional justice response also appears to be conditional on various specific factors (Nancarrow, 2006). Coker (2006), for example, argues that restorative processes may be bene-ficial for some women who experience domestic violence, but only if those processes meet five criteria: (1) prioritise victim safety over batterer rehabilitation; (2) offer material as well as social support for victims; (3) work as part of a co-ordinated community response; (4) engage normative judgments that oppose gendered domination as well as violence; and (5) do not make forgiveness a goal of the process. As outlined in the previous chapter, and as will be discussed in more detail below, several of these elements—in particular the balance between victim or community safety and offender rehabilitation, the emphasis on a co-ordinated community-based response, and the engagement of normative community judg-ments in the process of promoting offender accountability—are also embedded in the dynamics of restorative work with sex offenders. The majority of critiques have been formulated in the context of restorative systems involving adult victims and offenders of non-sexual offences. However, as will be discussed further below, application of the restorative approach to sexual offences, and to child sexual abuse in particular, add extra dimensions to the problem.

RESTORATIVE JUSTICE AND CHILD SEXUAL OFFENCES

It will be demonstrated that the case for restorative justice as applied to 'gendered and sexualised violence' (Hudson, 2002), or 'gendered harm' as Daly (2002a) prefers, commonly rests on the perceived weaknesses of the present criminal justice system in responding to these types of offences, and the greater potential of restorative justice for providing satisfactory outcomes in more cases (Hudson, 2002: 621). In this respect, retribution it seems may fall between two stools and is something of a double-edged sword. The leniency of traditional punitive reactions may give the impression that sexual violence is acceptable behaviour (Finstad, 1990; Braithwaite and Daly, 1994). At the same time, however, punitive sanctions may also serve to increase the level of violence and aggression in some offenders (Carlen, 1992; Sherman, 1992; Hudson, 1998; Morris and Gelsthorpe, 2000a: 415). Sim summarises the problem in relation to rape:

> The lenient sentences for such crimes and the symbolic messages which men take from leniency can be contrasted with the fact that longer prison sentences offer no solution to the problem of rape and indeed may simply exacerbate the problem at an individual level by placing the rapist in a masculine culture which reinforces the misogynist fantasies that were part of his behaviour patterns outside the walls (1990: 97).

Sim's words echo Garland's description of the 'tragic quality' of punishment: that it is simultaneously necessary to symbolise the state's authoritative disapproval of certain forms of behaviour and yet futile in its efforts at controlling that behaviour (Garland, 1990: 80).

Writers such as Finstad (1990) and Braithwaite and Daly (1994) also underline the need to devise more constructive ways of responding to sexualised violence, precisely because of its damaging, domineering and harmful nature (Herman, 1997). It has also been contended that the diversity and nature of sexual violence, as outlined in chapter 1, is an indication of the need for a range of responses rather than primary or sole reliance on the criminal justice system (Morris and Gelsthorpe, 2000a: 419).

Proponents such as Hudson (1998, 2002), Morris and Gelsthorpe (Morris and Gelsthorpe, 2000a; Morris, 2002a) and Daly (2002a), among others, have significantly advanced the case for the application of restorative justice to sexual and violent (and racial) crime. However, their work for the most part has been concentrated on domestic violence with brief reference to child sexual abuse. This chapter, and indeed this book, attempt to extend this thinking and apply the principles of restorative justice to the perpetrators of child sexual abuse (McAlinden, 2005).

Indeed, Morris and Gelsthorpe have summarised the particular set of characteristics which underlie family violence which, they argue, seem to be perpetuated by the use of conventional criminal justice processes and which make it particularly suitable for a restorative approach. Although these comments were initially made in the context of domestic abuse, it is argued here that these could apply equally to victims of child sexual abuse:

> The existence of a prior relationship between the parties; the fact that the parties have lived together and may wish to continue living together; the likelihood of repeat victimisation; the context of emotional abuse and ongoing power imbalances in the relationship; the victim's fear of the offender; the secrecy of the violence; the isolation of the victim; and the offender's minimising of the seriousness of the violence (2000a: 421).

It is proposed to further discuss several of these elements as they apply to child sexual abuse and the potential difficulties which they pose for restorative approaches.

Minimisation of Serious Criminal Offences

First, one of the main criticisms levelled against the use of restorative justice with sexual offences is that it may minimise or trivialise what are very serious criminal offences, particularly where children and the vulnerable are concerned (Hudson, 1998: 253; Morris and Gelsthorpe, 2000a: 417–8; Morris, 2002a: 603). Critics suggest that such offences are too grave or sensitive to be dealt with by means other than the traditional criminal justice system and that nothing should be done which might return them to the status of a 'private' matter. There is a concern that community disapproval, redress and attempts to change could be seen as a 'soft option' or 'getting away with it' (Hudson, 1998: 253) and that such approaches would be used as 'second-rate justice for offences that don't really matter' (Cain, 1985: 335).

Sexual offending, particularly against children, is a serious form of criminal behaviour and should be publicly recognised as such. To do otherwise would be to send a message to abusers that if they sexually abuse they may be able to escape prosecution and the consequences of their actions by agreeing to a treatment programme. The use of the restorative process, however, does not signify the decriminalisation of sexual offences. The criminal law remains as a signifier and a denouncer, but the belief within restorative processes is that the abuser's family and friends are far more potent agents to achieve this objective of denunciation and of mobilising censure (Morris and Gelsthorpe, 2000a: 418; Morris, 2002a: 603). In this way, restorative approaches also have the potential to challenge community norms and values about what is acceptable behaviour, and to make sure that deviant sexual behaviour is something which is strongly disapproved of and about which perpetrators feel a strong sense of shame (Hudson, 1998: 250, 254; Karp, 1998: 280; Morris and Gelsthorpe, 2000a: 418). Reintegrative shaming mechanisms, in particular, reaffirm normative standards and reinforce on offenders that their behaviour is unacceptable and will result in appropriate censure (Kelley, 1989: 781; Massaro, 1991: 1895; Karp, 1998: 280).[2] In addition, as

---

[2] American courts have noted that submitting defendants to public disgrace will often heighten the deterrent and rehabilitative impact of punishment. See *Goldschmitt v Florida*, 490 So. 2d 123 (Fla. Dist. Ct. App 1986), at 125 (quoting *United States v William Anderson Co.*, 698 F.2d 911, at 913 (8th Cir. 1982)).

discussed above, a system which makes provision for state intervention as the formal backdrop for more informal social processes is clearly workable within the restorative framework.

Failure to Promote Offender Accountability

A second concern is that restorative justice fails to promote offender accountability—it allows the offender to reject responsibility for the offence (Morris and Gelsthorpe, 2000a: 417) and is powerless to challenge the offender's attitudes. However, most offenders are not made accountable for acts of abuse or rape against intimates (Braithwaite and Daly, 1994: 191–92; Morris and Gelsthorpe, 2000a: 415). Criminalisation and penalisation only touches a minority of offenders (Morris and Gelsthorpe, 2000a: 415). For every paedophile known to the police there are ten more not identified (Leggett, 2000: 7). In addition, a high proportion of child victims, figures suggest between 80 (Grubin, 1998: 15) and 98 per cent (Leggett, 2000: 7), are abused by someone known to them rather than predatory strangers. In the case of intra-familial abuse, children or their carers do not report all incidents of abuse whether out of shame or fear. The possibility of a parent or other relative being labelled and singled out for public harassment and rejection may impede the sexually abused victim, particularly children, from coming forward in the first place and reporting the incident. This assertion is also supported empirically by the clinical literature which shows that many child victims do not want punishment or imprisonment for their offenders (Sauzier, 1989; Berliner and Conte, 1995).

As outlined in chapter 4, for example, in relation to 'grooming' techniques, sexual abuse thrives on secrecy, and the climate of fear which surrounds this form of offending only helps to perpetuate this secrecy. Restorative or reintegrative programmes may ultimately break cycles of abuse and help the offender to desist, more so than stigmatising the offender through punitive control in the community mechanisms such as registration and notification. If offenders knows that they may not face the possibility of a criminal prosecution or ultimately a prison sentence if they come forward, then more offenders may be willing to come out in the open, admit to their crimes and seek treatment. The availability of a restorative option may also encourage more victims to come forward and report the offence. Increasing numbers of offenders therefore would be made accountable for their offences. This in turn could have the net result of reducing the incidence of child sexual abuse.

Moreover, those offenders who are arrested and prosecuted for sexual abuse against children are likely to have got away with it before and may have ingrained patterns of abusing and assaulting the vulnerable which the criminal justice system does little to address (Braithwaite and Daly, 1994: 191–92). Even though criminal conviction is a rare event for sexual perpetrators, repeat offenders will often have an advanced pattern of offending by the time of their first conviction. The formal system of justice, however, does little to engage offenders and confront the under-lying causes of their offending behaviour. There is very little evidence to suggest, either generally with respect to criminal behaviour or specifically with respect to crimes of a violent or sexual nature, that increased penalties deter many offenders (Sherman, 1992; von Hirsch et al, 1999) or that rehabilitative sanctions 'work' (Edleson and Syers, 1990; Gendreau and Andrews, 1990). Indeed, as outlined in chapter 4, it could also be argued that persistent offenders are those most in need of a restorative response since many sex offenders are released from prison each year into the community without the benefit of effective treatment programmes.[3]

The restorative process has the potential to change the attitude and behaviour of offenders. It provides an opportunity for early intervention, and offers a way to confront offenders both about the factors underlying their offending and the con-sequences of their offending behaviour for the victim in particular (Morris, 2002a: 603). Community sanctions challenge criminal behaviour directly by demanding that offenders take ownership for the consequences of their actions. Rather than allowing someone else to speak for them, as a lawyer would in court, the offender is expected to accept responsibility for the abuse and techniques of neutralisation can be challenged (Morris and Gelsthorpe, 2000a: 417). Contrition and apology, key elements in the restorative approach, may be part of the cycle of abuse. The difference in restorative processes is that the 'public' nature of that contrition and apology and the shared monitoring of subsequent events help to ensure that it is 'real' (Morris and Gelsthorpe, 2000a: 417).

Reinforcement of the Power Imbalance in Abusive Relationships

A third major criticism which is often put forward against the use of restorative justice with sexual offences is that many forms of sexual violence and assault, such as rape or child sexual abuse, are about power and control. Rather than con-fronting the offender with the power of the state acting either on behalf of or in place of the victim, restorative justice makes the relationship between victim and offender central, displacing the relationship between offender and the state (Hudson, 1998: 247). To confront the victim of a sexual offence with their offender in this way may serve to increase the level of intimidation and emotional pressures. This, critics argue, could reproduce and reinforce the imbalance of power entrenched in abusive relationships and lead to possible revictimisation (Martin, 1996; Hudson, 1998: 247; Morris and Gelsthorpe, 2000a: 416–17).

Stubbs (2002), for example, has argued that it is dangerous to assume that vic-tims of domestic violence are able to assert their needs and promote their own interests in the presence of the person who has perpetuated violence against them,

---

[3] As outlined in ch 4, studies on the effectiveness of prison treatment programmes reveal a moder-ate success rate and, in general terms, show that treatment is only marginally effective with some groups as opposed to others. (See, eg: Beech et al, 1998; Friendship et al, 2003).

and that requiring victim participation in these circumstances may ultimately be disempowering and punitive. With children, in particular, there is the risk that the unequal power relationships between child victims and adult perpetrators of sexual offences may be further increased. Children may be fearful of confronting the parent or other adult relative who has abused them and may be subject to emotional abuse in the form of added pressure from other family members to keep the abuse secret or to discontinue the restorative process.

One could argue, however, that many victims of sexual violence already feel completely disempowered by abusive relationships (Hoyle and Sanders, 2000). There is always a power imbalance between offenders and victims, as offenders have 'taken' from victims (Morris and Gelsthorpe, 2000a: 424, n 18), and it is the conventions of present formal criminal law and punishment which reproduce the power relations that produce violent and sexual crime (Hudson, 1998: 249). Restorative justice processes and practices, however, routinely work towards removing this imbalance by focusing on the empowerment of victims. As Morris and Gelsthorpe (2000a: 417) argue, power imbalances can be addressed by ensuring procedural fairness, by supporting and empowering the less powerful, and by challenging the powerful (Morris, 2002a: 608).

With restorative justice there is also the potential to give victims a voice, and to help them feel more in control of the process. The victim's perspective is made central to the proceedings whereas it is only a source of evidence in criminal cases (Hulsman, 1991: 681; Hudson, 1998: 248). Restorative processes could provide a forum in which the victim can make clear to the offender, to their friends and to their family, the effects of the abuse on them (Morris, 2002a: 608). Friends and families can help to reduce the victim's feeling of isolation by providing a supportive basis for that voice to be heard or, if appropriate, may speak for the victim more powerfully than any prosecutor in a criminal trial (Morris and Gelsthorpe, 2000a: 417). Offenders can also give victims some insight into the reasons for their offending. The personal experience of seeing that the offender is affected by a genuine feeling of remorse and shame should have a healing and restorative effect for the victim (Walgrave and Acisten, 1996. 77).

Precipitation of Repeat Victimisation

A fourth and related criticism levelled against restorative justice in this context is that it may encourage victims to remain in abusive situations and cause repeat victimisation. An implicit or underlying assumption when parties seek legal remedies is that where there was a relationship, it has broken down and that contact is not desired (Morris and Gelsthorpe, 2000a: 419). However, as discussed in the previous chapter, this is not necessarily so when women are assaulted by their partners or children are abused by their parents (Sauzier, 1989; Berliner and Conte, 1995; Carbonatto, 1995, 1998; Hoyle, 1998). Indeed, a principal argument presented in support of the use of restorative processes with respect to child sexual abuse is that many children, for a range of reasons, wish to remain in or return to the family home and it is often desirable for them to do so (Hudson, 2002: 622). By offering constructive rather than penal solutions, restorative processes may also be opted for at an earlier stage in children's experience of sexual abuse (Morris and Gelsthorpe, 2000a: 422).

What restorative processes envisage is allowing children to make voluntary and supported choices about their future from a range of options. It may be argued that children, as minors, let alone children who have experienced abuse in a relationship founded on power and control, may be unable to make rational choices. On the other hand, to remove them from the professional decision-making process altogether does little to address children's concerns.

Moreover, restorative justice may actually increase the safety of child victims (Morris and Gelsthorpe, 2000a: 420). It has been argued throughout this book that the criminal justice system can do little to increase general victim safety and at best protects children or women from sexual abuse or attack by known perpetrators. As argued in some detail in the previous chapter, in the case of child sexual abuse, the friends and family of the offender are equally if not better placed than professionals to prevent the recurrence of abuse and to play a role in monitoring the offender's behaviour and the victim's safety. Restorative justice processes directly involve them, in contrast to the exclusion intrinsic to criminal justice interventions (Morris and Gelsthorpe, 2000a: 420).

Encouragement of Vigilantism

A fifth concern which has arisen is that restorative justice encourages vigilantism (Morris and Gelsthorpe, 2000a: 420) because of its association with community or popular justice.[4] As Ashenden puts it, 'The underside . . . is the "danger" of . . . vigilance turning into vigilante action' (2004: 203). As outlined in chapter 2, in relation to popular responses to sexual offending in the form of 'name and shame' campaigns, local community justice can be repressive, retributive and vengeful (Morris, 2002a: 609). These values, however, are fundamentally at odds with the defining values of restorative justice and cannot therefore be part of it (Morris and Gelsthorpe, 2000a: 420).

On the other hand, the schemes which have developed so far, albeit on an ad hoc basis, should inspire confidence that the community is capable of responding to the delicate issues surrounding the reintegration of sex offenders in the community in a responsible and constructive manner. As discussed in the previous chapter, the type of scheme envisaged is one which takes place within the criminal justice system in conjunction with statutory and voluntary agencies. Operating programmes on the basis of a referral by statutory agencies will ensure the

---

[4] Von Hirsch and Ashworth (1998: 303) certainly justify conventional justice practices on the grounds that they displace vigilantism and prevent people from taking the law into their own hands.

provision of adequate safeguards and standards, and that those individuals who claim that their human rights have been infringed may be able to seek a direct remedy against a public authority under human rights legislation. As Hudson argues, formal law could stand behind restorative justice procedures as a guarantor of rights which cannot be overridden by decisions arrived at by consensus or majority (1998: 256). It could mean, for example, that an offender's rights would be protected against a vengeful community; that a victim's rights would be protected against a community view which did not take the harm seriously; and that either party would have rights guaranteed against persuasion of the group by a stronger advocate (Hudson, 1998: 256). As such, if there were concerns about individuals or communities taking over this process for non-restorative processes, checks could be introduced.

Moreover, vigilantism does not require the introduction of restorative justice to emerge. Despite the lack of empirical research on the subject, Abrahams (1998) provides many examples of vigilantism from modern day Britain and elsewhere which seem to have been reactions against the failings of conventional criminal justice sanctions (Marx, 1989; Harrington, 1993; Johnston, 1996). As Morris and Gelsthorpe argue: 'the spectre of vigilantism in debates of restorative justice, therefore, is perhaps something of a red herring' (2000a: 420).

Furthermore, if properly operated and applied, restorative justice schemes may also provide a process of education and engagement for vigilante groups, as well as an opportunity for the wider community to approach the problem of managing sexual offenders in the community in a more considered way. Vigilantism, as Johnston suggests, represents:

> [A] public unconvinced by the security guarantees given to it by the formal system of justice. In those circumstances, private and popular solutions come to the fore (1996: 232).

As also outlined in the previous chapter, restorative approaches in this way, may serve to facilitate an effective partnership approach between the statutory, voluntary and community sectors in responding to contentious sexual offender issues. If communities were to be involved in the process of offender resettlement, this would give them some ownership of the problem and a relevant stake with formal justice agencies in securing offender reintegration. Again, consistent with Ericson and Haggerty's (1997) model of 'knowledge-risk-security,' being part of the information or knowledge loop would also reduce their feelings of being at risk and increase their feelings of security.

SHAMING

In addition to the broader commentary on restorative justice there is a related debate on shame within restorative justice literature. Critics of shame theory and practice also underline a number of specific conceptual and empirical difficulties.

A central critical tenet is the difficulty of implementing shaming sanctions in practice in contemporary Western society where four broad critiques emerge. [5]

Lack of Empirical Research

First, reintegrative shaming theory has been the subject of only limited empirical testing (Makkai and Braithwaite, 1994; Zhang, 1995; Vagg, 1998; Hay, 2001). Of these studies, only a few have explicitly examined the effects of reintegrative shaming on subsequent delinquent behaviour (Zhang, 1995; Vagg, 1998; Hay, 2001). Furthermore, studies have generally been confined to young offenders (Olthof, 2000; Maxwell and Morris, 2001, 2002) and to less serious crimes.

As mentioned in the previous chapter, the examples of reintegrative shaming practices with sex offenders which exist in the United States and Canada have not yet been subject to a thorough evaluation. What little research there is on shaming has been done in the context of classic shame cultures such as Iceland (Baumer et al, 2002), Japan (Japanese Ministry of Justice, 1998), Hong Kong (Vagg, 1998) and China (Lu, 1999) which bear many of the traditional hallmarks of a communitarian society—an homogeneous culture, with dense, cohesive social networks and which relies heavily on shaming as a method of social control (Magnusson, 1977; Miller, 1990; Gunnlaugsson and Galliher, 2000).[6] There is some evidence that communitarian societies, as defined by Braithwaite (1989: 84–85), have lower crime rates than other societies (Messner and Rosenfeld, 1997; Lu, 1999; Savolainen, 2000).[7] However, this research has in general provided contradictory or at best only partially supportive evidence.

In this respect, one of the most recent studies on shame theory, using survey data from Russia, where recent social changes have shifted the bases of official

---

[5] As discussed in ch 3, a number of other critical fronts have developed concerning shaming as a psychological process (Tomkins, 1987; Walgrave and Aersten, 1996; Maxwell and Morris, 1999; Olthof, 2000; Harris, 2001, 2003a). These relate chiefly to the theoretical distinctions between shame and related emotions such as guilt, humiliation and embarrassment (Lewis, 1971; Lindsay-Hartz, 1984; Scheff and Retzinger, 1991; Tangney et al, 1996; Sabini and Silver, 1997; Harris, 2001; Taylor, 2002; Harris et al, 2004; Harris and Maruna, 2006), and the importance of empathy and remorse, rather than shame, in achieving reparative outcomes (Karstedt, 2002; Maxwell and Morris, 2002, 2004; Morris, 2002b; Taylor, 2002; van Stokkom, 2002; Sherman, 2003).

[6] A number of other studies, however, have also been carried out on specific populations. See, eg: Zhang (1995) on shame in the ethnic context of Asian and African-American families; Hay (2001) on adolescent delinquency; and Zhang and Zhang (2004) on parental and peer disapproval of delinquency. As noted in ch 3, Ahmed (2001) and Harris (2001) have focused on school bullies and drunk drivers respectively, and have used this empirical data to clarify the fundamental concepts of the theory (Braithwaite and Braithwaite, 2001).

[7] It is not clear, for example, whether the nature of the sanctions employed, the extent of offender reintegration or some other mechanism accounts for the lower crime rates observed in these societies (Baumer et al, 2002). Research also shows that the recidivism rates of countries such as Iceland (Baumer et al, 2002) and Japan (Japanese Ministry of Justice, 1998) closely approximate those of other countries which were much less communitarian and socially integrated. Furthermore, Hong Kong has a high level of intolerance for deviant behaviour which results potentially in labelling and exclusion of those who are nonconformist (Vagg, 1998).

social control potentially making shaming more important, has also produced mixed results. It confirms, for example, that disintegrative shaming was likely to be related to the chances of future deviance, but reintegrative shaming was also positively predictive of projected crime and misconduct (Botchkovar and Tittle, 2005). As will be discussed further below, however, there are obvious limitations here in extrapolating these findings to mainstream Western society. Indeed, confidence in the validity of any general theory requires not only multiple tests with differently constituted samples, but confirmation in a range of cultural settings (Botchkovar and Tittle, 2005: 402).

Rates of reoffending are of course only one measure of offender reintegration. As discussed in the previous chapter in relation to restorative schemes as a whole, there is a need for careful experiment and periodical evaluation of reintegrative shaming mechanisms with sex offenders whose remit is broader than a consideration of recidivism rates. Many proponents of restorative justice do not see their main objective as the prevention of reoffending, but instead measure favourable outcomes in terms of the consequences of offending behaviour for all concerned—for families, communities and the victim, as well as the offender (Christie, 1977; Maxwell and Morris, 1999, 2002; Bazemore and Griffiths, 2003).

Lack of Social and Norm Cohesion

A second and related critical issue with implementing shaming mechanisms is that shame might not work optimally in the cultural conditions of post-modern society. Essentially, it is said that the cultural and societal conditions which are necessary for reintegrative shaming to work, such as norm cohesion and communitarianism (Braithwaite, 1989: 84–85) and which are evident in paradigmatic shame cultures like pre-Second World War Japan (Benedict, 1946), are lacking in modern society.

In Japan, citizens make frequent and conscious use of shaming as a means of behaviour control. There is a strong concern with social judgment which is ingrained from childhood and which takes primacy even over family approval or support. People live in close proximity in tightly knit communities with very little privacy so that misconduct does not go unnoticed. The structured and tight knit nature of Japanese society assures widespread agreement about moral and behavioural expectation and the terms of social disapproval—an essential condition of effective shaming and practices (Massaro, 1991: 1908–9).[8]

Instead, most Western societies are characterised more by individualism than communitarianism and they lack social and norm cohesion (Braithwaite, 1989:

---

[8] Contemporary studies of crime in Japan suggest that these informal sanctions, where clear and coherent cultural standards and the fear of shame produce conformity, continue to work (Haley, 1996; Komiya, 1999; Leonardsen, 2004). Indeed, the fear of shame and the attendant loss of status may help to explain the low crime rate in Japan (Massaro, 1991: 1909). However, at the same time, as mentioned in the previous note, this is accompanied by a high recidivism rate (Japanese Ministry of Justice, 1998). Thus, it may be that a distinct group of habitual offenders are responsible for what little crime there is.

84–85; Tavuchis, 1991). The extent of cultural pluralism and complexity also means that the cultural meaning of shame is highly ambiguous and amorphous (Massaro, 1991: 1922–24, 1939; Karp, 1998: 289). As Karp puts it:

> Shaming may be offensive to modern sensibilities because it implies conformity and consensus in a society that values individuality, diversity and freedom (1998: 289).

A related argument here in relation to community disapproval of deviant conduct, as will be discussed further below, is that there are also problems in identifying the relevant 'community' and securing its participation, representation and co-operation (Hudson, 1998: 251; Crawford, 1999: 148–201). Braithwaite acknowledges this relative absence of optimal cultural conditions in Western societies such as the United States. Nonetheless, he counters that even in highly individualistic cultures, shaming will still reduce crime more effectively than punishment which is unaccompanied by moralising and denunciation (1989: 86, 1993).

Moreover, it has also been questioned whether the community is likely to express strong enough disapproval to induce the necessary shame and whether the pomp and ceremony of the court is instead necessary for the shaming ritual (Hudson, 1998: 249). As Hacking (1999) has pointed out, however, in an age in which we are supposedly drowning in value-relativism, there is striking consensus concerning the wrongness of sexual contacts and relationships between adults and children. Popular responses to sexual offending show that the community is somewhat ahead of judicial attitudes with public criticism of lenient sentences for rape and the early release of high-risk offenders. Popular responses to sex offending in the form of 'name and shame' campaigns, discussed in chapter 2, show that the community is, if anything, too strong in its disapproval of offending behaviour, and would certainly be willing and able to provide guarantees of the enforcement of remedies and to express strong enough censure to induce the necessary shame in the offender (Hudson, 1998: 249).

Difficulties in Promoting Social Inclusion

A third pragmatic difficulty is the recovery of a culture of social inclusion which would underpin and support the development of processes whose outcome is shaming that is reintegrative rather than eliminative, and where the ultimate goal is the enhancement of social justice. It has been argued that the creation of such a culture, which is not easy to envisage in present day Britain and America,

> [I]s the most intractable problem in the path of restorative justice, and it is one that is beyond the ability of proponents of any theory of penal reform to solve (Hudson, 1998: 256).

This argument also underlines the necessity of a rigorous public education and awareness programme, driven by government, designed to provide accurate information about the nature of sex offending against children and approaches to it. As outlined in the previous chapter, such a programme would hopefully shift cultural attitudes, dispel the commonly held myths and misconceptions, and increase understanding of the real nature of sexual offenders and sexual offending, thereby promoting social inclusion (Grubin, 1998; Leggett, 2000).

As also suggested in the previous chapter, some of the issues in which the community should be educated include the following: the abuser is rarely the 'dirty old man' in the raincoat lurking in the school playground; most sexual abuse is committed by people known to the child; sexual abusers are men and women and, in a growing number of cases, adolescents or children; not all sex offenders pose the same degree of high-risk; and that sex offender recidivism research has shown that most will not reoffend given appropriate levels of treatment and support (Grubin, 1998). Involving the local community in reintegrative programmes will also reduce the social exclusion and stigmatisation of offenders that can increase the risk of further offending, and often the dangers for another unsuspecting community.

The Problematic Nature of 'Community' and 'Partnership'

A fourth broad critique, which in many ways cuts across the three previous ones is what is meant by 'community' in contemporary society. This is most clearly linked, in particular, to the previous critiques concerning the lack of social and norm cohesion in most Western societies and the related difficulties in fostering a culture of social inclusion. In the main there are problems in identifying the relevant 'community' and securing its participation, representation and co-operation (Crawford, 1999: 148- 201). From a conceptual point of view, as Hudson puts it:

> The weakest point of many of the restorative justice formulations is thus not the question of how can the power between victim and offender be balanced, but what is the community; what is the community interest, and how can it be represented? (1998: 251).

Indeed, securing community partnerships and the movement of 'the sites of power' (Crawford, 1999: viii) in crime control towards local crime prevention initiatives is far from being unproblematic. Crawford describes the realities behind the rhetoric of 'partnerships', and notes that movement towards systems of crime control and security based on appeals to local community involvement raises important political, social, organisational, definitional and legal issues which have yet to be fully appreciated (1999).

First, he draws attention to the 'contestable' nature of the term 'community' which has been deployed and manipulated in order to mobilise public participation in crime control and the way in which the normative and empirical understandings of the term collide and fuse (Crawford, 1999: 148–201). Indeed, the problematic nature of the notion of 'community' and how we in turn address its interests are issues that have been raised by a number of commentators (O'Malley,

1992, 1996; McCold, 1996; McCold and Wachtel, 1998; Walgrave, 2003: 74–77).[9]
As Hudson argues:

> The 'death of the social' having been proclaimed, most of us now inhabit not 'commun-
> ities' but shifting temporary alliances which come together on the basis of private pru-
> dentialism. Residents' associations; parents' associations; city-centre rate payers;
> shopping-mall retailers; share-holders' meetings; women's groups: these are the kinds of
> collectivities which claim people's allegiances now, rather than communities (1998: 251).

As outlined in chapter 3, different models of restorative justice propose different memberships of forums or conferences from victims, offenders and those close
to them, to selected expert groups. More often, however, reference is made to the
wider community. In the context of reintegrative shaming mechanisms the type of
community involvement envisaged here is primarily a geographical one. In relation to schemes such as circles of support and accountability in particular, as outlined in the previous chapter, members of the local community where the offender
resides after release from prison become involved in a practical way with the
offender's rehabilitation and reintegration. However, as will be discussed further
below, such extensive community involvement ultimately requires the commitment, co-operation and participation of the entire community to meet the needs
created by the crime (McCold, 1996: 92).

Secondly, there are inherent difficulties with the notions of 'local' or 'social
justice' and the possible consequences of a crime control philosophy and organisational model which places its prime emphasis on the needs of the community
(Crawford, 1999: 263–94). These could in certain circumstances result not in
communal harmony and social cohesion but in 'exclusion' (Pavlich, 2001: 3) or
'exclusivism' (Walgrave, 2003: 76–77) and the further spatial and social polarisa-
tion of deviants (Bottoms and Wiles, 1986) such as sex offenders. It could similarly
result in the reinforcement and exacerbation of inequalities inherent in the distribution of victimisation or the 'patterning of offence locations' (Bottoms and
Wiles, 2002: 628). Security, in such a context, can be identified with 'the degree of
personal insulation from "unsavoury" groups and individuals' (Davis, 1990: 224)
and is derived from the ability to find sanctuary in secure 'bubbles of governance'
(Shearing, 1995). Bottoms and Wiles note in a neo-medieval vision of the future:

> [T]he difficult question is whether these developments will continue to the point at
> which the city consists of defended locales, linked by protected routes, but with 'bad
> lands' elsewhere—the ultimate 'ghettoisation' of everyday life (1995: 36).

Indeed, a further and related danger here, as discussed above in relation to the
potential problems with restorative justice more generally, is that community

---

[9] Restorative advocates have also differed greatly in their conceptualisation of community.
Walgrave (2003), for instance, prefers the label 'communitariansim' to refer to a socio-ethical movement directed towards collectivity, but built into the rule of law, where members take responsibility
based on mutual respect and solidarity. McCold and Wachtel (1998) prefer a non-geographic,
'incident-based' definition which seeks to define community differently for each incident or problem
by including members from among the 'microcommunities' of concern for each particular incident.

groups may mutate into a form of vigilante justice where local popular responses to sex offending can become punitive and prejudicial, often resulting in vigilante activity and physical attacks on suspected paedophiles. The net result it has been argued, is that risky individuals are merely displaced elsewhere. Crawford summarises these problems with local or social justice thus:

> In the quest for a more socially just public sphere we need to be alert to the dangers of 'community' whilst acknowledging its potential. Strengthening communities is not always synonymous with the creation of social order and cohesion. An assertion of 'community' identity at a local level can be beautifully conciliatory, socially nuanced, and constructive but it can also be parochial, intolerant, oppressive and unjust (1999: 294).

In short, therefore, there is a need to develop forms of social cohesion which foster social solidarities while preserving an acceptance of difference (Crawford, 1999: 312). As outlined in some detail in the previous chapter, a mechanism such as circles, however, which lays joint emphasis on the prevention of further offending and the protection of the community's interests, represents an attempt to strike the appropriate balance between the needs and interests of the community and those of the offender.

A third and related contention is that shifts away from formal criminal justice institutions towards a new found emphasis on informal community partnerships as modes of crime control give rise to new patterns of local governance. These evoke key questions about the legitimate responsibilities of individuals, organisations and the state (Crawford, 1999: 63–93), the regulation of social conflict and the nature of individual and organisational democratic accountability (Crawford, 1999: 234–62). Rigorous criteria for combining the malign, darker side of 'community' involvement and its more benign attributes need to be constructed (Crawford, 1999: 313). As argued above in relation to concerns with vigilantism and restorative justice more generally, there is a need to build into the social fabric mechanisms which challenge and restrict the potential over-encroachment and abuse of such inherent capacities for persuasive or coercive powers. At the same time, however, and as will be discussed further below, the participation of the local community also has the potential to help ensure agency responsibility and accountability.

Fourthly, community partnerships need to ensure 'representativeness' of incorporated bodies and individuals, and to develop structures and processes that enable full participation and correspondence between community representatives and the communities they purport to represent. There must be multiple forms of openness and accountability—informational, organisational, managerial and political (Crawford, 1999: 311–12). These criteria are the necessary principles for genuine community responsibilisation (Crawford, 1999: 305). In addition, social institutions which mediate the impact of local or communal initiatives on other areas and groups need to be established at different sectoral and spatial levels such as local, city, regional and national levels. In this instance, the state has a fundamental empowering, mediatory, and regulatory role vis-à-vis communities, associations and partnerships (Crawford, 1999: 311). The involvement of statutory and voluntary agencies in community schemes will help to keep the community in check. Equally, community involvement in the reintegration of the offender also helps to ensure state and organisational accountability.

Finally, Crawford contends that crime alone may not be the most appropriate focus around which to organise open, tolerant and inclusive communities. Rather, it is more likely to lead to greater defensiveness, exclusivity and parochialism (1999: 312). The nurturing of tolerant communities, their institutions and structures, must be shaped around discussions that are integrating rather than exclusive and bifurcating, as is the case with 'crime.' In this respect, he argues that inculcating respect and tolerance for other community members or non-members can and should be encouraged around issues other than crime in its narrow sense (Bottoms, 1990). Prosocial patterns of behaviour in communities are more likely to be fostered around activities of care, nurturing and mutuality which may in turn have consequences for crime prevention (Crawford, 1999: 13). As outlined in the previous chapter, this is where community education and awareness programmes initially come into play which encourage, in part, parents and carers of children to take responsibility for the everyday protection of their own children, which may in turn serve to increase public safety and reduce the incidence of child sexual abuse.

CONCLUSION

It seems appropriate to end this chapter by returning to one of the arguments with which it began. The strengths of restorative approaches in responding to sexual offences lie chiefly in its advantages over the traditional retributive system. It has been argued that a restorative approach offers the prospect of providing a more effective response to managing the risk posed by sex offenders in the community than the one currently provided by the media, the public and ultimately by the legislature and the judiciary.

Without taking the community in particular on board via restorative measures, the result will be a compounding of the current problems faced by the statutory and voluntary sectors, and indeed the community itself, in placing and managing sex offenders in communities, as more sex offenders are released from custody at the end of their sentences every year. The only alternative to a future integrated approach aimed at developing more effective reintegrative partnerships between the statutory, voluntary and community sectors, is a Devil's Island penal colony for sex offenders of the sort envisaged in the film *Papillon*. This undesirable retrograde step would take us back to the days before we had a formal system of justice and the days of witch hunters where, to paraphrase the words of John Proctor in Arthur Miller's play *The Crucible*, 'vengeance wrote the law.'

9

Managing Risk: From Retribution to Reintegration

T HE CONTEMPORARY POPULAR and state-led responses to managing the risk posed by sex offenders in the community have largely been punitive and retributive in nature. These responses, however, have been far from effective. Instead of promoting the effective rehabilitation, risk management and reintegration of offenders they have often succeeded in achieving the opposite. The risk-based regulatory framework of offender reintegration has failed to manage risk effectively (Maruna and LeBel, 2002). Equally, the popular reaction to the presence of sex offenders in the community has served to displace risk management and even increase the risk of subsequent offending. Since conventional justice responses have been found lacking, the state and civil society need to consider and develop new and innovative ways to manage the risk posed by sex offenders in the community and promote their reintegration.

The essence of this book's argument has been that the future management of the risk posed by sex offenders is best secured through the integration of restorative and retributive philosophies rather than by simple retribution. The focus of this book, in tandem with popular and political concerns, has largely been on sexual offending against children. It has been stressed, however, that contrary to these dominant discourses, the primary issue is the management of offending by family and acquaintances, which often remains hidden, rather than by predatory strangers. In this respect, as will be discussed further below, the types of risk posed by sex offenders which need to be 'managed' may be classified into the following three typologies: 'known and high-risk'; 'known, but low-risk'; and 'unknown risk' (Soothill 2005, Soothill et al 2005a, 2005b). Each of these categories of risk must be meaningfully addressed in charting the way forward via restorative measures.

RETRIBUTIVE JUSTICE: THE FAILURE TO MANAGE RISK

The 'law and order' agenda in both the United States and the United Kingdom, which has closely followed suit (Jones and Newburn, 2002, 2006), has been premised on effective risk management, public protection (Kemshall and Maguire, 2001) and preventive governance (Ashenden, 2002, 2004), particularly in relation to dangerous offenders. It is becoming increasingly clear, however, that conventional mechanisms of control cannot adequately control risk and protect society from sex offenders. To a large extent, the legislature and the judiciary have so far relied almost exclusively on imprisonment, either in prisons or mental institutions, to curb sexual offending behaviour. Such approaches, however, have failed to deter or rehabilitate sex offenders and have been unsuccessful in reducing reoffending. There is a notable absence, in particular, of meaningful and effective therapeutic programmes in prisons (Furby et al, 1989; Beech et al, 1998). Traditional rehabilitative approaches tend not to work at all or are not wholeheartedly pursued. Chronic prison overcrowding, lack of resources and the various statutory release procedures often lead to the early release of sex offenders without the benefit of an effective treatment programme.

The criminal justice system is clearly failing to make sex offenders accountable for their offences. While overall levels of sexual offending are increasing, reconviction rates for sex offenders have declined (Friendship and Thornton, 2001). Moreover, sex offenders commit an alarming number of offences for which they are never arrested or convicted. Scholars have also contended that fewer than 5 per cent of sex offenders are ever apprehended (Salter, 2003) and that actual recidivism rates for sex offenders may be as much as 5.3 times the official reconviction rate (Falshaw et al, 2003). In sum, therefore, the current retributive response offers little hope for engaging individual offenders and making a real impact on the incidence and prevalence of sexual offending.

In conjunction with this, sexual offending, particularly against children, consistently makes news headlines causing public panic and fear and a general community intolerance for sex offenders (Silverman and Wilson, 2002). The popular response to sex offending is largely negative, vengeful and potentially destructive. The community's abhorrence and rejection of sex offenders when their identity becomes known means that risk is merely 'moved around' rather than being effectively managed. There is a pressing need therefore to think constructively about developing a more effective public response to the reintegration of sex offenders and for state agencies to work in a more networked way with the community and around sex offenders themselves. Sex offender recidivism rates will decrease only after effective reintegrative community treatment and support programmes are implemented to help promote social inclusion, to cure offenders of the urge to victimise and to support them in their rehabilitation and reintegration on release.

In response to the failure of traditional rehabilitative approaches and orchestrated media and public campaigns over the dangers posed by sex offenders living in the community, successive governments have enacted ever more punitive sanctions aimed at extending the didactics of control from prison into the community. These regulatory measures have included most notably, sex offender registration and community notification under 'Megan's Law' in the United States and Part 2 of the Sexual Offences Act 2003 in the United Kingdom (formerly Part I of the Sex Offenders Act 1997). Other jurisdictions have gone far beyond mere registration or community notification when a sex offender is released from custody. Various American states and many European countries have also implemented chemical castration legislation to reduce sexual deviance and deal effectively with these offenders. In addition, a minority of judges in the United States have begun to use 'shame' penalties in the form of signs and public exposure penalties as part of modern probation conditions for sex offenders. These policies may not only deflect from the concerns of intimate, non-stranger sexual assault, but they may dissuade the public from considering other viable policy options (Wright, 2003).

None of these measures on their own offer a panacea for the effective management of sex offenders in the community. It has been argued that all these measures are replete with moral and pragmatic issues. In this context, the arguments presented have highlighted the difficult and delicate task of balancing the rights of victims to protection on the one hand, and the rights of offenders to privacy and freedom from unlawful intervention in their lives on the other. Clearly, public protection and offender deterrence are at the heart of these official responses. The net result, however, of both popular and state-led responses to offender management and reintegration, has been the undermining of community safety.

Coercive criminal justice responses will not deter offenders, protect victims or make significant reductions in recidivism levels, except perhaps in the short term. These measures in common with popular 'name and shame' initiatives, individually and collectively, only serve to label and stigmatise offenders and isolate them from the rest of the community. Rather than promoting the offender's reintegration, these 'disintegrative shaming' (Braithwaite, 1989) mechanisms may actually impede it, and ultimately increase the risk of recidivism. As Simon (1998) argues, in the absence of a clear therapeutic focus for sex offenders, such legislative responses simply become mechanisms for 'managing the monstrous.' In fact, these measures represent a distinct failure to manage the monstrous. By stigmatising and ostracising offenders they put them on the trajectory of reoffending.

At the same time, for many victims of sexual violence, offender-focused prosecution is no solution (Finstad, 1990; Braithwaite and Daly, 1994). The criminal justice system often does too much and too little at the same time. It may do too much by putting the victim through the ordeal of the court process and driving a wedge between them and the perpetrator (Sanders and Young, 2002: 1068). A significant amount of sexual abuse or assault victims do not want to see their partner, father, mother or close family relative punished. They simply want the abuse to stop, especially if the abuser is their parent (Sauzier, 1989; Berliner and Conte, 1995; Carbonatto, 1995, 1998; Hoyle, 1998). It may do too little to protect the victim from reoffending by providing a reduction in charges, short sentences or an acquittal which minimises the harm done to the victim and does little to promote offender accountability (Sanders and Young, 2002: 1068).

The traditional justice system therefore fails too many victims and offenders. No matter how many aims are attributable to the criminal process (deterrence, retribution, rehabilitation, incapacitation), the overall rationale of the system is too simplistic: that of punishing the guilty. It is not clear, therefore, why a limited legal response has been expected to deal with this ever pervasive social issue. The endemic nature of sex offending against children requires an all encompassing solution to reflect the full complexity of the problem in which offences are properly understood in a far wider context than purely legal terms.

RETRIBUTION AND RESTORATION: BRIDGING THE GAP

The choice of justice responses, in this respect, has traditionally been presented in oppositional polar terms as being between either retributive or restorative approaches. Criminologists themselves, however, have begun to recognise that retributive and restorative frameworks are not diametrically opposed, but may rest easily side by side (Zedner, 1994; Walgrave and Aersten, 1996; Marshall, 1997; Daly and Immarigeon, 1998; Levrant et al, 1999; Daly, 2000; Duff, 2002; Hudson, 2002).

Indeed, there is a growing recognition that a purely punitive response is no longer sufficient for these types of offences and that there is a need to develop a more holistic response to the problem. Such an approach would address not just the punishment and control of offenders, but their rehabilitation and reintegration, while at the same time safeguarding the welfare of victims and addressing the concerns of the wider community. The reintegrative approach to sexual violence or sexual abuse cases is therefore less alienating than the punitive dichotomous approach currently embodied in the retributive system (Finstad, 1990; Braithwaite and Daly, 1994; Hudson, 2002: 621; Sanders and Young, 2002: 1068).

Recent initiatives also demonstrate that this choice does not have to be in such absolute terms. Schemes such as circles of support and accountability have developed dynamic treatment and support networks for high-risk sex offenders on release from prison, based firmly on restorative principles, which are 'community-based, volunteer driven and professionally supported' (Kirkegaard and Northey, 2000: 76). Circles have been presented as a holistic response to the sex offender problem, taking into account the needs of both the community and the offender. Early studies indicate that these schemes have been effective in reducing reoffending (Wilson et al, 2002) and promoting 'reintegrative shaming' (Braithwaite, 1989), and that communities are willing to play a constructive, supportive and positive role in the process (Quaker Peace and Social Witness, 2005: 5).

This, however, is not to deny a role for the symbolic condemnation of sexual violence through criminalisation and state intervention. Instead, restorative or reparative principles can be incorporated into the existing regulatory framework (Zedner, 1994; Dignan and Cavadino, 1996; Walther, 1996). In this respect, perhaps one of the most compelling approaches to reconciling restorative justice with the traditional regulatory framework is Braithwaite's (2002b) idea of 'responsive regulation.' As outlined in chapter 7, Braithwaite (Braithwaite, 1999, 2002b; Braithwaite and Braithwaite, 2001) endorses the presumption of a restorative response with deterrent and incapacitative back-up sanctions, although he specifically excludes retributive stigmatising punishment from this process.

Moreover such an approach would be firmly in keeping with current thinking on crime, justice and crime prevention along a number of dimensions. Criminal justice discourses have shifted focus towards evidence-based policy and practice and a 'what works' approach as demonstrated by the range of legislative mechanisms which now exist for social control (Rose, 2000). Furthermore, within the justice debate, public law discourses, and more specifically debates about social order, have embraced concepts such as 'governance' where it is acknowledged that justice can now no longer operate from the state down. As part of an integrated approach to crime prevention and control, there is a need to encourage community responsibility and to develop alliances horizontally and vertically between state agencies, civil society and the individual (Garland, 1996, 2001; Crawford, 1999; Garland and Sparks, 2000; Hirst, 2000; Rose, 2000; Shearing, 2000; Strang and Braithwaite, 2001). Emphasis is placed in particular on related concepts such as 'active citizenship,' 'partnership' and the need to develop co-ordinated responses to local crime problems which reflect the multiple interests in the problem (Crawford, 1999; Hope, 2001). Restorative or reintegrative approaches to offender resettlement also advocate a 'strengths-based' approach (Maruna and LeBel, 2002) which is characterised by the themes of repair, reconciliation and community partnership (Farrant and Levenson, 2002; Burnett and Maruna, 2006: 84).

Nowhere is this more urgent than in the management of sex offenders on release from custody into the community where there is a clear need for the community to work in partnership with statutory and voluntary agencies to develop more meaningful and effective approaches to the rehabilitation and reintegration of offenders. Such a participatory crime policy would not be intolerant and repressive as current retributive responses have been, but could help to develop and foster the qualities that people need to conceptualise, formulate and then implement more rational responses to local crime problems (Johnstone, 2000).

Such a move may initially be out of step with current public attitudes, and as such will not be achieved without a requisite degree of difficulty. Developing a relationship between statutory and voluntary agencies and the community, in this respect, which is all-encompassing, might appear to be quite ambitious. Indeed, 'engaging in a considered debate with the public . . . on the problems surrounding the managing of sex offenders' remains an intractable issue (Grange, 2003: 231). The first step in this process, however, is to raise public consciousness of how sex offenders actually operate. In this respect, some of the most recent research studies demonstrate that public opinion is much more nuanced and complex than initially appears from traditional data, and that victims are often less punitive than the media would have us believe (Roberts and Hough, 2002; Roberts et al, 2003; Hutton, 2005).[1]

---

[1] This argument can also be equated with a broader one made by Ashworth which says that victims of crime are not a homogeneous group and are certainly not all punitive—there are those in the 'service of offenders' as well as those in the 'service of severity' (2000: 186).

As people's awareness and knowledge of the issues grows then we can safely enlarge the net of people involved in making a contribution to offender management and reintegration. Restorative justice approaches recognise that the community can be a useful resource in preventing recidivism and managing the risk of reoffending, rather than the catalyst for the onset of future offending through the stigmatisation and ostracism of offenders. Indeed, the overall strength of restorative approaches to sexual offences lies in their ability to reintegrate sex offenders into the community and manage the risk they present more effectively or, as O'Malley (2006) prefers, to 'govern' sex offenders 'through the democratic minimization of harms.'

RESTORATIVE JUSTICE: THE EFFECTIVE MANAGEMENT OF RISK

A key critique of all the legislative efforts to manage sex offenders to date is that they constitute a response to managing known offenders and to abuse that has already occurred. As such, they can have little effect in preventing abuse which requires addressing abusers' problems or in impacting on overall levels of sex offending. Given that the majority of abuse occurs in the home where it often remains hidden, what is needed is a much broader approach to the management of risk.

Recent empirical research by Soothill et al (Soothill 2005, Soothill et al 2005a, 2005b) estimates that of sexual recidivists known to the police, under one third will come from convicted offenders in the high-risk category. The current focus of the retributive framework is firmly on the first of these categories as outlined at the outset of this chapter. These offenders will usually be captured by the MAPPP arrangements or their equivalent. It has been argued here that these 'known and high-risk' offenders could continue to be prosecuted via the criminal justice system, but then managed via reintegrative shaming mechanisms like circles of support and accountability on release.

Owing to the numbers of offenders involved, however, there will always be a larger number of the second category—'known, but low risk'—who are reconvicted. Indeed, of known sexual recidivists, around one third will come from convicted offenders in the more numerous low/ medium-risk categories (Soothill et al 2005b). Many of these offenders currently fall outside the traditional policing arrangements because of the resource implications of the numbers involved. For this category of offender, circles of support could be used as a fully-fledged alternative to prosecution and the formal sentencing process. More punitive sanctions however, could be retained as a backdrop or as an option of last resort with more persistent offenders, where restorative measures have failed to prevent reoffending, or with uncooperative offenders. It is the third category of offender however—those who pose an 'unknown risk'—comprising those offenders who have not been apprehended by the police or adjudicated on, who present the most problems.

Soothill et al's work (Soothill 2005, Soothill et al 2005a, 2005b), in this respect, has identified an important subset of this latter category of risk which has been termed those 'strongly suspected of serious sex crime and future danger' (Soothill, 2005)—those offenders thought by the police to be perpetrators, but who have not, for various reasons, been prosecuted. Their 15-year follow-up study compared sex offenders against children aged between 5 and 12 years who were convicted, with those who were suspected but not convicted in the Lancashire police force area over a 3-year period at the end of the 1980s. This grey area of people strongly suspected but not convicted covers cases such as that of Ian Huntley, convicted of murdering Soham schoolgirls Holly Wells and Jessica Chapman, where police forces failed to pass on relevant information about his offending past and the fact that he was strongly suspected of serious sexual offences.

The results show that offenders strongly suspected of, but not convicted for, a sexual offence also accounted for a third of repeat offenders coming to the attention of the police (Soothill et al, 2005b). As this book has also argued, these offenders therefore also fall outside the scope of traditional retributive measures of surveillance and control which are routinely in place for monitoring convicted and, to a lesser extent, cautioned sex offenders. In comparing the reconviction rates of those previously convicted of child sexual offences with those strongly suspected but not convicted, those with high-risk scores were almost identical in outcome regardless of whether they had been convicted. For the lower categories of risk, however, (low, low-medium, and medium-high) those with previous convictions were about twice as likely to be subsequently convicted of a sexual offence. Successful identification and subsequent conviction of the relatively small high-risk group will facilitate the targeting and appropriate use of traditional surveillance and management resources (Soothill et al 2005b: 41). As regards suspected offenders, however, as the authors readily acknowledge, 'There are considerable operational and ethical concerns to confront in dealing with such situations' (Soothill et al, 2005a: 226).

Having identified that detected but not convicted offenders provide a substantial source of future danger, the issue of how to manage this future risk must nonetheless be confronted. This category of 'unknown' or 'suspected risk' can essentially only be probed, using traditional methods, by improving the procedures for securing convictions, such as increased intelligence, investigation and subsequent surveillance. A restorative focus, however, would also help to identify the future risk posed by sex offenders against children. By removing the threat of public condemnation and punitive state sanctions, this would increase the willingness of perpetrators to come forward and seek help and encourage and support victims and communities to report the offence. Replacing formal prosecution with restoration for these offenders would also provide a meaningful way of effectively managing the future risk posed by repeat 'suspect' sex offenders, while at the same time negating such operational and ethical concerns.

In the longer term, if governments have a genuine aspiration to reduce the incidence of sexual offending significantly, in particular child sexual abuse, there will be a need to make a more concerted effort than targeting a relatively small number of perpetrators after they have offended (Geiran, 1996a: 153–54). Instead of 'knee-jerk reactions' in the form of sex offender registration and other legislative control in the community measures, there would be an opportunity to develop solutions to the problem of managing sex offenders in the community that would produce real change. Once this is recognised, then we can dispense with political rhetoric and quick fix solutions like registration, and go some way towards breaking cycles of abuse (Wilson, 1995; Flynn, 1996) and building genuine and effective child protection strategies.

The solution to the problem of managing sex offenders in the community therefore does not lie solely in the ever expansion of law, legislation and legal processes. The solution lies in helping the local community to take ownership of the problem and in developing community cohesion and strengthening working relationships between the community and statutory and voluntary agencies. In this way it would be possible for society to informally manage sexually deviant behaviour in the community and indicate their disapproval of such behaviour without stigmatising it (Braithwaite and Braithwaite, 2001). The legal mechanisms of management and control, however, can be used where necessary to establish programmes and as a remedy when normative and professional controls have broken down.

It is all very well, however, to call for opportunities for sex offenders to undergo restorative community treatment and support programmes. Without the necessary financial assistance to ensure effective programmes, the impact of any proposals will be slight. If the Government is committed to public protection and social inclusion beyond the level of rhetoric, adequate resources to extend the use of programmes like circles beyond a few isolated pilot schemes must be made available.

The restorative or reintegrative paradigm does not have all the answers. It is often met with controversy particularly where sexual offences and child victims are concerned. Such programmes may not be appropriate for all sex offenders, particularly high-risk offenders, but could provide an effective alternative for low-to-middle-risk offenders, particularly in the context of intra-familial abuse and when operated on a voluntary basis. Cases, therefore, would need to be carefully selected and managed and would also need a great deal of preparatory work and follow-up (Hoyle and Young, 2002: 537). However, its potential benefits for improving the safety of victims, for rehabilitating offenders, and for providing relief for communities mean it is worth careful implementation.

Restorative justice can be an effective means of affording protection to victims of sexual violence and abuse and enabling them to get on with their lives within communities that have been mobilised to care about them. At the same time, a vigilant community can increase the safety and welfare of children by maintaining informal social controls on abusers and limiting the offender's scope for offending. Not only are sex offences traumatic for victims and their families, but society as a whole has a substantial interest in the deterrence of such crimes. Restorative justice in this respect can also provide a measure of reassurance for communities that sex offenders are being effectively dealt with.

Such a collective response would ultimately represent proactive and anticipatory responses to managing the risk posed by sex offenders and reintegrating them into the community and not just reactive and defensive responses after specific cases occur. In short, it is contended that the argument for the fuller extension of the restorative paradigm to the domain of child sexual abuse and child sexual abusers should be recognised for what it is—a viable alternative in a justice system that has yet to come up with a better answer to an extremely difficult societal problem.

Bibliography

ABEL, GG, BECKER, JV, MITTLEMAN, MS, ROULEAU, JL and MURPHY, W (1987) 'Self-reported Sex Crimes of Non-incarcerated Paraphiliacs' 2 *Journal of Interpersonal Violence* 3.

ABRAHAMS, R (1998) *Vigilant Citizens* (Cambridge, Polity Press).

ACKER, JR (2006) 'Hearing the Victim's Voice Amidst the Cry for Capital Punishment' in D Sullivan and L Tifft (eds) *Handbook on Restorative Justice: A Global Perspective* (New York, Routledge).

ADLER, RA (1996) 'Estate of C.W.: A Pragmatic Approach to the Involuntary Sterilisation of the Mentally Disabled' 20 *Nova Law Review* 1323.

AERSTEN, I (2006) 'The Intermediate Position of Restorative Justice: The Case of Belgium' in I Aersten, T Daems and L Robert (eds) *Institutionalizing Restorative Justice* (Devon, Willan Publishing).

AHMED, E (2001) 'Part III. Shame Management: Regulating Bullying' in E Ahmed, N Harris, J Braithwaite and V Braithwaite (eds) *Shame Management Through Reintegration* (Cambridge, Cambridge University Press).

AHMED, E and BRAITHWAITE, V (2004) '"What, Me Ashamed?" Shame Management and School Bullying' 41 *Crime and Delinquency* 269.

AHMED, E HARRIS, N, BRAITHWAITE, J and BRAITHWAITE, V (eds) (2001) *Shame Management Through Reintegration* (Cambridge, Cambridge University Press).

ALEXANDER, R (1995) 'Employing the Mental Health System to Control Sex Offenders After Penal Incarceration' 17 *Law and Policy* 111.

ALLEN, FA (1981) *The Decline of the Rehabilitative Ideal: Penal Policy and Social Purpose* (Newhaven, CT, Yale University Press).

ANDERSON, S and KARP, DR (2004) 'Vermont's Restorative Re-entry Program: A Pilot in Burlington's Old North End' 4 *Kaleidscope of Justice* 7.

APPLEGATE, BK, CULLEN, FT and FISHER, BS (1997) 'Public Support for Correctional Treatment: The Continuing Appeal of the Rehabilitative Ideal' 77 *The Prison Journal* 237.

ASHENDEN, S (2002) 'Policing Perversion: The Contemporary Governance of Paedophilia' 6 *Cultural Values* 197.

—— (2004) *Governing Child Sexual Abuse: Negotiating the Boundaries of Public and Private, Law and Science* (London, Routledge).

ASHWORTH, A (1983) *Sentencing and Penal Policy* (London, Weidenfeld and Nicolson).

—— (1995) *Sentencing and Criminal Justice*, 2nd edn (London, Butterworths).

—— (2000) 'Victims' Rights, Defendants' Rights and Criminal Procedure' in A Crawford and J Goodey (eds) *Integrating a Victim Perspective within Criminal Justice* (Aldershot, Ashgate).

—— (2001) 'Is Restorative Justice the Way Forward for Criminal Justice?' 54 *Current Legal Issues* 347.

—— (2002) 'Responsibilities, Rights and Restorative Justice' 42 *British Journal of Criminology* 578.

ASHWORTH, A and BLAKE, M (1996) 'The Presumption of Innocence in English Criminal Law' *Criminal Law Review* 306.

ASHWORTH, A and PLAYER, E (2005) 'The Criminal Justice Act 2003: The Sentencing Provisions' 68 *The Modern Law Review* 822.

AULD, J, Gormally, B, McEVOY, K and RITCHIE, M (1997) *Designing a System of Restorative Justice in Northern Ireland: A Discussion Document* (Belfast, The Authors).

BAGLEY, C and KING, K (1990) *Child Sexual Abuse: The Search for Healing* (London and New York, Tavistock, Routledge).

BAGLEY, C and RAMSEY, R (1986) 'Sexual Abuse in Childhood: Psycho-Social Outcomes and Implications for Social Work Practice' 4 *Journal of Social Work and Human Sexuality* 33.

BAKER, E (1993) 'Dangerousness, Rights and Criminal Justice' 56 *Modern Law Review* 528.

BAKER, WL (1984) 'Castration of the Male Sexual Offender: A Legally Impermissible Alternative' 30 *Loyola Law Review* 377.

BALL, C (1999) 'The Youth Justice and Criminal Evidence Act 1999—Part I: A Significant Move Towards Restorative Justice, or a Recipe for Unintended Consequences?' *Criminal Law Review* 211.

BARAJAS, E (1995) 'Moving Toward Community Justice' *Topics in Community Corrections* (Washington DC, National Institute of Corrections).

BARAK, G (ed) (1994) *Media, Process, and the Social Construction of Crime* (New York, Garland Publishing).

BARBAREE, HE, MARSHALL, WL and HUDSON, SM (1993) *The Juvenile Sex Offender* (New York and London, Guildford Press).

BARBER, NW (1998) 'Privacy and the Police: Private Right, Public Right or Human Right?' *Public Law* 19.

BARKER, M and MORGAN, R (1993) *Sex Offenders: A Framework for the Evaluation of Community-based Treatment* (London, Home Office).

BARNES, HE (1930) *The Story of Punishment: A Record of Man's Inhumanity to Man* (Boston, Massachusetts: The Stratford Company).

BARNES, JM and PETERSON, KD (1997) *The Kentucky Sex Offender Treatment Program* (Kentucky, Department of Corrections).

BARNETT, RE (1977) 'Restitution: A New Paradigm of Criminal Justice' 87 *Ethics* 279.

—— (2003) 'Restitution: A New Paradigm of Criminal Justice' in G Johnstone (ed) *A Restorative Justice Reader: Texts, Sources, Context* (Devon, Willan Publishing).

BARR, R and PEASE, K (1990) 'Crime Placement, Displacement and Deflection' in M Tonry and N Morris (eds) *Crime and Justice: A Review of Research, Vol 12* (Chicago, University of Chicago Press).

BARTER, C (1999) 'Practitioners' Experiences and Perceptions of Investigating Allegations of Institutional Abuse' 8 *Child Abuse Review* 392.

BARTON, C (2000) 'Empowerment and Retribution in Criminal Justice' in H Strang and J Braithwaite (eds) *Restorative Justice: Philosophy to Practice* (Aldershot, Ashgate).

BATES, A, FALSHAW, L, CORBETT, C, PATEL, V, FRIENDSHIP, C (2004) 'A Follow-up Study of Sex Offenders Treated by Thames Valley Sex Offender Group Work Programme 1995-99' 10 *Journal of Sexual Aggression* 29.

BAUMER, EP, WRIGHT, R, KRISTINSDOTTIR, K and GUNNLAUGSSON, H (2002) 'Crime, Shame and Recidivism' 42 *British Journal of Criminology* 40.

BAUMER, T, MAXFIELD, G and MENDELSOHN, R (1993) 'A Comparative Analysis of Three Electronically Monitored Home Detention Programmes' 10 *Justice Quarterly* 1.

BAUMER, T and MENDELSOHN, R (1990) *The Electronic Monitoring of Non-violent Convicted Felons: An Experiment in Home Detection* (Washington DC, National Institute of Justice).

BAZEMORE, G (1996) 'Three Paradigms for Juvenile Justice' in B Galaway and J Hudson (eds) *Restorative Justice: International Perspectives* (Monsey, NY, Criminal Justice Press).

—— (1999) 'After Shaming, Whither Reintegration: Restorative Justice and Relational Rehabilitation' in G Bazemore and L Walgrave (eds) *Restorative Juvenile Justice: Repairing the Harm of Youth Crime* (Monsey, NY, Criminal Justice Press).

BAZEMORE, G and GRIFFITHS, CT (2003) 'Conferences, Circles, Boards, and Mediations: The "New Wave" of Community Justice Decision Making' in E McLaughlin, R Ferguson, G Hughes and L Westmarland (eds) *Restorative Justice: Critical Issues* (London, Sage).

BAZEMORE, G and SCHIFF, M (1996) 'Community Justice/Restorative Justice: Prospects for a New Social Ecology for Community Corrections' 20 *International Journal of Comparative and Applied Criminal Justice* 311.

BAZEMORE, G and UMBREIT, M (1995) 'Rethinking the Sanctioning Function in Juvenile Court: Retributive or Restorative Responses to Youth Crime' 41 *Crime and Delinquency* 296.

BAZEMORE, G and WALGRAVE, L (1999) 'Restorative Juvenile Justice: In Search of Fundamentals and an Outline for Systemic Reform' in G Bazemore and L Walgrave (eds) *Restorative Juvenile Justice: Repairing the Harm of Youth* Crime (Monsey, NY, Criminal Justice Press).

BEAN, P (1997) 'Paedophiles and the Proposed Register' 161 *Justice of the Peace and Local Government Law* 283.

BECK, AJ and SHIPLEY, BE (1989) *Recidivism of Prisoners Released in 1983* (Washington, US Department of Justice).

BECK, U (1992) *Risk Society: Towards a New Modernity* (London, Sage).

BECKER, H (1963) *Outsiders: Studies in the Sociology of Deviance* (New York, The Free Press of Glencoe).

—— (1974) 'Labelling Theory Reconsidered' in P Rock and M McIntosh (eds) *Deviance and Social Control* (London, Tavistock).

BECKETT, RC, BEECH, AR, FISHER, D and FORDHAM, AS (1994) *Community-based Treatment for Sex Offenders: An Evaluation of Seven Treatment Programmes* (London, Home Office).

BEDARF, A (1995) 'Examining Sex Offender Community Notification Laws' 83 *California Law Review* 885.

BEECH, A, BECKETT, RC, Fisher, D and Fordham, AS (1993) 'Community Based Sex Offender Treatment Provision' 103 *Prison Service Journal* 37.

BEECH, A, ERIKSON, M, FRIENDSHIP, C and DITCHFIELD, J (2001) *A Six Year Follow-up of Men Going Through Probation-based Sex Offender Treatment Programmes*, Home Office Research Findings No 144 (London, Home Office).

BEECH, A and FISHER, D (2004) 'Treatment of Sex Offenders in the UK in Prison and Probation Settings' in H Kemshall and G McIvor (eds) *Managing Sex Offender Risk* (London, Jessica Kingsley Publishers).

BEECH, A, FISHER, D and BECKETT, RC (1998) *STEP 3: An Evaluation of the Prison Sex Offender Treatment Programme*, A Report for the Home Office by the STEP Team (London, Home Office).

BEHLMER, GK (1982) *Child Abuse and Moral Reform in England 1870-1980* (Standford, CA, Stanford University Press).

BENEDICT, H (1992) *Virgin or Vamp: How the Press Covers Sex Crimes* (New York, Oxford University Press).

BENEDICT, R (1946) *The Chrysanthemum and the Sword: Patterns of Japanese Culture* (London, Routledge and Kegan Paul).

BENJAMIN, LS (1997) 'Special Feature: Personality Disorders: Models for Treatment and Strategies for Treatment Development' 11 *Journal of Personality Disorder* 307.

BEN-YEHUDA, N (2001) *Betrayal and Treason: Violations of Trust and Loyalty* (Boulder, Colorado, Westview).

BERLIN, FS (1989) 'The Paraphilias and Depo-Provera: Some Medical, Ethical and Legal Considerations' 17 *Bulletin of the American Academy of Psychiatry and Law* 233.

BERLIN, FS and KROUT, E (1986) 'Paedophilia: Diagnostic Concepts, Treatment and Ethical Considerations' 7 *American Journal of Forensic Psychiatry* 13.

BERLIN, FS and MALIN, MH (1991) 'Media Distortion of the Public's Perception of Recidivism and Psychiatric Rehabilitation' 148 *American Journal of Psychiatry* 1572.

Berlin, FS and MEINECKE, CF (1981) 'Treatment of Sex Offenders with Antiandrogenic Medication: Conceptualisation, Review of Treatment Modalities and Preliminary Findings' 138 *American Journal of Psychiatry* 601.

BERLINER, L (1996) 'Community Notification of Sex Offenders: A New Tool or a False Promise?' 11 *Journal of Interpersonal Violence* 294.

—— (1998) 'Sex Offenders: Policy and Practice' 92 *North Western University Law Review* 1203.

BERLINER, L and CONTE, JR (1990) 'The Process of Victimisation: The Victims' Perspective' 14 *Child Abuse and Neglect* 29.

—— (1995) 'The Effects of Disclosure and Intervention on Sexually Abused Children' 19 *Child Abuse and Neglect* 371.

BERRY, J (1992) *Lead Us Not Into Temptation* (London, Doubleday).

BESHAROV, DJ and VACHHS, A (1992) 'Sex Offenders: Is Castration an Acceptable Punishment?' *American Bar Association Journal* 43.

BICHARD, SIR M (2004) *The Bichard Inquiry Report* (London, Home Office).

BIRCH, D and TAYLOR, C (2003) '"People Like Us?": Responding to Allegations of Past Abuse in Care' *Criminal Law Review* 823.

BISHOP, N (1996) 'Intensive Supervision with Electronic Monitoring-A Swedish Alternative to Imprisonment' 3 *Vista* (Association of Chief Officers of Probation) 23.

BLAD, J (2006) 'Institutionalizing Restorative Justice? Transforming Criminal Justice? A Critical View on the Netherlands' in I Aertsen, T Daems and L Robert (eds) *Institutionalizing Restorative Justice* (Devon, Willan Publishing).

BLAGG, H, PEARSON, G, SAMPSON, A, SMITH, D and STUBBS, P (1988) 'Inter-agency Co-operation and Reality' in T Hope and M Shaw (eds) *Communities and Crime Reduction* (London, HMSO).

BLAKEY, KP (1996) 'The Indefinite Civil Commitment of Dangerous Sex Offenders Is An Appropriate Legal Compromise Between "Mad" and "Bad"—A Study of Minnesota's Sexual Psychopathic Personality Statute' 10 *Notre Dame Journal of Law, Ethics and Public Policy* 227.

BLUMSTEIN, A, COHEN, J MARTIN, SE and TONRY, MH (eds) (1983) *Research on Sentencing: The Search for Reform, Vols 1 & 2* (Washington, DC, National Academy Press).

BOELENS, R (1996) 'Does Electronic Monitoring Contribute to Community-based Penalties for Offenders?' 9 *New Technology in the Human Services* 2.

BOERNER, D (1992) 'Confronting Violence: In the Act and in the Word' 15 *University of Puget Sound Law Review* 525.

BONTA, J, ROONEY, J and WALLACE-CAPRETA, S (1999) *Electronic Monitoring in Canada* (Canada, Public Works and Government Services).

BOTCHKOVAR, EV and TITTLE, CR (2005) 'Crime, Shame and Reintegration in Russia' 9 *Theoretical Criminology* 401.

BOTTOMS, AE (1977) 'Reflections on the Renaissance of Dangerousness' 16 *The Howard Journal* 70.

—— (1987) 'Limiting Prison Use: Experience in England and Wales' 26 *The Howard Journal of Criminal Justice* 177.

—— (1990) 'Crime Prevention Facing the 1990s' 1 *Policing and Society* 3.

—— (1995) 'The Philosophy and Politics of Punishment and Sentencing' in C Clarkson and R Morgan (eds) *The Politics of Sentencing Reform* (Oxford, Oxford University Press).

—— (2003) 'Some Sociological Reflections on Restorative Justice' in A von Hirsch, JV Roberts, AE Bottoms, K Roach and M Schiff (eds) *Restorative Justice and Criminal Justice: Competing or Reconcilable Paradigms?* (Oxford, Hart Publishing).

BOTTOMS, AE and BROWNSWORD, R (1982) 'The Dangerousness Debate after the Floud Report' 22 *British Journal of Criminology* 229.

BOTTOMS, AE and PRESTON, RH (1981) *The Coming Penal Crisis: A Criminological and Theoretical Explanation* (Edinburgh, Scottish Academic Press).

BOTTOMS, AE and WILES, P (1986) 'Housing Tenure and Residential Community Crime Careers in Britain' in AJ Reiss and M Tonry (eds) *Communities and Crime: Crime and Justice a Review of Research, Vol 8* (Chicago, University of Chicago Press).

—— (1995) 'Crime and Insecurity in the City' in C Fijnaut, J Goethals, T Peters and L Walgrave (eds) *Changes in Society, Crime and Criminal Justice, Vol 1, Crime and Insecurity in the City* (The Hague, Kluwer).

—— (2002) 'Environmental Criminology' in M Maguire, R Morgan and R Reiner (eds) *The Oxford Handbook of Criminology*, 3rd edn (Oxford, Oxford University Press).

BOYES-WATSON, C (1999) 'In the Belly of the Beast? Exploring the Dilemmas of State-Sponsored Restorative Justice' 2 *Contemporary Justice Review* 261.

BRADFORD, JMW (1983) 'The Hormonal Treatment of Sexual Offenders' *Bulletin of the* 11 *American Academy of Psychiatry and Law* 159.

BRAITHWAITE, J (1989) *Crime, Shame and Reintegration* (Sydney, Cambridge University Press).

—— (1993) *'Shame and Modernity'* 33 British Journal of Criminology 1.

—— (1999) 'Restorative Justice: Assessing Optimistic and Pessimistic Accounts' in M Tonry (ed) *Crime and Justice: A Review of Research, Vol 25* (Chicago, University of Chicago Press).

—— (2000) 'The New Regulatory State and the Transformation of Criminology' 40 *British Journal of Criminology* 222.

—— (2002a) 'Setting Standards for Restorative Justice' 42 *British Journal of Criminology* 563.

—— (2002b) Restorative Justice and Responsive Regulation (Oxford, Oxford University Press).

BRAITHWAITE, J and BRAITHWAITE, V (2001) 'Part I. Shame, Shame Management and Regulation' in E Ahmed, N Harris, J Braithwaite and V Braithwaite (eds) *Shame Management Through Reintegration* (Cambridge, Cambridge University Press).

BRAITHWAITE, J and DALY, K (1994) 'Masculinities, Violence and Communitarian Control' in T Newburn and E Stanko (eds) *Just Boys Doing Business? Men, Masculinity and Crime* (London, Routledge).

BRAITHWAITE, J and MUGFORD, S (1994) 'Conditions of Successful Reintegration Ceremonies' 34 *British Journal of Criminology* 139.

BRAITHWAITE, J and PETIT, P (1990) *Not Just Deserts* (Melbourne, Oxford University Press).

BRANNAN, C, JONES, R and MURCH, J (1993) *Castle Hill Report: Practice Guide* (Shrewsbury, Shropshire County Council).

BREMER, J (1959) *Asexualisation: A Follow-Up Study of 244 Cases* (New York, Macmillan).

Brent Borough Council (1985) *A Child in Trust* (Brent, Brent Borough Council).

BRILLIANT, JA (1989) 'The Modern Day Scarlet Letter: A Critical Analysis of Modern Probation Conditions' *Duke Law Journal* 1361.

BROADHURST, R and MALLER, R (1992) 'The Recidivism of Sex Offenders in the Western Australian Prison Population' 32 *British Journal of Criminology* 54.

BRODY, AL and GREEN, R (1994) 'Washington State's Unscientific Approach to the Problem of Repeat Sexual Offenders' 22 *Bulletin of the American Academy of Psychiatry and Law* 343.

BRODY, SR (1975) *The Effectiveness of Sentencing*, Home Office Research Study No 35 (London, HMSO).

BRODY, SR and TARLING, R (1981) *Taking Offenders out of Circulation*, Home Office Research Study No 64 (London, HMSO).

BROMFIELD SMITH, D (2001) 'Electronic Monitoring of Offenders: The Scottish Experience' 1 *Criminal Justice* 201.

BROWN, M (1996) 'Serious Offending and the Management of Public Risk in New Zealand' 36 *British Journal of Criminology* 18.

BROWN, R and ELROD, T (1995) 'Electronic House Arrest: An Examination of Citizen Attitudes' 41 *Crime and Delinquency* 332.

BROWN, S (2005) *Treating Sex Offenders: An Introduction to Sex Offender Treatment Programmes* (Devon, Willan Publishing).

BROWNE, K and LYNCH, MA (1999) 'The Experiences of Children in Public Care' 8 *Child Abuse Review* 353.

BROWNLEE, I (1998) 'New Labour—New Penology? Punitive Rhetoric and the Limits of Managerialism in Criminal Justice Policy' 25 *Journal of Law and Society* 313.

BROWNLIE, J (2003) '"An Unsolvable Justice Problem"? Punishing Young People's Sexual Violence' 30 *Journal of Law and Society* 506.

BRYAN, T and DOYLE, P (2003) 'Developing Multi-Agency Public Protection Arrangements' in A Matravers (ed) *Sex Offenders in the Community: Managing and Reducing the Risks* (Devon, Willan Publishing, Cambridge Criminal Justice Series).

BUDIN, L and JOHNSON, C (1989) 'Sex Abuse Prevention Programs: Offenders' Attitudes About Their Efficacy' 13 *Child Abuse and Neglect* 77.

BURGOYNE, PH (1979) 'Recidivism Among Rapists' report to the Australian Criminology Research Council and the Victorian Department of Community Welfare Services.

BURNETT, R and MARUNA, S (2004) 'So "Prison Works", Does It? The Criminal Careers of 130 Men Released from Prison under Home Secretary, Michael Howard' 43 *The Howard Journal of Criminal Justice* 390.

—— (2006) 'The Kindness of Prisoners: Strengths-based Resettlement in Theory and in Action' 6 *Criminology & Criminal Justice* 83.

BUSCH, R (2002) 'Domestic Violence and Restorative Justice Initiatives: Who Pays if We Get it Wrong?' in H Strang and J Braithwaite (eds) *Restorative Justice and Family Violence* (Melbourne, Cambridge University Press).

CAIN, M (1985) 'Beyond Informal Justice' 9 *Contemporary Crises* 335.

CAMERON, A (2006) 'Stopping the Violence: Canadian Feminist Debates on Restorative Justice and Intimate Violence' 10 *Theoretical Criminology* 49.

CAMERON, H and TELFER, J (2004) 'Cognitive-Behavioural Group Work: Its Applications to Specific Offender Groups' 43 *The Howard Journal of Criminal Justice* 47.

CAPUTI, J (1987) *The Age of Sex Crime* (London, Women's Press).

CARBONATTO, H (1995) *Expanding Intervention Options for Spousal Abuse: The Use of Restorative Justice,* Occasional papers in Criminology New Series: No 4 (Wellington, New Zealand, Institute of Criminology, Victoria University of Wellington).

—— (1998) 'The Criminal Justice Response to Domestic Violence in New Zealand' 10 *Criminology New Zealand* 7 (A newsletter from the Institute of Criminology, Victoria University of Wellington).

CARLEN, P (1992) 'Criminal Women and Criminal Justice: The Limits to, and Potential of, Feminist and Left Realist Perspectives' in R Matthews and J Young (eds) *Realist Criminology* (London, Sage).

CARPENTER, AG (1998) 'Belgium, Germany, England, Denmark and the United States: The Implementation of Registration and Castration Laws as Protection Against Habitual Sex Offenders' 16 *Dickinson Journal of International Law* 435.

CASHMORE, J and PAXMAN, M (1999) *Family Decision Making: A Pilot Project by Burnside and DoCS, Evaluation Report* (New South Wales, Social Policy and Research Centre, University of New South Wales).

CAVADINO, M and DIGNAN, J (1992) *The Penal System: An Introduction* (London, Sage).

—— (1998) 'Reparation, Retribution and Rights' in A von Hirsch and A Ashworth (eds) *Principled Sentencing: Readings on Theory and Policy,* 2nd edn (Oxford, Hart Publishing).

CESARONI, C (2001) 'Releasing Sex Offenders into the Community Through "Circles of Support"—A Means of Reintegrating the "Worst of the Worst"' 34 *Journal of Offender Rehabilitation* 85.

CHALLINGER, D (1994) 'An Australian Case Study' in U Zvekic (ed) *Alternatives to Imprisonment in Comparative Perspective* (New York, Prentice-Hall).

CHESNAIS, JC (1981) *History of Violence in the West* (Paris, University of Paris).

CHRISTIANSEN, J and BLAKE, R (1990) 'The Grooming Process in Father-Daughter Incest' in A Horton, B Johnson, L Roundy and D Williams (eds) *The Incest Perpetrator: A Family Member No One Wants to Treat* (Newbury Park, Sage).

CHRISTIANSEN, K, ELERS-NIELSON, M, LAMAIRE, L and STÜRUP, GK (1965) 'Recidivism Among Sexual Offenders' in *Scandinavian Studies in Criminology* (London, Tavistock).

CHRISTIE, N (1977) 'Conflicts as Property' 17 *British Journal of Criminology* 1.

—— (2000) *Crime Control as Industry,* 3rd edn (London, Routledge).

CHRISTODOULIDIS, E (2000) '"Truth and Reconciliation" as Risks' 9 *Social & Legal Studies* 179.

CLARKSON, CMV (1997) 'Beyond Just Deserts: Sentencing Violent and Sexual Offenders' 36 *The Howard Journal* 284.

CLEAR, TR (2006) 'Community Justice Versus Restorative Justice: Contrasts in Family of Value' in D Sullivan and L Tifft (eds) *Handbook on Restorative Justice: A Global Perspective* (New York, Routledge).

CLEAR, TR, ROSE, D, WARING, E and SCULLY, K (2003) 'Coercive Mobility and Crime: A Preliminary Examination of Concentrated Incarceration and Social Disorganization' 20 *Justice Quarterly* 33.

COBLEY, C (1997a) 'Sentencing and Supervision of Sex Offenders' 98 *Journal of Social Welfare and Family Law* 98.

—— (1997b) 'Keeping Track of Sex Offenders: Part 1 of the Sex Offenders Act 1997' 60 *Modern Law Review* 690.

COBLEY, C (2000/2005) *Sex Offenders: Law, Policy and Practice* (Bristol, Jordans).

—— (2003) 'The Legislative Framework' in A Matravers (ed) *Sex Offenders in the Community: Managing and Reducing the Risks* (Devon, Willan Publishing, Cambridge Criminal Justice Series).

COCOZZA, JJ and STEADMAN, HJ (1976) 'The Failure of Psychiatric Predictions of Dangerousness: Clear and Convincing Evidence' 19 *Rutgers Law Review* 1081.

COHEN, F (1995) 'Sex Offender Registration Laws: Constitutional and Policy Issues' 31 *Criminal Law Bulletin* 151.

COHEN, S (1972/1980) *Folk Devils and Moral Panics* (London, Paladin).

—— (1985) *Visions of Social Control* (Cambridge, Polity Press).

COHEN, S and TAYLOR, L (1972/1981) Psychological Survival: The Experience of Long Term Imprisonment (Penguin, Harmondsworth).

COKER, D (1999) 'Enhancing Autonomy for Battered Women: Lessons from Navajo Peacemaking' 47 *UCLA Law Review* 1.

—— (2006) 'Restorative Justice, Navajo Peacemaking and Domestic Violence' 10 *Theoretical Criminology* 67.

COLEMAN, JS (1990) *Foundations of Social Theory* (Cambridge, Massachusetts, Harvard University Press).

COLLINS, P (1991) 'The Treatability of Psychopaths' 2 *Journal of Forensic Psychiatry* 103.

CONSEDINE, J (1995) *Restorative Justice: Healing the Effects of the Crime* (Lyttleton, Ploughshares Publications).

CONTE, JR, WOLF, S and SMITH, T (1989) 'What Sexual Offenders Tell Us About Prevention Strategies' 13 *Child Abuse and Neglect* 293.

CONWAY, P (1997) 'A Response to Paramilitary Policing in Northern Ireland' 8 *Critical Criminology: An International Journal* 109.

COOK, J and WALL, T (1980) 'New York Attitude Measures of Trust, Organization, Commitment, and Personal Need Non-fulfilment' 53 *Journal of Occupational Psychology* 39.

COOK, KJ (2006) 'Doing Difference and Accountability in Restorative Justice Conferences' 10 *Theoretical Criminology* 107.

COOMBES, R (2003) 'Adolescents Who Sexually Abuse' in A Matravers (ed) *Sex Offenders in the Community: Managing and Reducing the Risks* (Devon, Willan Publishing, Cambridge Criminal Justice Series).

COPE, R (1993) 'A Survey of Forensic Psychiatrists Views on Personality Disorder' 4 *Journal of Forensic Psychiatry* 215.

CORBY, B (1987) *Working With Child Abuse: Social Work Practice and The Child Abuse System* (Milton Keynes and Philadelphia, Open University Press).

CORBY, B, DOIG, A and ROBERTS, V (2001) *Public Inquiries into Abuse of Children in Residential Care* (London, Jessica Kingsley Publishers).

CORDNER, GW (1988) 'A Problem-Orientated Approach to Community-Orientated Policing' in JR Green and SD Mastrofski (eds) *Community Policing: Rhetoric or Reality?* (New York, Praeger).

COTTER, A, GEIRAN, V, RYAN, T and TALLON, M (1991) *A Therapeutic Programme for Sex Offenders in a Prison Setting* (unpublished report) (Dublin, Probation and Welfare Service).

COWAN, D (1997) *Homelessness: The (In-)Appropriate Applicant* (Aldershot, Dartmouth).

COWAN, D and GILROY, R (1999) 'Wicked Issues: The Role of the Housing Professional in Dealing with Sex Offenders,' paper presented at the Housing Studies Association Conference, *Managing Diversity*, University of Newcastle, September.

COWAN, D, GILROY, R, PANTAZIS, C and BEVAN, M (1999) *Allocating Social Housing to Sex Offenders: An Examination of Current Practice* (Coventry, Chartered Institute of Housing).

COWAN, D, PANTAZIS, C, GILROY, R (2001) 'Social Housing as Crime Control: An Examination of the Role of Housing Management in Policing Sex Offenders' 10 *Social & Legal Studies* 435.

COX, M (1997) 'The Lifetime Convictions of Child Sexual Abusers: Practice and Policy Dilemmas' 44 *Probation Journal* 19.

—— (ed) (1999) *Remorse and Reparation* (London, Jessica Kingsley Publishers).

CRAWFORD, A (1999) *The Local Governance of Crime: Appeals to Community and Partnerships* (Oxford, Oxford University Press).

—— (2002) 'The Prospects for Restorative Justice in England and Wales: A Tale of Two Acts' in K McEvoy and T Newburn (eds) *Criminology and Conflict Resolution* (London, Palgrave).

—— (2006) 'Institutionalizing Restorative Justice in a Cold, Punitive Climate' in I Aersten, T Daems and L Robert (eds) *Institutionalizing Restorative Justice* (Devon, Willan Publishing).

CRAWFORD, A and BLAIR, C (1999) *Review of the Community Safety Centre and a Crime Reduction Strategy for Northern Ireland,* Northern Ireland Criminal Justice Review, Research Report 7 (Belfast, HMSO).

CRAWFORD, A and CLEAR, TR (2003) 'Community Justice: Transforming Communities Through Restorative Justice?' in E McLaughlin, R Ferguson, G Hughes and L Westmarland (eds) *Restorative Justice: Critical Issues* (London, Sage).

CRAWFORD, A and GOODEY, J (eds) (2000) *Integrating a Victim Perspective Within Criminal Justice* (Aldershot, Ashgate).

CRAWFORD, A and JONES, M (1995) 'Inter-agency Co-operation and Community-Based Crime Prevention: Some Reflections on the Work of Pearson and Colleagues' 35 *British Journal of Criminology* 17.

—— (1996) 'Kirkholt Revisited: Some Reflections on the Transferability of Crime Prevention Initiatives' 35 *The Howard Journal* 21.

CRAWFORD, A and MATASSA, M (1999) *Community Safety Structures: An International Literature Review,* Northern Ireland Criminal Justice Review, Research Report 8 (Belfast, HMSO).

CRAWFORD, A and NEWBURN, T (2002) 'Recent Development in Restorative Justice for Young People in England and Wales' 42 *British Journal of Criminology* 476.

—— (2003) *Youth Offending and Restorative Justice: Implementing Reform in Youth Justice* (Devon, Willan Publishing).

CRAWLEY, E and SPARKS, R (2006) 'Is There Life After Punishment? How Elderly Men Talk About Imprisonment and Release' 6 *Criminology & Criminal Justice* 63.

Criminal Justice Inspection Northern Ireland (2005) *The Management of Sex Offenders in Northern Ireland: An Inspection of the MASRAM Process and Its Potential For Development* (Belfast, Criminal Justice Inspection Northern Ireland).

Criminal Justice Review Group (2000) *Review of the Criminal Justice System in Northern Ireland* (Belfast, HMSO).

CUNNEEN, C (1997) 'Community Conferencing and the Fiction of Indigenous Control' 30 *Australian and New Zealand Journal of Criminology* 292.

DALY, K (2000) 'Revisiting the Relationship Between Retributive and Restorative Justice' in H Strang and J Braithwaite (eds) *Restorative Justice: Philosophy to Practice* (Aldershot, Ashgate).

234   *Bibliography*

DALY, K (2001) 'Conferencing in Australia and New Zealand: Variations, Research Findings and Prospects' in A Morris and G Maxwell (eds) *Restorative Justice for Juveniles: Conferencing, Mediation and Circles* (Oxford, Hart Publishing).
—— (2002a) 'Sexual Assault and Restorative Justice' in H Strang and J Braithwaite (eds) *Restorative Justice and Family Violence* (Melbourne, Cambridge University Press).
—— (2002b) 'Restorative Justice: The Real Story' 4 *Punishment and Society* 55.
—— (2006) 'Restorative Justice and Sexual Assault: An Archival Study of Court and Conference Cases' 46 *British Journal of Criminology* 334.
DALY, K and IMMARIGEON, R (1998) 'The Past, Present and Future of Restorative Justice: Some Critical Reflections' 1 *Contemporary Justice Review* 21.
DALY, K and STUBBS, J (2006) 'Feminist Engagement with Restorative Justice' 10 *Theoretical Criminology* 9.
DASGUPTA, P (1988) 'Trust as Commodity' in D Gambetta (ed) *Trust: Making and Breaking Co-operative Relations* (Oxford, Basil Blackwell).
DAVIES, R (1997) 'Restorative Justice: A Window of Opportunity' 114 *Prison Service Journal* 27.
DAVIS, G (1992) *Making Amends: Mediation and Reparation in Criminal Justice* (London and New York, Routledge).
DAVIS, G, HOYANO, L, KEENAN, C, MAITLAND, L and MORGAN, R. (1999) *An Assessment of the Admissibility and Sufficiency of Evidence in Child Abuse Prosecutions*, A Report for the Home Office by the Department of Law, University of Bristol (London, Home Office).
DAVIS, M (1990) *City of Quartz: Excavating the Future in Los Angeles* (London, Verso).
DE HAAN, W and LOADER, I (2002) 'On the Emotions of Crime, Punishment and Social Control' 6 *Theoretical Criminology* 243.
Department of Corrections (1997) *Annual Report on The Sex Offender Treatment Program* (Washington, Department of Corrections).
Department for Education for Northern Ireland (DENI) (1999) *Pastoral Care in Schools: Child Protection* (Belfast, DENI).
Department of Health and Home Office (2000) *Reforming the Mental Health Act: Part II High Risk Patients*, Cm 5016-II (London, HMSO).
Department of Health and Social Services (DHSS) (1974) *Report of the Inquiry into the Child Care and Supervision Provided in Relation to Maria Colwell* (London, HMSO).
—— (1988) *Report of the Inquiry into Child Abuse in Cleveland* (The Butler-Sloss Report), Cmnd 412 (London, HMSO).
Department of Health and Social Services (Northern Ireland) (DHSS (NI)) (1982) *Report on Homes and Hostels for Children and Young People in Northern Ireland* (The Sheridan Report) (Belfast, DHSS).
—— (1993) *An Abuse of Trust: The Report of the Social Services Inspectorate into the case of Martin Huston* (Belfast, DHSS (SSI)).
Department of Justice, Equality and Law Reform (1997) *Tackling Crime: A Discussion Paper* (Dublin, The Stationery Office).
—— (1998) The Law On Sexual Offences: A Discussion Paper (Dublin, The Stationery Office).
—— (2000), Press Conference Speech by John O'Donoghue TD, Minister for Justice, Equality and Law Reform to Announce the Publication of the Sex Offenders Bill 2000, January 2000 (Dublin, Department of Justice).
DESCHENES, P, TURNER, S and PETERSILIA, J (1995) 'Dual Experiment in Intensive Community Supervision' 75 *Prison Journal* 3.

DIGNAN, J (1999) 'The Crime and Disorder Act and the Prospects for Restorative Justice' *Criminal Law Review* 48.

—— (2001) 'Restorative Justice and Crime Reduction: Are Policy Makers Barking Up the Wrong Tree?' in E Fattah and S Parmentier (eds) *Victim Policies and Criminal Justice on the Road to Restorative Justice* (Belgium, Leuven University Press).

—— (2003) 'Towards a Systemic Model of Restorative Justice' in A von Hirsch, JV Roberts, AE Bottoms, K Roach and M Schiff (eds) *Restorative Justice and Criminal Justice: Competing or Reconcilable Paradigms?* (Oxford, Hart Publishing).

DIGNAN, J and CAVADINO, M (1996) 'Towards a Framework for Conceptualising and Evaluating Models of Criminal Justice from a Victim's Perspective' 4 *International Review of Victimology* 153.

DIGNAN, J and LOWEY, K (1999) *Restorative Justice Options for Northern Ireland: A Comparative Overview*, Northern Ireland Criminal Justice Review, Research Report 10 (Belfast, HMSO).

DIGNAN, J and MARSH, P (2003) 'Restorative Justice and Family Group Conferences in England: Current State and Future Prospects' in E McLaughlin, R Ferguson, G Hughes and L Westmarland (eds) *Restorative Justice: Critical Issues* (London, Sage).

DINGWALL, G (1998) 'Selective Incapacitation After the Criminal Justice Act 1991: A Proportional Response to Protecting the Public?' 37 *The Howard Journal of Criminal Justice* 177.

DITCHFIELD, J and MARSHALL, WL (1991) 'A Review of Recent Literature Evaluating Treatments for Sex Offenders in Prisons and Comparable Institutional Settings' 81 *Prison Service Journal* 24.

DODGSON, K, GOODWIN, P, HOWARD, P, LLEWELLYN-THOMAS, S, MORTIMER, E, RUSSELL, N and WINER, M (2001) *Electronic Monitoring of Release Prisoners: An Evaluation of the Home Detention Curfew Scheme*, Home Office Research Study No 222 (London, Home Office).

DONZELOT, JD (1979) *The Policing of Families* (London, Hutchinson).

DRUMBL, M (2000) 'Sclerosis: Retributive Justice and the Rwandan Genocide' 2 *Punishment and Society* 287.

DUFF, A (2002) 'Restorative Punishment and Punitive Restoration' in L Walgrave (ed) *Restorative Justice and the Law* (Devon, Willan Publishing).

DUFF, RA and GARLAND, D (1994) 'Introduction: Thinking About Punishment' in RA Duff and D Garland (eds) *A Reader on Punishment* (Oxford, Oxford University Press).

EARL-HUBBARD, M (1996) 'The Child Sex Offender Registration Laws: The Punishment, Liberty, Deprivation and Unintended Results Associated with the Scarlet Letter Laws of the 1990s' 90 *North Western Law Review* 788.

EDLESON, J and SYERS, M (1990) 'Relative Effectiveness of Group Treatments for Men Who Batter' 26 *Social Work Research and Abstracts* 10.

EDWARDS, W and HENSLEY, C (2001a) 'Restructuring Sex Offender Sentencing: A Therapeutic Jurisprudence Approach to the Criminal Justice Process' 45 *International Journal of Offender Therapy and Comparative Criminology* 646.

—— (2001b) 'Contextualising Sex Offender Management Legislation and Policy: Evaluating the Problem of Latent Consequences in Community Notification Laws' 45 *International Journal of Offender Therapy and Comparative Criminology* 83.

EISENBERG, L (1981) 'Cross-cultural and Historical Perspectives on Child Abuse and Neglect' 5 *International Journal of Child Abuse and Neglect* 229.

ELDRIDGE, H and WYRE, R (1998) 'The Lucy Faithful Foundation Residential Programme for Sexual Offenders' in WL Marshall, YM Fernandez, SM Hudson and T Ward (eds) *Sourcebook of Treatment Programs for Sexual Offenders* (New York, Plenum Press).

ELLIOTT, M, BROWNE, K and KILCOYNE, J (1995) 'Child Abuse Prevention: What Offenders Tell Us' 19 *Child Abuse and Neglect* 579.

ENGLISH, K, CHADWICK, SM and PULLEN, SK (1994) *Colorado's Intensive Supervision Probation: Report of Findings* (Colorado, Department of Public Safety).

ERICSON, RV (1994) 'The Division of Expert Knowledge in Policing and Security' 45 *British Journal of Sociology* 149.

—— (1996) 'The Risk Society,' unpublished paper presented at the Australian and New Zealand Society of Criminology Conference, Victoria University of Wellington, January–February.

ERICSON, RV and HAGGERTY, KD (1997) *Policing the Risk Society* (Oxford, Clarendon Press).

ERLINDER, CP (1993) 'Minnesota's Gulag: Involuntary Treatment for the Politically Ill' 19 *William Mitchell Law Review* 99.

ETZIONI, A (1999) *The Limits of Privacy* (New York, Basic Books).

EVANS, R and PUECH, K (2001) 'Reprimands and Warnings: Populist Punitiveness or Restorative Justice?' *Criminal Law Review* 794.

EWALD, F (1986) *L'Etat Providence* (Paris, Grasset).

FAGAN, J, WEST, V and HOLLAND, J (2003) 'Reciprocal Effects of Crime and Incarceration in New York City' 30 *Fordham Urban Law Journal* 1551.

FALLON, P, BLUGLASS, R, EDWARDS, B and DANIELS, G (1999) *Report of the Inquiry Into the Personality Disorder Unit, Ashworth Special Hospital, Vol 1* (London, HMSO).

FALSHAW, L, FRIENDSHIP, C and BATES, A (2003) *Sexual Offenders—Measuring Reconviction, Reoffending and Recidivism*, Home Office Research Findings No 183 (London, Home Office).

FARRALL, S (2002) *Rethinking What Works with Offenders: Probation, Social Context and Desistance from Crime* (Devon, Willan Publishing).

—— (2003) '"J" accuse: Probation, Evaluation-Research Epistemologies (Part Two: This Time Its Personal and Social Factors)' 3 *Criminal Justice* 249.

FARRALL, S and BOWLING, B (1999) 'Structuration, Human Development and Desistance from Crime' 39 *British Journal of Criminology* 252.

FARRALL, S and CALVERLEY, A (2005) *Understanding Desistance From Crime* (London, Open University Press).

FARRALL, S and MALTBY, S (2003) 'The Victimisation of Probationers' 42 *The Howard Journal of Criminal Justice* 32.

FARRALL, S and SPARKS, S (2006) 'Introduction' 6 *Criminology & Criminal Justice* (Special Issue: What Lies Beyond? Problems, Prospects and Possibilities for Life After Punishment) 7.

FARRANT, F and LEVENSON, J (2002) *Barred Citizens: Volunteering and Active Citizenship by Prisoners* (London, Prison Reform Trust).

FAWCETT, J (1987) *The Application of the European Convention on Human Rights*, 2nd edn (Oxford, Clarendon Press).

FEELEY, M and SIMON, J (1992) 'The New Penology: Notes on the Emerging Strategy of Corrections and Its Implications' 30 *Criminology* 449.

—— (1994) 'Actuarial Justice: the Emerging New Criminal Law' in D Nelken (ed) *The Futures of Criminology* (London, Sage).

FELDMAN, DL (1997) 'The "Scarlet Letter Laws" of the 1990s: A Response to Critics' 60 *Albany Law Review* 1081.

FENNELL, P (2001) 'Reforming the Mental Health Act 1983: "Joined Up Compulsion"' *Journal of Mental Health Law* 5,

FERGUSON, H (1995) 'The Paedophile Priest: A Deconstruction' 84 *Studies* 247.

FERGUSSON, DM and MULLEN, PE (1999) 'Childhood Sexual Abuse: An Evidence-based Perspective' 40 *Developmental Clinical Psychology and Psychiatry* 581.

FIELDING, N (1995) *Community Policing* (Oxford, Clarendon Press).

FINKELHOR, D (1979) *Sexually Victimized Children* (New York, Sage).

—— (1984) *Child Sexual Abuse: New Theory and Research* (New York, Free Press).

FINKELHOR, D and ARAJI, S (1986) 'Explanations of Paedophilia: A Four Factor Model' 22 *Journal of Sexual Research* 145.

FINKELHOR, D and DZIUBA-LEATHERMAN, J (1994) 'Children as Victims of Violence: A National Survey' 94 *Child Abuse and Neglect* 413.

FINKELHOR, D, WILLIAMS, L, and BURNS, N (1988) *Nursery Crimes: A Study of Sexual Abuse in Day Care* (Newbury Park, CA, Sage).

FINN, P (1995) 'Do Sex Offender Treatment Programmes Work?' 78 *Judicature* 250.

FINSTAD, L (1990) 'Sexual Offenders Out of Prison: Principles for a Realistic Utopia' 18 *International Journal of the Sociology* 157.

FIONDA, J (1999) 'New Labour, Old Hat: Youth Justice and the Crime and Disorder Act 1998' *Criminal Law Review* 36.

FISCHER, AL (1997) 'Florida's Community Notification of Sex Offenders on the Internet' 45 *Cleveland State Law Review*, 505.

FISHER, D and BEECH, A (2004) 'Adult Male Sex Offenders' in H Kemshall and G McIvor (eds) *Managing Sex Offender Risk* (London, Jessica Kingsley Publishers).

FITZGERALD, EA (1990) 'Chemical Castration: MPA Treatment of the Sexual Offender' 18 *American Journal of Criminal Law* 1.

FLANNAGAN, T (1995) Long-Term Imprisonment: Policy, Science, and Correctional Practice (London, Sage).

FLOUD, J and YOUNG, W (1981) *Dangerousness and Criminal Justice* (London, Heinemann Educational Books).

FLOYD, J (1990) 'The Administration of Psychotropic Drugs to Prisoners: State of the Law and Beyond' 78 *California Law Review* 1243.

FLYNN, R (1996) 'Breaking the Cycle' 146 *New Law Journal* 1662.

FOLBERG, J and TAYLOR, A (1984) *Mediation: A Comprehensive Guide to Resolving Conflicts Without Litigation* (San Francisco, CA, Jossey-Bass).

FOUCAULT, M (1977) *Discipline and Punish: The Birth of the Prison* (London, Penguin).

FRANCIS, B, CROSLAND, P, HARMAN, J (2002) *The Police National Computer and the Offenders Index: Can They be Combined for Research Purposes?* Home Office Research Findings No 170 (London, Home Office).

FREEMAN-LONGO, RE, BIRD, SL, STEVENSON, WF and FISKE, JA (1995) *1994 Nationwide Survey of Treatment Programs and Models Serving Abusive-Reactive Children and Adolescent and Adult Sex Offenders* (Brandon, VT, Safer Society Press).

FREEMAN-LONGO, RE and KNOPP, FH (1992) 'State of the Art Sex Offender Treatment: Outcome and Issues' 5 *Annals of Sex Research* 141.

FREEMAN-LONGO, RE and WALL, RV (1986) 'Changing a Lifetime of Sexual Crime' 20 *Psychology Today* 58.

FREIBURG, A (2001) 'Affective Versus Effective Justice: Instrumentalism and Emotionalism in Criminal Justice' 3 *Punishment and Society* 265.

FRIEDRICHS, DO (1996) *Trusted Criminals: White-Collar Crime in Contemporary Society* (New York, Wadsworth Publishing Company).

FRIEL, C, VAUGHN, JB and DEL CARMEN, R (1987) *Electronic Monitoring and Correctional Policy*, Research Report (Washington, National Institute of Justice).

FRIENDSHIP, C, BEECH, AR, BROWNE, KD (2002) 'Reconviction as an Outcome Measure in Research: A Methodological Note' 42 *British Journal of Criminology* 442.

FRIENDSHIP, C, BLUD, L, ERIKSON, W and TRAVERS, R (2002) *An Evaluation of Cognitive Behavioural Treatment for Prisoners*, Home Office Research Findings No 161 (London, Home Office).

FRIENDSHIP, C, MANN, R, and BEECH, A (2003) *The Prison-Based Sex Offender Treatment Programme—An Evaluation*, Home Office Research Findings No 205 (London, Home Office).

FRIENDSHIP, C and THORNTON, D (2001) 'Sexual Reconviction for Sexual Offenders Discharged From Prison in England and Wales: Implications for Evaluating Treatment' 41 *British Society of Criminology* 285.

FRIENDSHIP, C, THORNTON, D, ERIKSON, M, BEECH, A (2001) 'Reconviction: A Critique and Comparison of Two Main Data Sources in England and Wales' 6 *Legal and Criminological Psychology* 121.

FROMSON, KB (1994) 'Beyond an Eye for an Eye: Castration as an Alternative Sentencing Measure' 8 *New York Law School Journal of Human Rights* 311.

FUJIMOTO, BK (1992) 'Sexual Violence, Sanity, and Safety: Constitutional Parameters for Involuntary Civil Commitment of Sex Offenders' 15 *University of Puget Sound Law Review* 879.

FURBY, L, WEINROTT, MR and BLACKSHAW, L (1989) 'Sex Offender Recidivism' 105 *Psychological Bulletin* 3.

GAGNE, P (1981) 'Treatment of Sex Offenders with Medroxyprogesterone Acetate' 138 *American Journal of Psychiatry* 644.

GALAWAY, B and HUDSON, B (eds) (1990) *Criminal Justice, Restitution, and Reconciliation* (Monsey, NY, Criminal Justice Press).

—— (eds) (1996) *Restorative Justice: International Perspectives* (Monsey, NY, Criminal Justice Press).

GALLAGHER, B (1998) *Grappling With Smoke: Investigating and Managing Organised Abuse A Good Practice Guide* (London, NSPCC).

—— (1999) 'Institutional Abuse' in N Parton and C Wattam (eds) *Child Sexual Abuse: Responding to the Experiences of Children* (New York, Wiley Publishers).

—— (2000) 'The Extent and Nature of Known Cases of Institutional Child Sexual Abuse' 30 *British Journal of Social Work* 795.

GALLAGHER, B, CHRISTMANN, K, FRASER, C and HODGSON, B (2003) 'International and Internet Child Sexual Abuse and Exploitation: Issues Emerging From Research' 15 *Child and Family Law Quarterly* 353.

GAMBETTA, D (1988) 'Can We Trust Trust?' in D Gambetta (ed) *Trust: Making and Breaking Co-operative Relations* (Oxford, Basil Blackwell).

GARBARINO, J and GILLIAM, G (1980) *Understanding Abusive Families* (Lexington, Massachusetts, Lexington Books).

GARFINKEL, H (1956) 'Conditions of Successful Degradation Ceremonies' 61 *American Journal of Criminology* 420.

GARLAND, D (1985) *Punishment and Welfare* (Aldershot, Gower).

—— (1990) *Punishment and Modern Society* (Oxford, Clarendon Press).

—— (1996) 'The Limits of the Sovereign State: Strategies of Crime Control in Contemporary Society' 36 *British Journal of Criminology* 445.

—— (2001) *The Culture of Control: Crime and Social Order in Contemporary Society* (Oxford, Oxford University Press).

GARLAND, D and SPARKS, R (2000) 'Criminology, Social Theory and the Challenge of Our Times' 40 *British Journal of Criminology* 189.

GEIRAN, V (1996a) 'Treatment of Sex Offenders in Ireland-The Development of Policy and Practice' 44 *Administration* 136.

—— (1996b) 'Sex Offender Treatment: A Case of Fools Rush In-Or Angels Fearing To Tread?' 14 *Irish Social Worker* 8.

GENDREAU, P and ANDREWS, D (1990) 'Tertiary Prevention: What the Meta-analysis of the Offender Treatment Literature Tells Us About "What Works"' 32 *Canadian Journal of Criminology* 173.

GHENT, JF (1990) 'Validity of Statutes Authorising Asexualisation or Sterilisation of Criminals or Mental Defectives' 53 *American Law Review* 960.

GIBBS, A (2003) 'Home Detention with Electronic Monitoring: The New Zealand Experience' 3 *Criminal Justice* 199.

GIBSON, B and WHITFIELD, D (1997) 'The Electronic Monitoring of Offenders' 161 *Justice of the Peace and Local Government Law* 1036.

GIDDENS, A (1984) *The Constitution of Society* (Cambridge, Polity Press).

—— (1990) *The Consequences of Modernity* (Cambridge, Polity Press).

GILLESPIE, A (2001) 'Children, Chatrooms and the Law' *Criminal Law Review* 435.

—— (2002) 'Child Protection on the Internet: Challenges for Criminal Law' 14 *Child and Family Law Quarterly* 411.

—— (2004) '"Grooming": Definitions and the Law' 154 *New Law Journal* 586.

GILLIGAN, J (1996) *Violence: Our Deadly Epidemic and Its Causes* (New York, A Grosset/ Putnam Books).

GINZBERG, JF (1992) 'Compulsory Contraception as a Condition of Probation: The Use and Abuse of Norplant' 58 *Brook Law Review* 979.

GIORDANO, P, Cernkovich, S and Rudolph, J (2002) 'Gender, Crime and Desistance: Toward a Theory of Cognitive Transformation' 107 *American Journal of Sociology* 990.

GLAZER, S (1996) 'Punishing Sex Offenders' 6 *Congressional Quarterly Researcher* 25.

GOFFMAN, E (1959) *The Presentation of the Self in Everyday Life* (Garden City, NJ, Doubleday-Anchor Books).

—— (1963) *Stigma: Notes on the Management of Spoiled Identity* (Englewood Cliffs, New Jersey, Prentice-Hall) (Harmondsworth, Penguin, 1968).

GOLDSTEIN, H (1990) *Problem-Orientated Policing* (London, McGraw-Hill).

GOOD, D (1988) 'Individuals, Interpersonal Relations and Trust' in D Gambetta (ed) *Trust: Making and Breaking Co-operative Relations* (Oxford, Basil Blackwell).

GOODEY, J (2000) 'An Over-view of Key Themes' in A Crawford and J Goodey (eds) *Integrating a Victim Perspective in Criminal Justice* (Aldershot, Ashgate).

GORDON, D (1990) *The Justice Juggernaut* (Brunswick, NJ, Rutgers University Press).

GORDON, RA (1982) 'Preventive Sentencing and the Dangerous Offender' 22 *British Journal of Criminology* 285.

GOWEN, D (1995) 'Electronic Monitoring in the Southern District of Mississippi' 59 *Federal Probation* 10.

GRANGE, T (2003) 'Challenges for the Police Service' in A Matravers (ed) *Sex Offenders in the Community: Managing and Reducing the Risks* (Devon, Willan Publishing, Cambridge Criminal Justice Series).

GRASMICK, HG and BURSIK, RJ (1990) 'Conscience, Significant Others, and Rational Choice: Extending the Deterrence Model' 24 *Law and Society Review* 837.

GRAY, P (2005) 'The Politics of Risk and Young Offenders: Experiences of Social Exclusion and Restorative Justice' 45 *British Journal of Criminology* 938.

GREEN, W (1986) 'Depo-Provera, Castration, and the Probation of Rape Offenders: Statutory and Constitutional Issues' 12 *University of Dayton Law Review* 1.

GREENFELD, L (1997) *Sex Offenses and Offenders: An Analysis of Data on Rape and Sexual Assault* (Washington, DC, US Department of Justice, Bureau of Justice Statistics).

GREENWOOD, PW with ABRAHAMSE, A (1982) *Selective Incapacitation*, Report prepared for the National Institute of Justice (Santa Monica, Ca, RAND).

GREER, C (2003) *Sex Crime and the Media: Sex Offending and the Press in a Divided Society* (Devon, Willan Publishing).

GRIFFITHS, A (1986) 'The Problem of Informal Justice: Family Dispute Processing Among the Bakwena-A Case Study' 14 *International Journal of the Sociology of Law* 359.

GRIFFITHS, CT and HAMILTON, R (1996) 'Spiritual Renewal, Community Revitalization and Healing: Experience in Traditional Aboriginal Justice in Canada' 20 *International Journal of Comparative and Applied Criminal Justice* 289.

GRISSO, T and APPELBAUM, P (1992) 'Is it Ethical to Offer Predictions of Future Violence?' 16 *Law and Human Behaviour* 621.

GROTH, AN, LONGO, RE and MCFADIN, JB (1982) 'Undetected Recidivism Among Rapists and Child Molesters' 23 *Crime and Delinquency* 450.

GRUBER, KJ and JONES, RJ (1983) 'Identifying Determinants of Risk of Sexual Victimization of Youth' 7 *Child Abuse and Neglect* 17.

GRUBIN, DH (1998) *Sex Offending Against Children: Understanding the Risk*, Police Research Series Paper No 99 (London, Home Office).

—— (2004) 'The Risk Assessment of Sex Offenders' in H Kemshall and G McIvor (eds) *Managing Sex Offender Risk* (London, Jessica Kingsley Publishers).

GRUBIN, DH and THORNTON, D (1994) 'A National Programme for the Assessment and Treatment of Sex Offenders in the English Prison System' 21 *Criminal Justice and Behaviour* 55.

GRUNFELD, B and NORIEK, K (1986) 'Recidivism among Sex Offenders: A Follow-up Study of 541 Norwegian Sex Offenders' 9 *International Journal of Law and Psychiatry* 95.

GUNNLAUGSSON, H and GALLIHER, JF (2000) *Wayward Icelanders: Punishment Boundary Maintenance, and the Creation of Crime* (Madison, WI, University of Wisconsin Press).

HACKING, I (1999) *The Social Construction of What?* (Cambridge, MA, Harvard University Press).

HAGAN, J (1997) 'Crime and Capitalization: Toward a Developmental Theory of Street Crime in America' in T Thornberry (ed) *Developmental Theories of Crime and Delinquency* (New Brunswick, Transaction Press).

HAKIM, S and RENGERT, GF (1981) *Crime Spill over* (Beverley Hills, CA, Sage).

HALEY, JO (1996) 'Crime Prevention Through Restorative Justice: Lessons from Japan' in B Galaway and J Hudson (eds) *Restorative Justice: International Perspectives* (Monsey, NY, Criminal Justice Press).

HALL, S, CRITCHER, C, JEFFERSON, T, CLARKE, J and ROBERTS, B (1978) *Policing the Crisis* (London, Macmillan).

HALLETT, C and BIRCHALL, E (1992) *Co-ordination and Child Protection* (London, HMSO).

HANSON, RF, RESNICK, HS, KILPATRICK, DG and BEST, C (1999) 'Factors Related to the Reporting of Childhood Rape' 23 *Child Abuse and Neglect* 559.

HANSON, RK (1997) *The Development of a Brief Actuarial Risk Scale for Sexual Offence Recidivism* (User Report 97-04) (Ottawa, Department of the Solicitor General of Canada).

HANSON, RK, STEFFY, RA and GAUTHIER, R (1993) 'Long-term Recidivism of Child Molesters' 61 *Journal of Clinical Psychology* 646.

HANSON, RK and THORNTON, D (1999) *Static-99: Improving Actuarial Risk Assessments for Sex Offenders* (User Report 99-02) (Ottawa, Department of the Solicitor General of Canada).

—— (2000) 'Improving Risk Assessments for Sex Offenders: A Comparison of Three Actuarial Scales' 24 *Law and Human Behaviour* 119.

HARRINGTON, C (1993) 'Community Organising Through Conflict Resolution' in SE Merry and N Milner (eds) *The Possibility of Popular Justice* (Michigan, University of Michigan Press).

HARRIS, DJ, O'BOYLE, M and WARBRICK, C (1995) *Law of the European Convention on Human Rights* (London, Butterworths).

HARRIS, MK (2003) 'Moving into the New Millennium: Toward a Feminist Vision of Justice' in E McLaughlin, R Ferguson, G Hughes and L Westmarland (eds) *Restorative Justice: Critical Issues* (London, Sage).

HARRIS, N (2001) 'Part II. Shaming and Shame: Regulating Drink-Driving' in E Ahmed, N Harris, J Braithwaite and V Braithwaite (eds) *Shame Management Through Reintegration* (Cambridge, Cambridge University Press).

—— (2003a) 'Reassessing the Dimensionality of Moral Emotions' 94 *British Journal of Psychology* 457.

—— (2003b) 'Evaluating the Practice of Restorative Justice: The Case of Family Group Conferencing' in L Walgrave (ed) *Repositioning Restorative Justice* (Devon, Willan Publishing).

HARRIS, N and MARUNA, S (2006) 'Shame, Shaming and Restorative Justice: A Critical Appraisal' in D Sullivan and L Tifft (eds) *Handbook on Restorative Justice: A Global Perspective* (New York, Routledge).

HARRIS, N, WALGRAVE, L, and BRAITHWAITE, J (2004) 'Emotional Dynamics in Restorative Conferences' 8 *Theoretical Criminology* 191.

HAWTHORNE, N (1994) *The Scarlet Letter*, first published in 1850 (London and New York, Penguin Books Ltd).

HAY, C (2001) 'An Exploratory Test of Braithwaite's Reintegrative Shaming Theory' 38 *Crime and Delinquency* 132.

HEBENTON, B (1997) 'Some Reflections on the US Experience of Sex Offender Registration and Notification,' paper presented at the panel 'Sex Offenders and the Justice System,' the British Criminology Conference, Queen's University Belfast, July.

HEBENTON, B and THOMAS, T (1993) *Criminal Records: State, Citizen and the Politics of Protection* (Aldershot, Avebury).

—— (1996a) 'Tracking Sex Offenders' 35 *The Howard Journal of Criminal Justice* 97.

—— (1996b) 'Sexual Offenders in the Community: Reflections on Problems of Law, Community and Risk Management in the USA and England and Wales' 24 *International Journal of the Sociology of Law* 427.

—— (1996c) 'Stranger Danger' *Criminal Justice Matters* 25.

—— (1997a) *Keeping Track? Observations on Sex Offenders Registers in the US*, Crime Detection and Prevention Series Paper No 83 (London: Home Office).

HEBENTON, B (1997b) 'Paedophiles, Privacy and Protecting the Public' *The Criminal Lawyer* 7.

—— (1997c) 'Some Observations on the Proposed Sex Offender Register' *The Criminal Lawyer* 5.

HEDDERMAN, C and SUGG, D (1996) *Does Treating Sex Offenders Reduce Offending*, Home Office Research Findings No 45 (London, Home Office).

HEIM, N (1981) 'Sexual Behaviour of Castrated Sex Offenders' 10 *Archives of Sexual Behaviour* 11.

HEIM, N and HURSCH, C (1979) 'Castration for Sex Offenders: Treatment or Punishment?' A Review and Critique of Recent European Literature' 8 *Archives of Sexual Behaviour* 281.

HENHAM, RJ (1998) 'Sentencing Sex Offenders: Some Implications of Recent Criminal Justice Policy' 37 *The Howard Journal* 70.

—— (2001) 'Sentencing Dangerous Offenders: Policy and Practice in the Crown Court' *Criminal Law Review* 693.

—— (2003) 'The Policy and Practice of Protective Sentencing' 3 *Criminal Justice* 57.

HENRY, F and TABACHNICK, J (2002) 'Stop it Now!: The Campaign to Prevent Child Sexual Abuse' in B Schwartz (ed) *The Sex Offender: Vol 4* (Kingston, New Jersey, Civic Research Institute).

Her Majesty's Prison Service (HMPS) (1994) *Release of Prisoners Convicted of Offences Against Children or Young Persons under the Age of 18*, Guidance Notes For Governors 545/94 (London, HM Prison Service).

Her Majesty's Stationery Office (HMSO) (1985) *Report of the Committee of Inquiry into Children's Homes and Hostels* (The Hughes Report) (London, HMSO).

HERMAN, J (1997) *Trauma and Recovery* (New York, Basic Books).

—— (1981) *Father-Daughter Incest* (Cambridge, Massachusetts, Harvard University Press).

HETHERTON, J (1999) 'The Idealisation of Women: Its Role in the Minimisation of Child Sexual Abuse by Females' 23 *Child Abuse and Neglect* 161.

HIBBERT, C (1963) *The Roots of Evil: A Social History of Crime and Punishment* (London, Weidenfeld and Nicolson)

HIRST, P (2000) 'Statism, Pluralism and Social Control' 40 *British Journal of Criminology* 279.

HOBBS, D (1988) *Doing the Business: Entrepreneurship, the Working Class, and Detectives in the East End of London* (Oxford, Clarendon Press).

HOLLIN, CR and HOWELLS, K (eds) (1991) *Clinical Approaches to Sex Offenders and their Victims* (Chichester, Wiley).

Home Office (1964) *Children and Young Persons Act 1963: Parts I and II*, Home Office Circular 22/64 (London, Home Office).

—— (1986) *The Sentence of the Court: A Handbook for Courts on the Treatment of Offenders* (London, HMSO)

—— (1988) *Punishment, Custody and the Community* (London, HMSO).

—— (1990) *Crime, Justice and Protecting the Public* (London, HMSO).

—— (1991) *Report of the Tripartite Seminar 1991 on the Effective Management of Sex Offenders* (London, Home Office).

—— (1995) *Availability of a New Community Sentence: Electronic Monitoring of Curfew Orders*, Home Office Circular 36/1995 (London, Home Office).

—— (1996a) *Protecting the Public: The Government's Strategy on Crime in England and Wales*, Cm 3190 (London, HMSO).

—— (1996b) *Sentencing and Supervision of Sex Offenders: A Consultation Document*, Cm 3304 (London, HMSO.)

—— (1997a) *No More Excuses: A New Approach to Tackling Youth Crime in England and Wales*, Cm 3809 (London, HMSO).

—— (1997b) *The Sex Offenders Act 1997*, Home Office Circular 39/97 (London, Home Office).

—— (1999) *Sex Offender Orders: Full Guidance (The Crime and Disorder Act)*, Home Office Circular 9/99 (London, Home Office).

—— (2000) *Setting the Boundaries: Reforming the Law on Sex Offences* (London, Home Office).

—— (2001a) *Making Punishments Work: Report of a Review of the Sentencing Framework for England and Wales* (Halliday Report) (London, Home Office).

—— (2001b) *Consultation Paper on the Review of Part I of the Sex Offenders Act 1997* (London, Home Office).

—— (2001c) *What Works: Second Report from the Joint Prison/Probation Accreditation Panel 2000-2001* (London: Home Office).

—— (2002) *Protecting the Public: Strengthening Protection Against Sex Offenders and Reforming the Law on Sexual Offences* Cm 5668 (London, HMSO).

Home Office and Department of Health (1975) *Mentally Abnormal Offenders: Report of the Committee*, Cm 6244, Chairman: Lord Butler of Saffron Walden, (London, HMSO).

—— (1999) *Managing Dangerous People with Severe Personality Disorder: Proposals for Policy Development* (London, HMSO).

Home Office, Department of Health, and Welsh Office (1995) *National Standards for the Supervision of Offenders in the Community* (London, Home Office, Department of Health and Welsh Office).

Home Office, HM Prison Service and Department of Health (2005) *Dangerous and Severe Personality Disorder (DSPD) High Secure Services For Men: Planning and Delivery Guide* (London, Home Office)

HOOD, R, SHUTE, S, FEILZER, M and WILCOX, A (2002) 'Sex Offenders Emerging from Long-Term Imprisonment: A Study of Their Long-term Reconviction Rates and of Parole Board Members' Judgements of Their Risk' 42 *British Journal of Criminology* 371.

HOOVER, EJ (1947) 'How Safe is Your Daughter?' CXLIV *American Magazine* 32.

HOPE, T (2001) 'Community Crime Prevention in Britain: A Strategic Overview' 1 *Criminal Justice* 421.

HOPE, T and MURPHY, DJI (1983) 'Problems of Implementing Crime Prevention: The Experience of a Demonstration Project' 22 *The Howard Journal* 38.

HOROWITZ, C (1996) 'Kids Who Prey on Kids' *Good Housekeeping*, October.

HOUGH, M (1996) 'People Talking About Punishment' 35 *The Howard Journal of Criminal Justice* 191.

HOUGH, M, ALLEN, R and PADEL, U (2006) *Reshaping Probation and Prisons: The New Offender Management Framework*, Researching Criminal Justice Series (Bristol, Policy Press).

HOUGH, M, LEWIS, H and WALKER, N (1988) 'Factors Associated with "Punitiveness"' in England and Wales' in N Walker and M Hough (eds) *Public Attitudes to Sentencing: Surveys from Five Countries* (Aldershot, Gower).

HOUSTON, JA (1994) 'Sex Offender Registration Acts: An Added Dimension to the War on Crime' 28 *Georgia Law Review* 729.

Howard League for Penal Reform (1995) *Unlawful Sex: Offences, Victims and Offenders in the Criminal Justice System of England and Wales,* Report of the Howard League Working Party (London, Waterlow).

Howitt, D (1996) *Paedophiles and Sexual Offences Against Children* (Chichester, Wiley).

Hoyle, C (1998) *Negotiating Domestic Violence: Police, Criminal Justice and Victims* (Oxford, Oxford University Press).

—— (2001) 'Restorative Justice in the Thames Valley: Changes in the Complaints and Discipline Process' 133 *Prison Service Journal* 37.

Hoyle, C and Rose, D (2001) 'Labour, Law and Order' 72 *The Political Quarterly* 76.

Hoyle, C and Sanders, A (2000) 'Police Response to Domestic Violence: From Victim Choice to Victim Empowerment?' 40 *British Journal of Criminology* 14.

Hoyle, C and Young, R (2002) 'Restorative Justice: Assessing the Prospects and Pitfalls' in M McConville and G Wilson (eds) *The Handbook of The Criminal Justice Process* (Oxford, Oxford University Press).

Hoyle, C, Young, R and Hill, R (2002) *Proceed With Caution: An Evaluation of the Thames Valley Police Initiative in Restorative Cautioning* (York, Joseph Rowntree Foundation).

Hudson, B (1998) 'Restorative Justice: The Challenge of Sexual and Racial Violence' 25 *Journal of Law and Society* 237.

—— (2001) 'Human Rights, Public Safety and the Probation Service: Defending Justice in the Risk Society' 40 *The Howard Journal of Criminal Justice* 103.

—— (2002) 'Restorative Justice and Gendered Violence: Diversion or Effective Justice?' 42 *British Journal of Criminology* 616.

Hudson, K (2005) *Offending Identities: Sex Offenders' Perspectives on their Treatment and Management* (Devon, Willan Publishing).

Hughes, B and Parker, H (1994) 'Saving the Children' *Community Care* 24.

Hughes, B, Parker, H and Gallagher, B (1996) *Policing Child Sexual Abuse: The View from Police Practitioners* (London, Home Office Police Research Group Report).

Hulsman, L (1991) 'The Abolitionist Case: Alternative Crime Policies' 25 *Israeli Law Review* 681.

Hunt, P (1994) *Report of the Inquiry into Multiple Abuse in Nursery Classes in Newcastle Upon Tyne* (Newcastle Upon Tyne, City Council of Newcastle Upon Tyne).

Hutton, N (2005) 'Beyond Populist Punitiveness?' 7 *Punishment and Society* 243.

Icenogle, DL (1994) 'Sentencing Male Sex Offenders to the Use of Biological Treatments' 15 *Journal of Legal Medicine* 279.

Irwin, B (1990) 'Old and New Tools for the Modern Probation Officer' 36 *Crime and Delinquency* 61.

Irwin, J and Austin, J (1994) *It's About Time: America's Imprisonment Binge* (Belmont, CA, Wadsworth).

Ives, G (1914) *A History of Penal Methods: Criminals, Witches, Lunatics* (Montclair, New Jersey: Patterson Smith).

Jackson, S and Scott, S (1999) 'Risk Anxiety and the Social Construction of Childhood' in D Lupton (ed) *Risk and Socio-cultural Theory: New Directions and Perspectives* (Cambridge, Cambridge University Press).

James, A and Jenks, C (1996) 'Public Perceptions of Childhood Criminality' 47 *British Journal of Sociology* 315.

Japanese Ministry of Justice (1998) *Summary of the White Paper on Crime, 1998* (Tokyo, Japan, Research and Training Institute).

JAY, M and DOGANIS, S (1987) *Battered: The Abuse of Children* (London, Weidenfeld and Nicolson).

JESSOP, B (1993) 'Towards a Schumpeterian Workfare State?: Preliminary Remarks on Post-Fordist Political Economy' 40 *Studies in Political Economy* 7.

JOHNSON-GEORGE, C and SWAP, W (1982) 'Measurement of Specific Inter-personal Trust: Construction and Validation of a Scale to Assess Trust in a Specific Other' 43 *Journal of Personality and Social Psychology* 1306.

JOHNSTON, L (1996) 'What is Vigilantism?' 36 *British Journal of Criminology* 220.

—— (2000) *Policing Britain: Risk, Security and Governance* (Essex, Longman Publishing).

JOHNSTONE, G (2000) 'Penal Policy Making: Elitist, Populist or Participatory?' 2 *Punishment and Society* 161.

—— (2001) *Restorative Justice: Ideas, Values, Debates* (Devon, Willan Publishing).

—— (2003) (ed) *A Restorative Justice Reader: Texts, Sources, Context* (Devon, Willan Publishing).

JOKOVICH, E (2003) 'Breaking the Silence on Abuse' 65 *Rattler* 11.

JONES, DM (ed), PICKETT, J, OATES, MR and BARBOR, P (1987) *Understanding Child Abuse*, 2nd edn (London, Macmillan Education Ltd).

JONES, T and NEWBURN, T (2002) 'Policy Convergence and Crime Control in the USA and the UK: Streams of Influence and Levels of Impact' 2 *Criminal Justice* 129.

—— (2006) 'Three Strikes and You're Out: Exploring Symbol and Substance in American and British Crime Control Politics' 46 *British Journal of Criminology* 781.

JÜLICH, S (2006) 'Views of Justice Among Survivors of Historical Child Sexual Abuse: Implications for Restorative Justice in New Zealand' 10 *Theoretical Criminology* 125.

KABAT, AR (1998) 'Scarlet Letter Sex Offender Databases and Community Notification: Sacrificing Personal Privacy for a Symbol's Sake' 35 *American Common Law Review* 333.

KAHAN, DM (1996) 'What Do Alternative Sanctions Mean?' 63 *University of Chicago Law Review* 591.

KAIHLA, P (1995) 'Sex Offenders: Is There a Cure?' *Maclean's* 56.

KALISCH, BJ (1978) *Child Abuse and Neglect: An Annotated Bibliography* (Westport, Connecticut, Greenwood).

KARP, DR (1998) 'The Judicial and the Judicious Use of Shame Penalties' 44 *Crime and Delinquency* 277.

KARP, DR and CLEAR, TR (2002) *What is Community Justice?* (Thousand Oaks, CA, Pine Forge Press).

KARP J (1996) 'Restitution of Victims by the Offenders' 30 *Israel Law Review* 331.

KARSTEDT, S (2002) 'Emotions and Criminal Justice' 6 *Theoretical Criminology* 299.

KAY, JW (2006) 'Murder Victims' Families for Reconciliation: Story-telling for Healing, as Witness, and in Public Policy' in D Sullivan and L Tifft (eds) *Handbook on Restorative Justice: A Global Perspective* (New York, Routledge).

KELLEY, RK (1989) (Comment) 'Sentenced to Wear the Scarlet Letter: Judicial Innovations in Sentencing' 93 *Dickinson Law Review* 759.

KELLY, L, LOVETT, J and REGAN, L (2005) *A Gap or a Chasm? Attrition in Reported Rape Cases*, Home Office Research Study No 293 (London, Home Office).

KEMPE, H (1978) 'Sexual Abuse: Another Hidden Pediatric Problem' 62 *Pediatrics* 382.

KEMPE, H, SILVERMAN, FN, STEELE, BF, DROGEMUELLER, W and SILVER, MK (1962) 'The Battered Child Syndrome' 181 *Journal of The American Medical Association* 17.

KEMSHALL, H (2001) *Risk Assessment and Management of Known Sexual and Violent Offenders: A Review of Current Issues*, Police Research Series Paper No 140 (London, Home Office).
—— (2004) 'Female Sex Offenders' in H Kemshall and G McIvor (eds) *Managing Sex Offender Risk* (London, Jessica Kingsley Publishers).
KEMSHALL, H and MAGUIRE, M (2001) 'Public Protection, Partnership and Risk Penalty: The Multi-agency Risk Management of Sexual and Violent Offenders' 3 *Punishment and Society* 237.
—— (2002) 'Community Justice, Risk Management and the Role of Multi-Agency Public Protection Panels' 1 *British Journal of Community Justice* 11.
—— (2003) 'Sex Offenders, Risk Penality and The Problem of Disclosure' in A Matravers (ed) *Sex Offenders in the Community: Managing and Reducing the Risks* (Devon, Willan Publishing, Cambridge Criminal Justice Series).
KEMSHALL, H, PARTON, N, WALSH, M and WATERSON, J (1997) 'Concepts of Risk in Relation to the Organisational Structure and Functioning within the Personal Social Services and Probation' 31 *Social Policy and Administration* 213.
KENNEDY, MT, MANWELL, MKC, MACKENZIE, G, BLANEY, R, CHIVERS, AT and MAY, I (1990) *Child Sexual Abuse in Northern Ireland: A Research Study of Incidence* (Antrim, Greystone Books).
KIERSCH, TA (1990) 'Treatment of Sex Offenders with Depo-Provera' 18 *Bulletin of the American Academy of Psychiatry and Law* 179.
KIMBALL, CM (1996) 'A Modern Day Arthur Dimmesdale: Public Notification When Sex Offenders Are Released into the Community' 12 *Georgia State University Law Review* 1187.
KINZIG, J (1997) 'Preventive Measures for Dangerous Recidivists' 5 *European Journal of Crime, Criminal Law and Criminal Justice* 25.
KIRKEGAARD, H and NORTHEY, W (2000) 'The Sex Offender as Scapegoat: Vigilante Violence and a Faith Community Response' 132 *Prison Service Journal* 71.
KIRKWOOD, A (1993) *The Report of the Inquiry into Aspects of the Management of Children's Homes in Leicestershire between 1973 and 1986* (Leicester, Leicestershire County Council).
KLEIN, A and TABACHNICK, J (2002) 'Framing a New Approach: Finding Ways to Effectively Prevent Sexual Abuse by Youth' 9 *The Prevention Researcher* 8.
KLEINHAMS, M-M (2002) 'Criminal Justice Approaches to Paedophilic Sex Offenders' 11 *Social & Legal Studies* 233.
KNOCK, K, SCHLESINGER, P, BOYLE, R and MAGOR, M (2002) 'The Police Perspective on Sex Offender Orders: A Preliminary Review of Policy and Practice', Police Research Series Paper No 155 (London, Home Office).
KNOPP, FH (1984) *Retraining Adult Sex Offenders: Methods and Models* (Orwell, Vermont: Safer Safety Press).
—— (1991) 'Community Solutions to Sexual Violence' in HE Pepinsky and R Quinney (eds) *Criminology as Peacemaking* (Bloomington, Indiana University Press).
KNOX, C (2002) 'See No Evil, Hear No Evil: Insidious Paramilitary Violence in Northern Ireland' 42 *British Journal of Criminology* 164.
KOMIYA, M (1999) 'A Cultural Study of the Low Crime Rate in Japan' 39 *British Journal of Criminology* 369.
KOSS, MP (2000) 'Blame, Shame, and Community: Justice Responses to Violence Against Women' 55 *American Psychologist* 1332.

Koss, MP, Bachar, KJ, Hopkins, CQ (2003) 'Restorative Justice for Sexual Violence: Repairing Victims, Building Community, and Holding Offenders Accountable' 989 *Annals New York Academy of Sciences* 384.

Kozol, HL, Boucher, RJ and Garofalo, RF (1972) 'The Diagnosis and Treatment of Dangerousness' 18 *Crime and Delinquency* 371.

Kramer, RM, Brewer MB and Hanna B (1996) 'Collective Trust and Collective Action: Trust as a Social Decision' in R Kramer and T Tyler (eds) *Trust in Organisations* (Thousand Oaks, CA, Sage).

Kravitz, HM, Haywood TW, Kelly JR, Liles, S and Cavanaugh, JL (1995) 'Medroxyprogesterone Treatment for Paraphiles' 23 *Bulletin of the American Academy of Psychiatry and the Law* 19.

Kurki, L (2003) 'Evaluating Restorative Justice Practices' in A von Hirsch, A Roberts and AE Bottoms (eds) *Restorative and Criminal Justice: An Exploratory Analysis* (Oxford, Hart Publishing).

Lacey, N (1988) *State Punishment: Political Principles and Community Values* (London and New York, Routledge).

—— (2001) 'Beset by Boundaries: The Home Office Review of Sex Offences' *Criminal Law Review* 3.

La Fond, JQ (1992) 'Washington's Sexually Violent Predator Law: A Deliberate Misuse of the Therapeutic State for Social Control' 15 *University of Puget Sound Law Review* 655.

La Fontaine, J (1990) *Child Sexual Abuse* (Cambridge, Polity Press).

La Fontaine, J and Morris, S (1991) *The Boarding School Line: January-July 1991. A Report from ChildLine to the DES* (London, ChildLine).

La Prairie, C (1994) 'Community Justice or Just Communities? Aboriginal Communities in Search of Justice,' unpublished paper (Ottawa, Department of Justice).

Laster, K and O'Malley, P (1996) 'Sensitive New-age Laws: The Reassertion of Emotionality in Law' 24 *International Journal of the Sociology of Law* 21.

Laub, JH, Nagin, D and Sampson, RJ (1998) 'Trajectories of Change in Criminal Offending: Good Marriages and the Desistance Process' 63 *American Sociological Review* 225.

Laub, JH and Sampson, RJ (2003) *Shared Beginnings, Divergent Lives* (Harvard, MA, Harvard University Press).

Law Commission of Canada (2000) *Restoring Dignity: Responding to Child Abuse in Canadian Institutions* (Canada, Law Commission of Canada).

Laws, DR (ed) (1989) *Relapse Intervention with Sex Offenders* (New York, Guilford Press).

Lee, H (1989) *To Kill A Mockingbird* (London, Mandarin, first published in 1960 by Heinemann Ltd).

Lees, S (1995) 'Media Reporting of Rape: The 1993 British "Date Rape" Controversy' in D Kidd-Hewitt and R Osborne (eds) *Crime and the Media* (London, Pluto).

Leggett, S (2000) 'Paedophiles and other Child Abusers' 5 *The Ulster Humanist* 7.

Leibrich, J (1996) 'The Role of Shame in Going Straight: A Study of Former Offenders' in B Galaway and J Hudson (eds) *Restorative Justice: International Perspectives* (Monsey, NY, Criminal Justice Press).

Leonardsen, D (2004) *Japan As a Low-Crime Nation* (New York, Palgrave Macmillan).

Levrant, S, Cullen, FT, Fulton, B and Wozniak, JF (1999) 'Reconsidering Restorative Justice: The Corruption of Benevolence Revisited?' 45 *Crime and Delinquency* 3.

Lewis, HB (1971) *Shame and Guilt in Neurosis* (New York, International Universities Press).

Lewis, L (1988) *Effectiveness of Statutory Requirements for the Registration of Sex Offenders*, Report to the California State Legislature (California, Department of Justice).

LEWIS, R, DOBASH, RE, DOBASH, RP and CAVANAGH, K (2001) 'Law's Progressive Potential: The Value of Engagement with the Law for Domestic Violence' 10 *Social & Legal Studies* 105.

LIDDLE, AM and GELSTHORPE, LR (1994) *Inter-agency Crime Prevention: Organising Local Delivery*, Police Research Group, Crime Prevention Unit Series Paper No 52 (London, Home Office).

LIEB, R (1996) 'Community Notification Laws: A Step Towards More Effective Solutions' 11 *Journal of Interpersonal Violence* 298.

—— (2003) 'Joined-up Worrying: the Multi-Agency Public Protection Panels' in A Matravers (ed) *Sex Offenders in the Community: Managing and Reducing the Risks* (Devon, Willan Publishing, Cambridge Criminal Justice Series).

LIEB, R, Quinsey, V and Berliner, L (1998) 'Sexual Predators and Social Policy' *Crime and Justice: A Review of Research*, Vol 23 (Chicago, University of Chicago Press).

LIEBLING, A (1992) *Suicides in Prison* (London, Routledge).

LILLES, H (2001) 'Circle Sentencing: Part of the Restorative Justice Continuum' in A Morris and G Maxwell (eds) *Restorative Justice for Juveniles: Conferencing, Mediation and Circles* (Oxford, Hart Publishing).

LINDSAY-HARTZ, J (1984) 'Contrasting Experiences of Shame and Guilt' 27 *American Behavioural Scientist* 689.

LINKS, PS (1996) Clinical Assessment and Management of Severe Personality Disorders (Washington, DC, American Psychiatric Press).

—— (1998) 'Developing Effective Services for People with Personality Disorders' 43 *Canadian Journal of Psychiatry* 251.

LOGAN, W (1999) 'Liberty Interests in The Preventive State: Procedural Due Process and Sex Offender Community Notification Laws' 89 *Journal of Criminal Law and Criminology* 1167.

LOMBARDO, RA (1997) 'California's Unconstitutional Punishment for Heinous Crimes: Chemical Castration of Sexual Offenders' 65 *Fordham Law Review* 2611.

LONG, B and McLACHLAN, B (2002) *The Hunt for Britain's Paedophiles* (London, Hodder and Stoughton).

Lord Chancellor's Department (2001) *The Review of the Criminal Justice System*, Chairman Sir Robin Auld (http://www/criminal-courts-review.org.uk).

LOVELAND, I (1996) 'The Unkindest Cut?' 146 *New Law Journal* 744.

Lu, II (1999) 'Bang Jiao and Reintegrative Shaming in China's Urban Neighborhoods' 23 *International Journal of Comparative and Applied Justice* 115.

LUHMANN, N (1988) 'Family, Confidence, Trust: Problems and Alternatives' in D Gambetta (ed) *Trust: Making and Breaking Co-operative Relations* (Oxford, Basil Blackwell).

LYON, D (1994) *The Electronic Eye: The Rise of Surveillance Society* (Cambridge, Polity Press).

MACINTYRE, D and CARR, A (2000) *Prevention of Child Sexual Abuse in Ireland: The Development and Evaluation of The Stay Safe Programme*, Studies in Health and Human Services, Vol 3. (Lewiston, Queeston and Lampeter, The Edwin Mellen Press).

MACKINNON, C (1987) *Feminism Unmodified: Discourses on Life and Law* (Cambridge, Massachusetts, Harvard University Press).

MACLEOD, J (1995) *Ain't No Makin' It*, 2nd edn (Oxford, Westview Press).

MAGNUSSON, SA (1977) *Northern Sphinx: Iceland and the Icelanders from the Settlement to the Present* (Montreal, McGill-Queen's University Press).

MAGUIRE, M and KEMSHALL, H (2004) 'Multi-Agency Public Protection Arrangements: Key Issues' in H Kemshall and G McIvor (eds) *Managing Sex Offender Risk* (London, Jessica Kingsley Publishers).

MAGUIRE, M, KEMSHALL, H, NOAKES, L, WINCUP, E and SHARPE, K (2001) *Risk Management of Sexual and Violent Offenders: The Work of Public Protection Panels*, Police Research Series Paper No 13 (London, Home Office).

MAGUIRE, M and RAYNOR, P (1997) 'The Revival of Through care: Rhetoric and Reality in Automatic Conditional Release' 37 *British Journal of Criminology* 1.

—— (2006) 'How the Resettlement of Prisoners Promotes Desistance from Crime: Or Does It?' 6 *Criminology & Criminal Justice* 19.

MAIR, G (2005) 'Electronic Monitoring in England and Wales' 5 *Criminal Justice* 257.

MAIR, G and MORTIMER, E (1996) *Curfew Orders with Electronic Monitoring: An Evaluation of the First Twelve Months of the Trials in Greater Manchester, Norfolk and Berkshire, 1995-1996*, Home Office Research Study No 163 (London, HMSO).

MAISCH, H (1973) *Incest* (London, Andre Deutsch).

MAKKAI, T and BRAITHWAITE, J (1994) 'Reintegrative Shaming and Compliance with Regulatory Standards' 32 *Criminology* 361.

MANN, RE and THORNTON, D (1998) 'The Evolution of a Multisite Sexual Offender Treatment Program' in WL Marshall, YM Fernandez, SM Hudson and T Ward (eds) *Sourcebook of Treatment Programs for Sexual Offenders* (New York, Plenum Press).

MARQUES, JK, DAY, DM, NELSON, C and WEST, MA (1994) 'The Effects of Cognitive-Behavioural Treatment on Sex Offender Recidivism: Preliminary Results of a Longitudinal Study' 21 *Criminal Justice and Behaviour* 10.

MARQUES, JK, NELSON, C, ALARCON, JM and DAY, DM (2000) 'Preventing Relapse in Sex Offenders: What We Learned From SOTEP's Experimental Treatment Program' in DR Laws, SM Hudson and T Ward (eds) *Remaking Relapse Prevention with Sex Offenders: A Sourcebook* (London, Sage).

MARSHALL, P (1994) *Reconviction of Imprisoned Sexual Offenders*, Home Office Research Bulletin No 36 (London, Home Office).

—— (1997) *The Prevalence of Convictions for Sexual Offending*, Home Office Research Bulletin No 55 (London, Home Office).

MARSHALL, T (1991) *Victim-Offender Mediation*, Home Office Research Bulletin No 30 (London, HMSO).

—— (1997) 'Seeking the Whole Justice', ISTD Conference, *Repairing the Damage: Restorative Justice in Action*, March.

—— (1999) *Restorative Justice: An Overview*. A Report by the Home Office Research Development and Statistics Directorate (London, HMSO).

MARSHALL, WL (1993) 'The Treatment of Sex Offenders: What Does the Outcome Data Tell Us? A Reply to Quinsey, Harris, Rice and Lalumiere' 8 *Journal of Interpersonal Violence* 524.

MARSHALL, WL and BARBAREE HE (1988) 'The Long-Term Evaluation of a Behavioural Treatment Program for Child Molesters' 6 *Behaviour Research and Therapy* 499.

MARSHALL, WL, JONES, R, WARD, T, JOHNSTON, P and BARBAREE, HE (1991) 'Treatment Outcome with Sex Offenders' 11 *Clinical Psychology Review* 465.

MARSHALL, WL, LAWS, DR, BARBAREE, HE (eds) (1990) *Handbook of Sexual Assault: Issues, Theories and Treatment of the Offender* (New York, Plenum Press).

MARTIN, P (1996) 'Restorative Justice-A Family Violence Perspective' 6 *Social Policy Journal of New Zealand* 56.

MARTIN, SE and SHERMAN, LW (1986) 'Selective Incapacitation: A Political Strategy for Repeat Offenders' 24 *Criminology* 155.

MARTINSON, R (1979) 'New Findings, New Views: A Note of Caution on Sentencing Reform' 7 *Hofstra Law Review* 242.

MARTINSON, R, LIPTON, D and WILKS, J (1974) 'What Works? Questions and Answers About Prison Reform' 10 *The Public Interest* 22.

MARUNA, S (2001) *Making Good: How Ex-Convicts Reform and Rebuild Their Lives* (Washington DC, APA Books).

MARUNA, S and FARRALL, S (2004) 'Desistance From Crime: A Theoretical Reformulation' 43 *KŒeitschrift fir Soziologie und sozialpsychologie* 171.

MARUNA, S and IMMARIGEON, R (eds) (2004) *After Crime and Punishment: Pathways to Offender Reintegration* (Devon, Willan Publishing).

MARUNA, S and LEBEL, TP (2002) 'Revisiting Ex-prisoner Re-entry: A Buzz-word in Search of a Narrative' in S Rex and M Tonry (eds) *Reform and Punishment* (Devon, Willan Publishing).

MARX, GT (1989) 'Commentary: Some Trends and Issues in Citizen Involvement in the Law Enforcement Process' 35 *Crime and Delinquency* 500.

MASSARO, TM (1991) 'Shame Culture and American Criminal Law' 89 *Michigan Law Review* 1880.

MASSON, H (2004) 'Young Sex Offenders' in H Kemshall and G McIvor (eds) *Managing Sex Offender Risk* (London, Jessica Kingsley Publishers).

MASSON, H and MORRISON, T (1999) 'Young Sexual Abusers: Conceptual Frameworks, Issues and Imperatives' 13 *Children and Society* 203.

MATHIESON, T (1965) *Defences of the Weak: A Sociological Study of A Norwegian Correctional Institution* (London, Tavistock).

—— (1997) 'The Viewer Society: Michel's Foucault's "Panoptican" Revisited' 1 *Theoretical Criminology* 215.

MATRAVERS, A (ed) (2003) *Sex Offenders in the Community: Managing and Reducing the Risks* (Devon, Willan Publishing, Cambridge Criminal Justice Series).

MATTHEWS, R (2005) 'The Myth of Punitiveness' 9 *Theoretical Criminology* 175.

—— (2006) 'Reintegrative Shaming and Restorative Justice: Reconciliation or Divorce?' in I Aersten, T Daems and L Robert (eds) *Institutionalizing Restorative Justice* (Devon, Willan Publishing).

MATTHEWS, R and PITTS, J (2000) 'Rehabilitation, Recidivism and Realism: Evaluating Violence Reduction Programmes in Prison in V Jupp, P Davis and P Francis (eds) *Doing Criminological Research* (London, Sage).

MATZA, D (1964) *Delinquency and Drift* (New York, Wiley).

—— (1969) *Becoming Deviant* (New Jersey, Prentice Hall).

MAXWELL, G and MORRIS, A (1993) *Family, Victims and Culture: Youth Justice in New Zealand* (Wellington, Social Policy Agency and the Institute of Criminology, Victoria University of Wellington).

—— (1999) *Understanding Re-offending* (Wellington, Institute of Criminology, Victoria University of Wellington).

—— (2000) 'Restorative Justice and Re-offending' in H Strang and J Braithwaite (eds) *Restorative Justice: Philosophy to Practice* (Aldershot, Ashgate).

—— (2001) 'Family Group Conferences and Reoffending' in A Morris and G Maxwell (eds) *Restorative Justice for Juveniles: Conferencing, Mediation and Circles* (Oxford, Hart Publishing).

—— (2002) 'The Role of Shame, Guilt and Remorse in Restorative Justice Processes for Young People' in E Weitekamp and HJ Kerner (eds) *Restorative Justice: Theoretical Foundations* (Devon, Willan Publishing).

—— (2004) 'What is the Place of Shame In Restorative Justice?' in H Zehr and B Toews (eds) *Critical Issues in Restorative Justice* (Monsey, New York, Criminal Justice Press and Devon, Willan Publishing).

MAYS, JB (1952) 'A Study of a Delinquent Community' 3 *British Journal of Delinquency* 5.

MCALINDEN, A (1999) 'Sex Offender Registration: Some Observations on "Megan's Law" and the Sex Offenders Act 1997' 1 *Crime Prevention and Community Safety: An International Journal* 41.

—— (2000), 'Sex Offender Registration: Implications and Difficulties for Ireland' 10 *Irish Journal of Sociology* (Special Issue: Crime and Policing) 102.

—— (2001) 'Indeterminate Sentences for the Severely Personality Disordered' *Criminal Law Review* 108.

—— (2005) 'The Use of "Shame" with Sexual Offenders' 45 *British Journal of Criminology* 373.

—— (2006a) 'Are There Limits to Restorative Justice? The Case of Child Sexual Abuse' in D Sullivan and L Tifft (eds) *Handbook on Restorative Justice: A Global Perspective* (New York, Routledge).

—— (2006b) 'Managing Risk: From Regulation to the Reintegration of Sexual Offenders' 6 *Criminology & Criminal Justice* 197.

—— (2006c) '"Setting 'Em Up": Personal, Social and Institutional Grooming in the Sexual Abuse of Children' 15 *Social & Legal Studies* 339.

MCCOLD, P (1996) 'Restorative Justice and the Role of the Community' in B Galaway and J Hudson (eds) *Restorative Justice: International Perspectives* (Monsey, NY, Criminal Justice Press)

—— (2000) 'Toward a Holistic Vision of Restorative Juvenile Justice: A Reply to the Maximalist Model' 3 *Contemporary Justice Review* 357.

—— (2001) 'Primary Restorative Justice Practices' in A Morris and G Maxwell (eds) *Restorative Justice for Juveniles: Conferencing, Mediation and Circles* (Oxford, Hart Publishing).

MCCOLD, P and WACHTEL, B (1998) 'Community is Not A Place: A New Look at Community Justice Initiatives' 1 *Contemporary Justice Review* 71.

MCDONALD, J, MOORE, D, O'CONNELL, T and THORSBORNE, M (1995) *Real Justice Training Manual: Coordinating Family Group Conferences* (Pipersville, PA, The Pipers' Press).

MCELREA, FWM (1994) 'Justice in the Community: The New Zealand Experience' in J Burnside and N Baker (eds) *Relational Justice: Repairing the Breach* (Winchester, Waterside Press).

MCEVOY, K and MIKA, H (2001) 'Policing, Punishment and Praxis: Restorative Justice and Non-violent Alternatives to Paramilitary Punishments in Northern Ireland' 11 *Policing and Society* 259.

—— (2002) 'Restorative Justice and the Critique of Informalism in Northern Ireland' 43 *British Journal of Criminology* 534.

MCEVOY, K, MIKA, H and HUDSON, B (2002) 'Introduction: Practice, Performance and Prospects for Restorative Justice' 42 *British Journal of Criminology* (Special Issue: Restorative Justice) 469.

MCGRATH, K (1992) 'Inter-agency Co-operation in the Provision of Group Therapy for Adolescent Sex Offenders and their Parents,' unpublished paper presented to the Ninth International Conference on *Child Abuse and Neglect*, Chicago, IL, September.

MCGRATH, RJ (1995), 'Sex Offender Treatment: Does It Work?' 19 *Perspectives* 24.

McGRATH, RJ, CUMMING, G, LIVINGSTON, JA, HOKE, SE (2003) 'Outcome of A Treatment Program For adult Sex Offenders: From Prison to Community' 18 *Journal of Interpersonal Violence* 3.

McGRATH, RJ, HOKE, SE and VOJTSEK, SE (1998) 'Cognitive-behavioural Treatment of Sex Offenders: A Treatment Comparison and Long-term Follow-Up Study' 25 *Criminal Justice and Behaviour* 203.

McGUIRE, J (1995) *What Works: Reducing Re-offending?—Guidelines from Research and Practice* (Chichester, John Wiley).

—— (2000) *An Introduction to Theory and Research: Cognitive-behavioural Approaches*, HM Inspectorate of Probation Report (London, Home Office).

McIVOR, G (1992) *Sentenced to Serve?* (Aldershot, Gower).

McLAREN, K (1992) *Reducing Re-offending: What Works Now?* (Wellington, New Zealand, Department of Justice).

McLAUGHLIN, E and JOHANSEN, A (2002) 'A Force for Change? The Prospects for Applying Restorative Justice to Citizen Complaints against the Police in England and Wales' 42 *British Journal of Criminology* 635.

McNEILL, F (2006) 'A Desistance Paradigm for Offender Management' 6 *Criminology & Criminal Justice* 39.

MEAD, M (1937) *Cooperation and Competitions Among Primitive Peoples* (New York, McGraw-Hill).

MEIER, B (1998) 'Restorative Justice: A New Paradigm in Criminal Law?' 6 *European Journal of Crime, Criminal Law and Criminal Justice* 125.

MEISENHELDER, T (1977) 'An Exploratory Study of Exiting From Criminal Careers' 15 *Criminology* 319.

MELELLA, JT, TRAVIN, S and CULLEN, K (1989) 'Legal and Ethical Issues in the Use of Anti-androgens in Treating Sex Offenders' 17 *Bulletin of the American Academy of Psychiatry and Law* 223.

MELIA, P (1999) 'Ashworth and After' 2 *Mental Health Care* 205.

MENZIES, R, WEBSTER, C, McMAIN, S, STALEY, S and SCAGLIONE, R (1994) 'The Dimensions of Dangerousness Revisited: Assessing Forensic Predictions About Violence' 18 *Law and Human Behaviour* 1.

MERTON, RK (1993, first published 1938) 'Social Structure and Anomie' in C Lemert (ed) *Social Theory: The Multicultural Readings* (Boulder, Colorado, Westview Press).

MESSNER, SF and ROSENFELD, R (1977) 'Political Restraint of the Market and Levels of Criminal Homicide: A Cross-National Application of Institutional Anomie Theory' 75 *Social Forces* 1393.

MEYER, M (2005) 'Family Decision Making and Child Sexual Abuse: A Restorative Process?,' paper presented at the Sixth International Conference on *Conferencing, Circles and Other Restorative Practices*, Penrith Australia, March.

MIERS, D (1991) *Compensation for Criminal Injuries* (London, Butterworths).

—— (2004) 'Situating and Researching Restorative Justice in Great Britain' 6 *Punishment and Society* 23.

MIERS, D, MAGUIRE, M, GOLDIE, S, SHAROE, K, HALE, C, NETTEN, A, DOOLIN, K, UGLOW, S, ENTERKIN, J and NEWBURN, T (2001) *An Exploratory Evaluation of Restorative Justice Schemes*, Crime Reduction Research Series Paper No 9 (London, Home Office).

MIKA, H (1992) 'Mediation Interventions and Restorative Justice: Responding to the Astructural Bias' in H Messmer and H-U Otto (eds) *Restorative Justice on Trial* (Dordrecht, Neth, Kluwer Academic Publishers).

MIKA, H and McEVOY, K (2001) 'Restorative Justice in Conflict: Paramilitarism, Community and the Construct of Legitimacy in Northern Ireland' 4 *Contemporary Justice Review* 292.

MILLER, A (2000) *The Crucible*, (London, Penguin Books Ltd, first published in 1953 by New York, Penguin Putnam Inc).

MILLER, S and BLACKLER, J (2000) 'Restorative Justice: Retribution, Confession and Shame' in H Strang and J Braithwaite (eds) *Restorative Justice: Philosophy to Practice* (Aldershot, Ashgate).

MILLER, WI (1990) *Bloodtaking and Peacemaking: Feud, Law, and Society in Saga Iceland* (Chicago, University of Chicago Press).

MILLS, LG (2003) *Insult to Injury: Rethinking Our Responses to Intimate Abuse* (Princeton, Princeton University Press).

MONAHAN, J (1973) 'Dangerous Offenders: A Critique of Kozol et al' 19 *Crime and Delinquency* 418.

—— (1981) *Predicting Violent Behaviour* (Beverley Hills and London, Sage).

MONEY, J (1970) 'Use of an Androgen-Depleting Hormone in the Treatment of Male Sex Offenders' 6 *Journal of Sexual Research* 165.

MOORE, C (1995) *Betrayal of Trust: The Father Brendan Smyth Affair and the Catholic Church* (Dublin, Marino).

—— (1996) *Kincora Scandal: Political Cover-up and Intrigue in Ulster* (Dublin, Marino).

MOORE, DB (1993) 'Shame, Forgiveness and Juvenile Justice' 12 *Criminal Justice Ethics* 3.

MOORE, DB, FORSYTHE, L and O'CONNELL, T (1995) *A New Approach to Juvenile Justice: An Evaluation of Family Conferencing in Wagga Wagga* (Wagga Wagga, Australia, Charles Stuart University).

MORRIS, A (2002a) 'Critiquing the Critics: A Brief Response to Critics of Restorative Justice' 42 *British Journal of Criminology* 596.

—— (2002b) 'Shame, Guilt and Remorse: Experiences from Family Group Conferences in New Zealand' in I Weijers and A Duff (eds) *Punishing Juveniles: Principles and Critique* (Oxford, Hart Publishing).

MORRIS, A and GELSTHORPE, L (2000a) 'Re-visioning Men's Violence Against Female Partners' 39 *The Howard Journal* 412.

—— (2000b) 'Something Old, Something Borrowed, Something Blue, But Something New? A Comment on the Prospects for Restorative Justice under the Crime and Disorder Act 1998' *Criminal Law Review* 18.

MORRIS, A and MAXWELL, G (2000) 'The Practice of Family Group Conferences in New Zealand: Assessing the Place, Potential and Pitfalls of Restorative Justice' in A Crawford and J Goodey (eds) *Integrating a Victim Perspective in Criminal Justice* (Aldershot, Ashgate).

—— (2001) 'Implementing Restorative Justice: What Works?' in A Morris and G Maxwell (eds) *Restorative Justice for Juveniles: Conferencing, Mediation and Circles* (Oxford, Hart Publishing).

—— (2003) 'Restorative Justice For Adult Offenders: The New Zealand Experience' in L Walgrave (ed) *Repositioning Restorative Justice* (Devon, Willan Publishing).

MORRIS, A, Maxwell, G and Robertson, J (1993) 'Giving Victims a Voice: A New Zealand Experiment' 32 *The Howard Journal of Criminal Justice* 304.

MORRIS, N (1994) 'Dangerousness and Incapacitation' in A Duff and D Garland (eds) *A Reader on Punishment* (Oxford, Oxford University Press).

MORRIS, N and MILLER, M (1986) 'Predictions of Dangerousness' in N Morris and M Tonry (eds) *Crime and Justice: A Review of Research Vol 10* (Chicago, University of Chicago Press).

MORRIS, N and ROTHMAN, DJ (1995) *The Oxford History of the Prison: The Practice of Punishment Western Society* (New York and Oxford, Oxford University Press).

MORRIS, R (1994) *A Practical Path to Restorative Justice* (Toronto, Rittenshouse).

MORTIMER, E and MAY, C (1998) *Electronic Monitoring of Curfew Orders: The Second Year of Trials*, Home Office Research Findings No 66 (London, Home Office).

MORTIMER, E, PEREIRA, E and WALTER, I (1999) *Making the Tag Fit: Further Analysis From the First Two Years of the Trials of Curfew Orders*, Home Office Research Study No 105 (London, Home Office).

MRAZEK, PB, LYNCH, M and BENTOVIM, A (1981) 'A Recognition of Child Sexual Abuse in the United Kingdom' in PB Mrazek and C Kempe (eds) *Sexually Abused Children and Their Families* (Oxford, Pergamon).

MULLENDER, R (1998) 'Privacy, Paedophilia and the European Convention on Human Rights: A Deontological Approach' *Public Law* 384.

MURDOCH, J (1993) 'Safeguarding the Liberty of the Person: Recent Strasbourg Jurisprudence' 42 *International Comparative Law Quarterly* 494.

MURPHY, FD, BUCKLEY, H and JOYCE, L (2005) *The Ferns Report*, presented by the Ferns Inquiry to the Minister for Health and Children (Dublin, Government Publications).

MURPHY, M (1995) *Working Together in Child Protection: An Exploration of the Multi-Disciplinary Task and System* (Aldershot, Arena).

MURPHY, P (1995) *Blackstone's Criminal Practice* (London, Blackstone Press).

—— (1998) 'A Therapeutic Programme for Imprisoned Sex Offenders: Progress to Date and Issues for the Future' 19 *Irish Journal of Psychology* 190.

MURRAY, JS (1998) 'California's Chemical Castration Law: A Model for Massachusetts?' 24 *Criminal and Civil Confinement* 731.

MYHILL, A and ALLEN, J (2002) *Rape and Sexual Assault of Women: The Extent and Nature of the Problem-Findings from the British Crime Survey*, Home Office Research Study No 237 (London, Home Office).

NAFFINE, N (1997) *Feminism and Criminology* (Cambridge, Polity Press).

NAGAYAMA HALL, GC (1995) 'Sexual Offending Recidivism Revisited: A Meta-Analysis of Recent Treatment Studies' 63 *Journal of Consulting and Clinical Psychology* 802.

NANCARROW, H (2006) 'In Search of Justice for Domestic and Family Violence: Indigenous and Non-indigenous Australian Women's Perspectives' 10 *Theoretical Criminology* 87.

NASH, M (1999) *Police, Probation and Protecting the Public* (London, Blackstone Press).

NATHANSON, DL (1992) *Shame and Pride: Affect, Sex and the Birth of the Self* (New York, WW Norton).

National Criminal Intelligence Service (NCIS) (2003) *United Kingdom Threat Assessment of Serious and Organised Crime* (London, NCIS).

National Organisation for the Treatment of Abusers (NOTA) (1995) 'The National Commission of Enquiry into the Prevention of Child Abuse: An Executive Summary of the Key Themes and Recommendations' 14 *NOTA News* 30.

NAVA, M (1988) 'Cleveland and the Press: Outrage and Anxiety in the Reporting of Child Sexual Abuse' 28 *Feminist Review* 103.

NELLIS, M (1991) 'The Electronic Monitoring of Offenders in England and Wales' 31 *British Journal of Criminology* 165.

—— (2005) 'Out of this World: The Advent of Satellite Tracking of Offenders in England and Wales' 44 *The Howard Journal of Criminal Justice* 125.

NEWBURN, T (2002) 'Atlantic Crossings: "Policy Transfer" and Crime Control in the USA and Britain' 4 *Punishment and Society* 165.

NEWBURN, T, CRAWFORD, A, EARLE, R, GOLDIE, S, HALE, C, MASTERS, G, NETTEN, A, SAUNDERS, R, SHARPE, K and UGLOW, S (2002) *The Introduction of Referral Orders into the Youth Justice System*, Home Office Research Study No 242 (London, Home Office)

New Jersey Commission on the Habitual Sex Offender (1950) *The Habitual Sex* Offender (New Jersey, Commission on the Habitual Sex Offender).

NICKOLAICHUK, T, and GORDON, A (1996) 'Treatment Reduces Sexual Recidivism: Clearwater Outcome Data Summary,' paper presented at the Annual ATSA Meeting: Outcome of the Clearwater Sex Offender Treatment Program; A Matched Comparison Between Treated and Untreated Offenders, Chicago, IL.

NOLAN, L (2001) *Report of the Review on Child Protection in the Catholic Church in England and Wales: A Programme for Action* (www.nolanreview.org.uk).

NORTON, K and HINSHELWOOD, RD (1996) 'Severe Personality Disorder: Treatment Issues and Selection for Inpatient Psychotherapy' 168 *British Journal of Psychiatry* 723.

O'CONNELL, T (2000) 'Restorative Justice for Police: Foundations for Change,' Tenth United Nations Congress of the Prevention of Crime and the Treatment of Offenders, Vienna, Austria, April.

O'CONNOR, A, KEARNEY, T, SHORTS and MCCORMACK, J (1994) *Sexual Offender Programme, Central Mental Hospital: 5 Year Report, April 1989-April 1994* (Dublin, National Forensic Psychiatric Service).

O'DONOVAN, K (1985) *Sexual Divisions in Law* (London, Weidenfeld and Nicolson).

OLAFSON, E, CORWIN, DL and SUMMITT, RC (1993) 'Modern History of Child Sexual Abuse Awareness: Cycles of Discovery and Suppression' 17 *Child Abuse and Neglect* 7.

OLIVER, AL (1997) 'On the Nexus of Organizations and Professions: Networking Through Trust' 67 *Sociological Inquiry* 227.

OLIVER, I (1978) *The Metropolitan Police Approach to the Prosecution of Offenders* (London, Peel Press).

OLTHOF, T (2000) 'Shame, Guilt, Antisocial Behaviour and Juvenile Justice' in I Weijers and A Duff (eds), *Punishing Juveniles: Principles and Critique* (Oxford, Hart Publishing).

O'MALLEY, P (1992) 'Risk, Power and Crime Prevention' 21 *Economy and Society* 252.

—— (1996) 'Post-Social Criminologies: Some Implications of Current Political Trends for Criminological Theory and Practice' 8 *Current Issues in Criminal Justice* 26.

—— (1999) 'Volatile Punishments: Contemporary Penality and the Neo-Liberal Government' 3 *Theoretical Criminology* 175.

—— (2002) 'Globalizing Risk? Distinguishing Styles of "Neo-liberal" Criminal Justice in Australia and the USA' 2 *Criminal Justice* 205.

—— (2006) 'Risk and Restorative Justice: Governing Through the Democratic Minimization of Harms' in I Aersten, T Daems and L Robert (eds) *Institutionalizing Restorative Justice* (Devon, Willan Publishing).

O'MALLEY, T (1996) *Sexual Offences: Law, Policy and Punishment* (Dublin, Round Hall Sweet & Maxwell).

Oregon Department of Corrections (1995) *Sex Offenders Community Notification in Oregon* (Dallas, Oregon, Department of Corrections).

ORTMANN, J (1980) 'The Treatment of Sexual Offenders' 3 *International Journal of Law and Psychiatry* 443.

OSBORN, SG (1980) 'Moving Home, Leaving London and Delinquent Trends' 20 *British Journal of Criminology* 54.

OSBORNE, D and GAEBLER, T (1992) Reinventing Government: How the Entrepreneurial Spirit is Transforming the Public Sector (Reading, Massachusetts, Addison-Wesley).

OST, S (2002) 'Children at Risk: Legal and Societal Perceptions of the Potential Threat that the Possession of Child Pornography Poses to Society' 29 *Journal of Law and Society* 436.

—— (2004) 'Getting to Grips with Sexual Grooming? The New Offence under the Sexual Offences Act 2003' 26 *Journal of Social Welfare and Family* 147.

PADFIELD, N (1996) 'Bailing and Sentencing the Dangerous' in N Walker (ed) *Dangerous People* (London, Blackstone Press).

—— (2003) 'Indeterminate Sentences ... Again' 62 *Cambridge Law Journal* 247.

PALLONE, NJ (2003) 'Without Plea-Bargaining, Megan Kanka Would Be Alive Today' 3 *Criminology and Public Policy* 83.

PARKE, RD and COLLMER, CW (1975) 'Child Abuse: An Inter-disciplinary Analysis' in EM Hetherington (ed) *Review of Child Development Research, Vol 5* (Chicago, University of Chicago Press).

Parliament of the Commonwealth of Australia (1995) *Organised Criminal Paedophile Activity*, A Report by the Parliamentary Joint Committee on the National Crime Authority (Canberra, Parliament House).

PARTON, N (1985) *The Politics of Child Abuse* (Basingstoke, Macmillan).

—— (2004) 'From Maria Colwell to Victoria Climbié: Reflections on Public Inquiries into Child Abuse A Generation Apart' 13 *Child Abuse Review* 80.

PARTON, N, THORPE, D and WATTAM, C (1997) *Child Protection: Risk and the Moral Order* (Hampshire, Macmillan).

PATERNOSTER, R, BACKMAN, R, BRAME, R and SHERMAN, L (1997) 'Do Fair Procedures Matter? The Effect of Procedural Justice on Spousal Assault' 31 *Law and Society Review* 163.

PAVLICH, G (2001) 'The Force of Community' in H Strang and J Braithwaite (eds) *Restorative Justice and Civil Society* (Cambridge, Cambridge University Press).

PEARSON, G (1983) *Hooligan: A History of Respectable Fears* (London, Macmillan).

PEARSON, G, BLAGG, H, SMITH, D, SAMPSON, A and STUBBS, P (1992) 'Crime, Community and Conflict: The Multi-Agency Approach' in D Downes (ed) *Unravelling Criminal Justice* (London, Macmillan).

PEASE, K (1995) *The Future of Imprisonment and Its Alternatives*, paper to the Council of Europe.

—— (2002) 'Crime Reduction' in M Maguire, R Morgan and R Reiner (eds) *The Oxford Handbook of Criminology*, 3rd edn (Oxford, Oxford University Press).

PENNELL, J (2006) 'Stopping Domestic Violence or Protecting Children? Contributions from Restorative Justice' in D Sullivan and L Tifft (eds) *Handbook on Restorative Justice: A Global Perspective* (New York, Routledge).

PENNELL, J and BURFORD, G (2001) 'Family Group Decision Making: Resolving Child Sexual Abuse' in G Burford (ed) *Broken Icons* (St John's, NF, Jesperson Press).

PERKINS, D (1991) 'Clinical Work with Sex Offenders in Secure Settings' in CR *Hollin* and K Howell (eds) *Clinical Approaches to Sex Offenders and their Victims* (Chichester, John Wiley and Sons Ltd).

PETERS, KA (1993) 'Chemical Castration: An Alternative to Incarceration' 31 *Duquesne Law Review* 307.

PETERSILIA, J (2003) *When Prisoners Come Home* (Oxford, Oxford University Press).

PETERSILIA, J and TURNER, S (1990) 'Comparing Intensive and Regular Supervision' 36 *Crime and Delinquency* 87.

PETRUNIK, MG (2002) 'Managing Unacceptable Risk: Sex Offenders, Community Response, and Social Policy in the United States and Canada' 46 *International Journal of Offender Therapy and Comparative Criminology* 483.

PFOHL, SJ (1977) 'The Discovery of Child Abuse' 24 *Social Problems* 310.

PHELAN, P (1995) 'Incest and its Meaning: The Perspectives of Fathers and Daughters' 19 *Child Abuse and Neglect* 7.

PLANTE, TG (1999) *Bless Me Father for I Have Sinned: Perspectives on Sexual Abuse Committed by Roman Catholic Priests* (Westport, Connecticut and London, Praeger).

PLOTNIKOFF, J and WOOLFSON, R. (2000), *Where Are They Now?: An Evaluation of Sex Offender Registration in England and Wales*, Police Research Series Paper No 126 (London, Home Office).

PORPORINO, F and ZAMBLE, E (1984) 'Coping with Imprisonment' 26 *Canadian Journal of Criminology* 403.

POWER, H (1999) 'The Crime and Disorder Act 1998: (1) Sex Offenders, Privacy and the Police' *Criminal Law Review* 3.

—— (2003) 'Disclosing Information on Sex Offenders: The Human Rights Implications' in A Matravers (ed) *Sex Offenders in the Community: Managing and Reducing the Risks* (Devon, Willan Publishing, Cambridge Criminal Justice Series).

PRANIS, K (1998) 'Conferencing and the Community,' paper presented at 'Conferencing: A New Response to Wrongdoing,' Minneapolis, MN, August (www.realjustice.org.)

PRATT, J (2000) 'The Return of the Wheelbarrow Men; or, the Arrival of Postmodern Penality?' 40 *British Journal of Criminology* 127.

PRATT, J and CLARK, M (2005) 'Penal Populism in New Zealand' 7 *Punishment and Society* 303.

PRENTKY, RA (1996) 'Community Notification and Constructive Risk Reduction' 11 *Journal of Interpersonal Violence* 295.

PRESSER, L and GAARDER, E (2000) 'Can Restorative Justice Reduce Battering? Some Preliminary Considerations' 27 *Social Justice* 175.

PRESSER, L and GUNNISON, E (1999) 'Strange Bedfellows: Is Sex Offender Notification a Form of Community Justice?' 45 *Crime and Delinquency* 299.

PRINS, H (1990) 'Dangerousness: A Review' in R Bluglass and R Bowden (eds) *Principles and Practice of Forensic Psychology* (Edinburgh, Churchill Livingstone).

—— (2001) 'Offenders, Deviants or Patients—Comments on Part Two of the White Paper' *Journal of Mental Health Law* 21.

Quaker Peace and Social Witness (2005) *Circles of Support and Accountability in the Thames Valley: The First Three Years—April 2002 to March 2005* (London, Quaker Communications).

QUINSEY, VL, HARRIS, GT, RICE, ME and LALUMIERE, ML (1993) 'Assessing Treatment Efficacy in Outcome Studies of Sex Offenders' 8 *Journal of Interpersonal Violence* 512.

RADBILL, SX (1968) 'A History of Child Abuse and Infanticide' in RE Helfer and CH Kempe (eds) *The Battered Child* (Chicago, University Press).

RADZINOWICZ, L (1957) *Sexual Offences* (London, Macmillan).

—— (1999) *Adventures in Criminology* (London, Routledge).

RADZINOWICZ, L and HOOD, R (1990) *The Emergence of Penal Policy in Edwardian and Victorian England* (Oxford, Clarendon Press).

RAINEAR, DH (1984) 'The Use of Depo-Provera for Treating Male Sex Offenders: A Review of the Constitutional and Medical Issues' 16 *University of Toledo Law Review* 181.

RAITT, F (1997) 'Informal Justice and The Ethics of Mediating in Abusive Relationships' 2 *Juridical Review* 76.

REINER, R (1991) *Chief Constables* (Oxford, Oxford University Press).

REISS, A (1989) 'The Institutionalisation of Risk' 11 *Law and Policy* 392.

REJTMAN, R (1997) 'Notification Requirements Under the Sex Offenders Act 1997: Do They Really Protect Children and Young People in the United Kingdom from Sexual Abuse and Exploitation' 139 *Child Right* 11.

RETZINGER, SM and SCHEFF, TJ (1996) 'Strategy for Community Conferences: Emotions and Social Bonds' in B Galaway and J Hudson (eds) *Restorative Justice: International Perspectives* (Monsey, NY, Criminal Justice Press).

RHODES, RAW (1995) *The New Governance: Governing Without Government,* ESRC State of Britain Seminar II (Swindon, ESRC).

RICE, ME, HARRIS, GT, QUINSEY, VL (1989) 'A Follow-up of Rapists Assessed in a Maximum Security Psychiatric Facility' 5 *Journal of Interpersonal Violence* 435.

RICE, ME, QUINSEY, VL and HARRIS, G (1991), 'Sexual Recidivism Among Child Molesters Released From a Maximum Security Psychiatric Institution' 59 *Journal of Consulting and Clinical Psychology* 381.

RICHARDS, E (1989) 'The Jurisprudence of Prevention: The Right of Societal Self-defence Against Dangerous Individuals' 16 *Hastings Constitutional Law Quarterly* 320.

RICHARDSON, E and FREIBERG, A (2004) 'Protecting Dangerous Offenders from the Community: The Application of Protective Sentencing Laws in Victoria' 4 *Criminal Justice* 81.

RICHARDSON, F (1999) 'Electronic Tagging of Offenders: Trials in England' 38 *The Howard Journal of Criminal Justice* 158.

RICHARDSON, G, KELLY, TP, BHATE, SR, GRAHAM, F (1997) 'Group Differences in Abuser and Abuse Characteristics in a British Sample of Sexually Abusive Adolescents' 9 *Sexual Abuse: A Journal of Research and Treatment* 239.

RIESENBERG, D (1987) 'Motivations Studied and Treatment Devised in Attempt to Change Rapists' Behaviour' 257 *Journal of the American Medical Association* 899.

RITCHIE, J and O'CONNELL, T (2001) 'Restorative Justice and the Need for Restorative Environments in Bureaucratic Corporations' in H Strang and J Braithwaite (eds) *Restorative Justice and Civil Society* (Cambridge, Cambridge University Press).

ROBERTS, JV (2002) 'Alchemy in Sentencing: An Analysis of Sentencing Reform Proposals in England and Wales' 4 *Punishment and Society* 425.

—— (2003) 'Evaluating the Pluses and Minuses of Custody: Sentencing Reform in England and Wales' 42 *The Howard Journal of Criminal Justice* 229.

ROBERTS, JV and HOUGH, M (eds) (2002) *Changing Attitudes to Punishment: Public Opinion, Crime and Justice* (Devon, Willan Publishing).

ROBERTS, JV and ROACH, K (2003) 'Restorative Justice in Canada: From Sentencing Circles to Sentencing Principles' in A von Hirsch, JV Roberts, AE Bottoms, K Roach and M Schiff (eds) *Restorative Justice and Criminal Justice: Competing or Reconcilable Paradigms?* (Oxford, Hart Publishing).

ROBERTS, JV, STALANS, L, INDERMAUR, D and HOUGH, M (2003) *Penal Populist and Public Opinion: Findings from Five Countries* (New York, Oxford University Press).

ROBERTS, JV and WHITE, NR (1986) 'Public Estimates of Recidivism Rates: Consequences of a Criminal Stereotype' 28 *Canadian Journal of Criminology* 229.

ROBERTS, P (1995) 'Taking the Burden of Proof Seriously' *Criminal Law Review* 783.

ROBINSON, G (2002) 'Exploring Risk Management in Probation Practice: Contemporary Developments in England and Wales' 4 *Punishment and Society* 5.

ROCHE, D (2003) *Accountability in Restorative Justice* (Oxford, Oxford University Press, Clarendon Studies in Criminology).

ROMERO, JJ and WILLIAMS, LM (1985) 'Recidivism Among Convicted Sex Offenders: A 10-year Follow-up Study' 49 *Federal Probation* 58.

ROSE, N (1996) 'The Death of the Social? Refiguring the Territory of Government' 25 *Economy and Society* 327.

—— (2000) 'Government and Control' 40 *British Journal of Criminology* 321.

RUSSELL, DEH (1986) *The Secret Trauma: Incest in the Lives of Girls and Women.* (New York, Basic Books).

RUSSELL, S (1997) 'Castration for Repeat Sexual Offenders: An International Comparative Analysis' 19 *Houston Journal of International Law* 425.

RUTHERFORD, A (1997) 'Women, Sentencing and Prisons' 147 *New Law Journal* 424.

—— (2000) 'Holding the Line on Sex Offender Notification' 150 *New Law Journal* 1359.

RUTTER, M and GILLER, H (1983) *Juvenile Delinquency: Trends & Perspectives* (New York, Guildford).

SABINI, J and SILVER, M (1997) 'In Defense of Shame: Shame in the Context of Guilt and Embarrassment' 27 *Journal for the Theory of Social Behaviour* 1.

SALTER, A (1995) *Transforming Trauma: A Guide to Understanding and Treating Adult Survivors of Child Sexual Abuse* (Newbury Park, CA, Sage).

—— (2003) *Predators, Pedophiles, Rapists, and Other Sex Offenders: Who They Are, How They Operate, and How We Can Protect Ourselves and Our Children* (New York, Basic Books).

SAMPLE, LL and BRAY, TM (2003) 'Are Sex Offenders Dangerous?' 3 *Criminology and Public Policy* 59.

SAMPSON, A (1994) *Acts of Abuse: Sex Offenders and the Criminal Justice System* (London, Routledge).

SAMPSON, A, SMITH, D, PEARSON, G, BLAGG, H and STUBBS, P (1991) 'Gender Issues in Inter-agency Relations: Police, Probation and Social Services' in P Abbott, and C Wallace (eds) *Gender, Power and Sexuality* (Bastingstoke, Macmillan).

SAMPSON, A, STUBBS, P SMITH, D, PEARSON, G and BLAGG, H (1988) 'Crime, Localities and the Multi-Agency Approach' 28 *British Journal of Criminology* 478.

SAMPSON, RJ and LAUB, JH (1993) *Crime in the Making: Pathways and Turning Points Through Life* (London, Harvard University Press).

—— (1994) 'Urban Poverty and the Family Context of Delinquency' 65 *Child Development* 523.

—— (1997) 'A Life-Course Theory of Cumulative Disadvantage and the Stability of Delinquency' in T Thornberry (ed) *Developmental Theories of Crime and Delinquency* (London, Transaction).

SANDERS, A and YOUNG, R (2002) 'From Suspect to Trial' in M Maguire, R Morgan and R Reiner (eds) *The Oxford Handbook of Criminology*, 3rd edn (Oxford, Oxford University Press).

SANDERS, R and LADWA-THOMAS, U (1997) 'Inter-agency Perspectives on Child Sexual Abuse Perpetrated by Juveniles' 2 *Child Maltreatment* 264.

SANDOR, D (1994) 'The Thickening Blue Wedge in Juvenile Justice' in C Alder and J Wundersitz (eds) *Family Conferencing and Juvenile Justice: The Way Forward or Misplaced Optimism?* (Canberra, Australian Institute of Criminology).

SANISLOW, CA and MCGLASHAN, TH (1998) 'Treatment Outcome of Personality Disorders' 43 *Canadian Journal of Psychiatry* 237.

SARAGA, E (2001) 'Dangerous Places: The Family as a Site of Crime' in J Muncie and E McLaughlin (eds) *The Problem of Crime*, 2nd edn (London, Sage).

SAUZIER, M (1989) 'Disclosure of Child Sexual Abuse: For Better for Worse' 12 *Psychiatric Clinics of North America* 455.

SAVOLAINEN, J (2000) 'Inequality, Welfare State, and Homicide: Further Support for the Institutional Anomie Theory' 38 *Criminology* 1021.

SAWYER, B (2000) *An Evaluation of the SACRO (Fife) Young Offender Mediation Project*, Scottish Executive Crime and Criminal Justice Research Findings No 43 (Edinburgh, Scottish Executive).

SCHEFF, TJ and RETZINGER, SM (1991) *Emotions and Violence: Shame and Rage in Destructive Conflicts* (Lexington, MA, Lexington Books/ DC Heath & Company).

SCHEINGOLD, S, OLSON, T and PERSHING, J (1992) 'The Politics of Sexual Psychopathy: Washington State's Sexual Predator Legislation' 15 *University of Puget Sound Law Review* 809.

SCHIFF, M (2003) 'Models, Challenges and the Promise of Restorative Conferencing Strategies' in A von Hirsch, A Roberts and AE Bottoms (eds) *Restorative Justice and Criminal Justice: An Exploratory Analysis* (Oxford, Hart Publishing).

SCHMIDT, A (1989) 'The Use of Electronic Monitoring of Offenders' in K Russell and R Lilly (eds) *The Electronic Monitoring of Offenders* (Leicester, Leicester Polytechnic Law School).

SCHULTZ, K (1995) *Electronic Monitoring and Corrections* (Vancouver BC, Simon Fraser University).

SCORER, R (2006) 'Blacklisted' 156 *New Law Journal* 125.

SEMPLE, W (1994) 'Alternative Dispute Resolution' 39 *Journal of Legal Studies* 406.

SHAPLAND, J (2001) 'Restorative Justice and Criminal Justice: Just Responses to Crime?,' draft paper for the Toronto Symposium on Restorative Justice, May.

SHAPLAND, J, ATKINSON, A, COLLEDGE, E, DIGNAN, J, HOWES, M, JOHNSTONE, J, PENNANT, R, ROBINSON, G, SCORESBY, A (2002) 'Evaluating the Fit: Restorative Justice and Criminal Justice,' British Criminology Conference, July.

SHAW, R (1997) 'Electronic Monitoring: What are the Real Issues?' 161 *Justice of the Peace and Local Government Law Review* 620.

SHEARING, C (1995) 'Governing Diversity: Explorations in Policing,' unpublished presented to the Socio Legal Studies Association Conference, University of Leeds, March.

—— (2000) 'Punishment and the Changing Face of Governance' 3 *Punishment and Society* 203.

SHERMAN, L (1992) *Policing Domestic Violence* (New York, The Free Press).

—— (2003) 'Reason for Emotion: Reinventing Justice with Theories, Innovations and Research—the American Society of Criminology 2002 Presidential Address' 41 *Criminology* 1.

SHERMAN, L, STRANG, H and WOODS, D (2000) *Recidivism Patterns in the Canberra Reintegrative Shaming Experiments (RISE)* (Canberra, Centre for Restorative Justice, Research School of Social Sciences, Australia National University).

SHICHOR, D (1992) 'Following the Penological Pendulum: The Survival of Rehabilitation' 56 *Federal Probation* 19.

SHICHOR, D and SECHREST, DK (eds) (1996) *Three Strikes and You're Out: Vengeance as Public Policy* (London, Sage).

SHUTE, S (2004) 'The Sexual Offences Act 2003: (4) New Civil Preventative Orders—Sexual Offences Prevention Orders; Foreign Travel Orders; Risk of Sexual Harm Orders' *Criminal Law Review* 417.

SILVERMAN, J and WILSON, D (2002) *Innocence Betrayed: Paedophilia, the Media and Society* (Cambridge, Polity Press).

SIM J (1990) 'Review of H Bianchi and R Van Swaaningen (eds) Abolitionism: Towards a Non-Repressive Approach to Crime (1986)' 18 *International Journal of the Sociology of Law* 97.

SIMON, J (1993) *Poor Discipline* (Chicago, University of Chicago).

—— (1998) 'Managing the Monstrous: Sex Offenders and the New Penology' 4 *Psychology, Public Policy and Law* 452.

SKELTON, A and FRANK, C (2001) 'Conferencing in South Africa: Returning to Our Future' in A Morris and G Maxwell (eds) *Restorative Justice for Juveniles: Conferencing, Mediation and Circles* (Oxford, Hart Publishing).

SKIDMORE, P (1995) 'Telling Tales: Media Power, Ideology and the Reporting of Child Sexual Abuse in Britain' in D Kidd-Hewitt and R Osborne (eds) *Crime and the Media* (London, Pluto).

SKUSE, DH (1985) 'Non-organic Failure to Thrive: A Re-appraisal' 60 *Archives of Disease in Childhood* 173.

SMALLBONE, S and WORTLEY, R (2000) *Child Sexual Abuse in Queensland: Offender Characteristics and Modus Operandi* (Brisbane, Queensland Crime Commission, Project Axis).

SMITH, DR (1993) *Safe From Harm: A Code of Practice for Safeguarding the Welfare of Children in Voluntary Organisations in England and Wales* (London, Home Office).

SMITH, DW, LETOURNEAU, EJ, SAUNDERS, BE, KILPATRICK, DG, RESNICK, HS and BEST, CL (2000) 'Delay in Disclosure of Childhood Rape: Results from a National Survey' 24 *Child Abuse and Neglect* 273.

SOOTHILL, K (1974) *The Prisoner's Release* (London, Allen and Unwin).

—— (1993) 'The Serial Killer Industry' 4 *Journal of Forensic Psychiatry* 341.

—— (2005) 'Strongly Suspected of Serious Sex Crime and Future Danger' 16 *Journal of Forensic Psychiatry & Psychology* 221.

SOOTHILL, K and FRANCIS, B (1997) 'Sexual Reconvictions and the Sex Offenders Act, 1997' 147 *New Law Journal* 1285 and 1324.

—— (1998) 'Poisoned Chalice or Just Deserts? (The Sex Offenders Act 1997)' 9 *Journal of Forensic Psychiatry* 281.

SOOTHILL, K, FRANCIS, B and ACKERLEY, E (1998) 'Paedophilia and Paedophiles' 148 *New Law Journal* 882.

SOOTHILL, K, FRANCIS, B and SANDERSON, B (1997) 'A Cautionary Tale: the Sex Offenders Act 1997, the Police and Cautions' *Criminal Law Review* 482.

SOOTHILL, K, FRANCIS, B, and SANDERSON, B and ACKERLEY, E (2000) 'Sex Offenders: Specialists, Generalists—or Both? A 32-year Criminological Study' 40 *British Journal of Criminology* 56.

SOOTHILL, K and GIBBENS, TCN (1978) 'Recidivism of Sexual Offenders: A Re-appraisal' 18 *British Journal of Criminology* 267.

SOOTHILL, K and GROVER, C (1995) *Changes in the Newspaper Reporting of Rape Trials Since the Second World War*, Home Office Research Bulletin No 37 (London, Home Office).

SOOTHILL, K, HARMAN, J, FRANCIS, B and KIRBY, S (2005a) 'Identifying Future Repeat Danger from Sexual Offenders Against Children: A Focus on those Convicted and those Strongly Suspected of Such Crime' 16 *Journal of Forensic Psychiatry & Psychology* 225.

—— (2005b) 'What is the Future Repeat Danger from Sexual Offenders Against Children? Implications for Policing' 78 *The Police Journal* 37.

Soothill, K, Jack, A, Gibbens, TCN (1976) 'Rape: A 22-year Cohort Study' 16 *Medicine, Science and the Law* 62.

Soothill, K and Walby, S (1991) *Sex Crime in the News* (London, Routledge).

Spencer, JR (2004) 'The Sexual Offences Act 2003: (2) Child and Family Offences' *Criminal Law Review* 347.

Stadler, A (1997) 'California Injects New Life Into An Old Idea: Taking A Shot At Recidivism, Chemical Castration, and The Constitution' 46 *Emory Law Journal* 1285.

Stanley, N (1999) *Institutional Abuse: Perspectives Across the Life Course* (London, Routledge).

Steadman, HJ and Cocozza, JJ (1974) *Careers of the Criminally Insane* (Lexington, Lexington Books, DC Heath & Co).

Stelzer, GL (1997) 'Chemical Castration and the Right to Generate Ideas: Does the First Amendment Protect the Fantasies of Convicted Paedophiles? 81 *Minnesota Law Review* 1675.

Stenson, K and Watt, P (1999) 'Crime, Risk and Governance in a Southern English Village' in G Dingwall and S Moody (eds) *Crime and Conflict in the Country-side* (Cardiff, University of Wales Press).

Stockdale, E and Devlin, K (1987) *Sentencing* (London, Waterlow).

Strain, C and Sheath, M (1993) 'Group Work as a Basis for Assessing Sex Offenders' 103 *Prison Service Journal* 40.

Strang, H (2001) 'Justice for Victims of Young Offenders: The Centrality of Emotional Harm and Restoration' in A Morris and G Maxwell (eds) *Restorative Justice for Juveniles: Conferencing, Mediation and Circles* (Oxford, Hart Publishing).

—— (2002) *Repair or Revenge: Victims and Restorative Justice* (Oxford, Clarendon Press).

Strang, H and Braithwaite, J (eds) (2001) *Restorative Justice and Civil Society* (Cambridge, Cambridge University Press).

—— (2002) *Restorative Justice and Family Violence* (Melbourne, Cambridge University Press).

Strang, H, Sherman, LW, Barnes, GC and Braithwaite, J (1999) *Experiments in Restorative Policing: A Progress Report to the National Police Research Unit on the Canberra Reintegrative Shaming Experiments (RISE)* (Canberra, Centre for Restorative Justice, Australian National University).

Straus, MA (1974) 'Forward' in RJ Gelles (ed) *The Violent Home: A Study of Physical Violence Between Husbands and Wives* (Beverly Hills, CA, Sage).

Stubbs, J (1997) 'Shame, Defiance, and Violence against Women: A Critical Analysis of "Communitarian" Conferencing' in S Cook and J Bessant (eds) *Women's Encounters with Violence: Australian Experiences* (London, Sage).

—— (2002) 'Domestic Violence and Women's Safety: Feminist Challenges to Restorative Justice' in H Strang and J Braithwaite (eds) *Restorative Justice and Family Violence* (Melbourne, Cambridge University Press).

Sugg, D, Moore, L and Howard, P (2001) *Electronic Monitoring and Offending Behaviour-Reconviction Results for the Second Year of Trials of Curfew Orders,* Home Office Research Study No 141 (London, Home Office).

Sullivan, D and Tifft, L (2000) *Restorative Justice s a Transformative Process: The Application of Restorative Justice Principles to Our Everyday Lives* (Voorheesville, NY, Mutual Aid Press).

—— (2001) *Restorative Justice: Healing the Foundations of Our Everyday Lives* (Monsey, NY, Willowtree Press).

Sullivan, J and Beech, A (2002) 'Professional Perpetrators' 11 *Child Abuse Review* 153.

Sutherland, EH (1950) 'The Diffusion of Sexual Psychopath Laws' 56 *American Journal of Sociology* 142.

Symonds, E (1980) 'Mental Patients' Rights to Refuse Drugs: Involuntary Medication as Cruel and Unusual Punishment' 7 *Hastings Constitutional Law Quarterly* 701.

Tabachnick, J and Chasan-Taber, L (1999) 'Evaluation of a Child Sexual Abuse Prevention Program' 11 *Sexual Abuse: A Journal of Research and Treatment* 279.

Tabachnick, J, Chasan-Taber, L and McMahon, P (2001) 'Evaluation of a Child Sexual Abuse Prevention Program—Vermont, 1995-1999' 285 *Journal of the American Medical Association* 114.

Tangney, JP, Miller, RS, Flicker, L and Barlow, DH (1996) 'Are Shame, Guilt and Embarrassment Distinct Emotions?' 70 *Journal of Personality and Social Psychology* 1256.

Tardieu, A (1878) *Étude Médico-Légale sur Les Attentats au Moeurs* (Paris and London, Ballière et Fils).

Tavuchis, N (1991) *Mea Culpa: A Sociology of Apology and Reconciliation* (Stanford, CA, Stanford University Press).

Taylor, G (1985) *Pride, Shame and Guilt: Emotions of Self-Assessment* (Oxford, Oxford University Press).

—— (2002) 'Guilt, Shame and Shaming' in I Weijers and A Duff (eds) *Punishing Juveniles: Principle and Critique* (Oxford, Hart Publishing).

Taylor, R (2000) *A Seven-Year Reconviction Study of HMP Grendon Therapeutic Community*, Home Office Research Findings No115 (London, Home Office).

Thomas, C (1989) 'Electronic Monitoring Supervision' in R Russell and R Lilly (eds) *The Electronic Monitoring of Offenders* (Leicester, Leicester Polytechnic Law School).

Thomas, DA (1998) 'The Crime (Sentences) Act 1997' *Criminal Law Review* 83.

—— (2004) 'The Criminal Justice Act 2003: Custodial Sentences' *Criminal Law Review* 702.

Thomas, S and Lieb, R (1995) *Sex Offender Registration: A Review of State Laws* (Washington State Institute for Public Policy, Olympia).

Thomas, T (1997) 'A Sex Offender Register-Will it Help?' 133 *Childright* 11.

—— (2000/2005) *Sex Crime: Sex Offending and Society* (Devon, Willan Publishing).

—— (2001) 'Sex Offenders, the Home Office and the Sunday Papers' 23 *Journal of Social Welfare and Family Law* 103.

—— (2003) 'Sex Offender Community Notification: Experiences from America' 42 *The Howard Journal of Criminal Justice* 217.

Thornberry, TP and Jacoby, JE (1979) *The Criminally Insane: A Community Follow-up of Mentally Ill Offenders* (Chicago, University of Chicago Press).

Thornton, D (2002) 'Constructing and Testing A Framework for Dynamic Risk Assessment' 14 *Sexual Abuse: A Journal of Research and Treatment* 139.

—— (2003) 'The Machiavellian Sex Offender' in A Matravers (ed), *Sex Offenders in the Community: Managing and Reducing the Risks* (Devon, Willan Publishing, Cambridge Criminal Justice Series).

Thornton, D and Hogue, T (1993) 'The Large-scale Provision of Programmes for Imprisoned Sex Offenders: Issues, Dilemmas and Progress' 3 *Criminal Behaviour and Mental Health* 371.

Tierney, J (1996) *Criminology: Theory and Context* (Hempel Hempstead, PrenticeHall/ Harvester Wheatsheaf).

Tobias, JJ (1972) *Crime and Industrial Society in the Nineteenth Century* (Penguin, Harmondsworth).

264 *Bibliography*

TOMKINS, SS (1987) 'Shame' in DL Nathanson (ed) *The Many Faces of Shame* (New York, Guildford Press).
TONRY, M (1988) 'Structuring Sentencing' in M Tonry and N Morris (eds) *Crime and Justice: A Review of Research, Vol 12* (Chicago, University of Chicago Press).
—— (2006) 'The Prospects for Institutionalization of Restorative Justice Initiatives in Western Countries' in I Aersten, T Daems and L Robert (eds) *Institutionalizing Restorative Justice* (Devon, Willan Publishing).
TRAVIS, J (1994) *Twenty-Five Years of Criminal Justice Research* (Washington DC, National Institute of Justice).
TRAVIS, J and PETERSILIA, J (2001) 'Re-entry Reconsidered: A New Look at an Old Question' 47 *Crime and Delinquency* 291.
TRESCHEL, S (1980) 'The Right to Liberty and Security of the Person—Article 5 of the European Convention on Human Rights in Strasbourg Case Law' 1 *Human Rights Law Journal* 88.
TUCKER, S and CADORA, E (2003) *Justice Reinventment* (New York, Open Society Institute).
TURNER, JWC (ed) (1952) *Kenny's Outlines of Criminal Law* (Cambridge, University Press).
UEKERT, BK (2003) 'The Value of Co-ordinated Community Responses' 3 *Criminology and Public Policy* 133.
UMBREIT, M (1994) *Victim Meets the Offender: The Impact of Restorative Justice and Mediation* (Monsey, NY, Criminal Justice Press).
UMBREIT, M, BRADSHAW, W and COATES, RB (1999) 'Victims of Severe Violence Meet the Offender: Restorative Justice Through Dialogue' 6 *International Review of Victimology* 321.
UMBREIT, M, COATES, RB and VOS, B (2001) 'Victim Impact of Meeting with Young Offenders: Two Decades of Victim Offender Mediation Practice and Research' in A Morris and G Maxwell (eds) *Restorative Justice for Juveniles: Conferencing, Mediation and Circles* (Oxford, Hart Publishing).
UMBREIT, M and ZEHR, H (2003) 'Restorative Family Group Conferences: Differing Models and Guidelines for Practice' in E McLaughlin, R Ferguson, G Hughes and L Westmarland (eds) *Restorative Justice: Critical Issues* (London, Sage).
US State of Maryland, Department of Public Safety and Correctional Services (1973) *Maryland's Defective Delinquency Statute: A Progress Report* (unpublished).
UTTING, W (1998) *People Like Us: The Report of the Review of the Safeguards for Children Living Away From Home* (London, HMSO).
VAGG, J (1998) 'Delinquency and Shame: Data from Hong Kong' 38 *British Journal of Criminology* 247.
VAN DAM, C (2002) *Identifying Child Abusers: Preventing Child Sexual Abuse by Recognizing the Patterns of Offenders* (New York, The Haworth Press).
VAN DER WERFF, C (1989) *Recidivism 1977* (Netherlands, Ministry of Justice, Research Documentation Centre).
VANDERZYL, KA (1994) 'Castration as an Alternative to Incarceration' 15 *Northern Illinois University Law Review* 107.
VANDIVER, DM and WALKER, JT (2002) 'Female Sex Offenders: An Overview and Analysis of 40 Cases' 27 *Criminal Justice Review* 284.
VAN DUJN, AL (1999) 'The Scarlet Letter Branding' 47 *Drake Law Review* 635.
VAN NESS, D (1993) 'New Wine and Old Wineskins: Four Challenges of Restorative Justice' 4 *Criminal Law Forum* 251.
—— (1998) 'Legal Principles and Process' in L Walgrave and G Bazemore (eds) *Restoring Juvenile Justice* (Amsterdam, Kugler Publishers).

VAN NESS, D, MORRIS, A and MAXWELL, G (2001) 'Introducing Restorative Justice' in A Morris and G Maxwell (eds) *Restorative Justice for Juveniles: Conferencing, Mediation and Circles* (Oxford, Hart Publishing).

VAN NESS, D and STRONG, KH (1997/2002) *Restoring Justice* (Cincinnati, Ohio, Anderson Publishing Co).

VAN STOKKOM, B (2002) 'Moral Emotions in Restorative Justice Conferences: Managing Shame, Designing Empathy' 6 *Theoretical Criminology* 339.

VANSTONE, M (2000) 'Cognitive-Behavioural Work with Offenders in the UK: A History of Influential Endeavour' 39 *The Howard Journal of Criminal Justice* 171.

VENNARD, J, SUGG, D and HEDDERMAN, C (1997) *Changing Offenders' Attitudes and Behaviour: What Works?* Home Office Research Study No 171 (London, Home Office).

VILLA VINCENZO, C (1999) 'A Different Kind of Justice: The South African Truth and Reconciliation Commission' 1 *Contemporary Justice Review* 403.

VIZARD, E and HAWKES, C (1997) 'Dealing with Paedophiles' 15 *Criminal Justice* 6.

Voluntary Sector Sex Offender Working Group (1997a) *Sex Offenders in the Community: The Interface Between Statutory and Voluntary Agencies in the Effective Monitoring and Treatment of Sex Offenders*, Report by the Voluntary Sector Sex Offender Working Group (Belfast, NIACRO).

—— (1997b) *Sex Offenders in the Community*, Conference Report from the Voluntary Sector Sex Offender Working Group, Belfast Castle, February (Belfast, NIACRO).

VON HIRSCH, A (1976) *Doing Justice: The Choice of Punishments* (NewYork, Oxford University Press).

—— (1985) *Past or Future Crime: Deservedness and Dangerousness in the Sentencing of Criminals* (NewBrunswick, NJ, Rutgers University Press).

—— (1993) *Censure and Sanctions* (Oxford, Oxford University Press).

—— (1994) 'Censure and Proportionality' in RA Duff and D Garland (eds) *A Reader On Punishment* (Oxford, Oxford University Press).

—— (2002) 'Record-enhanced Sentencing in England and Wales' 4 *Punishment and Society* 443.

VON HIRSCH, A and ASHWORTH (1996) 'Protective Sentencing under s.2(2)(b): The Criteria for Dangerousness' *Criminal Law Review* 175.

—— (eds) (1998) *Principled Sentencing: Readings on Theory and Policy*, 2nd edn (Oxford, Hart Publishing).

VON HIRSCH, A, ASHWORTH, A and SHEARING, C (2003) 'Specifying Aims and Limits for Restorative Justice: A "Making Amends" Model?' in A von Hirsch, JV Roberts, AE Bottoms, K Roach and M Schiff (eds) *Restorative Justice and Criminal Justice: Competing or Reconcilable Paradigms?* (Oxford, Hart Publishing).

VON HIRSCH, A, BOTTOMS, AE, BURNEY, E and WIKSTROM, P (1999) *Criminal Deterrence and Sentence Severity* (Oxford, Hart Publishing).

VON HIRSCH, A, ROBERTS, J, BOTTOMS, AE, ROACH, K and SCHIFF, M (eds) (2003) *Restorative Justice and Criminal Justice: Competing or Reconcilable Paradigms?* (Oxford, Hart Publishing).

WALBY, S and ALLEN, J (2004) *Domestic Violence, Sexual Assault and Stalking: Findings from the British Crime Survey*, Home Office Research Study No 276 (London, Home Office).

WALGRAVE, L (2000) 'How Pure Can A Maximalist Approach to Restorative Justice Remain? Or Can a Purist Model of Restorative Justice Become Maximalist?' 3 *Contemporary Justice Review* 415.

WALGRAVE, L (2001) 'On Restoration and Punishment: Favourable Similarities and Fortunate Differences' in A Morris and G Maxwell (eds) *Restorative Justice for Juveniles: Conferencing, Mediation and Circles* (Oxford, Hart Publishing).

—— (2003) 'Imposing Restoration Instead of Inflicting Pain' in A von Hirsch, JV Roberts, AE Bottoms, K Roach and M Schiff (eds) *Restorative Justice and Criminal Justice: Competing or Reconcilable Paradigms?* (Oxford, Hart Publishing).

WALGRAVE, L and AERSTEN, A (1996) 'Reintegrative Shaming and Restorative Justice: Interchangeable, Complementary or Different?' 4 *European Journal of Criminal Policy and Research* 67.

WALKER, N (1985) *Sentencing: Theory, Law and Practice* (London, Butterworths).

—— 1987) 'The Unwanted Effects of Imprisonment' in AE Bottoms and R Light (eds) *Problems of Long-Term Imprisonment* (Cambridge, Institute of Criminology).

—— (1996) *Dangerous People* (London, Blackstone Press).

WALKER, N and MARSH, C (1984) 'Do Sentences Affect Public Disapproval' 24 *British Journal of Criminology* 27.

WALTER, I, SUGG, S and MOORE, L (2001) *A Year on the Tag: Interviews with Criminal Justice Practitioners and Electronic Monitoring Staff about Curfew Orders*, Home Office Research Findings No 140 (London, Home Office).

WALTHER, S (1996) 'Reparation and Criminal Justice: Can They Be Integrated?' 4 *European Journal of Crime, Criminal Law and Criminal Justice* 163.

WARBRICK, C (1998) 'The Structure of Article 8' *European Human Rights Law Review* 32.

WARGENT, M (2002) 'The New Governance of Probation' 41 *The Howard Journal of Criminal Justice* 182.

WARNER, K (1994) 'The Rights of the Offender in Family Conferences' in C Alder and J Wundersitz (eds) *Family Conferencing and Juvenile Justice: The Way Forward or Misplaced Optimism?* (Canberra, Australian Institute of Criminology).

WARNER, N (1992) *Choosing With Care* (London, HMSO).

WASIK, M (1999) 'Reparation: Sentencing and the Victim' *Criminal Law Review* 470.

—— (2004) 'Going Round in Circles: Reflecting on 50 Years of Change in Sentencing' *Criminal Law Review* 253.

WASIK, M and TAYLOR, RD (1991) *Blackstone's Guide to the Criminal Justice Act 1991* (London, Blackstone Press).

WATERHOUSE, R (2000) *Lost In Care* (London, HMSO).

WEITEKAMP, EGM, KERNER, H-J, MEIER, U (2003) 'Community and Problem-Oriented Policing in the Context of Restorative Justice' in EGM Weitekamp and H-J Kerner (eds) *Restorative Justice in Context: International Practice and Directions* (Devon, Willan Publishing).

WEST, DJ (1969) *Present Conduct & Future Delinquency* (London, Heinemann).

WESTCOTT, H (1991) *Institutional Abuse of Children—From Research to Policy: A Review* (London, NSPCC).

WHITE, IA and HART, K (1995) *Report of the Inquiry Into the Management of Child Care in the London Borough of Islington* (London, Borough of Islington).

WHITE, R (1994) 'Shame and Reintegration Strategies: Individuals, State Power and Social Interests' in C Alder and J Wundersitz (eds) *Family Conferencing and Juvenile Justice: The Way Forward or Misplaced Optimism?* (Canberra, Australian Institute of Criminology).

—— (2003) 'Communities, Conferences and Restorative Social Justice' 3 *Criminal Justice* 139.

WHITFIELD, D (1997) *Tackling the Tag* (Winchester, Waterside Press).

WILCOX, A, YOUNG, R and HOYLE, C (2004) *An Evaluation of the Impact of Restorative Cautioning: Findings from a Reconviction Study*, Home Office Research Findings No 255 (London, Home Office).

WILKINS, L (1964) *Social Deviance: Social Policy, Action and Research* (London, Tavistock).

WILLEMSENS, J (2003) 'Restorative Justice: A Discussion of Punishment' in L Walgrave (ed) *Repositioning Restorative Justice* (Devon, Willan Publishing).

WILLIAMS, A and THOMPSON, B (2004) 'Vigilance or Vigilantes: The Paulsgrove Riots and Policing Paedophiles in the Community: Part 1: The Long Slow Fuse' and 'Part 2: The Lessons of Paulsgrove' 77 *Police Journal* 99 and 193.

WILLIAMS, B (1993) *Shame and Necessity* (Berkeley, CA University of California Press).

WILLIAMS, G and MCCREADIE, J (1992) *Ty Mawr Community Home Inquiry* (Gwent County Council).

WILSON, D and MCCABE, S (2002) 'How HMP Grendon "Works" in the Words of Those Undergoing Therapy' 41 *The Howard Journal of Criminal Justice* 229.

WILSON, K (1995) 'Facts and Fables about Sexual Offending,' paper presented to *The Abuse of Trust Conference*, Belfast, January.

WILSON, RJ, HUCULAK, B and MCWHINNIE, A (2002) 'Restorative Justice Innovations in Canada' 20 *Behavioural Sciences and the Law* 363.

WINICK, B (1998) 'Sex Offender Law in the 1990s: A Therapeutic Analysis' 4 *Psychology, Public Policy and Law* 505.

WINSTON, T (1997) 'Alternatives to Punishment Beatings and Shootings in a Loyalist Community in Belfast' 8 *Critical Criminology: An International Journal* 122.

WOLFRAM, S (1983) 'Eugenics and the Punishment of Incest Act 1908' *Criminal Law Review* 508.

WOOD, D (1988) 'Dangerous Offenders and the Morality of Protective Sentencing' *Criminal Law Review* 424.

Woolf Report (1991) *Prison Disturbances 1990: Report of an Inquiry by the Rt. Hon. Lord Justice Woolf (parts I and II), and His Honour Judge Stephen Tumin (part II)* Cmnd 1456 (London, HMSO).

WORTLEY, R and SMALLBONE, S (2006) *Situational Prevention of Child Sexual Abuse*, Crime Prevention Studies, Vol 19 (Monsey, New York, Criminal Justice Press and Devon, Willan Publishing).

WRIGHT, M (1996) *Justice for Victims and Offenders: A Restorative Response to Crime* (Bristol, PA, Open University Press).

—— (1999) *Restoring Respect for Justice* (Winchester, Waterside Press).

—— (2002) 'The Court as Last Resort' 42 *British Journal of Criminology* 654.

WRIGHT, RG (2003) 'Sex Offender Registration and Notification: Public Attention, Political Emphasis, and Fear' 3 *Criminology and Public Policy* 97.

WYRE, R (2000) 'Paedophile Characteristics and Patterns of Behaviour in C Itzin (ed) *Home Truths About Sexual Abuse Influencing Policy and Practice: A Reader* (London, Routledge).

YOUNG, J (1971) *The Drugtakers* (London, Paladin).

—— (1974) 'Mass Media, Drugs and Deviance' in P Rock and M McIntosh (eds) *Deviance and Social Control* (London, Tavistock).

—— (1991) 'Left Realism and the Priorities of Crime Control' in K Stenson and D Cowell (eds) *The Politics of Crime Control* (London, Sage).

—— (1992) 'Ten Points in Realism' in J Young and R Matthews (eds) *Rethinking Criminology: The Realist Debate* (London, Sage).

YOUNG, PW (1998) 'Paedophiles—Right to Privacy' 72 *Australian Law Journal* 29.

YOUNG, R (2001) 'Just Cops doing "Shameful" Business? Police-led Restorative Justice and the Lessons of Research' in A Morris and G Maxwell (eds) *Restorative Justice for Juveniles: Conferencing, Mediation and Circle* (Oxford, Hart Publishing).

YOUNG, R and GOOLD, B (1999) 'Restorative Police Cautioning in Aylesbury-From Degrading to Reintegrative Shaming Ceremonies' *Criminal Law Review* 126.

YOUNG, R, HOYLE, C, COOPER, K and HILLS, R (2005) 'Informal Resolution of Complaints Against the Police' 5 *Criminal Justice* 279.

ZAMBLE, E and QUINSEY, V (1997) *The Criminal Recidivism Process* (Cambridge, Cambridge University Press).

ZEDNER, L (1994) 'Reparation and Retribution: Are They Reconcilable?' 57 *Modern Law Review* 228.

—— (2002) 'Victims' in M Maguire, R Morgan and R Reiner (eds) *The Oxford Handbook of Criminology*, 3rd edn (Oxford, Oxford University Press).

ZEHR, H (1990) *Changing Lenses: A New Focus for Crime and Justice* (Scottdale, PA, Herald Press).

—— (1995) 'Justice Paradigm Shift? Values and Vision in the Reform Process' 12 *Mediation Quarterly* 207.

—— (2002) 'Journey to Belonging' in EGM Weitekamp and HJ Kerner (eds) *Restorative Justice: Theoretical Foundations* (Devon, Willan Publishing).

ZEHR, H and MIKA, H (1998) 'Fundamental Concepts of Restorative Justice' 1 *Contemporary Justice Review* 47.

ZHANG, L and ZHANG, S (2004) 'Reintegrative Shaming and Predatory Delinquency' 41 *Journal of Research in Crime and Delinquency* 433.

ZHANG, SX (1995) 'Measuring Shame in an Ethnic Context' 35 *British Journal of Criminology* 248.

ZIMRING, FE (2001) 'Imprisonment Rates and the New Politics of Criminal Punishment' 3 *Punishment and Society* 161.

ZIMRING, FE and HAWKINS, G (1995) *Incapacitation: Penal Confinement and the Restraint of Crime* (New York, Oxford University Press).

Index

Abuse of trust, *see also* Grooming, Trust 10, 30, **85–8**
Accommodation, 130, 187
Accountability and engagement, *see* Restorative justice, benefits, critiques
  of communities, *see* Community
  of offenders, *see* Sex offenders
Active citizenship, *see also* Community, Partnership approach 29, 219
Adapted Core programme, SOTP, 65
Australia, 5, 19, 40–1, 62, 64, 81, 82, 84, 113, 119, 121–3, 138, 177, 178–9, 186
Automatic life sentences, 156
Avenol, *see also* Treatment 64

Balance of rights, *see also* Registration, competing perspectives, ECHR jurisprudence 32
BBC News Online, 19, 20, 21, 76, 77, 104, 105,
Beckford, Jasmine, 17
Bichard Inquiry, 20, 76, 77, 83, 104, 144
Bifurcated policy, 26
Booster programmes, SOTP, 65
Butler Committee, 156

Canada, *see also* COSA i, 5, 7, 14, 17, 19, 32, 41, 64, 67–8, 84, 95, 138, 165, 168, 174, 177, 207
Castration,
  chemical, 14, 26, 63, 65, 71, 127, 142, **145–51**, 194, 217
  effectiveness, *see also* practical issues 146
  effects of, 147–9
  ethical and legal concerns, *see also* Constitutional challenge, ECHR jurisprudence, Treatment, versus punishment 142, 145–7, **149–51**
  practical issues 146, **147–9**
  pre-screening for, *see also* Sex offenders, types of 146
  surgical, 63, 145–6
  use in conjunction with traditional therapy, 148
  use in reintegrative shaming programmes, 217
Charter For Our Children Campaign, 21, 109
Chemical castration, *see* Castration
Child pornography 10, 87
Child protection 136

in institutional settings, *see also* Grooming, Institutional abuse, Institutional grooming 19, 75–77, 89
in the community, 94, 193
in the home, 27
strategies, 18, 35, 166, 167, 187, 222
Children, grooming of, *see* Grooming
Children's homes, *see* Institutional abuse, Institutional grooming
  investigations into, *see individual inquiry or review reports*
Children's rights, *see also* UN Convention on the Rights of the Child (1989) 17
Child sexual abuse, 8
  hidden nature of, 4, 12, 166
  historical recognition of, 10, 15–18, 199
  prevention of, *see also* Stop It Now! 74, 161, 166, 202, 205, 213, 221
  see also Sexual offending, statistics on 17, 20, 87
Child sexual abusers,
  see also Paedophiles, Sex offenders, Young sexual offenders 152, 167–8, 210, 223
Civil commitment, *see also* Indeterminate detention 26, **154–5**
Civil liberties and human rights, *see* ECHR jurisprudence, Sex offenders' rights
Circles of support and accountability (COSA), 9, 49, **180–3**
  as reintegrative shaming, 14
  as resettlement, 181
  as restorative justice, 180–3
  Canada, 182
  England and Wales, 181
  effectiveness of, *see* Restorative justice 180–1, 183
  extending the use of, **174–7**
  future evaluation of, *see* Restorative justice
  origins of, 95
  relationship with MAPPPs, *see also* MAPPPs, Thames Valley Project 182
  role of community in, *see also* Community Responsibility, Public education and awareness 49, 182–3
Cleveland Inquiry, 18
Cognitive behavioural therapy, *see* Treatment 70
Colwell, Maria, 17–18
Communitarian societies, *see also* Reintegrative shaming 43, 162, 171, 207

Community, *see also* Public, Popular responses
    to sex offenders, Vigilantism
  activities against sex offenders, 93–4
  benefits of restorative justice for, *see also*
    Accountability and engagement,
    Empowering, Restorative justice,
    Supporting 6, 14, 39, 95, 192
  expectations of law and agencies, 92
  fears, *see also* Media, 'Moral panic' 90–1
  grooming of, *see* Grooming
  partnership with statutory and voluntary
    agencies, *see* Partnership approach 95
  responsibility, 92
  role in offender reintegration, *see also*
    Resettlement 12, **90–5**
Community crime prevention, *see* Crime
    prevention
Community disposals, 24, 138
Community justice, *see* Restorative justice
Community notification, 3, 6, 13, 21, 25–6, 32,
    93, **97–125**, 127, 172, 188, 216–7
  forms of, 117
  See also Public disclosure of information, *R v
    Chief Constable of North Wales Police, ex
    parte Thorpe* [1999], Registration and
    notification
  Public demand for, *see* Sarah's Law
Community-based treatment, *see* Treatment
Community policing, *see also* Informal policing
    40, 192
Community re-entry, *see* Reintegration,
    Resettlement
Community Reintegration Project, *see* COSA,
    Canada
Community safety, *see* Public protection
Constitutional challenge, *see also* Castration,
    Electronic tagging, Registration and
    notification **116**, 117, 129, 149
Control in the community, *See* Electronic
    tagging, Preventive orders, Registration,
    Shame penalties
  what happens when this fails?, *see* Chemical
    castration, Indeterminate detention,
    Secure accommodation
Cooke, Sydney, 20, 140, 152
Co-operation, *see* Multi-agency working,
    Partnership approach
Core programme, SOTP, 65, 67
COSA, *see* Circles of Support and
    Accountability,
Children and Young Persons Act 1968, 16
Crime and Disorder Act 1998, 7, 29, 53, 72, 131,
    139, 156, 192
Crime control, 3, 15, 23–4, 29, 34, 43, 47, 53, 62,
    93–4, 99, 101, 111, 156, 183, 191,   194,
    210–2
Crime prevention, 3, 33, 93, 118, 191–2, 210,
    213, 219

Crime (Sentences) Act 1997, 26, 28, 138, 156
Criminal Evidence (Amendment) Act 1997), 28
Criminal Justice Act 1948, 155
Criminal Justice Act 1967, 155
Criminal Justice Act 1991, 26, 71, 82, 138–9,
    155–6
Criminal Justice Act 2003, 27, 31, 72, 157
Criminal Justice and Court Services Act 2000,
    28, 139
Criminal Justice and Public Order Act 1994, 10,
    138, 140
Criminal justice policy, *see also* New Labour,
    New penology, Risk penality 3, 9, 12, 15,
    18, 23, 26, 30, 34, 53, 108, 110–1, 140,
    144, 194
Criminal justice system, **61–77**
  problems with, *see* Managing risk, Formal
    criminal justice, failure of
Criminal Records Bureau, 28, 76
Criminal records system, 74
Custodial sentences, 26, 41, 72, 97, 133
Custody Plus, 27
Cycle of abuse, 6, 202–3, 222
Czechoslovakia, 146

Daily Mail, 20, 76, 119
Daily Record, 21, 109
Dangerousness, 25, **112–3**, 155–60
  debate, *see also* Predictive judgements, Risk
    prediction
  management of, *see* Managing Risk
Dangerous Severe Personality Disorder (DSPD),
    157, 160
Deception, *see* Grooming
Denier's Programme, SOTP, 65
Denmark, 146, 150
Department of Education, *see also* List 99 28, 30,
    76
Department of Health, *see also* PECS 16, 28, 76,
    156, 157
Depo-provera, *see* Castration, chemical
    145–51
Deterrence, *see also* Registration and
    notification, rationale 9, 27, 55, 62,
    71, 97, **107-8**, 116, 134, 137, 139, 147,
    185, 217
Deviancy amplification, *see also* Labelling, Media
    18, 130
Discretionary life sentences, 156
Disintegrative Shaming, *see* Shaming
Domestic violence, 4, 14, 17, 41, 42, 142, 199,
    200, 203
DSPD, *see* Dangerous Severe Personality
    Disorder
DSPD Bill 2000, 157
Due process, 55, 56–7, 116, 142, 149, 155
Dunblane shootings, 21
Dutroux, Marc, 20

ECHR jurisprudence, *see* European Convention
   on Human Rights
Electronic Tagging, 14, 35, 92, 127, 134, **137–44**,
   153
   ethical and legal concerns, *see also*
      Constitutional challenge, ECHR
      jurisprudence **142–4**
   practical issues, **140–2**
   public attitudes to, 143–4
   tagging programmes, **137–9**
   use with sex offenders, **139–44**
Empathy and remorse, *see also* Restorative
   justice 43, 46–7, 64, 180, 207
Empowering, *see also* Community, Sex
   offenders, Victims, Restorative justice,
   benefits 8, 38–9, 40, 50–1, 55, 57, 166,
   169, 174, 190, 197–8, 204, 212
End-to-end management of offenders, *see*
   NOMS
Enforcement pyramid, 9, 185
Engagement, *see* Restorative justice, benefits
   of sex offenders, *see also* Sex Offenders 8, 68,
      70, 165
   of communities, *see also* Communities 165,
      171
European Convention on Human Rights
   (ECHR), *see also* Castration, Electronic
      tagging, Indeterminate detention,
      Registration and notification, Secure
      accommodation, Sex offenders' rights
   Article 2, 143
   Article 3, 150
   Article 5, 134, 142
   Article 6, 160
   Article 7, 112
   Article 8, 150
   Article 11, 134
Evidence-based policy and practice, 3, 140, 219
Extended programme, SOTP, 65
Extended sentences, 26–7, 73, 156
Extended supervision, 28, 47
Extra-familial abuse, 81, 184
Extra licence conditions, 74

Fallon Inquiry, 156
Family Decision-making model, 41
Family, grooming of, *see* Grooming
Family Group Conferencing (FGC), 44, 46,
   177–80
   use, 40
   effectiveness, *see also* Restorative justice
      177–8, 180
Family violence, *see also* Child sexual abuse,
   Domestic violence 17, 199, 200
Female sex offenders, 11
Feminism, 17, 63, 197
Ferns Inquiry, 20
FGC, *see* Family Group Conferencing

Finland, 146
Floud Committee, 156, 158–9
Foreign travel orders, *see also* Registration and
   notification 103, 131
Formal criminal justice, *see also* Retributive
   justice, Traditional Justice, State justice
   failure of, **4–7**
France, 17, 114, 192

Gatekeeping, 86
Germany, 17, 40, 146
Grendon Underwood, *see also* Treatment 65
Grooming, 77–8, **84–90**, 137
   effects of, 84, 87–8
   failure of criminal law, 85
   judicial recognition of, 135
   meaning of, **84–5**, 86
   of children, 4, 10, 92, 135, 182, 202
   of families and communities, 4, 86, **87–8**, 182
   of institutions, *see also* Institutional Abuse, 86,
      89–90
   parliamentary debates on, 85
   role of trust, *see also* Abuse of Trust, Trust,
      4
   targeting of, *see also* Risk of sexual harm
      orders 135–6
   use of internet, 10, 136, 182
   see also Vetting procedures
Guardian, 19, 20, 21, 147

Habitual Criminals Act 1869, 100
Habitual Criminals Register, 100
Halliday Report, 13, 27
Hamilton, Thomas, 21
Hook, Sophie 20
Hostels, *see also* Housing 83, 94, 152
Housing, 93, 152, 161, 172, 175
Hughes, Howard 20
Huston, Martin, 19
Human Rights Act 1998, *see also* ECHR
      jurisprudence 143
Huntley, Ian, *see also* Soham murders 20, 83,
      104, 144, 181, 221

Incapacitation, *see also* Public protection 9, 15,
      23–4, 26, 55, 62, 70–1, 110, 111, 155–6,
      158, 159, 162, 186, 194, 217
Indeterminate detention, *see also* Civil
      commitment, Protective sentencing 14,
      145, **154–60**
   ethical and legal concerns, *see also* ECHR
      jurisprudence, Article 5 **159–60**
   practical issues, **157–9**
   for the severely personality disordered, *see*
      DSPD
Informal justice, *see* Restorative justice
Informal policing, *see also* Community policing,
      Northern Ireland, paramilitaries 91

Informal sanctioning of deviance, *see* Informal policing, Shaming
Information sharing, *see* MAPPPs
Institutional abuse, *see also individual inquiry and review reports,* Institutional grooming, Organisational culture 89
Institutional grooming, *see* Grooming
Integration of retributive and restorative justice, *see also* Restorative justice, relationship with formal criminal law 215
Intelligence, *see also* Policing 20, 76–7, 104–5, 114, 144, 221
Internet, *see* Grooming 10, 84, 89, 102, 117, 136, 137, 182
Intra-familial abuse, 4, 11, 17, 69, 81, 90, 137, 184, 185, 202, 222
Investigation, *see also* Policing 99, 105, 107, 121, 158, 221
Irish Independent, 20

Just-deserts, *see also* Proportionality 26, 108

Kelly, Ruth, 76, 77
Kincora scandal, 19
Knowledge, 24–5, 31, 34, 91, 122, 190
'Knowledge-risk-security', 24, 121, 189, 206
Known offenders, *see also* Risk, categories of 11, 106, 121, 190, 220

'Law and order', 3, 15, 27, 34, 62, 107, 124, 156, 194, 215
Labelling, *see also* Deviancy amplification, Disintegrative shaming 6, 18–9, 44, 98, 118, 122–3, 127–8, 130, 202, 207, 217
Law enforcement, *see also* Policing 5, 78, 92, 99, 101, 117, 119
Legislative framework, *see also individual Acts* 5, 25–9
Leicestershire Inquiry, 75
Life imprisonment, 73, 156
Life sentences, 26, 71, 73, 156–7
Life sentence procedures, *see* Release on licence
List 99, 28, 76–7, 102

Managing risk, *see also* Risk
   current problems with, *see* Community, Criminal justice system, Sex offenders, and Recidivism data, Release on licence, Tracking, Treatment, Vetting procedures 82, 90
   via restorative justice, 7–9
   via retributive justice, 215–220
Mandatory life sentences, 26
MAPPPs, *see* Multi-agency working
MASRAM, *see* Multi-agency working
Media,
   amplifying activities of, *see also* Deviancy amplification, Labelling

coverage of high profile cases, *see also individual cases* 5, 15, 20
creation of myths and misconceptions, 188, 210
influence on popular imagination, *see also* Public 19, 22–3
'moral panic', 3, **18–23**
see also 'Name and Shame' campaign, *individual newspapers*
'Megan's Law', *see* Registration and notification
Mental health provision, 26, 27
Mental Health Bill 2004, 27, 157
Mental Health legislation, review of, 27, 156–7
Mirror, 19, 22
Miscarriages of justice, 119, 160
Monitoring, *see* Sex Offenders, Surveillance, Tracking
'Moral panic', *see* Media 3, 18–23, 90, 190
Multi-agency working, *see also* Risk 24, **29–32**
   MAPPPs (multi-agency public protection panels), 28, 31, 32, 114, 175–6, 192, 220
   role of community in, 95–6, 194
   MASRAM (multi-agency procedures for the assessment and management of sex offenders) 32
   the problematic nature of, 118, 123
   see also Partnership approach

NACRO, *see* National Society for the Care and Resettlement of Offenders
'Name and Shame' campaign, 3, 6, 21, 22, 98, 127, 128, 130, 181, 205, 209, 217
National Criminal Intelligence Service (NCIS), 105
National Offender Management Service (NOMS), 29, 73, 105, 176
National Society for the Care and Resettlement of Offenders (NACRO), 30
National Society for the Prevention of Cruelty to Children (NSPCC) 16
NCIS, *see* National Criminal Intelligence Service
Netherlands, the 17, 138, 192
New Labour, *see also* Criminal justice policy, Managerialism, New Penology, Youth justice 26–7, 53
New Penology, 18, **23–5**, 161
News of the World, see also 'Name and Shame' campaign 21, 22, 90, 181
New Zealand, 5, 23, 40–1, 64, 84, 137, 138, 143, 155, 158, 177–9, 192
'NIMBY' (Not in My Back Yard), *see also* Risk displacement 92
Nolan Report, 19, 20, 75
No More Excuses, 26
NOMS, *see* National Offender Management Service
No punishment without law, *see* ECHR jurisprudence, Article 7

Northern Ireland, 32, 65, 69, 83, 105, 176
  high profile cases, 19, 20, 42
  paramilitary 'policing' of sex offenders, 38, 91
  voluntary sector, 30
  See also ViSOR,
Norway,17, 146
Notification orders, *see also* Registration and
    notification 103
NSPCC, *see* National Society for the Prevention
    of Cruelty to Children
Nurseries, 89

Oliver, Robert, 20
On-line abuse, *see* Grooming, use of internet
Organisational culture, *see also* Institutional
    abuse, Institutional grooming 20, 83,
    89–90
Ostracism, of offenders, *see* Disintegrative
    Shaming, Social exclusion

Paedophile(s), 3, 15
  definition of, 10
  popular use of term, 19–20
Paedophile rings, 19
Paedophilia, 19, 146, 189
Panoptican, 23
Paramilitary groups, *see* Northern Ireland
Paraphilia, *see also* Paedophilia 146–50
Parole, *see* Release on licence
Partnership approach, 5, 184, **191–4**
  benefits of, 176, 206
  problematic nature of, *see also* Shaming,
    critiques 32–4
Payne, Sarah, *see also* Sarah's Law, Whiting, Roy
    5, 21, 22, 91, 106, 118, 181
PECS, *see* Pre-Employment Consultancy Service
Penal policy,
  transfer of, *see* Criminal justice policy 15
Penal provision, **26–7**
Persistent offending, 7, 9, 14, 48–9, 53, 110, 127,
    144, 156, 186, 203, 220
Personality disorders, *see* DSPD
PNC, *see* Police National Computer
Police Act 1997, 28, 74, 76
Police checks, 76
Policing, of sex offenders, *see also* Intelligence,
    Investigation, Surveillance 33
Police National Computer, *see also* ViSOR 102,
    104
Police supervision, *see* Supervision
Popular responses to sex offending, *see also*
    Community, Public, Vigilantism 8, 130,
    209, 212
'Populist punitiveness', **18–23**, 25, 97, 110,
    194
Post-release control, **28–9**, 44
Post-release supervision, *see* Supervision 73–4,
    83, 141

Power imbalance, *see* Restorative justice,
    critiques of
Powers of Criminal Courts Act 1973, 156
Powers of Criminal Courts (Sentencing) Act
    2000, 26, 53, 72, 138, 156
Pre-Employment Consultancy Service (PECS),
    28, 76
Pre-employment vetting, *see* Vetting procedures
    76, 90
Predictive judgements, *see also* Dangerousness
    debate, Risk Prediction 32, 113, 157–8
Presumption of innocence, *see* ECHR
    jurisprudence, Article 6
Preventative governance, 182
Prevention,
  of child sexual abuse, 161, 166, 188, 202, 213,
    222–3
  of crime, 3, 33, 93, 115, 118, 191, 213, 219
Prevention of Crime Act 1908, 100, 155
Preventive detention, *see* Indeterminate
    detention, Secure Accommodation 24,
    27
Preventive orders, *see also* Sexual Offences Act
    2003 127, **131–7**
  as public shaming,
  risk of sexual harm orders, **135**, 161
    potential problems, **136–7**
    use to target grooming, *see* Grooming
  sexual offences prevention orders, 11, **131–4**,
    139, 142, 161, 170
    ethical and legal concerns, **134**
    practical issues, **133–4**
Preventive strategies, 24
Priests, abuse of children, 20, 147
Prison-based treatment, *see* Treatment
Prison service, 30–2, 105, 175–6
Prison works, 26
Private sphere, sexual offending, *see also*
    Intra-familial abuse 17
Probation service, 30, 31, 33, 69–70, 73, 74, 114,
    141, 176
Probation orders, 69, 72, 82
'Professional perpetrators', *see also* Institutional
    abuse 19
Prohibition on torture, inhuman or degrading
    treatment or punishment, *see* ECHR
    jurisprudence, Article 3
Proportionality, *see also* Just-deserts 26, 55, 57,
    64, 113
Protection from Harassment Act 1997, 10,
    28
Protecting the Public, 28
Protection of Children Act 1978, 10
Protection of Children Act 1999, 28, 74, 76
Protective sentencing, *see also* Indeterminate
    detention 155–7
  history of, 113, 155
  recent approach, 154, 156

Public,
  concerns, *see also* Popular response to sex
    offending 124, 168
  demonstrations, 3, 22
  hostility towards and rejection of sex
    offenders, *see also* Sex offenders, Popular
    responses to sex offending, Vigilantism
    90
  hysteria, 20, 22, 25, 118, 119, 152
  perception of risk, *see* Sex Offenders, Risk
  punitive attitudes, 3, 5, 9, 13, 15, 18, **19–23**,
    25, 27, 34, 91, 97, 110, 129, 194
Public disclosure of information, *see also*
    Community notification, *R v Chief
    Constable of North Wales Police, ex parte
    Thorpe* [1999], Registration and
    notification, Sarah's Law 93, **105–6**, 124
Public education and awareness, 6, 84, 94, 96,
    106, 174–5, 184, **188–91**, 209
Public exposure penalties, *see* Shame penalties
Public inquiries and reviews, *see Individual
    reports*
Public protection, 30–4
  Imprisonment for, 73, 157
  See also Incapacitation, Registration and
    notification, rationale
Public shaming of the offender, *see* Shaming
Punishment,
  role of, in retributive and restorative justice, 5,
    27, 55, 115, 161, 185
  theoretical aims of, 23, 52, 54, 108, 128, 184
  versus treatment of offenders, *see also*
    Treatment, versus punishment 13, 62,
    66, 149
Punishment deficit, 27
Punishment of Incest Act 1908, 16

Quaker Community, *see also* Circles of support
    and accountability, 176

*R v Chief Constable of North Wales Police, ex
    parte Thorpe* [1999] QB 396 (CA), *see
    also* Public disclosure of information,
    Registration and notification 32, 106
Rape, 4, 7, 10, 16, 42, 69, 79, 87, 145, 200, 202,
    203, 209
Recidivism data, 5, 31–2, 67–9, 79–81, 140, 144,
    147–8, 178, 181–2, 189, 195, 207, 216
Reconviction rates, 4, 5, 66–8, 79, 80–1, 144,
    158, 180, 181, 182, 183, 216, 221
Registers, *See* List 99, PECS, Registration and
    notification
Registration and notification, 3, 6, 13, 32,
    97–125
  as an investigative tool, *see also* ViSOR 119
  as a punishment?, *see also* ECHR jurispru-
    dence, Article 7 **111–2**
  as public shaming, *see* Shaming

civil liberties and human rights, *see also* ECHR
    jurisprudence **113–116**
competing perspectives of the victim and
    offender, *see also* Children's rights,
    Protection, Dangerousness debate,
    Registration as a punishment,
    Stigmatisation **108–16**
constitutional challenge, **116**
detrimental effects of, 121
history of, **98–100**
main provisions, **101–106**
'Megan's Law', vii, 13, 21, 26, 75, 97, 98, 99,
    101–2, 103, 117, 216
  The Sexual Offences Act 2003, Part 2,
    102–4
parliamentary debates on, 85
practical limitations of, 25, **119–24**
The police, *see also*, Policing,
  efficacy of the response, **119–22**
  official compliance with, 120
  powers and resources, 120–1
The public,
  abuse in the home, *see also* Child protection
    in the home, Intra-familial abuse **122–4**
  problems of scope, 122
  protection, *see also* Public protection **122–4**
rationale, *see also*, Deterrence, Protection 24,
    107–108
requirements of, *see* main provisions
see also, Community notification, Public
    disclosure of information,ViSOR
Registration periods, *see also* Registration and
    notification, main provisions, Young
    sexual offenders 120
Regulatory framework, *see also* Retributive
    framework 5, 7, 9, 26, 28, 29, 34, 44, 55,
    144, 184–5, 215, 218
Rehabilitation, 6, 47, 49, 50, 54–5, 61, 3, 66, 71,
    94–6, 98, 118, 130, 160, 173, 192, 199,
    211, 216
  decline of, *see also* Treatment 61, 62
Reintegration, *See* Community re-entry,
    Resettlement, Restorative justice,
    Shaming
Reintegrative justice, *see also* Community
    Justice, Restorative Justice 39, 44, 54, 56,
    58, 153, 169, **177–85**, 192, 194, **197–213**
Reintegrative Shaming, *see* Shaming
  an additional or an alternative form of
    justice?, **184–7**
  implementation of practices, **184–94**
  See also Partnership approach, Public
    education and awareness
Reintegrative Shaming Experiment (RISE), 178
Release on licence, *see also* Parole, Supervision
    70–75
Re-offending, *see also* Disintegrative shaming,
    Recidivism rates 123, 173

Repeat victimisation, *see* Restorative justice, critiques
Republic of Ireland, 5, 19, 29, 69, 72, 73, 83, 104, 132, 176, 192
Resettlement, **47–51, 173**
  individual factors, 49
  redemption script, 49
  risk-based model, 47
  role of community in, *see also* Community 12
  role of hope, 49
  social or structural variables, 45
  strengths-based model, 51, 174, 219
  support with, 168
Responsive regulation, 55, 185, 218
Restorative cautioning, 178
Restorative justice, 5, 6, **7– 12, 37–42**, 43, 46, 91, 177–80, 197–9, 211, **220–3**
  aims and values, 57, 168
  an additional or an alternative form of justice?, *see also* Reintegrative shaming, 184
  and coercion, 56, 187
  and grooming, *see* Grooming
  and vigilantism, *see also* Vigilantism 212
  and young sexual offenders, *see also* Young sexual offenders, Youth justice 123–4, 178
  as a regulatory approach, 9
  as diversion, *see also* Reintegrative shaming 177
  as sanctioning, *see also* Reintegrative shaming, Circles, as restorative justice 55
  benefits, *see* Community, Sex offenders, Victims
  critiques of, 199, 201, **203–4**
    effective management of risk, *see* Managing risk, via restorative justice, Risk, categories of
    general, 197
    of shaming, *see* Shaming
    particular concerns when applied to child sexual abuse, 5, 8, **200–6**
  effectiveness of, 191
    circles of support and accountability, 7, **180–3**
    victim offender mediation and family group conferencing, 40–1, 44, 46, **177–80**
  future evaluation of, 68
  programmes and practices, *see also* COSA, FGC, Restorative cautioning, RESTORE, RISE, SAJJ, VOM 39, 180
  relationship with formal criminal justice, *see also* Integration of retributive and restorative justice 9, 38, **51–7**, 169, 185, role of empathy and remorse, 43, 46, 180
  role of shaming, *see* Shaming
  role of the state in, 52, 58

transformative potential of, 170
understandings of, 37
use with low-level offences, 7, 14, 55
use with serious forms of offending, 5, 12, 37, 41, 55–6, 58
use with serious social problems, 7, 42
Restorative paradigm, 14, 170, 223
Restraining orders (RO), 131
Retributive justice, 6, 13, 44, 53–4, 57, 113, 177 **215–18**
  contemporary perspective, **18– 34**, 61
  failure to manage risk, *see* Managing risk, via retributive justice
  historical perspective, **16–18**
Retributive framework, *see also* Regulatory Framework, Retributive justice 5–6, 12, 13, 29, 37, 52, 70, 110, 127, 184, 186, 220
Retribution, 9, 12, **15–35**, 38, 52, 54–5, 62, 71, 108, 169, 185, 200, **215–223**
RESTORE programme, *see also* Restorative justice, programmes and practices 42
Retribution, 9, 12, **15–35**, 54–5, 200, **215–223**
Review of Part I of the Sex Offenders Act 1997, 29
Review of the Criminal Justice System in Northern Ireland, 83
Rights of the child, *see* Children's rights **109**
Right to a fair trial, *see* ECHR jurisprudence, Article 6 134
Right to freedom of peaceful assembly and association with others, *see* ECHR jurisprudence, Article 11
Right to liberty and security of person, *see* ECHR jurisprudence, Article 5 115, 134, 142
Right to respect for private and family life, *see* ECHR jurisprudence, Article 8 114
Rights-based philosophy, 114
RISE, *see* Reintegrative Shaming Experiment
Risk,
  categories of, 9, 185, 215, 221
  displacement, 93
  institutionalisation of, 23
  management, *see* Managing risk
  popular conceptions of, *see also* Sex Offenders 22, 44
Risk assessment and management, *see also*, Multi-agency working, MAPPPs 3, 12, 24, 25, **29–32**, 34, 61, 65, 73, 104, 114, 119, 157, 161, 187
  tools, 105
Risk-based approach, 9, 131
Risk penality, *see also* Criminal justice policy, New penology 15, 24, 136
Risk prediction, *see also* Dangerousness debate, Predictive judgements 23
Risk society, 24, 110, 191
Risk of sexual harm orders, *see* Preventive orders 135, 161

RO, *see* Restriction orders,
Rolling Programme, SOTP, 65
ROSOs, *see* Risk of sexual harm orders
Rwanda, 7, 42

Safer Society Foundation, 165
SAJJ, *see* South Australia Juvenile Justice Project
Sarah's Law, *see* Payne, Sarah, *News of the World*
Satellite tracking, *see also* Electronic tagging,
    Tracking 139
Scarlet letter sentencing, 117, 129
Schools, 19, 32, 40, 46, 76, 77, 89, 132, 133, 139,
    144, 207, 210
Scotland, 21, 84, 104, 109, 176, 192
Secure accommodation, 14, 127, 145, **151–4**
    as disintegrative shaming, *see also*
        Disintegrative shaming 194
    as social exclusion, *see also* Social exclusion
        152
    benefits of, 140, 152
    ethical and legal concerns, 134
    practical issues, *see also* ECHR jurisprudence,
        Article 5 142, 154
Selective incapacitation, *see also* Criminal justice
    policy, Indeterminate detention 24, 26,
    159
Self-report studies, 4, 80
Sentencing and Supervision of Sex Offenders, 28
Sentencing circles, 41
Setting the Boundaries,
Severe personality disorders, *see* DSPD,
    Indeterminate detention 27
Sexual Offences Act 2003, *see also* Registration
    and notification, Preventive orders   10,
    13, 14, 28–9, 31, 44, 75, 76, 82, 85, 97, 98,
    100, **102–4**, 125, 127, **131–137**, 216
Sexual Offences (Amendment) Act 2000, 10, 28,
    76,
Sexual Offences (Conspiracy and Incitement)
    Act 1996, 28
Sexual offences prevention orders (SOPO), *see*
    Preventive orders 11, **131–4**, 139, 142,
    161, 170
Sexual Offences (Protected Material) Act 1997,
    28
Sex offender orders (SOO), 35, 112, 131–4, 143,
Sex offenders,
    as a special risk, 97, 155
    benefits of restorative justice for, 178, 192,
        194, 222
    see also Accountability and engagement,
        Empowering, Restorative justice,
        Supporting
    community hostility to, 6, 90, 142, 168, 173–4
    demonology of, 72
    management of, 12–15, 24–5, 28–30, 32–4, 61,
        73, 75, 84, 90, 92, 95, 105, 131, 143, 170,
        175–6, 195, 217, 219

mobility of, 83
monitoring of, 24, 26, 28, 71, 75, 83, 95–7,
    108, 118, 137–44, 175
policing of, 29, 74, 91, 117
politicisation of, 15, 109
popular conceptions of, 21
problems with reintegration, *see also*
    Grooming, Recidivism, tracking, 48
restriction on movement of, *see also*
    monitoring, tracking, 28. 35, 47, 100,
    131, 134, 143
rights, *see also* ECHR jurisprudence 12, 13, 32,
    55, 106–8, 111–6, 134, 140, 149–51, 198,
    206, 217
segregation of, 130, 152, 161
supervision of, 28, 47, 71–4, 83, 100, 139–43,
    172, 187
tracking of, *see also* Tracking, problems with
    21, 24, 97, 99, 104, 139
types of, *see also*, Risk, categories of 41
Sex offenders register, *see* Registration and
    notification
Sex Offenders Act 1997, *see also* Registration and
    notification vii, 28–9, 31, 35, 82, 97, 100,
    102, 112, 120, 132, 216
parliamentary debates on,
reform of, 114, 131
Sex Offenders Act 2001, *see also* Republic of
    Ireland 29, 73, 83, 104, 132
Sex Offender Treatment Evaluation Project
    (STEP), 67
Sex Offender Treatment Programmes (SOTP),
    see also Treatment 63–70
Sex trafficking, 83
Sexual offending,
    definitional matters, **10–12**
    media coverage of, *see* Media, 'Name and
        Shame' campaign, *individual news papers*
    myths and misconceptions, *see also* Media,
        Public 21–2
    public perception of, *see also* Public, Risk 92
    statistics on, 4, 69, 79, 144, 174
    see also Popular responses to, State-led
        responses to
Sexual predators, 11, 121
Shame penalties, **127–31**
    history of, 127–8
    signs and apologies, as public exposure
        128–30
    see also Disintegrative shaming, Social
        exclusion, Stigmatisation
Shame Management, *see also* Shaming, as a
    psychological process 46
Shaming,
    as a psychological process, *see also* Shame
        Management 46–7
    conceptualisations of shame and shaming, 45
    critiques of, 13

disintegrative shaming, 44, 47
  reintegrative shaming, i, 3, 7,14, 24, 37, 40,
    42–44, 45–7, 50–1, 55, 90, 131, 151,
    161–2, **165–95**, 201, 207–8, 211, 218, 220
  implementation of, **184**, 191
  practices, 43
  theory, 8, 40, 43, 184, 206–7
    RISE, *see* Reintegrative Shaming
      Experiment
Signs and apologies, *see* Shame penalties
Singapore, 138
Sites of danger, 11, 92
Situational crime prevention, *see also* Crime
    prevention 161
Smyth, Fr Brendan, 20
Social control, *see also* Social exclusion, Social
    inclusion 23–4, 30, 48, 142, 161, 170–1,
    207–8, 219, 222
Social inclusion, *see also* Shaming, critiques 8,
    53, 188, 194, **209–10**, 216, 222
Social exclusion, 54, 129, 152, 193, 210
Social services, 30
Soham murders, *see also* Huntley, Ian 5, 20, 76,
    77, 83, 104, 144, 221
SOOs, *see* Sex offender orders
SOPOs, *see* Sexual offences prevention orders
SOTP, *see* Sex Offender Treatment Programme
South Africa, 7, 42, 192
South Australia Juvenile Justice Project (SAJJ),
    179
Spatial separation, *see also* Situational crime
    prevention 132
Special Sex Offender Sentencing Alternative
    (SSOSA), 69
SSOSA, *see* Special Sex Offender Sentencing
    Alternative
STEP, *see* Sex Offender Treatment Evaluation
    Project
State justice, *see also* Formal Criminal Justice,
    Retributive Justice, Traditional Justice, 3,
    38, 52, 198
State-led responses to sex offending, I, 6, 12,
    215, 217
Statistics, *see* Sexual offending
Statutory agencies, 30, 94–5, 175, 182, 187, 205
Stigmatisation, 43–4, 47–8
Stop It Now! **165–8**
  as a prevention programme, 166
  effectiveness of, 167
  key projects, 167
  restorative or reintegrative potential, 14, 167
Stop It Now! UK & Ireland, 167
Strain theory, 48
Stranger danger, 10–11, 20, 22, 84
Strengths-based approach, 51, 174, 219
Supervision, 27–8, 47, 71–2, 187
  aims of, 73–4, 100
  criticisms of, 61, 71, 124, 142

  see also Ticket-of-leave system
Supporting, *see also* Community, Sex offenders,
    Victims, Restorative Justice, benefits,
    7, 14, 50, 57, 74, 81, 95, 159, 161, 166–8,
    186, 189, 193–4, 204, 210
Surveillance, *see also* Policing 23, 28
Suspect offenders, *see also* Risk, categories of 114
Sweden, 17, 138, 146

Thames Valley Police, 178
Thames Valley Project, *see also* Circles of
    Support 69, 167, 175–6
Ticket-of-leave system, 100
The Boston Globe, 20
The Crucible, 118, 213
The Irish News, 20
The Irish Times, 19, 20
*The Sex Offenders Act 1997, Home Office Circular
    39/97*, ii, 28, 29, 31, 35, 84, 97, 100, 102,
    112, 114, 120, 131, 132, 216
The Sunday Times, 20, 21, 128
The Times, 19, 21, 72, 82, 94, 118, 128, 140, 147,
    152
'The Third Way', *see also* Youth Justice 26
Three strikes and you're out, 25, 110
Tracking, *see* Sex Offenders
  problems with, 75, **81–4**, 100, 121, 142
Traditional Justice, *see also* Formal Criminal
    Justice, Retributive Justice, State Justice
    4, 61, 64, 155, 160, 169, 177, 199, 217
Trafficking, 10, 83
Training and employment, 25, 30
Treatment,
  community-based treatment, 7 24, 40, **69–70**,
    96, 112, 151, 165, 187, 191, 193–4, 222
  decline of, 61
  effectiveness of programmes, 97, 148, 189, 203
  prison-based treatment, *see also* SOTP, STEP,
    4, **64–9**, 74, 172
  therapeutic approaches to, *see also* Cognitive
    behavioural therapy 62, **63–4**, 154–5
  versus punishment, 13, 62, 66, 149–50, 218
Trust, *see also* Abuse of Trust, Grooming 171,
    173, 188, 191
'Twin track' policy, 26, 156
Ty Mawr Inquiry, 75

UN Convention on the Rights of the Child
    (1989), 109
Utting Report, 19, 75–7
Vetting procedures, 75–77
Victims,
  benefits of restorative justice, *see also*
    Empowering, Protecting, Supporting,
    46
  rights of, versus rights of offenders, *see*
    Balance of rights 12–13, 32, 37, 107,
    108–116, 217

Victims (*cont.*):
    views of, *see also* Public, punitive attitudes 5,
        8, 39, 43, 179, 184, 192
Victim-Offender Mediation (VOM),
    use, 40–1
    effectiveness, **177–80**
Vigilance, 95, 189, 205, 222
Vigilantism, *see also* Restorative justice,
        critiques, 6, 8, 22, 91, 98, 109, 118, 130,
        137, 152, **205–6**, 212
    impact on multi-agency work, *see also*
        Housing 94–5, 193–4
Violent and Sex Offender Register (ViSOR), 75,
    83, **104–5**, 114,
ViSOR, *see* Violent and Sex Offender Register
Voluntary agencies, 7, 9, 19, 30, 32, 42, 56, 92–3,
    96, 106, 165–6, 168, 170, 172, 183,
    188–93, 205, 213, 219, 222
Voluntary sector working group, *see* Northern
    Ireland
VOM, *see* Victim Offender Mediation
Vulnerability,
    of children, 11, 17, 19, 88

    of women, 11, 88, 182
Wagga Wagga model, 40
Warner Report, 19, 57, 75, 76
Waterhouse Report, 75, 76
'What works', 3, 47, 66–7, 144, 183, 219
Whiting, Roy, *see also* Payne, Sarah 21, 91

Youth justice, 9
    the 'third way', 26
    see also Crime and Disorder Act 1998,
        Restorative justice, Youth Justice and
        Criminal Evidence Act 1999 26
Young sexual offenders, 7, 48, 53, 141,
    early intervention, 123
    need for special response, 40, 123–4
    registration periods, *see also* Registration and
        notification 103-04, 120
    'risky children or children at risk', 123
    use of restorative justice with, *see also*
        Restorative justice 56, 178, 180,
        207
Youth Justice and Criminal Evidence Act 1999,
    53